WITHDRAWN

Cities of the Nations
Historic Metropolitan
Core

Publisher's note: This book is one of a four-book series comprising Vol. 1 of the AAG Project.

The four books are:
1. Cities of the Nation's Historic Metropolitan Core
2. Nineteenth Century Ports
3. Nineteenth Century Inland Centers and Ports
4. Twentieth Century Cities

Association of American Geographers

Comparative Metropolitan Analysis Project

Vol. 1   Contemporary Metropolitan America: Twenty Geographical Vignettes. Cambridge: Ballinger Publishing Company, 1976.
Vol. 2. Urban Policymaking and Metropolitan Dynamics: A Comparative Geographical Analysis. Cambridge: Ballinger Publishing Company, 1976.
Vol. 3. A Comparative Atlas of America's Great Cities: Twenty Metropolitan Regions. Minneapolis: University of Minnesota Press, 1976.

Vignettes of the following metropolitan regions are also published by Ballinger Publishing Company as separate monographs:

- Boston
- New York-New Jersey
- Philadelphia
- Hartford-Central Connecticut
- Baltimore
- New Orleans
- Atlanta
- Chicago
- St. Paul-Minneapolis
- Seattle
- Miami
- Los Angeles
- Detroit

Research Director:
John S. Adams, University of Minnesota

Associate Director and Atlas Editor:
Ronald Abler, Pennsylvania State University

Chief Cartographer:
Ki–Suk Lee, University of Minnesota

Steering Committee and Editorial Board:
Brian J.L. Berry, Chairman, Harvard University
John R. Borchert, University of Minnesota
Frank E. Horton, Southern Illinois University
J. Warren Nystrom, Association of American Geographers
James E. Vance, Jr., University of California, Berkeley
David Ward, University of Wisconsin

Supported by a grant from the National Science Foundation.

CONTEMPORARY METROPOLITAN AMERICA

1

Cities of the Nation's Historic Metropolitan Core

Association of American Geographers
Comparative Metropolitan Analysis Project

John S. Adams, Editor
University of Minnesota

Ballinger Publishing Company • **Cambridge, Massachusetts**
A Subsidiary of J.B. Lippincott Company

International Standard Book Number: 0-88410-425-7 (set)

Library of Congress Catalog Card Number: 76-56167

Printed in the United States of America

Library of Congress Cataloging in Publication Data
Main entry under title:

   Contemporary metropolitan America.

   Includes bibliographies and index.
   CONTENTS: pt. 1. Cities of the Nation's historic metropolitan core.—pt. 2. Nineteenth century ports.—pt. 3. Nineteenth century inland centers and ports.—pt. 4. Twentieth century cities.
   1. Cities and towns—United States. I. Adams, John S., 1938–   II. Association of American Geographers. Comparative Metropolitan Analysis Project.
HT123.C635   301.36'3'0973   76-56167
ISBN 0-88410-425-7 (set)
      0-88410-467-2 (pt. 1)
      0-88410-464-8 (pt. 2)
      0-88410-465-6 (pt. 3)
      0-88410-466-4 (pt. 4)

Contents

Chapter Three
The New York-New Jersey Metropolitan Region
George W. Carey, Rutgers University

Chapter Four
Metropolitan Philadelphia: A Study of Conflicts and Social Cleavages
Peter O. Muller, Kenneth C. Meyer, Roman A. Cybriwsky,
Temple University

List of Figures

CHAPTER THREE–NEW YORK-NEW JERSEY

CHAPTER FOUR-PHILADELPHIA

CHAPTER FIVE–HARTFORD-CENTRAL CONNECTICUT

List of Tables

CHAPTER ONE-INTRODUCTION

CHAPTER TWO-BOSTON

Cities of the Nations
Historic Metropolitan
Core

Chapter 1

The American City: Workshop for a National Culture

James E. Vance, Jr.
University of California
Berkeley

The collection of short monographs appraising the physical, social, and economic natures of the twenty largest American metropolitan areas, which this essay seeks to introduce, cannot fail to present the reader with what must be one of the basic conflicts of modern life—the finding of a reassuring human path through a richness of detail that seems at times to force the vision of the traveler to so short a prospect that he becomes lost, through not understanding the basic pattern of the woodland and the fundamental geography of the land. The explorer must understand these relations if he seeks in the end to understand a larger reality, and perhaps in turn to be able ultimately to reach the forest fringe and look upon the world beyond, and the future. In the end the complex tale of national development and evolution falls into place on a page that remains untorn but far from unchanged in the writing that we can read. During our first century of national existence it was in our fields and on our frontier that the story of the nature of the American character and the evolution of her geography was most clearly written.

It is on a different palimpsest—the city— that we must seek the story of the second century of our national life. Again there is both a geographical interaction and a functional interdependence that must be recorded, and the erasures of urban revision never fundamentally destroy the writing of the past. Change is itself unchanging, ever-present, and the most normal of dynamics, even though we must reiterate that change is seldom if ever so complete as to destroy the influence of what it transforms. Yet when we read the writing of a particular moment or a specific paragraph in both the national account and that of a particular city we may gain a confusing view of the tale itself. The beauty and genius of that story is in its telling, in the present instance in the words of the twenty vignettes of individual and quite characterful metropolises; but there is a need for an exegesis that may help us to understand how the score of distinctive tales go together to make a sweeping allegory of America's second century. The allegory is there but, as is so often the case in such fundamental writings, the meaning may not be readily discernible in the individual part. The history of the nation since the Centennial of 1876 can as validly be roughed out on an ever-lasting urban sheet as could the account of our first century be written in the trees and the fields. And, as was the case with that earlier account, we must be careful to avoid the notion that any one geographical area exists independently of another; if the danger of parochialism during our early history lies in thinking that the city grew only out of the American countryside, as is so commonly misconceived, the peril of our later history lies in believing that the city was ever narrow, constrained, and unchanging. There may always have been city centers but there never have been centers that were either stable over time or inclusive of all elements of city life. Our colonial history leaves no doubt that the outward spread of the urban occupation of land began even before our political revolution in 1776, and at least a half century ahead of our industrial revolution. This truth must be emphasized because, next to the notion that the natural state of mankind in America was rural, the most egregiously false notion about cities is that there is somehow a moral rectitude and historical primacy that reposes in the central cities, which are often simplistically thought to have been compact and self-contained until the last half century, only recently to be surrounded by a great band of "sin in the suburbs." It must be made plain that movement to the suburbs is a long-standing element of the American urban growth process and in no way simply a process of fear and detachment from present-day central city problems.

The purpose of this introductory essay is to establish some rough generalizations about the growth process in American cities in order to gain joint objectives—to begin to understand how the various parts of a particular city are both interrelated and integrated in their evolution; and to seek to understand how the nature of twenty massive, complex, and widely scattered cities might be viewed within a broad general context as furnishing a summary view of the American city and its current state.

THE GROWTH OF AMERICAN URBANISM

This is not the place to detail the evolution of American life within the city that has taken place since the 1876 Centennial. We must, however, gain some understanding of the degree to which the urban experience is the American experience. To do so we may reflect on the fact that of the four million people in the United States recorded in the first census, in 1790, only 200,000, just under 5 percent in precise figures, lived in an urban situation —then as now defined so as to include rather

small towns. Only when industrialization and foreign trade had gained momentum enough to cause cities to grow more rapidly than the countryside, as was true in 1840, did the urban population amount to more than one-tenth of the national total (1840 urban population was 10.6 percent). When the United States population first exceeded thirty million in 1860, the urban portion was essentially one out of five residents (19.7 percent), a proportion that grew rather rapidly in the succeeding decades. A century ago, in 1870, one-quarter of our population was classed as urban, showing a fivefold growth in proportion during our first century of national existence. Obviously, the percentage growth could not continue so spectacularly, but absolute numbers expanded more strikingly. The nation's cities contained only 200,000 in 1790, little more than half a million in 1810, and only a million in 1830. In the decade of the 1840s the cities grew from less than two million to more than three and a half million. By the time of the Civil War over six million lived in cities, and only a decade later, in 1870, nearly ten million were housed there. The rise was rapid indeed thereafter—over twenty million in 1890, over thirty million in 1900, forty in 1910, fifty in 1920, and nearly seventy million in 1930. Already for the first time in 1890 more than half the Americans lived in cities, a figure that now stands at just under three-quarters. But the numbers involved have expanded most inexorably, from twenty-two million in 1890 to essentially 150 million in 1970.

The previous figures represent all cities. Perhaps more germane to our present concern is the growth of larger places. If we use half a million people as the divide between good size and what are really large cities, we find that it was not until 1850 that New York became our first city to reach half a million; there were two large cities in 1860, and the progression was as follows (Tables 1, 2, 3).

Table 1. Number of Large American Cities at Selected Census Dates

Cities with Population:	1850	1860	1870	1880	1890	1900	1910	1920	1930	1940	1950	1960	1970
500,000 to 999,999	1	2	2	3	1	3	5	9	8	9	13	16	20
1,000,000 and over	–	–	–	1	3	3	3	3	5	5	5	5	6
Total Number of Large Cities	1	2	2	4	4	6	8	12	13	14	18	21	26

Source: US Bureau of the Census.

Table 2. Political Cities of Half a Million or More, 1970

City	Population in Thousands	City	Population in Thousands
1. New York City	7,894.8	14. San Diego	696.7
2. Chicago	3,366.9	15. San Antonio	654.1
3. Los Angeles	2,816.0	16. Boston	641.0
4. Philadelphia	1,948.6	17. Memphis	623.5
5. Detroit	1,511.4	18. St. Louis	622.2
6. Houston	1,232.8	19. New Orleans	593.4
7. Baltimore	905.7	20. Columbus	539.6
8. Dallas	844.4	21. Seattle	530.8
9. Washington	756.5	22. Jacksonville	528.8
10. Cleveland	750.9	23. Pittsburgh	520.1
11. Indianapolis	744.6	24. Denver	514.6
12. Milwaukee	717.0	25. Kansas City	507.0
13. San Francisco	715.6		

Source: US Bureau of the Census.

Clearly the growth of large cities came during our second century (1870-1970), leading to the populating of the greatest number of major cities to be found in any western country. In 1970 there were in this country twenty-five central cities of more than half a million population and a similar twenty-five physically delimited "cities" Urbanized Areas) with a million people or more.

Although suffering several major geographical faults, the Standard Metropolitan Statistical Area (SMSA) is the most widely used measure of metropolitanism in the United States. We find in 1970 there were sixty-five SMSAs with half a million or more, with half that number of SMSAs housing more than a million people (Table 4).

These figures have interest in themselves, but for our purpose their main use is that of demonstrating the complexity of American urbanization and its wide geographical spread. Unlike a number of other advanced countries (wherein urbanization is both highly concentrated and geographically clustered), in the United States cities are in a sense more widespread than either dense population or clustered economic activity. It is true to say that there is an American manufacturing belt, though less validly so today than when it was first bruited in the 1920s, but it is much more

Table 3. Urbanized Areas of One Million or More, 1970

Urbanized Area	Population in Thousands	Urbanized Area	Population in Thousands
1. New York-Northeastern New Jersey	16,206	12. Pittsburgh	1,846
2. Los Angeles-Long Beach	8,351	13. Minneapolis-St. Paul	1,704
3. Chicago-Northwestern Indiana	6,714	14. Houston	1,677
		15. Baltimore	1,579
4. Philadelphia	4,021	16. Milwaukee	1,252
5. San Francisco-Oakland-San Jose	4,013	17. Seattle-Everett	1,238
		18. Miami	1,219
6. Detroit	3,970	19. San Diego	1,198
7. Boston	2,652	20. Atlanta	1,172
8. Washington	2,481	21. Cincinnati	1,110
9. Dallas-Fort Worth	2,015	22. Kansas City	1,101
10. Cleveland	1,959	23. Buffalo	1,086
11. St. Louis	1,882	24. Denver	1,047
		[25. San Jose here lumped with San Francisco-Oakland]	1,025

Source: US Bureau of the Census.

Table 4.   SMSAs with Half a Million Population or More in 1970

SMSA	Population in Thousands	SMSA	Population in Thousands
1. New York	11,571.8	34. Phoenix	967.5
2. Los Angeles-Long Beach	7,032.0	35. Columbus, Ohio	916.2
3. Chicago	6,978.9	36. Providence-Pawtucket	910.7
4. Philadelphia	4,817.9	37. Rochester	882.6
5. Detroit	4,199.9	38. San Antonio	864.0
6. San Francisco-Oakland	3,109.5	39. Dayton	850.2
7. Washington	2,861.1	40. Louisville	826.5
8. Boston	2,753.7	41. Sacramento	800.5
9. Pittsburgh	2,401.2	42. Memphis	770.1
10. St. Louis	2,363.0	43. Ft. Worth	762.0
11. Baltimore	2,070.6	44. Birmingham	739.2
12. Cleveland	2,064.1	45. Albany-Schenectady-	
13. Houston	1,985.0	Troy	721.9
14. Newark	1,856.5	46. Toledo	692.5
15. Minneapolis-St. Paul	1,813.6	47. Norfolk-Portsmouth	680.6
16. Dallas	1,555.9	48. Akron	679.2
17. Seattle-Everett	1,421.8	49. Hartford	663.8
18. Anaheim-Santa Ana	1,420.3	50. Oklahoma City	640.8
19. Milwaukee	1,403.6	51. Syracuse	636.5
20. Atlanta	1,390.1	52. Gary-Hammond	633.3
21. Cincinnati	1,384.8	53. Honolulu	626.1
22. Paterson-Clifton	1,358.7	54. Ft. Lauderdale	620.1
23. San Diego	1,357.8	55. Jersey City	609.2
24. Buffalo	1,349.2	56. Greensboro-Winston	
25. Miami	1,267.7	Salem-High Point	602.8
26. Kansas City	1,253.9	57. Salt Lake City	557.6
27. Denver	1,227.5	58. Allentown-Bethlehem	543.5
28. San Bernardino-Riverside	1,143.1	59. Nashville	541.1
29. Indianapolis	1,109.8	60. Omaha	540.1
30. San Jose	1,064.7	61. Grand Rapids	539.2
31. New Orleans	1,045.8	62. Youngstown-Warren	536.0
32. Tampa-St. Petersburg	1,012.5	63. Springfield, Ma.	529.9
33. Portland, Ore.	1,009.1	64. Jacksonville	528.8
		65. Richmond, Va.	518.3

Source: US Bureau of the Census.

questionable to argue an urban belt and an urban ecumene. To demonstrate that fact we may take the data contained in the last three tables and assign them by the census geographical regions of the United States (Table 5).

Given the very considerable differential in population density, state and regional totals of population, economic activity, and "domination" by centers of corporate control we might expect that the United States would be rather like Britain or France in demonstrating an urban core and sparsely settled fringe. Yet the data lead us to argue otherwise. If we take large cities as here defined, there is a rather unusual balance among the regions, and even, to a lesser degree, among the divisions of regions. A few qualifications emerge but none controverts the generalization. The Northeast,

East North Central, and Pacific regions are characterized by larger large cities than the other regions and divisions but the under-represented areas largely right the balance in having more places in the smaller range of the great cities. The suggestion comes through that there is a certain element of staging in the growth of these important places—whatever definition of urbanization we use—and that perhaps the urban process in America is tending to produce a reasonable geographical spread of great towns.

THE PROCESS OF REGIONAL CONGREGATION IN AMERICAN URBANISM

The seeming progression from a partial to a full development of cities, which we find in

Table 5. Assignment of Cities, Urbanized Areas, and SMSAs to Census Geographical Regions, 1970

REGIONS Divisions	Cities over 500,000	Urbanized Areas Over 1 Million	SMSAs 500,000–999,999	SMSAs Over 1 Million
NORTHEAST	6	7	9	8
New England	1	1	1	3
Middle Atlantic	5	6	8	5
NORTH CENTRAL	8	8	9	8
East North Central	6	5	6	7
West North Central	2	3	3	1
SOUTH	6	4	6	12
South Atlantic	1	2	3	5
East South Central	1	–	–	5
West South Central	4	2	3	2
WEST	5	6	9	4
Mountain	1	1	1	1
Pacific	4	5	8	3
UNITED STATES	25	25	33	32

Source: US Bureau of the Census.

the regional pattern of the United States, provides us with a useful suggestion in our search for the nature of the urbanization process. In colonial times the data with which to judge the pattern of urbanization are scarce, but in 1790 the first federal census was conducted and from it we gain a view of our early urban structure. For a study such as this, which seeks to understand the twenty largest cities of the United States, there is a direct pertinence in asking, What were the twenty more important towns of 1790 (Table 6)?

The domination of the category of great

towns by ports is indeed striking; the first thirteen places were greatly important harbors heavily engaged in the colonial trade. Even up to the twenty-seventh town, Cambridge, all places were at the least, in their era, quite usable river ports, if not, as in most cases, true seaports. Albany, Petersburg, Alexandria, and Haverhill were at or near the lowest falls on their respective rivers, and only when we reach Worcester and Pittsfield were these federal period towns truly inland.

The pattern of great towns in the America of 1790 was that of an alignment at what Jean

Table 6. The Great Towns of 1790

Rank	Town	Population in Thousands	Rank	Town	Population in Thousands
1	New York, N.Y.	33.1	16	Albany, N.Y.	3.4
2	Philadelphia, Pa.	28.5	17	New Bedford, Ma.	3.3
3	Boston, Ma.	18.3	18	Beverly, Ma.	3.2
4	Charleston, S.C.	16.3	19	Norfolk, Va.	2.9
5	Baltimore, Md.	13.5	20	Petersburg, Va.	2.8
6	Salem, Ma.	7.9	[21	Alexandria, Va.	2.7]
7	Newport, R.I.	6.7	[22	Hartford, Ct.	2.6]
8	Providence, R.I.	6.3	[23	Hudson, N.Y.	2.5]
9.	Gloucester, Ma.	5.3	[24	Haverhill, Ma.	2.4]
10	Newburyport, Ma.	4.8	[25	Lynn, Ma.	2.2]
11	Portsmouth, N.H.	4.7	[27	Portland, Me.	2.2]
12	Brooklyn, N.Y.	4.4	[27	Cambridge, Ma.	2.1]
13	New Haven, Ct.	4.4	[28	Worcester, Ma.	2.0]
14	Taunton, Ma.	3.8	[29	Pittsfield, Ma.	1.9]
15	Richmond, Va.	3.7	[30	Northampton, Ma.	1.6]

Source: US Bureau of the Census.

Gottmann has called even today the "economic hinge" between this nation and the rest of the world. In our first national decade the tie was more powerful still; America was the creation of the European kingdoms whose trade flowed largely through, or at least in, the ships at home in these ports on "the distant shore." Initially a series of quite separate planted ports had been staked out on the American shore, and they had become the basis for the early urban development in this country, because the trading activity that was consistently the vector of exploration and development existed through the agency of city men—in counting houses, in warehouses, on the ship's bridge, and in the shrouds above it. The trading function that was so considerably our national life required a level of social concentration in cities and the physical alignment of great towns along the northeastern coast such as to produce a distinctive urban pattern, quite different from that in Europe. The cities thus shaped in our early history are still of such surpassing importance that much of the rest of the world must view the alignment as an "economic hinge." It is too strong to argue that today the world is merely our "distant shore," but, then again, certainly we no longer are their's.

Because cities had a specific and narrowly focused purpose with little variation during federal times, they tended to cluster in a particular part of the national geography. This process of regional congregation became the initial one at work in our great towns, and its local expression remains the most powerful force at work shaping our cities even today. Unfortunately, local congregation is paired with another force—segregation—which has in recent decades seemed much more the dominant force at work in destroying those same cities. But a careful weighing of the two local processes may help to give us both a bit more confidence as to the outcome of our third century and a better understanding of how cities develop the physical build they present to us each day we reside and work in them.

Both within the geographical extent of the nation and the physical extent of the city there is little that is evenly distributed in space: clustering, with its concomitant of empty areas, becomes the common geographical pattern in almost all things that are spread about the earth's surface.

This is the pattern that may be observed, but it raises immediately in the enquiring mind the question of the process that produced the effect. Such a pattern can come in one of two ways: certain features may be collected together, in a congregation, by the active working of particular social, economic, cultural, or physical "forces"; or it may come from the external operation of such forces, wherein the cluster that results is the outcome of segregation, exercised in a negative way, by forcing the exclusion of particular persons, animals, plants, or other entities from the areas in which they are not to be found and, presumably, are not desired. Our attention in individual cities, and particularly in recent times, has focused on the negative process, that of segregation, with little thought given to the much more common, and healthy, positive process of congregation. Here some attempt will be made both to right the balance and to demonstrate how attention to the process of congregation is very useful in seeking an understanding of the order that emerges from the seemingly infinite individual decisions that go to make up life in the city.

Returning to our consideration of America in 1790, we may observe the direct impact of congregation, both in the case of the clustering of most of the developing economic activities in the hands of a relatively small number of great towns and in the alignment of those towns in a particular hinge pattern on the coast between Portland and Norfolk. These ports grew up from small germinal towns "planted" from England to forward her national economy. Elsewhere (in *The Merchant's World*) I have discussed at length the fact that the location and function of these towns on the distant shore can be understood only in terms of the economic and social activities of the mercantilist mother country that was doing the planting. The location of the planted towns was the one best able to serve the colonial trade that justified the undertaking and that prospered so mightily that large numbers of Englishmen migrated to America, only to revolt against the mother country when she refused them full participation in the life-giving trade. In America the flow of migrants was great enough to shape a new English-speaking land, as was later the case in Canada, Australia, and New Zealand. Where the flow was less large, or the indigenous population was too great—as in India, Nigeria, Ghana, and, in a different way, South Africa—the process had a different result, because the relative numbers were reversed. But because in all these cases the process of mercantilist implantation of cities was at work, in time the nations' largest towns came to be located in a fashion similar to those of the United States in 1790. Only as countries have developed internalized economies—perhaps for political reasons, as is so strikingly shown in South Africa—has the coastal congregation of towns been reduced, as it was in the United States in the nineteenth century.

We may justifiably hold that when there is but a single, and therefore a rather specialized, purpose for towns, there will be a characteristic—typical—location pattern for them. In 1790 it was the landing of overseas trade routes on our Atlantic shore that aligned the towns in a distinctive regional congregation.

To add further to this principle we may examine the remaining seven of the twenty larger cities of 1790, and perhaps an additional ten to sharpen the detail of the process at work in locating them. Of these seventeen towns (given in Table 6), nine were located in such a way as to represent a logical extension of the mercantile implantation that had first emerged in the seventeenth century; they were river ports connected by naturally navigable water with the ocean (Taunton, Richmond, Albany, Petersburg, Alexandria, Hartford, Hudson, Haverhill, and Cambridge). Five were smaller coastal

ports (New Bedford, Beverly, Norfolk, Portland, and Lynn), and only three were interior towns hard to reach by water (Worcester, Pittsfield, and Northampton). It seems reasonable to argue that the focus in town founding and town filling was still largely that of external trade. If we were to consider the total pattern of American economic activity in 1790, we would discover that those areas engaged in commercial production were working for the securing of goods largely, or at least importantly, destined for export—tobacco (our largest export) and rice in the South, grain and pickled meat in the Middle Atlantic states, and fish, whale oil, and timber in New England.

Let us add at this point that in such a trading economy the towns that develop away from the coast would tend to congregate along the lines of interconnection between the ports of foreign trade and the raw-material-producing interior. When we examine the largest twenty American cities in 1830 there can be little doubt as to the validity of this view (Table 7). The ports still dominated as America's largest places, providing the first six cities, but the interior river ports were increasing in relative importance, furnishing four of the twenty cities. Two new elements emerged in 1830, each of which represented a new form of regional congregation. The national capital city, not in existence in 1790, had forty years later become our tenth city. As the Washington D.C. vignette shows, in 1830 Washington was a specialized city of political activity, yet that

Table 7. The Great Towns of 1830

Rank	Town	Population in Thousands	Rank	Town	Population in Thousands
1	New York, N.Y.	202.5	16	Troy, N.Y.	11.5
2	Baltimore, Md.	80.6	17	Newark, N.J.	10.9
3	Philadelphia, Pa.	80.4	18	Louisville, Ky.	10.3
4	Boston, Ma.	61.3	19	New Haven, Conn.	10.1
5	New Orleans, La.	46.0	20	Norfolk, Va.	9.8
6	Charleston, S.C.	30.2	[21	Buffalo, N.Y.	8.6]
7	Cincinnati, Ohio	24.8	[22	Petersburg, Va.	8.3]
8	Albany, N.Y.	24.2	[23	Alexandria, Va.	8.2]
9	Brooklyn, N.Y.	20.5	[24	Portsmouth, N.H.	8.0]
10	Washington, D.C.	18.8	[25	Newport, R.I.	8.0]
11	Providence, R.I.	16.8	[26	Gloucester, Ma.	7.5]
12	Richmond, Va.	16.0	[27	Hartford, Conn.	7.0]
13	Pittsburgh, Pa.	15.3	[28	Springfield, Ma.	6.7]
14.	Salem, Ma.	13.8	[29	Newburyport, Ma.	6.3]
15	Portland, Me.	12.5	[20	Lynn, Ma.	6.1]

Source: US Bureau of the Census.

activity had so congregated there as to make
the town a major place. And, after a faltering start in 1791 in Providence, industrialization in factories had come rather quickly in
the United States. Just after 1800, the secre-
tary of the treasury, Alexander Hamilton, had
surveyed the United States with respect to this
factory industry and had concluded that most
of it congregated in a few places, most dominantly around Providence and in northeastern
New Jersey. By 1830, Providence and Newark
were industrial cities strongly evident in the
first twenty places, and Hartford, Connecticut,
and Springfield and Lynn, Massachusetts, stood
as smaller manufacturing places of dominating
position in the rapidly expanding industry of
America. Even today, as our vignette on Hartford shows, it is the manufacturing congregated around that place that raises a modest
city to rank as the center of one of the twenty
largest Daily Urban Systems used as the geographical units in this project.

The first supports of urbanization to be
added to the founding one of overseas mercantile trade were those of political activity and
industrialization. There was a remarkable clustering of towns in particularly favored sites—
New York, Brooklyn, and Newark; Boston,
Lynn, Salem, Gloucester, Newburyport, Ports-
mouth, and Portland; Providence and Newport;
Hartford and Springfield; Alexandria and Washington; Norfolk and Richmond, with Petersburg
nearby; Albany and Troy. We are forced to
conclude that not only was there a pattern of
distinctive locations for larger towns, but that
a pattern of internal specialization also appeared
to be emerging within regions that were becoming urbanized on a scale larger than the
individual city. To cite merely two examples:
Newport remained even in 1830 a rather
specialized port on the colonial model, but
Providence was growing by its nearby industrialization. Alexandria was the traditional
town of the Potomac, but, nonetheless, Washington could grow in its literal shadow by there
congregating political functions. The same
localized pattern of city specialization could
be seen in Albany-Troy and in the James River
development in Virginia. It seems that as
cities became more common in America, so
might they begin to undertake a locally particular specialization in activities. There were
clusters of towns located nearby each other
wherein the distribution of those activities

that founded and filled towns varied among
the individual places. In 1830 there still seems
to have been a physical separation of one town
from another, but obviously, as growth came,
the discrete city might well yield to the conurbation—the growing together of a number of
places that were originally geographically distinct. Until that adhesion came, however, we
are justified in using the figures on the population of individual political cities as a rough
measure of the size and importance of American
cities.

The great towns of 1870, another forty
years on in our national life, were rather different places from those of the brand new
republic (Table 8). The regional metropolises
had begun to emerge, taking on a pattern that
has not changed so very greatly during the succeeding century. New York, Philadelphia, St.
Louis, Chicago, Baltimore, Boston, Cincinnati,
New Orleans, and San Francisco were nine of
the first ten cities; and all were regional centers of complex support. Of these, all but Cincinnati appear as vignettes in this series, and in
those individual studies the conditions for continued growth are clearly stated. Because Cincinnati is missing from our twenty cities it is
necessary to account for its departure, which
seems to stem from greater development of
manufacturing elsewhere in the Middle West
and the declining relative importance of the
river transportation that first filled the city.
If we link Brooklyn, the third city, with New
York in such a complexity, then half of the
great towns of that census year were just such
increasingly diverse places. There is no real
element of chance in the fact that all were
originally ports—Boston, New York, Philadelphia, Baltimore, New Orleans, and San Francisco on the sea; and St. Louis, Chicago, and
Cincinnati on the by then integrated Great
Lakes-Mississippi waterways. In the second ten
cities, seven were part of this vast inland
navigation network—Pittsburgh and Louisville
on the Ohio River, Albany at the beginning
of the Erie Canal and Buffalo where it reached
Lake Erie, Cleveland where the Ohio and Erie
Canal left Lake Erie, Detroit at the first narrows going up those Great Lakes, and Milwaukee
where a harbor could collect commodities being
raised and mined beyond the head of Lake
Michigan.

The location for American cities remained
the place where water commerce congregated

Table 8. The Great Towns of 1870

Rank	Town	Population in Thousands	Rank	Town	Population in Thousands
1	New York, N.Y.	942.2	16	Cleveland, Ohio	92.8
2	Philadelphia, Pa.	674.0	17	Jersey City, N.J.	82.5
3	Brooklyn, N.Y.	719.9	18	Detroit, Mich.	79.5
4	St. Louis, Mo.	310.8	19	Milwaukee, Wisc.	71.4
5	Chicago, Ill.	298.9	20	Albany, N.Y.	69.4
6	Baltimore, Md.	276.3	[21	Providence, R.I.	68.9]
7	Boston, Ma.	250.5	[22	Rochester, N.Y.	62.3]
8	Cincinnati, Ohio	216.2	[23	Richmond, Va.	51.0]
9	New Orleans, La.	191.4	[24	New Haven, Conn.	50.8]
10	San Francisco, Calif.	149.4	[25	Charleston, S.C.	48.9]
11	Pittsburgh, Pa.	139.2	[26	Indianapolis, Ind.	48.2]
12	Buffalo, N.Y.	117.7	[27	Troy, N.Y.	46.4]
13	Washington, D.C.	109.1	[28	Syracuse, N.Y.	43.0]
14	Newark, N.J.	105.0	[29	Worcester, Ma.	41.1]
15	Louisville, Ky.	100.7	[30	Lowell, Ma.	40.9]

Source: US Bureau of the Census.

mercantile activity and people, but we would be in error if we thought that it was only that commerce that filled the city. Industry was fast overtaking water-borne trade as a maker of towns. In all of the ports, factories had clustered first near the wharves but ultimately in many parts of the city. And in those regions where manufacturing was most at home—metropolitan New York, Philadelphia, the forks of the Ohio River, and New England—there were actual factory towns emerging into prominence of position as roughly measured by population. Newark and Jersey City were part of the great cluster of activity that was New York, and they were sited on that continental side of the harbor where we would logically expect manufacturing to be located. As the vignette on New York so clearly shows, there was a major shift in the port of New York from the city itself to the New Jersey shore, a trend that has in fact quickened in recent years. Providence still held its own, though no longer the absolute center of factories it had been a half century before. In the third ten cities the mix was largely that of declining ports from earlier times—Richmond, New Haven, and Charleston—with the emerging factory towns—Rochester, Syracuse, Worcester, and Lowell. Indianapolis was a regional center that was growing as railroads came to supplant canals and rivers in inland freight haulage. As it grew it also industrialized so that in the end its development pulled the western boundary of the factory belt farther toward the interior to

the point that it ultimately spread to include the separate clusters of manufacturing that had grown up around Chicago and St. Louis into a single manufacturing belt that extended from northeast of Boston to west of St. Louis and Chicago.

Here we may take count of stock sufficiently to point out that no longer was any great town a place of a simple specialization. Old ports were now great manufacturing places and newer manufacturing towns were becoming important transportation hubs when the more easily ramified railroad took over from the inland waterway as the basic means of American haulage. Particularly during the Civil War, with its dislocation of the previous waterways system in a time of greatly enhanced demand for the movement of goods and persons, the greater utility of rail lines was fully demonstrated. As might be expected, when complexity replaced specialty there was a strong tendency for specialization to be expressed areally within the city. The existence of Brooklyn, Jersey City, and Newark in a cluster of great towns was merely a symptom of the future.

In the period between the Civil War and the First World War the American economy came of age, becoming the greatest industrial power in existence, while American society took on the job of integrating a diverse and continuing flood of immigrants into the largest democratic republic ever undertaken. It was in the city that these heroic activities were most notably to take place, a fact that makes the television mythology that locates the American frontier in the distant countryside seem so artificial and romantically tangential. The notion that the American character was forged in Fort Laramie or Virginia City rather than in Chicago or East Boston is as foolish as the one that holds that it was religious freedom alone that planted colonists on our shores.

In 1910 we can take a summary look at the outcome of this forty years of rather fiery tempering of American society and its economic support (Table 9). Obviously the long-established pattern of regional metropolises persisted so that the first thirteen cities were supported by the complexity of activity that such a status implied. In general there had been a shift in ranking, which meant that the ports had lost their utter dominance and the cities of great congregation of manufacturing were gaining in rank: Cleveland, Pittsburgh, Detroit, and Buffalo had all come up in rank, whereas Cincinnati, Baltimore, New Orleans, and San Francisco had dropped. It would be as unwise as it is inaccurate to categorize the large American cities as either ports or manufacturing towns; the major metropolis by 1910 had taken on a diversity of functions. There is, however, considerable justification for reassigning the main instrument of growth from the transportation functions to those of factory production. But, of course, any goods produced would in turn lead to increased demands for the transport of the materials and finished products.

The most striking arrival that may be perceived from the ranking of great towns in 1910 is that of the regional metropolises of previously rather underdeveloped regions: Minneapolis, Kansas City, and Seattle all occupied new ground and had reached the status of one of the top twenty towns. In the next ten ranks, Indianapolis, Denver, Portland, Oregon, and Atlanta took on new status as large towns, certainly as the dominant transportation hubs for increasingly important regions. Indianapolis was without contest the national leader in the development of the interurban railway, a form of "farmer's railroad" that was by 1910 enjoying what turned out to be a most ephemeral development. Atlanta had been the rail center of the South for many years, but only by 1910 was the region up to supporting a nearly great town. That support has been strengthened in more recent years, as our vignette shows, by Atlanta's becoming the air hub of the old South. The case for Portland, with the westward shift of the lumber boom after the opening in the 1880s and 1890s of the "northern lines" of railroads, was similarly that of rail center and emerging industrial town. And the considerable export of lumber brought on the rapid growth of ports in Portland and Seattle. Seattle had also prospered mightily with the development of Alaska and the Yukon after the gold discoveries of 1897 in the Klondike.

In 1910 the evidence was clear that the United States was not to be a country of mighty urban contrasts. While New York and

Table 9. The Great Towns of 1910

Rank	Town	Population in Thousands	Rank	Town	Population in Thousands
1	New York, N.Y.	4,766.8	17	Los Angeles, Calif.	319.1
2	Chicago, Ill.	2,185.2	18	Minneapolis, Minn.	301.4
3	Philadelphia, Pa.	2,071.6	19	Kansas City, Mo.	248.3
4	St. Louis, Mo.	687.0	20	Seattle, Wash.	237.1
5	Boston, Mass.	670.5	[21	Indianapolis, Ind.	233.6]
6	Cleveland, Ohio	560.6	[22	Providence, R.I.	224.3]
7	Baltimore, Md.	558.4	[23	Louisville, Ky.	223.9]
8	Pittsburgh, Pa.	533.9	[24	Rochester, N.Y.	218.1]
9	Detroit, Mich.	465.7	[25	St. Paul, Minn.	214.7]
10	Buffalo, N.Y.	423.7	[27	Denver, Colo.	213.3]
11	San Francisco, Calif.	416.9	[27	Portland, Ore.	207.2]
12	Milwaukee, Wisc.	373.8	[28	Columbus, Ohio	181.5]
13	Cincinnati, Ohio	363.5	[29	Toledo, Ohio	168.4]
14	Newark, N.J.	347.4	[30	Atlanta, Ga.	154.8]
15	New Orleans, La.	339.0	[31	Oakland, Calif.	150.1]
16	Washington, D.C.	331.0			

Source: US Bureau of the Census.

the Northeast might be the heart of urban life, each region was to have a great town, some of them ultimately nearly so great as the old places in the Northeast. The Paris-and-France or London-and-England model was not to rule in America. Here the city was an utterly essential element of the Americanization process, as much for the Chinese and Japanese arriving on the West Coast, or the Poles and Bohemians filling Chicago and Buffalo, as for the Italians and Irish flocking to New York and Boston. The great "urbanization" was intimately tied up with the great "migration" to America. In this fact lies much of the misfortune that we suffer from the popular equation of the frontier and pioneering states of life with the agricultural-mining expansion into open land. It should be clearly understood that the city has always been a frontier in American life, first in the English plantations of the seventeenth and eighteenth century, as Carl Bridenbaugh (*Cities in the Wilderness*) has shown us; then in the melting pots of mass foreign immigration in the nineteenth century, as Oscar Handlin (*The Uprooted*) and Moses Rischin (*The American Gospel of Success*) prove to us; and now as the crucibles in which we seek to create a stable and socially acceptable alloy of persons of diverse ethnicity and rural as well as urban origin.

If 1910 was the beginning of the present, it was after another forty years, in 1950, that the pattern begins to show true definition (Table 10). By then the growth of central cities

in older areas had pretty much ceased or those places had even begun to decline. In the twenty years since 1950, New York, Chicago, Detroit, Baltimore, Cleveland, St. Louis, Boston, San Francisco, Pittsburgh, Buffalo, New Orleans, Minneapolis, Cincinnati, and even Washington, D.C., have all lost population in the central city, so that their 1970 totals are below those of 1950 (Table 11). In fact, Pittsburgh, Buffalo, Cincinnati, and Minneapolis are no longer among the twenty largest cities when narrowly limited to the political city at the core. The simple truth is that between 1950 and 1970 it became clear that in most parts of the country the concept of the city as summed up by its central political entity lost validity. Only where massive annexation was possible did these core towns continue to grow. The rise of Houston, Dallas, Indianapolis, San Diego, San Antonio, Memphis, and Columbus came from the combination of two forces—the growth of American cities in general, and the ability of those places in particular to expand their political boundaries (or to occupy previously overgenerous annexations) in the face of population growth. In other places—New York, Chicago, Philadelphia, Detroit, Washington, Cleveland, and Boston in particular—there was radical change, rather than internal growth, with a vast expansion of the role of the central city as America's social frontier. The activities on this new frontier grew quickly and in the face of constraining political boundaries that limited the part of the metropolitan area that had

Table 10. The Great Towns of 1950

Rank	Town	Central City Population in Thousands	Rank	Town	Central City Population in Thousands
1	New York, N.Y.	7,891.9	16	New Orleans, La.	570.4
2	Chicago, Ill.	3,620.9	17	Minneapolis, Minn.	521.7
3	Philadelphia, Pa.	2,071.6	18	Cincinnati, Ohio	503.9
4	Los Angeles, Cal.	1,970.3	19	Seattle, Wash.	467.5
5	Detroit, Mich.	1,849.5	20	Kansas City, Mo.	456.6
6	Baltimore, Md.	949.7	[21	Newark, N.J.	438.7]
7	Cleveland, Ohio	914.8	[22	Dallas, Texas	434.4]
8	St. Louis, Mo.	856.7	[23	Indianapolis, Ind.	427.1]
9	Washington, D.C.	802.1	[24	Denver, Col.	415.7]
10	Boston, Mass.	801.4	[25	San Antonio, Texas	408.4]
11	San Francisco, Cal.	775.3	[26	Memphis, Tenn.	396.0]
12	Pittsburgh, Pa.	676.8	[27	Oakland, Cal.	384.5]
13	Milwaukee, Wisc.	637.3	[28	Columbus, Ohio	375.9]
14	Houston, Texas	596.1	[29	Portland, Ore.	373.6]
15	Buffalo, N.Y.	580.1	[30	Louisville, Ky.	369.1]

Source: US Bureau of the Census.

Table 11. The Great Towns of 1970

Rank	Central City	Population in Thousands	Rank	Central City	Population in Thousands
1	New York, N.Y.	7,894.8	16	Boston, Mass.	641.0
2	Chicago, Ill.	3,366.9	17	Memphis, Tenn.	623.5
3	Los Angeles, Cal.	2,816.0	18	St. Louis, Mo.	622.2
4	Philadelphia, Pa.	1,948.6	19	New Orleans, La.	593.4
5	Detroit, Mich.	1,511.4	20	Phoenix, Ariz.	582.0
6	Houston, Texas	1,232.8	[21	Columbus, Ohio	539.6]
7	Baltimore, Md.	905.7	[22	Seattle, Wash.	530.8]
8	Dallas, Texas	844.4	[23	Jacksonville, Fla.	528.8]
9	Washington, D.C.	756.5	[24	Pittsburgh, Pa.	520.1]
10	Cleveland, Ohio	750.9	[25	Denver, Col.	514.6]
11	Indianapolis, Ind.	744.6	[26	Kansas City, Mo.	507.0]
12	Milwaukee, Wisc.	717.0	[27	Atlanta, Ga.	496.9]
13	San Francisco, Calif.	715.6	[28	Buffalo, N.Y.	462.7]
14	San Diego, Calif.	696.7	[29	Cincinnati, Ohio	452.5]
15	San Antonio, Texas	654.1	[30	Nashville, Tenn.	448.0]

Source: US Bureau of the Census.

to bear the burdens of social adjustment and valid financial responsibility in a nation and time when social justice could not be forgotten. The problems so prominently presented in our studies of Philadelphia, Cleveland, St. Louis, and Detroit show this role of the confining city boundary.

The new central city isolation contrasted with the situation of the nineteenth century cities, which could spread their borders to encompass the growth of the city as an entity of regional or national purpose. Whatever financial responsibilities for social problems there then were could be spread over virtually all citizen groups. In the 1860s Philadelphia had extended its jurisdiction over a large area fast becoming a city when it engaged in a massive annexation of the towns on its borders. In 1899 New York had operated even more grandly, taking in Brooklyn (which was then the fourth city in the country) and three other counties that surrounded Manhattan. It was common for cities to grow in area as well as in population. But around the time of the First World War, for a variety of reasons, some of them viewed as encouraging political reform, annexation became difficult for most of the major cities that were then in existence. These places came to be ringed by suburbs of separate incorporation and increasingly distinctive social and economic class.

THE SUBURB IS OF ANCIENT LINEAGE BUT CHANGED STATUS

At this point it must be emphasized that the change was not in the residence of the more well-to-do at the edge of the city that had been a characteristic of American cities from nearly their beginning—and of Anglo-Saxon society at least from the thirteenth century when Peter of Savoy built his palace outside the city's walls in London. What was new was the fact that massive international and interregional trade and manufacturing had so enlarged the population of cities that it was difficult to provide accommodation within their boundaries save by greatly increasing the densities of people on the land. That solution had to be taken in the first half of the nineteenth century in the largest places, so we find overcrowding widespread in New York in the 1840s and 1850s. So long as there was no mechanical transport for passengers within the city, crowding and deterioration of public health were unavoidable. But the hearty efforts at improving the health of urban Americans, marked by the reforms and zealous undertakings of the three decades just before 1920, had convinced those Americans who could gain space, openness, better air, and newer and less contaminated housing that it was their familial, societal, and economic duty to do so. In a society where basic prosperity was spreading more widely among city people, there could be no outcome other than the rapid and extensive suburban spread that the 1920s and 1930s witnessed. In fact, when the federal government finally came to grips with the enunciation of a national housing policy, as expressed in the faltering efforts of the late Hoover administration and the more fruitful ones in the New Deal, that policy sought to encourage the average American to seek private, single family housing of reasonable physical quality. The practices that had sent prosperous Boston merchants to live in suburban Milton as early as the time of the China Trade; which had caused the merchant A.T. Stewart to lay out Garden City on Long Island as a workers' suburb in 1869; which had made Chicago a city of gardens when Ebenezer Howard came there to work as a court reporter in the 1870s; and which had led medical, social, and political reformers to crusade for the relief of the honest workman's burden through movement to the new housing areas near the edge of the city were not the result of base and craven motives now argued by some as the main basis for suburbanization. And so long as those peripheral areas came ultimately to be part of the city, there was little change from the conditions that had always operated in cities. Phrased slightly differently, so long as the process of annexation could operate, the process that led to a congregation of inmigrants to the city in its older core areas and of longer term residents in the suburbs was thought both natural and desirable.

When the Chicago School of Sociologists in the 1920s were describing their model of the American city, they pictured it as characterized by a densely developed core, where the first settlement had taken place only to be crowded out by business. Ranged round that central business district were bands of housing of increasing newness and elevating social status and income. No remark of moral condemnation was entered; this was the way cities had always been, and it was assumed that in a socially mobile and decreasingly ethnically specific population, this was the way they should continue to be.

But there were two particular difficulties. One was specific to the healthy functioning of the city as a political and social organism. Just at the time the Chicago sociologists were shaping their model on concentric zones, those gripped with political reform instincts were campaigning for smaller units of government, which would create better supervision and a geography of "community." We now realize how disastrous this well-meaning but little-informed activity really was. Just at the time when a new form of urban frontiersmanship—that of rural blacks from the South and rural Spanish-Americans, from Puerto Rico in particular—was beginning, the normal processes of American urbanization were put out of operation. The city was to be constrained in area; thus the process of frontier congregation within the city would affect only part of the physical metropolis when it came to social interaction and political and financial responsibility. The other difficulty came from the effort to work a revolution in the basic cultural attitudes toward housing within cities. This revolution was one of trying to convince Americans that they should adopt the higher densities of urban housing that had long been characteristic of continental European cities—but not of Britain. Thus we found during the 1930s the adoption of a national housing policy that was comprised of two distinct parts—one for the central city person, either well-to-do or the average man, which called for very high densities of people in large apartment houses; and one for the more traditional member of American society, who might aspire, after the Federal Housing Administration was created in 1934, to a suburban residence so long as he was an honest working man.

There were "two cities" in America, one for the core area residents—who had always been most numerously the inmigrants from overseas or the countryside of America—and one for the more traditional social element whose acculturation had already been accomplished and who had, in the very long-standing practice, moved outward from the center to gain space, health, and what was viewed as the ideal urban environment. The efforts in the 1930s to shape a national housing policy had managed to create "two cities" in America much like the "two nations" that Benjamin Disraeli wrote about in his social novels of the 1840s, before he turned directly to politics. In the last century Britain was made up of a small "nation" of the rich aristocracy and a vast "nation" of the poor working class.

Fortunately, in the 1930s in America the numbers were reversed. The larger "city" was the extensive one of the working class and middle class suburbs, whereas the smaller "city" was that of the densely housed and still to be acculturated central area poor. Unfortunately, while all of this was going on, the legal bar to annexation, which was constraining in a permanent way the older cities, was beginning to form a boundary between the smaller but more impoverished core city and the larger and more prosperous suburbia. But again it should be emphasized that it was the imposition of this boundary between the two cities rather than the process of suburbanization that was new. In a nation that has been happily free of external boundary problems since the middle of the last century, this internalized conflict has tended to defy clear understanding and to lead to the adoption of rather simple and "nationalistic" arguments of the case for each of these "cities."

In several of the studies of individual cities that follow this chapter, the central city case is advanced with fervor and a sense of outrage; in none of these studies has anyone seemed to feel free to argue with equal force the suburb's case. Social science in American universities has so thoroughly taken up the cudgels of the central city that there is little recognition that people across the boundary in the suburbs are certainly human and probably rather humane, that they ended up there by the operation of a process of urban growth (morphogenesis) that has been true of our cities from their origin, and that the urban goals of housing laid down in the 1930s gave those suburban settlers a valid expectation that their acts were consonant with national social and economic policies.

It is in such a context that we should examine the concept of "white flight" so often alluded to today. The confusion and guilt we encounter is the product of looking at a present-day pattern of cities and immediately assuming that it is the result only of current forces, even of only a single force from among those present-day determinants. Faced with such an oversimplification of reality, the best course would seem to be to turn back to that reality itself. In a short essay such as this, however, the reflective view must be clearly focused to be completed. Here we will concentrate on the single question: Is there a general process of city growth in America? If there is, then perhaps a consideration of its current operation may help us to deal with the border warfare between the two cities that is becoming both more dangerous and more doctrinaire.

IS THERE A GENERAL PROCESS OF CITY GROWTH?

The twenty vignettes that follow discuss in considerable detail the nature of the largest cities of the United States. The picture is one of a distinctive settlement structure and at the same time a particular society that is resident therein. Here no attempt is made to resolve the question of whether the physical structure of the city is totally the creation of society or society a creation utterly independent of the physical build of the city. Instead it is assumed that there is sufficient impress of form on society and society on form to deal with both as cause and effect (dependent and independent variables). Unfortunately it is part of the presentation of the picture of a specific city that the distinctive is emphasized and that the characteristics shared with other cities are left to the reader's assumption. These necessary generalizations can best be presented in the nature of processes at work in shaping the form of the city.

Already we have seen one process at work in the establishment of cities in the American land—the one called regional congregation, which led to distinctive geographical patterns of cities at various times in our history. What we may now ask is whether this process can serve as well to help to explain the physical build within cities, or at least to provide an analytical system for relating that physical build from one time to another and from one place to a distant one? I believe a notion of local congregation can serve our integrative purpose. In the sections that follow an attempt is made to sketch the way the process of congregation can serve as a guide to understanding and as a tool of analysis.

The central question is very simple: Are there common characteristics, among the welter of details that we may see in an individual city, and certainly in twenty of the largest cities of America? If there are such common characteristics, then it seems that there are likely to be shared processes that produce such identities. For that reason it is most useful, and certainly more intellectually exciting, to look for the process from which common responses come than it is merely to catalog the way in which American cities are alike. Particularly as the study of an individual city is a difficult way to find processes at work, and to present them to your view, we have believed that it is in the introduction to this volume of vast and exciting detail that we must seek to provide a key to whence came that richness and where might it be leading. Only through some idea as to what the process at work may be can we really answer why we are the way we are today and what we may be at the end of the century.

The Placement of American Cities

The United States furnishes us with a realm in which to study cities that can hardly be equaled elsewhere. At first it might seem that a 350 year urban history is short by world experience, and thus to be regretted in a search for a central process such as we seek. There can be no doubt that truths about cities were learned before our nation was founded and that there are other processes and practices of urbanization than those we employ; but there is validity to the argument that in the United States we have the not so common opportunity to look at urbanization from its local beginnings and in a time for which historical records are available. We may begin by asking, What was the first process of urbanization to operate within the lands that now make up the United States?

It was a very simple process, that of *placement,* but we should not be misguided into thinking that the simplicity makes this an unimportant act. Rather the reverse in fact; once a city is emplaced, the facts of its location and environment become the reality of life, which may be transformed to a degree but never denied. To take two examples: In our consideration of Chicago it transpires that the city was sited largely as the lake terminus of the Illinois and Michigan Canal when it was being built in the 1830s. Such a terminus needed a harbor on the lake and access to the canal leading to the Illinois River and, ultimately, to the Mississippi. The mouth of the Chicago River joined these qualities. It also was a vile site for a city,

subject to flooding and unable to furnish drainage for storm waters that tend to collect in areas so subject to sharp thunderstorm activity. But once Chicago was set down on the ground it was unlikely to be moved and, instead, it was the ground that had to change, as it did through filling in the 1850s and 1860s. And the city had literally to rise out of the mud to match that level, particularly at the hands of George Pullman, whose first success was that of jacking up the buildings along Lake Street as the ground was filled in 1857. Over the years even the initial transportation purpose changed and Chicago became first the world's greatest rail hub and more recently the premier air focus; yet it was the Illinois and Michigan Canal that determined its emplacement, and on a water-soaked site mainly suitable to that function but few others.

In another instance of a limited decision's becoming the controlling factor in the life of a great city long after the decision itself had much meaning we may look briefly at San Francisco. When the discovery of gold in California in 1848 led quickly to a great rush thence of miners, it was important to establish an entrepôt somewhere on San Francisco Bay from which they might be fed and supplied and through which the gold could be sent to the money markets of the world where it gained its main use and value. Because the inshipment of food and mining materials was nearly exclusively by sea, and by sailing vessels given the state of steamboating at that time, the best place for an entrepôt became Yerba Buena Cove just to the south inside the Golden Gate. There warehouses were set up from which transshipment up the rivers to the mines could be undertaken using shallow draft steamboats. The site of San Francisco was ideal as a juncture between oceanic sailing and riverine steamboating; it was far less desirable as the core of a large metropolitan area. The years since 1869, when the railroad reached the east side of the Bay at Oakland, as our vignette on the Bay Area shows, have been characterized by the continuous effort of San Francisco city to overcome its eccentric location in the face of the emergence of a diverse metropolitan area of great extent and many undertakings. Ferries of large capacity had to be pressed into service until bridges were opened to the east in 1936 and to the north in 1937. And since then several billion dollars have been poured into trying to overcome a position so offside as to be explicable only by looking back to the conditions of the original emplacement. It has been this continuing effort to update a past act of emplacement that accounts for the "innovation" of the Bay Area Rapid Transit construction during the last decade, rather more than any essential response to the overall needs of the metropolis and its diverse peoples. But the full detail of that case must wait on the San Francisco-Oakland vignette.

Competitive Congregation: The Special Case of Megalopolis

In our discussion of the great towns at various times in history the role of the congregation of functions emerged with clarity. The original towns of America were her trading ports—entrepôts if you will—whose implantation on this shore was the beginning not only of European settlement but of urbanization as well. The emplacement of the towns was where the initial trading purpose would have had it; in the case of New York, Boston, Philadelphia, and Baltimore we must deal with sites ideal for such colonial activities but far less desirable for the operation of the modern city. A further aspect of this trading orientation of the colonial entrepôts, which persists somewhat to our discomfort, is the competitive nature of the towns. Various English trading companies and aristocratic proprietors were given grants of land normally centering on a coastal estuary on which a port could be built whose hinterland extended inland to tap the assumed wealth of natural produce and potential farming settlement. The result was that the thirteen colonies were to varying degrees directly competitive one with another in the beginning and have tended to remain so even today. The areal extent of the individual colonies was originally thought adequate for the activities they undertook but the passage of time has meant that the more successful foci of the individual colonies —the great towns and present-day metropolises —have grown so fat as to spread across political boundaries into other states. New York is the most striking case but Philadelphia, Boston, and Washington (a specialized congregation adjacent to colonial Alexandria) share the problem. The modest goals of the colonial plantations shaped a political geography of states on the northeast coast that does not conform well with the ultimate growth there of a number of great cities.

The very number of those northeastern cities, for which Jean Gottmann resurrected the name of an ancient city—Megalopolis—is a distinctive feature of American urban geography. There has been the most casual, and certainly most inappropriate, projection of the idea of the American Megalopolis to other parts of the United States, and to other countries, in complete defiance of the genetic qualities of the original example. Megalopolis is the way it is because of its colonial history. The creation by the Stuart kings of competitive trading colonies, each centering on an entrepôt, meant, first, a specialization of functions that led in turn to the creation of a great town at the very earliest stage of settlement, and, second, to a competitive alignment of those places which became the string of cities of Megalopolis. As Carl Bridenbaugh showed forty years ago, the colonies grew out of the implanted town and they grew up in a fiercely competitive alignment along the northeastern coast. When the American Revolution ended the direct ties to England it did not destroy the competition within the United States; so much remained that the economic history of the nineteenth century was that of parallel striving among cities that might be no more than ninety miles apart—for example, New York and Philadelphia. The result was the attempt of each city to capture part of the trans-Appalachian West for its own benefit and support. The success that met these efforts maintained the entrepôts right up to the present, with the notable exception of Charleston (South Carolina), though the nineteenth century successes produced new types of activities which came to reside alongside the colonial interests of long distance trade. The outcome was a city of several types of congregations rather than the single-minded one found before the Revolution.

In the Beginning There Was Mercantile Activity

Within the colonial town most persons were fairly directly tied to the overseas trading functions of the place. Even the retail trade tended to reflect that trade in a very direct way. The goods for sale were what the ships had brought, and those unavailable were those still on the high seas. These were not central places where country men brought goods and bought others in exchange. These were towns where men and women earned their living by facilitating an extensive system of trade that might reach from the first Corn Belt in Lancaster County, Pennsylvania, to the Royal Exchange in London. Esther Forbes, in her vivid picture of *Paul Revere and The World He lived In,* presents us with an unmistakable view of a city on the frontier but still very much a part of the wider Atlantic world. In the same way, as a townsman Benjamin Franklin was a man of his times and his place in the cosmos, far more worldly than we view most of our Founding Fathers and far more gifted in social and geographical comprehension that those semibackwoodsmen of Virginia. When he migrated it was from the largest early colonial town to the largest late colonial town.

The nineteenth century mixed the purposes of towns, adding manufacturing and political administration to trade; and as more people came to reside in cities, the needs of daily provision increased to the point that it was necessary for increasing groups of workers to cater to retail, as opposed to long distance wholesale, trade. With the increasing complexity of urban support came the separation of urban land uses into distinctive clusters for a specific purpose. In colonial towns there had been an intermixture of activities—of shops in houses and houses next to churches and state houses and wharves as in Boston—not, it should be emphasized, in a jumble as is sometimes alleged but in a quite rational reflection of the relatively simple social and economic structure of these towns. Houses were shops and workshops as well as residences. And if all buildings were more or less alike, there was little need for locational distinctions. It was the absence of specialization with distinctive streets, rather than the mythical wandering cow, that made our cities seem rather formless in a way complex medieval towns were not.

At this point we must look ahead in time to the other cities that form part of this comparative survey. Simple congregation for a single specific purpose might have been true of the colonial towns but it certainly has not been for the cities that have sprung up later. Yet, when we examine the initial stages of any of our twenty cities, we find that their sites were normally set by some mercantile objective and that that objective tended to be a

projection of business activity from outside the area. In other words, these towns did not emerge from the countryside in accordance with the precepts of central place theory; rather, the towns were sited in largely undeveloped country in the interests of "opening it up," an act not comprehended by central placement.

Running through the list of places outside the urban Northeast, we find Atlanta mushrooming in the late 1830s, when it became the terminus of rail lines from the Atlantic coast. New Orleans, St. Louis, Pittsburgh, and Minneapolis-St. Paul were sited in various ways in direct response to the first of the interior waterways—the Mississippi system. In these river ports trade was the main—probably nearly the exclusive—concern in the first years of settlement. When the Erie Canal, in 1825, opened the Great Lakes to an integration with the American East Coast ports, Cleveland and Chicago were founded as canal ports on the lakes and Detroit was resuscitated from a disrupted past to become another lake port. Turning to the Pacific coast, San Francisco, and later Seattle, became an entrepôt for the supply of gold fields. Los Angeles tried such an undertaking with respect to the Panamint Rush of the 1860s but it lost out to San Francisco, only to slumber as a failed trading town for another decade. Finally, even the Texas boom towns—Houston, Fort Worth, and Dallas—began as centers for the trading in an export product, first cotton and then oil. It was the opportunity to establish the innermost port to handle cotton exports which caused Houston to be sited on Buffalo Bayou, just as the coming of the railroads to the north edge of the Waxahatchie cotton belt helped to site Dallas and Fort Worth. In our list of great cities only two seem somewhat apart from this initial mercantile specialization—Hartford and Miami. In the instance of Hartford a case can be made for it as a colonial port (on the Connecticut River which was deep enough for the small colonial ships). But in the last hundred years it has ceased to be an important place for long distance ties save in the office and factory industries spread over an extensive district in central Connecticut. It is the density of suburban and exurban settlement and economic activity that raises the area to the status of one of the twenty most populous "daily urban systems" in the United States;

Hartford as a city is so unlike the other nineteen in this group as to defy, and make unmeaningful, comparison with the others. Miami does not fit very well historically, but it belongs in the first twenty metropolises. It began in seriousness as a city when it became a terminus, for a time, of the rail line down the Florida peninsula; as the vignette shows, only later did Miami become a port. It was as a real estate boom town that it grew. With eighteen out of the twenty largest cities fairly clearly growing on emplacements set out originally for distant trading purposes, there seems no need to add further to the argument that it was in these mercantile towns that the foundation of American metropolitanism was laid.

Initially in most cities there was a specialized local congregation of economic activities located near the transportation terminus of the connection to the outside world; these were the docks of the coastal and river ports and the rail lines of the few interior cities (Atlanta, Fort Worth, Dallas, and Minneapolis). Only in Los Angeles was the focus different. There it was a peculiar hydrographic situation in a semi-arid basin that sited the city where the flow of the Los Angeles River, which passed in the dry season through the bed gravels of the stream, was forced by a sill of rock to flow for a short distance above the surface of those gravels. When the Spaniards located the town they did so because of this surface flow of water. But the city did not grow with much vigor until local merchants were successful in bribing the Southern Pacific Railroad to pass through the town in 1876. It is symbolic that the Mexican plaza and the railroad station adjoin.

If these towns in their early years had no differentiation in internal structure—only a street pattern—once other functions came to reside there (alongside the traders) the new force of local congregation began to operate. In discovering why that was the case we may profitably recall briefly the process itself. Settlement of Europeans in North America had initially been an undertaking intimately tied to economic and social activities and concerns in Europe itself. The ports of the Atlantic seaboard had advanced the economic frontier of the several European countries that planted them—England, Holland, and France —and had been backed up by activities in larger and older cities of the homeland. Only a single purpose attached initially to these ports on the

western shore of the Atlantic—that of serving as distant correspondent in trade to the more complex city in the mother country. But as the American town grew it enlarged its role in functions other than distant trade, domesticating the sale of goods and services at retail within itself rather than far away across the Atlantic. When America gained her independence in 1783 a much more considerable wave of domestication in colonial ports took place, requiring the creation of several distinct local congregations, each to serve its own particular purpose and thereby separated from another internalized clustering. In truth, the entrepôts in America which at first were specialized extensions of the activities in distant places such as London or Amsterdam became economically complex cities in their own right. The same general pattern held for the other towns that came to be planted in the interior of the United States during the nineteenth century—the river and lake ports and later the railroad towns that first merely tied the developing countryside with a national system of intercommunication but came in the end to be complex regional metropolises. A town on any frontier was a place for supplying capital goods to that frontier and for collecting from it its early produce. It became a center of a greater range of activiites.

Towns and Townsmen as Pioneers

Only as development within the region took place were most of the functions that had earlier been carried out in the distant "homeland" cities brought forward to be nearer the producer and consumer. In part the ranks of this geographical advance were filled by those supplying the repeating retail and wholesale needs of the producers of basic raw products—minerals, furs, timbers, and crops—but perhaps more importantly those ranks were filled by the collectors, traders, and processors of the products of the countryside. Buffalo became preeminently a milling center for the wheat that opened farming in Ohio; Cincinnati arose as "porkopolis," the butcher and renderer of the hogs that replaced wheat to increase the prosperity of the Ohio farmer; and Cleveland grew as the maker of iron and steel for a railroad-building and manufacturing economy that came, at the end of the last century, to overshadow the agricultural economy of the eastern Middle West. In all these activities these city men were pioneers contemporaneous with those slashing the forest, turning the untilled sod, and laying the first tracks. From 1620 on, there was always a group of persons moving directly to the frontier town to begin the process of urbanization ahead of, or at least at the same time as, the country's advancing frontier. Because this is a commonly overlooked fact, I hope that emphasis may be placed on it.

The best test of the proposition of contemporaneity of urban with rural frontier is the continually noted transformation of the countryside, over a very short time, from general farming—almost subsistence agriculture—to quite specialized agriculture depending heavily on outshipment of crops, usually with processing in nearby cities. Where towns were not the companions of the agricultural pioneering—as in the Selkirk settlements of 1811 in the Red River valley of Manitoba or in some of the isolated areas of the Appalachians—nearly subsistence farming continued for many decades. A further test of this proposition is furnished by the chronology of American settlement which finds the town often planted before there were any fields around it to receive the same treatment. Boston, New York, Philadelphia, Savannah, New Orleans, St. Louis, Pittsburgh, San Francisco, and Seattle all came before their adjacent agricultural "hinterland" was put to any use. It is unfortunately the case that most of the theory of city founding and location comes from Europe where the earliest history of towns is lost in obscurity and where inference by scholars from conditions during the last century and a half has been substituted. Thus, in the 1820s the Pomeranian aristocratic farmer, Johann Heinrich von Thünen, reasoned that a city must have an agricultural hinterland to support itself, and a century later the Bavarian geographer, Walter Christaller, reasoned that the location of cities is determined by the supplying of a rural population with goods and services. American *experience,* not scholarly inference, belies such reasoning and we must argue that cities are pioneers as much as the backwoodsmen with whose course so much American mythology has dwelt.

The Locational Split Between Wholesaling and Retailing

Because towns do rapidly transform the countryside around themselves, the towns are in turn transformed. If at first they were sim-

ple entrepôts tying distant developed economic areas with developing frontier regions—note I did not say supplying the needs of that developing region, because it seems it is the linkage with the outside that is necessary for the region to evolve to the point that it can economically express a demand for goods and services—some of these pioneering towns did then begin to serve their regions more directly. Merchants who first dealt with collecting pot ashes, fish, and furs (in Boston and Hartford), furs and minerals (in St. Louis), or gold and silver (in San Francisco and Seattle) soon began to specialize in their trade, with some continuing to deal at wholesale with the products of the land whereas others found their abilities most particularly in the provision of individual needs of customers resident in or visiting the city. In Chicago at the middle of the last century most merchants were wholesalers who turned on occasion to retail trade. A generation later these entrepreneurs divided into two groups—those dealing with distant customers by express (and later mail) and those showing goods to customers who came into their shops. At that point there were two different conditions of access to customers, the first wherein the establishment wished to be near the railroad freight house and express office and the second wherein the establishment wished to be located on State Street, Main Street, or whatever thoroughfare was the resort of the customers seeking to fill their own wants.

From initially a single, simple congregation of urban pioneers there had developed a more complex and specialized society, but a society in which the process of local congregation remained as strong a determinant of the location of activities as it had been when the town had but a single function. Now there were several distinct congregations—that of traders with the outside, who were likely to be at the original center of the town near the docks or the railroad station; that of the establishments that came to specialize in retail trade, a clustering that depended on access to customers who were physically present in the town and whose energies would be conserved by a specialized clustering of shops in which goods would be shown to them, and sold; and that of those engaged in processing materials for large scale markets, either those far away and yet using the local produce or those nearby, consuming goods often brought in return from that distance. Each of these congregations tended to have supporting activities that enlarged its particular demand for space.

As the export trade from a city increased, which was commonly the first crank of the ratchet that began to raise the town's population, there was a demand for specialized services to lend support. In Boston, New York, Philadelphia, Baltimore, New Orleans, San Francisco, and Seattle these included shipping companies, customs agents, and a great array of those who facilitated long distance trade. In some places commodity exchanges were established, serving to set the prices for goods handled from a multiplicity of sources and dispatched to a number of customers. Boston handled leather this way; New York cotton, sugar, coffee, wool, and a number of other items; St. Louis became a center for the trade in furs; San Francisco dealt with metals; Chicago's Board of Trade handled grain and meat, later dropping meat; and most cities had at least some firms whose distant connections carried on commodity trading. The result was a specialized congregation of traders in titles to goods rather than in their physical possession. In a more specialized sense these titles were the stocks and bonds of corporations whose value was given through a consensus of "the market" rather than a determinate, immutable sum. But the market in titles to shares and commodities had such needs for congregation, and such dangers from isolation, that stock and commodity exchange and brokerage firms dealing with those legal titles became the most obviously geographically congregated of all urban functions, and thereby the most competitive seekers for locations in the heart of the financial congregation. The result was that the first skyscrapers were thrust up on sites central to the financial congregation. And today the last remnant of fierce spatial competition in major cities remains the jostling for land and office in these financial districts. Tall buildings respond more to a need for highly localized congregation than to the highest of land values as is sometimes assumed.

Internal Transportation
and Congregation

The competition for space in the retail congregation was equally as fierce in the nine-

teenth century because then the market served was smaller in total numbers and less mobile than it has subsequently become. When potential shoppers were of necessity channeled along lines of public transportation there was a focus of shoppers where those lines came together. It should not surprise us that in the beginning retail trade tended to be rather mixed up in space with other types of mercantile activity. After all, the merchant of colonial America dealt in various activities, but as he might come to specialize in retailing, his concern for commodity trading would be likely to slacken and even depart. No longer would he need to be near the exchanges; instead he would wish to be where the customers for retail goods were most numerous. The result was a separation of local congregations into financial districts and shopping districts. This geographical characteristic is observable in any American city of good size. In truth it depends upon the simple fatigue that grips people moving on foot; they seek to minimize the walking they must do to carry on their activities. Before there was vehicular transport in cities—that is, before about 1830 in New York and 1850 in other large towns—there was a certain incoherence in the separation of activities because there was no mass channeling of movement. Once fixed lines of public transport were established—particularly once there were mechanical means of transport, with their emphasis on established and reasonably spaced "stops"—there was a tendency for certain "stops" to be the center of one congregation, whereas another would serve as the pole of attraction for a different congregation. In the vignettes dealing with the core areas of San Francisco and New York we are presented evidence of specialized congregations of offices and stores rather separated geographically from each other.

To present an illustrative explanation of the tie between transport and congregation we may look for a moment at the way the introduction of street railways into already rather large American cities reshaped those places after 1887. The first important mechanical transport in American cities was more truthfully transport *to* cities, which came when railroads were built outward from those larger towns that existed in the 1830s. Boston was the first "hub" of railroads, having three radiating lines by 1835. Philadelphia and Baltimore followed soon after and even New York was reasonably served by the 1840s. As interior cities grew in importance, railroads fast focused on them. Chicago, though originally a canal port, came, as every school boy knows, to be the world's great railroad town by the end of the last century. If we ask how these incoming railroads affected the movement within the city, the answer must be not very much. What they did do was increase the area from which people could reach the city with physical ease. Visitors to the city increased and persons of means could begin to think of suburban residence. Visitor or commuter, the person arriving by train obviously reached the city at the train station. But fatigue and time demands were different between the two groups. The visitor was an occasional or even one time participant in urban life, but the commuter came daily. Thus we find that the demands of the commuters came to take precedence over those of the visitors. Stated another way, the land use around the passenger stations tended to become heavily dominated by those activities that were associated with the middle class who were the main body of commuters. It was the financial workers—bankers, brokers, traders, insurance workers, and their legal and transport servants—whose congregation could benefit most from location adjacent to the station. The recent completion of the world's tallest building—the Sear's Tower—near Union Station in Chicago merely demonstrates the continuing truth of the greater utility to commuters of sites near the station. The visitors were quite often in the beginning housed in hotels near the station, but as the financial congregation grew there was a tendency for the hotels to be pushed farther away, a movement that was further encouraged by the absolute eviction of shopping quarters to streets at some remove from the station.

We find when we look at our great towns that this is the case. In Boston, New York, Philadelphia, Chicago—in fact in most of the world's great financial centers—the stations are in or near the financial district; if not originally so, they are certainly ultimately thus located. In London the railroads were drawn to The City; in New York much administrative and financial activity was drawn to the stations located in midtown.

When a system of transport for use internal to the city was finally hammered out in the late 1880s, with Frank Sprague's successful development of traction motors, multiple unit control, and the other mechanical features that made electric traction possible, both the lower income group of workers and the visitor-shopper suddenly entered into consideration. No longer was there a single or at best a couple of "stops" for mechanical transport in the city; now there could be stops for several congregations. And in those cities that gained important railway transit systems—most notably Boston, New York, Philadelphia, and Chicago with their elevated or subway systems—there emerged new geographical congregations, particularly for retail trade. The sociologist Walter Firey in a monumental study of *Land Use in Central Boston* notes, among many brilliant conclusions, what he termed a process of "contractualism" which drew together, at Washington Street and Summer-Winter streets, the main department stores of the city. This was, to use our term here, the congregation of retail trade at the crossing of two of the main subway lines, a situation soon to be reproduced near Herald Square in New York, with a similar impact on those leaders of retail trade who moved thence from an earlier congregation near Eighth Street after the subways had been built and opened. In city after city street railways, even of a less fixed type than those with subways and elevateds, reshaped the location of retail trade in a way that the railroad had not done. The reason is precisely the one we are considering—that the railroad station became the locale for financial district congregation, leaving the retail trade to wander aimlessly for several decades, as the history of department store locations in New York City strikingly demonstrates. When the street railway was introduced it not only offered new stops around which congregation could be taken up but it also expanded the size of the body of users to include occasional visitors and shoppers and the great mass of lower income workers whose individual purchases might be small but whose massed consumption was indeed compelling. The massing of their modest demands was such that a whole new range of goods, priced to capture their trade, could be introduced. And with its introduction came the halcyon days of the central city department store, the only place the masses could then afford to shop and the easiest, most accessible place for the more prosperous to shop as well. Today this overpowering congregation of shoppers has been split: the prosperous have mobility and drive elsewhere to shop, but the masses, particularly those of recent urbanization—Blacks, Spanish-Americans, and Puerto Ricans—still tend to congregate on the central city department stores because there their specialized demands can still best and most cheaply be met.

The conditions that lead to congregation of activities within the city lead, as strongly, to separation therein, for it is the benefits of clustering one activity that suggest to those coming together the necessity to reserve what limited space there is in the particular area to that specific land use. Such an effort to utilize space for a particular purpose has, in our society and its economy, been enforced by the operation of economic practices of competitive bidding for land and morphological practices of specialized design of buildings. In the first instance it is what economists call "the land rent gradient" that does the job. The mechanism envisaged is one wherein the most anxious seeker of space at a particular point will there pay the highest rent (assuming his use of land is for productive purposes and his reasoning as to the value of the location is correct). Other users who either prize the land less highly or can use it only less productively will offer lower rents for it and, thus, be forced to look elsewhere. Because a site near a railroad passenger station is most "productive" in terms of reducing effort and time waste for commuters rather than occasional shoppers, and because shopping involves the central city population as a whole (for whom the station for train services to the suburbs is not of much interest), then some other site has higher relative value for retail businesses than does the vicinity of the railroad station. It is important to realize that land value does not operate on a single scale geographically, much as in the past it was thought to operate on a continuous scale economically. What is the "best site" for financial offices may in all likelihood not be the "best site" for department stores. This fact emerges clearly when we observe how several "best sites" are to be found in the city when the multiplicity of activities within the city are considered. Thus, the oversimplification of desire for and valuation of location that emerges from the rigidity of a single-centered land-rent gradient analysis is a poor explanation of the siting of various

activities within the city. If we wish to know what is the process at work in establishing the internal structure of cities, as we do in this introductory essay, then I believe we can gain far more understanding from thinking about the various types of congregation within the city and the changes in the conditions of congregation that may be observed during the history of our cities than from myopic consideration of land rent alone.

Specialization of Structure Creates Residential Congregation

In the preceding paragraph it was noted that morphological specialization in city buildings also helps to account for the existence of several discrete land use congregations. To understand this point it is necessary to look back briefly at the build of American cities in the last century. Then there were certain physical characteristics of buildings in great towns that helped determine the land use pattern of the time; characteristics that are themselves of interest because some of those buildings have with good fortune survived. The nineteenth century city building was normally less structurally specialized than is the building today, in part because construction techniques were rather simple and generally applied and in part because the experience on which planning for new building was based was not itself very diverse. In the colonial town the business of a merchant was carried on in his counting house which commonly might merely be the front room of his dwelling house, a situation also common when it came to the location of a retail shop. The scale of business, the volume of goods handled, and the employment of persons outside the family were such that the domestic building could serve in addition as the business building. In terms of architecture, the use of timber framing was so universal (save in a small number of church and governmental buildings) as to mean that the modular size of timbers of common availability dictated a modest scale for the spans and heights of rooms and the use of repeated roomlike units to gain additional space within the building. Thus houses grew by adding ells, and various functions were comprehended within the same general structure.

Even when construction technology began to change—to utilize brick and stone masonry and in turn to use iron columns in the compression members of structures—little effort was made to change the size of rooms and thereby foreclose the easy transformation of use from one activity to another. It was a common practice in the city of the first two-thirds of the nineteenth century for people to live behind or above shops; and for offices, particularly those dealing with the general population of the city, to be intermixed on the ground floor of buildings with shops or else housed on upper stories above those shops. Shops themselves were normally of sufficiently modest size that they could be located in a dwelling house if it sood on a handy site. But in the last third of the century the physical build of our cities began to change to such a degree that structures were planned quite specifically for the need that first occupied them. And residential properties began to be notably more varied in form and size than they had been before. At the same time that the mansions on Fifth Avenue in New York were being constructed at the edge of the city core, the single room tenements in tall dumb-bell buildings were built in more southerly reaches of Manhattan. Lest this be thought the way it was earlier in time, it is well to look into the houses of important men in the colonial city, particularly in comparison with those of simple honest workmen of their time. The dis-cussion of architecture in New York contained in the vignette on that city brings this out well.

This is not the place to try to continue an analysis of the specialization of structures in American cities. Rather, we may make only a couple of general points. We should realize that the process of specialization has become ever more obvious, to the point that we now find it very difficult to reemploy buildings from other times and other uses. What happens to the movie theaters of the prewar years; what will happen to the surplus of gasoline stations we now know that we have? In turn we realize that both the housing of the poor in the past and that of the rich find little value for us today—that of the poor because its grim auster-ity is beyond the necessity of virtually all today, and that of the rich because its maintenance is literally beyond the competence of virtually any private citizen. When housing is refur-bished in the centers of cities it tends to have been that initially occupied by middle rather than upper class people and it shows a strong tendency to be early nineteenth century, rather

than later in that period. Beacon Hill never waned; Society Hill in Philadelphia and the inner South End in Boston have returned to favor. These were modular houses from an earlier time whose variety of usefulness has never really been lost.

Occupation Early Basis of American Housing

The cities that the English settlers in North America planted on her shores were patterned after the merchant towns of the Middle Ages, as much in social structure as in the physical layout, which intrudes more clearly on our view and is, therefore, more widely understood. As quite workaday settlements, their main purpose was the conduct of various craftsmen's jobs in manufacture and of long distance and local activity in trade: the grandiose or pompous functions of the Continental court city of the lay prince or the prince bishop were for the most part missing. If one English town was to serve as the model for American urbanism it was the city of London, whose nature, we should not forget, was neither that of county capital—that was Westminster standing outside its walls to the west—nor religious capital—that was Canterbury in the country off to the east. The city of London was a merchant's town wherein the internal physical structure was almost entirely concerned with caring for the needs of the various trades and the urban social structure was far less classbound and polarized than was that in the countryside. What social geography there was was largely the product of the congregation of the workers in different trades within distinct districts of the city. To take just one example, the nature of trade was such that neither the poor nor the pros-perous could move out of the heart of the city—the poor because their labor tended to be on a day-to-day basis that required their resi-dence, such as it was, near the docks, ware-houses, and shops that were the source of casual employment; and the prosperous be-cause they had to be in the thick of the particu-lar trade in which they were engaged, both to gain the business information so essential to its success in an era of word-of-mouth intelli-gence and to sell goods in an era when geo-graphical location rather than advertising announced the probable source of goods.

It would be too strong to say there was no social class in these merchants' towns that were brought to America: it is not too strong to say that they were for their time and our time relatively classless. The result was an occupational congregation at work in trades that tended to have all practitioners living near together. The master, the journeyman, and the apprentice tended to occupy the same or adjacent houses, and in proximity to other groupings of the type within the trade. As a result, the city implanted in America tended to avoid economic and social class division in its geography.

Two crucial changes came in these cities as they evolved between colonial times and the present and each was a specific expression of congregation. As the scale of economic activity expanded in the cities of the United States, particularly during the nineteenth century, there was a tendency for the various occupation districts of the city to grow so large that they tended to become little towns within the city, a development that was strongly reinforced if particular ethnic groups were associated with the trade. The tie between brewing and German quarters was most obvious in St. Louis but was found elsewhere, as was the association of textile trades with French Canadian districts in New England cities and of later immigrant groups with the iron and steel industry in Pittsburgh, Cleveland, and Chicago. In many of our twenty cities the ties between the Chinese, Jewish, and Spanish-American ethnic groups and the needle trades that make clothing were strong, and, as those trades grew, ethnic work quarters emerged whose location might create a Chinese or Jewish district, or else the prior existence of such a district might draw to it the workshop quarter.

There were as well functional requirements in the various use districts in cities that tended to encourage, if not actually enforce, separation from other districts. If an era proved unusually desirable to one activity or group of residents, for whatever reason, the process of local congregation would be likely to begin, leading in the end to such a concentration of activity of that particular sort that other uses would either (1) be driven out, or (2) themselves be drawn out by the desire to shape another congregation, of necessity elsewhere. There is an important point that is being made that should not be overlooked: it is that congregation is a process at work influencing all locational decisions made within metropolitan areas *and* that there can never, after the initial, usually most simple, stage of urbanization, be a single congregation that will serve the expressed and valid needs of all activities and groups. Thus, the single-centered city model so favored by economists and normative geographers is a mental abstraction rather than an urban geographical observation, and largely unreflective of the social forces and desires that must be placed alongside economic forces in the shaping of the city.

The second crucial change that came to American cities in the shift from the colonial town to the great modern metropolis was the introduction of transportation internal to the city itself. Once there was internal transport, the benefits of residence tied to workplace, which had been the tradition from the Middle Ages to the onset of the industrial revolution, could be reappraised. The conclusion was similar to that drawn with respect to the tie between wholesaling and retailing or shopping and office functions—that is, that there were considerable benefits to be derived from separation of functions and recongregation of each function in its new center. Factories could then vastly enlarge and seek sites strongly serviced by external transport, shopping districts could become central business districts piling sales space high on the ground and requiring shoppers to take mechanical transport from dispersed housing areas to a congregated shopping area, and offices could be piled even higher into the air because fewer visitors to their premises were needed but more complex relations between offices were involved and benefits were gained from density of clustering among offices themselves.

The Role of Class in a Nativist Culture

What was the effect on residential conditions when housing developed an independent congregation—that is, distinct from workplace congregations such as had been traditional forces shaping cities? The direct effect was that of establishing distinct local congregations within residence based not on occupation as before but rather on economic and social class. The main exception to this general truth came in the matter of domestic servants who, in a direct fashion, continued the sort of occupational grouping that had been true of medieval and early modern society. The significance of this fact is shown in the long history of racial "integration" in southern cities (such as Atlanta and New Orleans) where, until quite recently, it could be shown that there was greater residential mixing of blacks and whites than in the North. What they did was to live in a time-honored occupational pattern, a fact made manifest by the recent "disintegration" of housing in just those southern cities: now servants either have disappeared from the scene or else "live out."

Caste and class became the congregating forces in American cities once there was transportation internal to the city. There were class distinctions in earlier times but their geographical expression was slight; if different economic classes were not resident in adjacent houses, they were resident in neighboring streets. Blacks in the city were likely to be in the serving class and thus an integral part of the higher income households. There were otherwise rather few immigrants to America who did not melt fairly quickly into an emerging native culture that was neither English nor not-English. The accounts of European—and particularly English—travelers in the nineteenth century make much of the existence of a distinctly American culture, to which new arrivals sought earnestly to attach themselves. There were exceptions—the religious Germans of Pennsylvania and the French in New Orleans—though for the most part ethnic identity was not a very significant feature of the emerging great towns of the earlier years of the republic. This fact is worth emphasis because it was not to an English culture, as in English Canada, that the immigrants were adhering; instead adherence was to a native product, of which those denizens were inordinately proud and, in youthful insouciance, of which they were greatly assertive. But as most people coming to the United States in the last century were voluntarily and thankfully leaving cultures "that had failed them," they tended to join the natives in America in asserting the virtues both of the local culture and of a single culture. Influenced by such desires, our cities were true melting pots, as the countryside was not then and the city is no longer.

The increase in urban activity, which brought in its wake the enlargement and re-sorting of functional congregations, forced attention to be given to internal transportation. To collect workers at large factories, warehouses, and transportation facilities; to gather customers at the quickly expanding shops in the city center; and to assemble the large work forces needed for expanding office activities meant the introduction and daily use of trolley and rapid transit lines. Those lines led, however, in two directions, though, with contrasting geographical patterns at the two ends: at the objective of the daily journey to work there were large, densely occupied workplaces whereas at the destination of the homeward journey there was a vast, disaggregated pattern of housing spread extensively over an everexpanding urban region. The important thing to note is that this spreading carpet of housing was both extensive and of thin depth; in colonial America families had resided in houses aligned together along adjacent streets in the city, closer in spacing than was true of rural housing, but not in itself so very different from the country module.

Partly as a result of the original migration to the New World, and certainly as a consequence of the national restlessness that has gripped Americans throughout their history, there was a stronger tendency for the existence of nuclear families than would have been true in the lands whence came the settlers. As a result the vast, rural almost-apartment houses that were characteristic of the Alpine lands and Germany were uncommon in America, and so were similarly commodious urban houses. The urban history of America had stages that sufficiently corresponded with transportation development to allow the preference for single family detached housing to be expressed by a society that still to a larger degree than elsewhere was typified by relatively small, nuclear families, particularly as they lived in cities.

The Nativist Culture of the Suburbs
Let us try to assemble the various conditions and forces that entered into the shaping of a social geography of housing in the late nineteenth century American city. There was a great expansion of urban population, that, in turn, was typically nuclear in family structure, nativist in culture, and no longer characterized by great occupational congregation. As economic historians have shown, these Americans were relatively better off than their European or Asian relatives. In particular, they were better able to use the developing mechanical transport that was giving the chance for increased

mobility within the city. In Europe the working class could ill afford to commute until much later in the evolution of the city form, so its congregation in close-in overcrowded working class quarters was a necessity. Only the upper middle class in Europe could move to the suburbs. In America even in the last half of the last century some workers were able to command the transport that permitted the maintenance of those three cultural goals that show through the seemingly inchoate spread of urban housing: (1) the persistence of the nuclear family, (2) the desire to continue the detached and relatively roomy single family housing, and (3) the search to find the product of the melting pot process in the native culture of the suburbs. The last goal, that of living within a native culture, is an entirely logical outgrowth of what had become a national social philosophy; simply stated, that was the forging of a new culture to replace in every case those that had been left behind geographically. Once the distant origins had been left behind, it was fully consonant with the goals of migration that the new melting pot culture would be readily accepted, since it was viewed as a product of diverse contributions, not merely those of a single homeland. Anyone who knew both Victorian England and the America of the Civil War could have no reasonable question that they were at all the same in culture. The very fact that those in power in Britain sided with the losers in that War should be an enlightening reflection.

Taking up the point about the search for adherence to a native culture, it should be shown how this already led in the late nineteenth century to a movement into the suburbs. The critical fact to note is that in the period after the Civil War immigration to America both expanded greatly in numbers and shifted strikingly in source. As every student knows, the "old immigration" to the United States, particularly before 1840 but even measurably before 1865, was comprised of persons coming mainly from the British Isles and, to a lesser extent, Germany, whose dynastic ties with the English kings played some part. After 1865 the focus shifted to northern and central Europe and then to southern and eastern Europe, bringing large groups of persons to America who had previously lived far apart from one another and whose culture was very different between the various groups by origin.

This "new immigration" introduced language and cultural adjustment problems that had been somewhat less in earlier periods, as much because of the more modest numbers of immigrants as for any innate adaptability on the parts of those arriving. Whatever the reasons, there is little question that the new immigrants came to America and took up life in a diaspora of their past culture. The Irish, probably mainly because of religion, had been congregated together in Boston, New York, and Philadelphia even before the Civil War. After that conflict additional groups took up joint residence in the heart of the cities. Sometimes it was religion that may have encouraged this congregation— as among Catholics in a then even more Protestant land and Jews in a Gentile world—other times it was no doubt language—as with northern Europeans—and in the most stark of cases it was a cultural differentiation that made it exceedingly difficult for the immigrant to live integrated in American society—as with the Chinese in cities of the West.

This may be a sufficient explanation of the origin of the famous model of urban form and growth in America—that of the Chicago School of Social Ecology—which has it that the central part of the city is the zone wherein acculturation of immigrants takes place and whence, once the immigrant's sons are Americans, those men start families and take up residence in the nativist suburbs. The "concentric zones" that were thought to be seen in a city such as Chicago seemed to bear out the truth of this model. Perhaps they did in the 1920s, but today we realize that the model is no longer sufficient to explain the persistence of some ethnic clusterings "unto the third, fourth, and fifth generations."

A CONGREGATIONAL RESIDENTIAL MODEL

What model of residential structure, then, would allow us to analyze both the disappearance of original culture, with the substitution for it of a native form, and the continuation of that distinctively ethnic culture in other instances? I would argue that our view of the city as a place of distinctive but evolving groupings of people will serve nicely.

The residential structure of American cities is the product of two basic forces—one the separation of residence and workplace, and the other the clustering in social groupings. Most of us having grown up in a time when people live relatively distant from their work, we may not appreciate how very uncommon this situation was until fairly recent times. In rural life, in all times and most places, people lived close by their fields—at least some of those fields even in farms comprised of small, dispersed parcels—and certainly adjacent to their domestic animals, even when farm housing was collected into villages as in Luxembourg and the Rhineland. In classical and medieval towns, workmen lived in or over their shops and their assistants commonly lived within their extended occupational households. It is a great truth that there were occupational location decisions but few residential ones. But with the growth in scale of production, trading, and various services that came under the industrial revolution of the late eighteenth and nineteenth centuries residence was separated out and subjected to a new set of controls and for the first time by an independent set of location decisions. With occupation no longer serving as the guide, most of those decisions came to be made on cultural and social grounds. Because a shared nativist culture came to be common to most Americans, it was social class structuring that determined most, but not all, residential locations. For those groups that for one reason or another sought to or could not avoid maintaining a distinctive "culture," culture might continue to be the context of choice; but for most it was the congregation of persons of similar social status and attitudes that shaped the selection. What we find then is that before we consider the process of general residential congregation we must take up the question of the maintenance of a particular culture distinct from the generally evolved culture produced in the melting pot.

It is obvious that at least two forces will tend to produce a situation in which original culture will be maintained by a group resident within the broader American culture. The first is one where the initial location decision was made outside the group when they were forced into a segregated existence wherein the normal acculturation process became difficult or impossible of accomplishment. It is, after all, living together that leads to cultural exchange, and commonly the emergence of a shared composite culture in the end. In taking several specific cases of the effect of ethnic segrega-

tion on the social geography of American city, we may make the relationship of segregated clustering to residential structure most clear.

Up to the Second World War there were three distinctive ethnic groups that were to a very considerable degree forced through legal constraints into a segregated residential pattern. These were blacks, most particularly in the South but also to a large degree elsewhere in the country; and Japanese and Chinese in California and the West in general. I will not attempt here to account for all the reasons there were for this segregation or, on the other hand, to salve our collective conscience by condemning it. Such condemnation solves no problems, so let us use our space for such understanding as may solve problems. Let it suffice to note the existence of the residential separation, which in turn led to segregated residential patterns for each of these groups in the cities where their numbers were at all large. The question we must ask is, Does the existence of such a segregated "congregation" come entirely from forces outside the group involved? In other words, Is it totally forced on unwilling recipients? The experience since the war helps us to perceive at least part of an answer. In the thirty years since the close of the Second World War, residential discrimination against Japanese-Americans has to a most healthy degree declined. As we would expect, in West Coast cities the level of congregation of those groups is relatively small, as shown by the maps prepared for this comparative analysis. In the case of the Chinese, however, the case is rather different. Much as the ending of discriminatory practices came first with respect to the Chinese-Americans, their "integration" with the general population has been less. Or has it? Perhaps it is merely that congregation is a positive force among Chinese-Americans to the extent that they have not given up the living together in urban space to the same degree that most Americans of Japanese parentage have done. Recent investigations of the Chinese in Oakland and San Francisco have suggested that the reason for this contrast may lie in conditions of continuing immigration. Because of the Communist takeover of mainland China in 1949, and later changes in the immigration laws that also reflected that situation, there has been a fairly large new migration of Chinese to the United States in the last two decades. Because many of these people are relatives of American Chinese they are beyond their youth and find it hard to move into the native culture of the Bay Area or the country as a whole. Instead, the traditional central city ethnic congregation serves their needs best, furnishing shops where Chinese foods and goods are sold and where transactions can be conducted in Cantonese. Thus, we must conclude that there can be a positive aspect to ethnic congregation as well as a negative one, with the Japanese-Americans showing what happens when there is little positive attraction and no negatively based congregation" while the Chinese-Americans give us an insight into what happens when bars are removed but the desire to congregate remains.

The Two Expressions of Congregation Among Blacks

In the larger and more important case of black Americans, the process is the same but the outcome is complexly different, probably for two critical reasons—that the group is vastly larger, a tenth of the nation's population, and that its original ethnic culture has been lost through a grim past of slavery, particularly in the face of a discrimination even more complete and persistent than that suffered by Asian-Americans. We must begin by asking what is the culture of black Americans, and thereby confronting immediately the truth that it is on the one hand derived largely from our general native culture and on the other divided within itself between a small and long-standing urban black culture, the situation that W.E.B. Dubois described at the turn of the century, and a large and newly interjected rural culture that has been carried to cities mainly since the 1930s. If it were not tragic enough that their original culture was largely lost through enslavement of blacks, it is additionally a misfortune that there must be division within the replacement culture that has been shaped. This division is mainly the concern of sociologists, who have shown the split between the female house servants of slavery and the male field hands, between the small educated elite of the post–Civil War years and the vast ill-educated and badly treated body of share-croppers, and between the emergent black bourgeoisie and the continuing flood of rural migrants evicted from the countryside by economic changes in field agriculture.

Here, however, we must take note of the complexity that exists in black culture and the consequent differences of appeal that ethnic congregation will have for various groups of black people. For the black college graduate of the 1920s and 1930s, who has lived in cities for a generation or more, class congregation may be far more appealing than ethnic congregation. But for the badly educated migrant family from the South, constantly faced with poverty, the real desire is probably to be resident in a "black community"—that is, an ethnic geographical congregation where confusion, fear, insecurity, and friendlessness are somewhat reduced. As a group never expecting to rise above poverty, these residents often have quite specialized institutional needs—welfare offices, food programs, credit facilities, and churches—that make life possible, as it would not be within a more general native culture, even one of fair financial austerity.

Usually it is held that wealth leads to in-group feelings and the desire to be isolated from the rest of urban society, but I think it is nearly as certain that poverty leads as well to the needs for congregation—and, as is always the case with poverty, its exactions, even for congregation, are grinding. The wealthy can live anywhere, but can the poor? The supporting activities for the poor are so very much more critically needful that it seems unlikely that they can. Differences in welfare practices, availability of food stamps, public charity hospitalization, remedial education, and a number of other institutional situations are certainly more important to the poor than to the middle and upper classes for the simple and obvious reason that the poor have little chance either to find other solutions or to live without those institutions. Thus, the importance of class or ethnic congregation, in a peculiar fashion, may well be greatest at the bottom of the economic pile.

The geographical expression of this contrasting condition of the educated black middle class and the greatly disadvantaged black lower class is found in two distinctive programs for remedying the condition of black powerlessness within segregated areas of residence, too casually known as "ghettos." In the early striving for social justice, the drive was very much for "integration"—in housing, in schools, in shopping facilities, and in all those expressions of social congregation that had become the symbols of discrimination and segregation.

When the rights movement with respect to black housing began, its spokesmen were a rather elitist group—the small black middle class and a much larger and certainly more confident white liberal group. Viewing the problem from their own perspective, as we all do, the middle class call was for ethnic integration in housing. When middle class reformers viewed the situation of housing segregation they did it considerably from an economic perspective, whatever component of ethnic identification they also might bring to the operation. The result was a push for "open housing" under a really enforceable equal housing law. This was the product of middle class thought and understanding of the operation of congregation. For that group, black or white, it was the opportunity to live with educational and economic peers that seemed most important, a view that was quite predictably enforced for the nation as a whole in the Supreme Court decisions in the late 1960s. Supreme Court justices have always been drawn from the middle class, and for them equality in housing would imply access to all economic classes of housing for all individuals.

In the late 1960s and the 1970s there has been great confusion and not a little disillusionment with "integration" among its most ardent supporters. Few of us would question the justice and desirableness of integration, so the fact that even when some semblance of integration was reached not all blacks were happy has confused middle class reformers, black or white. In the same way it has been hard for some of these people to understand why the most violent and implacable opposition to integration has come in working class areas, not merely those with white residents but also those with residents of other ethnic minorities. Yet the two situations are fundamentally interrelated. For the lower economic classes there is much more appeal in ethnic congregation than there is in more prosperous groups. But for a healthy society these must be congregations not segregations: the people must take up a quarter within the city *by their own choice* and gain there control of their own lives, economically and politically. It is at that state that the push for urban social equality has arrived. The result has been that now we have a strong drive for political power for ethnic congregations more than for the abstract programs for integration which characterized the 1960s.

This drive for ethnic political power has taken a number of expressions, but it remains tightly woven with a fabric of congregation, which must stand somewhat at odds with one of integration. We have already examined the needs that people with low or hazardous incomes have for institutions of social welfare. In such a context we must look with extreme care at proposals for "spreading the poor around" the city or the metropolis, as envisaged under the extensive plans such as in Dayton, Ohio. This caution is entered not in the interests of the more prosperous but rather, of the less. In addition, the drive for ethnic political power raises a series of questions about two favorite reform proposals for cities—the forced integration of classes and ethnic groups and the imposition of metropolitan government. As members of the middle class, most academic geographers have tended to be philosophically in favor of integration and to have worked for that end. But the more they reflect on the question and examine the structure of cities, the more they must question the absolute validity of such ideas. Specifically, the problem becomes one of democratic expression of attitudes and interests. The United States, and the metropolitan areas where most of its citizens live, is dominantly a white, middle class society. The absolute numbers are there, whatever notions one may have about "soul," "justice," and other qualifications that might be entered. Thus, if economic congregation (another expression of ethnic integration) were to take place completely, all social geographical areas would tend to be dominated by white ethnics. Even among the poor, there are more whites than blacks in the country as a whole, and certainly, short of a Marxian revolution, we are not going to abolish economic class in what is probably the most socially mobile of the world's societies. So, if the drive of "civil rights" is for ethnic political power, as it now seems to be, then ethnic congregation will tend to be the practical basis for its support, and commonly favored over economic congregation.

Political Activism Darkens the Hue

The test of this notion comes easily to hand in the activities within the twenty cities we are here considering. From early mixed black and white middle class cooperative drives for "integration," a considerable proletarianization and darkening of the hue of activism recently has developed. In the late 1960s, white radicals entered black areas seeking to guide, or lead if necessary, battles for civil rights as then defined. The outcome startled the whites when there was a very successful movement by blacks to segregate most whites out of those movements. White advocate-planners have been told to leave, in words without the niceties of middle class behavior with which they had grown up. Students in general and social scientists in particular have not been as welcome as they had expected, and certainly they have been evicted from leadership positions. There is clear understanding by various ethnic groups that solidarity is the watchword, but that the definition of solidarity tends to be in ethnic terms. There can be alliances among ethnic solidarities, but there are few integrations within them. Campus politics today tend to substitute skin color for the arm bands that used to symbolize political attitudes, a fact of importance, as the university campus is about the only place in America where the full range of social and ethnic groups can be observed participating in a single integrated political system. The system is integrated, but if campuses tell us anything, they tell us that the parties are broken first by ethnic identity and only then, and to a lesser degree, by economic class.

Political Activism
Opposes Metropolitanism

The political activism within large cities in the United States has been almost entirely toward greater atomism rather than greater metropolitanism. A certain commentary on the nature of academic professionals is afforded by the fact that this Comparative Metropolitan Analysis Project contains two monographs on "metropolitan government" and none on the "neighborhood or community government" drive that is the cry of central city ethnics and the lower economic classes. The argument for metropolitan government is strongly based on "efficiency," "environmental protection," and the general concept of planning and orderliness. These are white, middle class, academic virtues that seem odd indeed, and almost certainly disenfranchising, to the central city ethnic congregations. They want more division, not less; more ability for the small group to throw

its weight around, however slight it may be, rather than less; more concern for the rights of the individual and less for a society that is viewed as both statistically and philosophically against them. As in campus politics today, there can be alliances among municipalities for defined and limited purposes, but there can be no reduction in the solidarity of the atomic unit. The drive for solidarity has taken a strongly ethnic direction in recent years. "Community school boards" in several cities have tended to equate community with ethnic congregation rather more than geographical division of the city, and only where the congregation tends to occupy a geographical area that becomes one of the "communities" for election of boards is this identification avoided. Black leaders in Boston have looked upon busing of school children as "tokenism" without accompanying creation of "community school boards." Perhaps it was such words that brought the violent reaction to the actual implementation to integrative busing that came in the fall of 1974. There have as well been strident demands for "community control" of police, of fire and other protective services, and of welfare administration and planning. The notion is always that these are concerns of the "community" alone and must therefore be controlled by it. The Economic Opportunity Program and Model Cities undertakings have been forced by the federal government to be "community controlled" if they are to have access to funds.

Whatever the merits of the case, and they are far from acid clean as the virtual collapse of the initial experimental program in New Haven that set the pattern for the country shows us, there can be no doubt that there are two fundamental attitudes toward the future organization of metropolises: one is that of academic life and those convinced of the virtue and necessity of efficiency and planning, which seeks metropolitan government; and the other, which seeks community government, is that of working class life and those convinced that the "rights" of the individual must rule, whatever the outcome for society and however inefficient. All that need be added is that each of these attitudes toward the future has associated with it a particular characteristic geographical congregation. For metropolitan government the congregation tends to be middle class residential areas of weak ethnic identity in the central city and inner suburbs. For community government the congregation tends to be either lower class, strongly ethnic neighborhoods in the heart of the central city or else distant outer suburbs of rather high economic class and no very open ethnicity.

For clear understanding of the present pass we should emphasize that there is a differential that exists within the black ethnic grouping, which is at least two "communities." The larger, more vocal, and clearly now dominant community is that of lower income people living in geographical congregation in the inner parts of the central cities. This is what is loosely termed "the ghetto"—where community school boards, control of police, and neighborhood government are strongly advocated. In essence, this is the area where the second of the battles for black rights has come to focus—that is, this is the area that became the substantial basis for black political power in the campaign that followed the earlier struggle for "open housing" for blacks. That opening of housing really meant two rather different things to the distinct black grouping— for the poor it meant the legal ability to expand the supply of housing open to the dominantly black congregation so that at least the most aggravated forms of central city slum crowding might be worked against, and for the black middle class it meant the legal opening to move into ethnically integrated but economically congregated suburbs where they could hope to overcome what were until recently discriminatory constraints placed on their economic and social mobility. Under a program that meant different things to different groups within the black population, it is not surprising that those outside (who tended to look upon the black housing problem as one entirely of the discrimination by segregation) were deceived and confused by the outcome. If we add an analysis of the quite contrasting meaning of congregation to the black lower class and the black middle class, perhaps some of the confusion may be overcome.

Congregation by Lifestyle: Oppositional Districts

If congregation is a process common to all of social geography, then we must ask how it has affected groups other than blacks living within our cities? The general answer seems to lie in the matter of lifestyle wherein we assume

that people congregate together with others of similar state, either economic or social, or perhaps more precisely economic *and* social. Poor blacks congregate with poor blacks and poor whites with their peers, but not by choice I suspect in either case with those who are poor without having the same race. Lifestyle is a summary term that may serve us well in implying a certain context of attitudes and attributes that create social groupings that have, in turn, social geographical areas associated with them. The previous discussion may have suggested that ethnicity or income are the dominant forces shaping lifestyle, and it seems likely that that is the case for the working and lower middle classes, with both ethnic origin and income being factors. But for some considerable number of Americans, certainly probably a majority, ethnicity is a lost concept; they are Americans of forgotten origin. For them income and a complex of nonethnic social attitudes will have to suffice.

Before going on we must return to a point made earlier, the distinction that exists between the specifically ethnic complexes of culture in America and that complex that is without definite ethnic attribution—the nativist American culture. Some think it English, but no one thinks so who knows that English culture really is beyond the simple matter of language. In the traditional model of society in American cities, that designed by the Chicago School, once families moved out of the central city, they were assumed to have joined that omniumgatherum that was American culture, wherein the divisions were those of economic and social class. Yet today we realize that there is a new component, a rather wild yeast that is at work in the fermentation. Most people still move out of the city to gain the physical and social environments that they crave, and have always craved, near the city's edge in our society. The result is that the suburbs are the home not of ethnic congregation but instead of the vast mass that is a nativist congregation. Due to the great numbers involved, there has always been more than a single congregation in the suburbs: some have been the communities of the rich, others of the very poor, and most have been the communities of those between, the majority in our society, which because of the large numbers involved have tended to be further divided into congregations based on other criteria—workplace and type of work, physical environmental desires, and simple birthplace or "hometown" of the residents. With these several bases for clustering within the vast mass of the suburban native culture, a set of individual congregations grew up.

Social critics, planners in particular, have tended to inveigh against suburbia because it was so massive and so seemingly undifferentiated. Most planners and social critics were, or have become, upper middle class people with a strong shudder that grips them when they think of the lack of "taste" that is to be found in popular American culture. This trait is shown by the obsession that planners have with European and Asian, specifically Japanese, solutions to urban problems. Instead of accepting that the physical build of American cities is so strongly cast in terms of automotive transportation that the whole fabric of our life would be forced to change by any very heavy reliance on a rigid rapid transit system, they tend to advocate it because it would force the changes necessary to bring to America the virtues they see in European cities. It is a favorite cliché that San Francisco "is everybody's favorite city" because it is so different from all other American cities.

We seem to end up with a great mass of critics of suburbia exceeded in numbers only by the people who live there and do not think the life so bad. With reason we can expect the ethnic political groups of the central city to criticize the suburbs; the minority party always does that to the majority party, and there are quite valid questions of economic and social equity as between city centers and their edges. But the most strident claim of the critics is that the suburbs represent a running away from the city and its problems. It must be said how silly this argument really is. In the first place, American cities have been characterized by this outward movement from the very beginning, and on the part of almost all ethnic groups. The black population is different, but where it has normal income mobility, it also has shown the desire to join in the alleged "white flight" from the center. Much of the criticism of the suburbs is based not on their discriminatory qualities as much as on the success they have had in submerging previous ethnic and cultural distinctions into a single native culture. If your object is to maintain ethnic or lifestyle congregations of great and continuing dis-

tinctions, then the suburbs are threats through their very success in destroying that identity. This however is not a moral question; it is as valid to argue for a shared culture as it is to work for distinctions, for a melting pot culture as for a plural society. And in a democracy it cannot be permitted that one viewpoint will submerge all others. This says that not all our cities may be transformed to suburban qualities—that is nativist, economically classified, areas—but it also says that for those who wish that form of congregation, it is right to do so. If the civil rights of the central city black require concern for his individual wishes with respect to culture, so equally those rights require concern for the individual wishes of suburban whites even if they serve to create vast rather uniform cultures. Only if they exclude previous ethnics who wish to join their nonethnic culture can society cry foul.

What is new in all of this is that there are a number of people who were raised in the majority culture of America—that is, nonethnic suburbia—who reject that lifestyle. No doubt social critics and ethnic activists have convinced them of the great deprivation they have suffered, a conclusion supported by the fact that the group most likely to encounter social critics and committed ethnics—college students—is also the one most likely to take up what has variously been termed an "alternative lifestyle" or a "counterculture"—the latter a poor term as there are enough cultures in America so all may be thought running somewhat counter to another. What is of most interest to a geographer is that an individual's joining a new lifestyle has meant shifting residence. If any further proof were needed to support the notion that the process of geographical congregation is central to the shaping of our cities, the actions of "the counterculture" lend evidentiary support out of all proportion to the actual significance of that cultural grouping. The central city black, it may be argued, lived in congregation because he cannot live in integration, though that argument loses force as time passes, but it cannot be argued that the Patricia Hearsts are forced by society rather than by their own lifestyle decision to live in or near the core area black "ghetto."

In many American cities the "alternative lifestyle area," the oppositional district, has become as much a part of the local urban geography as the central business district. This is not merely the South End of Boston, the South Campus of Berkeley, or Capitol Hill in Seattle, places where the large local student population would seem to be the raw material for self-inflicted segregation; it is as well the inner Westheimer district of Houston, the middle Peachtree Street quarter of Atlanta, and sections adjacent to the central business district of other large cities. There, where large residences or older apartment houses have been transformed in scale of occupation to single rooms, has emerged a new congregation, or at least one much more clearly seen today than it was in the past. This is the quarter of social autonomy, autonomous in two ways: first, that individuals are there the fundamental element of society, living totally separated from other individuals, or living in periodic, and usually rather ephemeral, communalism as their personal spirit moves them; and, second, as a congregation autonomous from the collective civic society of a city, often arguing that they must defend themselves from outside "interference" by divorcing themselves from concern with those outside. To this group philistinism is a complete reality and one likely to spread menacingly over the suburbs.

It is certainly unfair and incorrect to leave the impression that these districts of alternative lifestyle are all fundamentally antisocial: however it does seem justified to argue that they have grown up by deliberately creating some conflict between themselves and the mass, nativist culture of America. Roszak coined a battle cry as well as a name for them when he termed them the "counterculture." They have not been segregated by society at large, they have been congregated by their own interests. Because they view their relationship to society as strained and even antipathetic, it was possible for a virulently antisocial group such as the SLA to move about California with an ease of camouflage that still surprises many. Whatever its qualities, that splinter group understood the cultural basis of geographical congregation and was able to employ that understanding with remarkable brilliance to avoid capture. Where they misunderstood society was in the white working class suburb of Concord in the area east of Oakland where notions of Marxian class struggle may have blinded the SLA to the true meaning of economic class congregation within a nativist culture.

It follows from the deliberate congregation of autonomous people that they do possess some basic sharing of attitudes; what seems to be missing is any desire to be part of a national society or economy. The range of departures from those integrated structures is remarkable, commonly including style of dress (hip-chic), food ("natural" or "organic"), housing (communal or periodically compatible), politics (protest and the philosophically pristine), education (alternative and individual fulfillment), governmental organization ("community"), religion (anything that is not too clearly Judeo-Christian), interior decoration (nonfurniture and plants), and architecture (preferably architectonic and idosyncratic so as to avoid attribution to any widely accepted style). It will be noted that in each instance the persons entering the counterculture do so as an individual act and probably think that their social atomization becomes the critical social fact, yet once they have taken up the geographical congregation that must accompany any workable and durable social act, they lose identity and become part of a group large enough to create its own pattern of shopping, housing, political action, religious experience, education, and the like. To the outside world the main expression comes in the goods that sustain the autonomous society—their health foods, leatherworks, drawings, handicrafts, and items most notably designed to be different. It has come as a shock for many to discover that for all its protest against society in the mass, this autonomous society has shown remarkable adeptness at continuing the economic practices they thought they had left behind. Perhaps the survival of the profit motive is the most divisive element in the New Eden.

Because of the frequent geographical proximity of the oppositional district to student housing, it is often thought that they are one and the same. Fortunately the American people are beginning to understand that "student protests" may be undertaken by only a small minority of local students and be made up only in small part by actual students. It is the alternative lifestyle group who are the radicals of the present and who conflict with nativist society and culture on any target of opportunity. Students and ethnics protest specific conditions while those of the counterculture protest the totality of American life. It is only because the protestors have to have

a congregation to survive, and that congregation must exist geographically, that the confusion has arisen. The same general morphological
and social conditions that are common to
student housing are also common to oppositional society housing. In both instances we are
dealing with a society of individuals. Is it surprising that they exist in the city cheek by
jowl? Perhaps if the reason for this physical
proximity of counterculture and universities
is understood, we will be better off within
universities; the American electorate may begin to understand that rather than our having
created the counterculture, the general society
created it and that the rejection of that society, which is implied, has forced the countercultural group into a residential pattern of
roominghouses in the city, or their rural equivalent, the jack rabbit homesteads in the country.

There Are Congregations in Suburbia

To complete our view of the function of
congregation in shaping the physical pattern
of housing in our large cities a brief consideration of the groupings in the suburbs is
necessary. Those extensive bands of housing
that represent the outward spread of building
to accommodate the ever-increasing populations of our larger cities have not grown without form and pattern, though in the suburban
band it is minor differences *within* a majority
culture rather than either ethnicity or opposition lifestyle that do the shaping. The traditional views of the residential pattern in cities
—the writing of Burgess and McKenzie, of
Homer Hoyt, and of Chauncy Harris and Edward Ullman—have dealt with this surrounding
ring of native culture as an outgrowth of
acculturation of immigrant groups who first
took up residence in the city center. It has
been assumed that all persons would progress
from ethnicity to native culture, and that
there would as well be a modicum of economic
and social mobility operating in the emergent
American society. Thus Burgess and McKenzie
and Homer Hoyt organized their two proposals—respectively the concentric zone hypothesis and the sector hypothesis—with the
idea that once "Americanization" had taken
place, residential patterns would mainly be
structured by economic class.

Is that in fact the way American suburbs
work? Any answer must be a partial yes, which
is obviously a partial no as well. What we find

is that there is broad scale sorting of housing
by *cost of occupation,* which is not quite the
same thing as cost of construction. It is possible for housing to be rather expensive when
built but to decline in value over the years so
its purchase at any particular time may be considerably cheaper than replacement cost would
be. This is the essence of the classical land rent
and sociological theory of "filtering down"
of housing, which envisages the housing of
the well-to-do passing with later generations
to the middle and finally the lower class. The
specifically sociological notion is that of succession in housing with a lower economic class
occupying after each property exchange;
sometimes with the notion, largely unfound in
fact, that it is the invasion of a lower class that
forces the higher class to move out, hardly an
economically believable process. The geographical pattern that we might anticipate in
the suburbs would, under this thinking, be one
of increasing prosperity with movement toward
the city's edge, accompanied by ever newer
housing.

There are two predications in this thinking
that deserve some appraisal, particularly with
respect to the very large cities such as those we
are here considering. The first is that there is a
single focus of the city, presumably the central
business district, around which all sorting takes
place. The second is that there is no sense of
community, of socially deliberate congregation,
within the suburbs, only an income-oriented
rush to have the newest housing. Both these
predications are at best half truths: for some
people in the suburbs their location with
respect to the metropolitan core is an important factor, even in a small minority of
cases, the most important factor; but for
many others, the largest group in most cities,
their lives are lived entirely in the suburbs so
it is the system of daily movement therein
that matters. And for most people in the
suburbs there are social forces that shape
their housing choice, even if it is not directly
ethnic or countercultural reasons that enter
in. We know that the largest populations of
American cities, viewed in terms of locations,
are in the suburbs, and, in turn, the majority of
jobs in most cities are in those suburbs. The
commonest movement in cities is normally
from one suburb to another rather than from
the suburbs to the central city. For these
reasons, theories that explain urban residential

structure in terms of a single core focus are doomed to inaccuracy.

Because metropolitan areas are now so large in area, there is a real problem of daily access when the object of travel is in one suburban quadrant while residence is in another. If a resident of the northwest quadrant seeks to work in the southeast, his journey to work becomes unduly elongated. If, however, he lives and works in the northwest quadrant, it is more than likely that he commutes less far than he would if he were working in the central business district. Thus, there is a real tendency for an outlying workplace to determine in which quadrant the employee will live; or, in turn, for one living in a quadrant energetically to seek work there. As the cost of gasoline continues to climb, the operation of this determinant will almost inexorably increase, taking over much of the role that has formerly been assigned to the filtering and succession processes.

The other predication on which our residential location theory has been based is that of strictly economic sorting of social classes in geographical space, with little innately social content. It is assumed that people live where their jobs take them in the city and find in that place housing suitable to their income. Studies of the journey to work belie such nice economist's formulations. We are forced to conclude from the long and inefficient commuting in which a number of people engage that they *must* decide where to live on grounds other than occupational, suggesting that it is a social purpose that their residence seeks to fulfill. Without here presenting the evidence, it may be stated that to a considerable degree in America today people are "to the suburb born," either having grown up where they live or else having moved there along with their friends or family from some other suburb. Their parents often moved to the suburb to demonstrate without question that they had passed from an immigrant ethnic congregation in the central city to a nativist economic congregation in the suburb. Those parents' children may well stay in that suburb for an equally social but different reason—that of remaining with friends in the general quadrant of the city that seems home to them and where probability would make it likely that their employment would be found. It is as well not to overlook that fact that most persons,

even though at home in the native culture of the suburbs, are somewhat overcome by the personal anonymity that comes from moving to a new community, even though still within that general culture, and will tend to remain where they feel at home if to do so is financially feasible.

THE APARTMENT BELT AT THE EDGE OF THE CITY

This association of society and place has begun to appear in a different guise in the last ten years when mortgage financing has forced a shift from single family owner-occupied housing to multifamily condominium or rental housing. If we reflect on the problem of the geographical expression of a tight money market for housing mortgages, it is clear that the ethnic and oppositional congregations of the central city will be less affected than will the native suburbs. In the core housing is largely either filtered down or publicly provided, but in the suburbs the housing has not been around long enough to be passed on through many generations. In addition, the Americanization process still works in cities producing a number of migrants outward from the central city who seek thereby both an improvement in physical housing and admission to a general American culture. For them, as well as the natural increase of families previously resident in the suburbs, housing provision is "normally" sought in those self-same suburbs, thus creating there the main pressure for housing expansion in the metropolis. To balance the books completely, the main loss from the suburbs comes either through migration to the suburbs of a different metropolis, which hardly changes the national pattern, or through adoption of an alternative lifestyle that takes suburbanites back into the city or else into the distant countryside. As the latter process is still rather uncommon, even despite the excess coverage it has had at the hands of the professional writers, the increment to the suburbs has been great and utterly normal. "White flight" is a contentious and self-serving view expressed largely by (1) core area ethnic politicians seeking to instill an unjustified sense of guilt among suburbanites and thereby gain a power out of measure to the numbers of their own followers, or (2) the body of social critics and social scientists who feel themselves saved from the "philistinism" of the suburbs and the "blatant Americanism" of its culture through their continuing residence in the central residential areas of the metropolis.

There are people, many people indeed, who still strive to live in the suburbs and not at all for base and craven desires. For them that great geographical segment of the city is both home and the location of the social congregations they wish to join or in which they were reared. Yet housing does not filter well in this locale for the reasons noted, so it is here that the housing problem of the private sector of the economy is likely to concentrate. The outcome has been that it is in the suburbs that new morphologies of housing have emerged in response, in the main, to the money situation. The "garden apartment" complex of rental housing was an early attempted solution but more recent expressions of relief from the problem have been the condominium as a general form, with the row house or cluster housing as specific cases. The result furnishes an interesting support for the notion of congregation: the great area for new multifamily housing construction has become the edge of the city, that belt that a number of land economists and sociologists view as the preserve of the rich country club set. What that belt is instead is the outlet for the growing suburban population which seeks in reasonable geographical approximation to its own congregational area the maintenance of the lifestyle it desires; if the entrants to this housing market cannot have single family houses in the suburbs of their choice, they then seek multifamily housing, hopefully owned units, in the general geographical congregation they desire.

The message of this situation seems more clear than well understood. It is that people within nativist culture do have very strong social attitudes that shape their perception of suburbia and that determine the congregations in which they strive with strong will to live. It is not the form of housing that stops their return to the central city—a condominium in suburbia probably has physical conditions not appreciably different from one in the central city—it is the social congregation found there. Lest that be taken as final proof that "white flight" is true after all, let it be noted that congregation is more cultural than ethnic. When we visit the suburbs of Atlanta or the Bay Area it is difficult indeed to tell the race of

their occupants until the children get up in the morning. If they are upper middle class houses, the same European cars will fill the garages, and the domestic architecture, school plant layout, and shopping center design will hold. These may as well be blacks as whites who have taken over a suburban generalized American culture. In the central city "ghetto" rather a different situation prevails; there it will be a specifically black, considerably rural, and highly disintegrated society that is found. Neither black nor white suburbanites seek to make congregation with it. If we take Atlanta to be the most important of American cities from the viewpoint of an understanding of a fully developed black urban society as our vignette on that city shows (and I believe we should), then we can read straight from Atlanta's urban landscape the truth that suburban congregation is as normal to blacks as it is to whites. When social scientists and planners try to force the joining in a single congregation of those who have left inmigrant culture and those who remain within it (ethnics from overseas or rural blacks from the plantation and their unacculturated descendents), they are seeking to overturn perhaps the most central process at work in the shaping of our cities.

This thinking does raise quite real, and thereby controversial, questions in the matter of the physical layout and social geography of cities. It may well seem that a case is being made for continued segregation of economic and ethnic groups, yet no contentious assertion is intended. The purpose is that of showing the way that physical structure evolves in America's cities, and what forces are at work. It is far safer and wiser to project future actions on such a basis of understanding, even if its attitudes ultimately are rejected, than on doctrinaire assumptions of "natural order" and abstract justice which are not automatic urban processes. We may decide that mixing matriarchal welfare families with nuclear, two parent, upper middle class families is an imperative to obtain social justice: but does the justice come in aiding the poor, who desperately need it, or in dogmatically confronting the prosperous, who usually have options open to them that largely divert the impact? We should take account of the great supportive role of congregation in social geography. Once the tight rein that tied residence to workplace was released at the end of the last century, all groups began to search for some replacement process in the shaping of residential geography and congregation has come to take the place of the occupational link that had previously been so commanding.

THE EMERGENCE OF URBAN PAROCHIALISM IN SHOPPING

The meaning of local congregation is largely an expression of the intraurban mobility that the particular group enjoys, as is shown by the patterns of "social space" that have been discerned by geographers and sociologists during the last decade. In their studies they have shown that few people, perhaps no people, use the entire city even in relatively small places. Each of us has "the city" that he individually uses, leaving much of the physical settlement and urban society untouched by his activities and interests. This was always true it seems, though in a rather different way. We know, for example, that medieval Italian cities had districts that contained the activity of most persons, often to the extent that it was literally unsafe for the resident of one district to stray too far into another's domain, a situation that is clearly evident in the poorer and most ethnic of districts in large cities today. It was the group loyalty of the residents of an area that protected medieval people just as it is the might of the city gang, tied to its geographically defined turf, that protects youths in New York and Philadelphia today.

Even when there was no physical threat met by those straying from the district, there was likely to be uncertainty and physical and social discomfort. It was easier to shop nearby, and likely to be more pleasant to do so. We should not overlook the role that belonging to the local congregation that normally supports a shopping district plays in determining its clientele. In some instances that clientele may be determined by economic and ethnic class, in others by the neighborhood of residence. The neighborhood bar or cafe are accepted symbols of this regionalization of shopping within cities, but the separation is nearly as well defined in clothing and some other types of shops. The result is that the stores of a neighborhood tend to reflect the

nature of the social congregation found there and to reinforce its functional appeal.

Traditionally it was in the heart of the city that the parochial quality in shopping disappeared, by the conscious design of merchants who realized that to operate in the center they must pay rents of such height that they had to appeal to a mass market—that is, unless their striving was for high income exclusivity, which could carry mark-ups on prices beyond the capacity for most shoppers to bear. There are two different conditions involved in this combination, which seeks in the core area location to maximize customer access in (1) mass appeal shops, and (2) high priced exclusive shops as well; in each case it was to tap the total market of the city for that price range of goods that they located there. To keep prices down, the mass appeal store could hope in the central business district to gain the highest volume, thereby spreading overhead costs over the greatest volume of sales.

Transportation and Selling

Mass appeal selling has moved out as mass housing was moved out, that is, since there has been democratically used internal transportation in cities. It was a requisite for continued growth of cities that people could move about them from collected workplaces to dispersed housing areas. Once the transportation system was developed for that purpose it could be used for shopping in the city center. But when the next phase of transportation was introduced, that of individual means—the bicycle and the automobile—which gave greater flexibility in practicable destinations, it was possible to think in terms of new congregations of shops closer to the places people lived. If we ask which shops would be able to move out first and to maintain the closest ties with housing, the answer is clear that it would be in the selling of goods widely consumed by the population as a whole, or at least generally consumed by a social or ethnic group congregated in the suburbs. Standard articles of utility clothing and household goods are examples of those items of almost universal purchase that might be sold in any suburban area, whereas supplies for boating, riding, and other special activities illustrate selling that may be both narrowly focused in its social and geographical market.

The last two decades have been a time of new commercial congregation to go along with the great transformation of residential geography that came with the nearly universal use of cars, the development of a national housing policy of encouraging private ownership of single family houses, and the creation of mass production methods of house construction to keep down the cost of the product. Class-specific housing tracts were the outcome of mass production in much the same way that various "models" of automobile have come off assembly lines to meet the demands of various price brackets of buyers. The fact to be noted is that it is possible to mass produce all price levels of automobile if it is practicable to collect together in one place the actual production. In housing, this same practical consideration means that there is much stronger tendency today for rather uniform economic class housing areas than was the case in earlier eras when the actual housing was built unit by unit for the ultimate occupant.

Mass Production of Housing and Shopping Centers

This point needs amplification: it was the practice in American cities, from at least the middle of the nineteenth century on, to have speculation in lands for housing and subdivision of large parcels into lots that were then sold mostly to potential residents. Once a family bought a lot they then usually engaged a builder to construct on it the house that they could afford. We should not envisage a vast variety of houses just because they were built often on contract for individual buyers; finally, even in the last century, construction costs encouraged a certain standardization of architecture and the use of mass-produced components, a development of American lumber industries that was widely noted by European visitors. What did happen was that the residential areas built before the FHA period of the 1930s were much more likely to have a greater range of economic class living within them than do tracts today. There were more variables at work: a family of modest income might struggle to buy a rather expensive lot only to place on it a modest house more in accordance with their income, or a wealthy person might for several reasons place an expensive house on a modest lot. Any visit to a nineteenth century residential area by a person with a practiced eye for morphogenesis will show the much greater economic mixing true of that time than of today.

Because housing in almost all income class areas is now at least locally mass produced, there is a much greater congregation of income-specific groups than was true in the past. And, in turn, the vast increase in the overall size of urban populations has meant that there are congregations of enough families of a particular type in a specific tract or suburb to make more localized retail congregation possible. The mass appeal selling that formerly concentrated in the central business district has been able to move to the suburbs and there to find a threshold of support sufficient to allow the development of an integrated shopping center with its suburban department store accompanied by a cluster of standardized "specialty shops." As housing expands, the potential for new outlying shopping centers is itself expanded, and there is no longer either the need for or virtue in congregating this type of shopping in the city center. The exception to this rule comes in the matter of truly specialized shopping, notably that for the very well-to-do. Because their numbers are relatively small, even where they are congregated, they lack the numbers to support outlying high income shopping. Instead, the expensive specialty shops tend to remain in or near the central business district—on North Michigan Avenue in Chicago, on Newbury Street in Boston, on Grant Avenue in San Francisco, around 57th Street in New York—where they are central to a potential market that still has to focus its demands on one metropolitan core to gain the viable size for a retailing district, thus perpetuating a situation that was true even for mass shopping in the last century.

The main exception to this congregation of high price specialty shops in the city core is found in those cities where the number of wealthy is high and where their congregation within the metropolis is pronounced. In Houston the well-to-do are numerous, ostentatious, and congregated, so the River Oaks area is also the locale of the most obviously high priced of American shopping centers—Galleria Post Oak. Both Los Angeles—in the Beverly Hills-Westwood area—and San Francisco—on the peninsula—have similar congregations of the wealthy and, in turn, have developed outlying shopping facilities specialized to their needs —in Beverly Hills and in the Stanford Shopping Center in Palo Alto. Few other cities have quite the build-up of massed housing for the very prosperous; the congregation of the high income residences is usually to be found but it is impossible to decentralize specialty shopping unless the added support of a university community can be found—as in Wellesley, Evanston, the university district of Seattle, and Berkeley.

There has been a similar restriction to central business districts of shopping for groups with low disposable incomes. In those districts it has been possible for merchants to turn their attention to the sale of merchandise aimed at another restricted market, that of ethnic groups that have been fairly recent migrants to the city from rural areas and have both incomes and tastes different from the mass market. To keep markups down, the scale of the market possible only at the city center is a critical factor, along with the focus on the central business district that is characteristic of most public transit systems. The Puerto Rican in the Northeast, the black in most of our larger cities, and the Spanish-American in Texas and California, when a woman, is more dependent upon public transit than is any other group of adult shoppers. The result is that State Street in Chicago, Broadway in Los Angeles and Oakland, and downtown Atlanta have become increasingly "ethnic" in their clientele not merely by the outward shift of white customers to suburban centers but due as well to the rising disposable income of blacks and Spanish-Americans. As that disposable income rises it comes into play in the retail market first in the central business district, though as time progresses we may anticipate that a more suburban congregation of blacks will lead to more reliance on outlying centers, as in the case in the new Eastmont Mall of Oakland. At the moment there is a real question whether suburbanization of black housing, which is fast taking place in the larger cities, will cause this distinction in shopping places (between whites and blacks) to disappear. In the same period that fair housing has finally allowed the black residential area to expand into the suburbs, there has been a strong movement for distinctive black clothing and furniture styles that has tended to maintain ethnic identity in shopping in the suburban as well as the central city areas.

CLUSTERING OF MANUFACTURING

A final form of clustering of activity that needs mention is that of manufacturing in cities. In the nineteenth century town, which represented the first fruit of the industrialization of America, manufacturing tended to be highly congregated, at first near sources of water power—as in Lowell, Holyoke, and Paterson—and later in an intimate association with railroads for the receipt and dispatch of goods. When the railroad factory became the norm for manufacturing, there was little difference in the siting of plants and the warehouses of wholesaling distributors and collectors of raw materials. There were districts within cities where space became highly valued and where plants and warehouses were built to considerable heights, occasionally six or seven stories. In part such a massive productive congregation depended upon the existence of mechanical transportation within the town that could bring large numbers of workers from their homes to the places of employment. As we have seen, the workers had, in turn, to cluster their housing at no very distant remove from the factory-warehouse quarter or along trolley lines reaching to it. So long as mass transport was required, one productive congregation led directly to another residential congregation.

With the use of individual cars and trucks, the whole nature of clustering changed. The plants and warehouses might still be dependent upon rail for inshipment of raw materials or goods but there was an increasing chance that finished product or disassembled sales would be shipped out by truck. Without going into detail, this meant that there was a strong possibility that a site away from the city's heart would be more attractive to industry and wholesaling than one near the city center. Particularly, as freeways and toll roads were built to care for intermediate and longer distance movements, there would be a strong pull toward placing the factory or warehouse where rail line and freeway intersected or were at least adjacent. Only if no rail shipments were involved would this vary, and then only to the extent that it would be a simple site near a freeway that would attract industry and wholesaling. This new location for industry and warehousing became equally as much an instance of local congregation as the factory or warehouse district of the nineteenth century had been in the inner city. Now, however, the need for high density of construction would be decreased leading to the building of single story plants and warehouses, which in turn tended to become far more mechanized than their multi-story predecessors had been. The result was a less dense demand for workers, which was matched in time to a greatly increased mobility for those employees, who were likely now to be automobile commuters. Because the number of workers in relation to building space was very small, parking on the site was seldom a great problem, a fact sharply in contrast to the situation in the center office district where employee densities were high per square foot of building and per ground acre of development.

What this tells us is simple: mass transit has very great appeal for office workers whereas it has very little for industrial workers. Given the convergence of routes on the city core, the high densities of office workers found there, and the high economic cost of parking in the central district, the relative appeal of urban mass transit in the central commuting journey is at its strongest. It is in factory-warehouse districts—normally located toward the edge of the city, and today almost universally located on major arterial highways (most commonly on freeways) and on sites where the small relative employee parking space demands of modern industry are rather easily met—that urban mass transit makes its weakest appeal. There is as well the psychology of the worker to be considered. One of the great problems of modern industry is the high level of worker regimentation that it implies. In such a situation, the worker when he punches out at the end of his shift is most reluctant to substitute a successor regimentation by mass transit in his journey home. Even stalled in his car on the freeway, he feels emancipated from a mechanistic existence in a way that the planner, whose job is lacking in regimentation, finds hard to understand.

SUBSIDIES AS AN INDUCEMENT TO HYPERMOTILITY

The outward shift of industry and wholesaling adds a further inducement to move to the suburbs, and, so long as there is any reasonable accordance between the location of work and that of residence, this situation can reduce the total journey to work of individuals and of the total urban work force. As yet we have not done very well at rationalizing the location of residence and workplace—there is one form of congregation working on factories and quite another on the housing of their workers. But this situation is not without reasonable solution, perhaps even automatic solution. The recent large increases in the cost of automobile operation, particularly in the cost of gas, interpose a force that should encourage an individually initiated reduction in the journey to work. This reduction is more likely to come with the continued use of cars than it is, the planners notwithstanding, with a shift to mass transit. As that is a seemingly contradictory notion, it needs further examination.

Recent efforts toward transportation change and "reform" in cities have taken a particular form—that of substituting mass for individual transport—and have been encouraged by a nearly universal practice of public subvention to public transit. The upshot has been to charge the user less than it costs to provide the service, while on the highway in most places he is paying in more than it costs to provide the highway for his use. Thus, the urban car driver is subsidizing rural highways in virtually all states and other forms of governmental service in many states. Yet in most cities today it is the general taxpayer who is picking up part of the bill for bus riders and the main part of the bill for rapid transit riders. In such a context, it is likely that the car driver will be the first to feel the increase in operating costs stemming from rising fuel costs and that any increases will bear more heavily on him than on the transit rider. Almost without exception the argument advanced by politicians and planners today is that society in general should subsidize public transit and penalize private. There are arguments of social justice—the aid necessary to the poor who have no use of cars—and of public benefit—cities with nineteenth century morphology may be sorely taxed to deal with floods of cars. Yet when we examine that social justice argument we find that large parts of the subsidy to commuters goes to the well-to-do living in the suburbs rather than the poor living in the center. This is glaringly true of most "innovative" transportation experiments today. Just to take one instance, in the Bay Area a new rapid transit system, BART, has been designed specifically for commuters, with widely spaced stations, high speeds, and lines greatly extended into the outer suburbs. This system is planned for commuting above all other uses, and as of 1973 there was an annual operating subsidy of over $4 per passenger entering the turnstile and a construction subsidy of somewhere between $1.75 and $2 billion. The subvention for upper middle class commuters living at most questionable distances from their workplaces far exceeds any subsidy to provide socially necessary transportation for the poor. The first figures on the use of BART show most disappointing general use, a real absence of riders within the poor and ethnic congregations at the center of the metropolis, and the main use of the system for extremely long commuting journeys from the outer and more affluent suburbs to downtown San Francisco's financial district. In the same city, the Bay Area, a freeway system has been built and is being operated entirely on user taxes and charges. Thus, if we examine the two forms of transport—freeways and rapid transit—and ask in which is there a greater likelihood for hypermotility, excessive use of transportation, and unwise location of workplace or residence, I believe the answer has to be that it is more likely in the rapid transit situation.

If we accept that the fuel crisis of 1973-1975 will continue in one form or another, it seems most likely that it will persist as a situation of greatly increased costs of fuel. In car driving we have learned that that cost has almost instantaneously been passed on. In mass transit it has a tendency to become an increased public charge, and there are strong groups that fight the transfer of the increased costs to the rider, arguing instead that the general society must shoulder them. If this view is to prevail, there seems little doubt that the continuing spread of the city is inevitable. When the "cost of distance" is shifted to the general taxpayer, including the less affluent who tend to occupy the central cities with their more rational potential for mass transit, the individual pinch of distance will be less real. We seem badly to have mixed up the argument of social justice and maintenance of particular congregations with the consideration of transportation policy. Let us try to sort out the truths.

There is a real question of how to provide intraurban mobility for the central city population of modest income, which suggests that the general public should bear part of the cost of transportation. The result has been the shaping of a policy of public support for mass transit based on two asserted goals—that of aiding the

population of lower income to enjoy a mobility that is assumed to increase their chances of social justice and employment; and that of maintaining a "centered" city, which is the same thing as saying preserving the existing congregations that we have noted in this essay. If we accept these goals as valid, which they certainly are at least in part, we still must ask what is the effect of a general subsidy to mass transit and particularly of transit lines to the suburbs? This is not a simple academic's question. In a recent *New York Times* article two proponents of rail transportation hold out the Bay Area Rapid Transit system and the Lindenwold line out of Philadelphia as the "couple of bright spots" in the return of rails. And much of the national effort in transit focuses on aiding the outer suburban commuter by speeding up and softening his journey to work. These are the main elements of rapid transit research, and there is as well the institution of a subsidy program that accepts part of the burden of costs of his commuting. Thus, in the guise of aiding the poor, we are today spending as much —or in the case of Oakland and San Francisco far more—to move the more prosperous in their journey to work. Our vignette on the Bay Area amplifies the details and makes these same conclusions.

Many may find this situation disturbing, but there is often a fatalism that holds that we must accept this mixed outcome to gain the specific one of justice for the poor. It seems, however, that we may question that conclusion and enter this essay as an analytical argument for variation and adaptability in the physical design of cities. In the conclusions that follow, the question of freezing the structural form of the metropolis will be discussed, but here it is necessary to consider the question of justice in city transportation. Accepting that there must be some form of subsidy to the central city poor, we still need not accept that there must as well be a subsidy to the outer suburban areas as there is in BART and other transit proposals. In the food stamp program so widely used to feed the poor at a better standard we have a model that might well be used to provide the poor with greater mobility. The precedent is there in most cities where the fares are reduced for the elderly, the young, and sometimes the physically handicapped. Why could we not do the same for those below the poverty line in income, or even modestly above it? In this way we would gain the social objective of giving the poor mobility without at the same time subsidizing the undesirably dispersive tendencies of the most prosperous. This policy is not merely a question of removing a subsidy from a group that seem doubtfully worthy of one, but also one of seeking to gain the other objective of current urban transportation policy—that of maintaining current congregations. If, as seems probable, the cost of car travel in cities will rise rapidly, there is a new force for containment of driving far more real and far more just than that of subsidizing the mass transit of those groups who can perfectly well afford the costs of their voluntary acts of moving to the distant suburbs. And, additionally, this policy of forcing them to accept the costs of the mobility they demand would help to overcome what is the greatest physical problem of cities —shifts in the operation of processes of segregation and congregation that leave parts of the urban fabric strained by overuse or slack by abandonment.

LOS ANGELES STANDS AS THE LABORATORY OF CONGREGATION

Space is lacking in any survey of such broad historical and geographical scope as this to engage in a detailed test of the central concepts presented. We may, however, attempt a quite summary test if an appropriate geographical laboratory can be found; and such a laboratory exists in the Los Angeles metropolitan area. Our vignette supplies greater and different insights, but here we may look at Los Angeles as a city of congregations. The appropriateness of the southern California conurbation as a test area lies in the fundamental simplicity it affords with respect to some of the possible variables other than congregation, thus offering a reasonable chance of observing the specific working of that particular urban morphogenetic process. The Los Angeles basin is large and reasonably usable; it was thinly settled when urbanization began and little affected by political and agricultural constraints; the populating of the metropolis came quickly and from a great diversity of geographical and cultural regions; and much of the growth took place under the working of a transportation technology which forced the cost of movement pretty directly upon the participants in that movement, avoiding the skew of subsidized

movement that has encouraged the prosperous to live far removed from the center of the city and has tended to cluster the urban poor in their abandoned neighborhoods.

The impress of congregation is widely visible in Los Angeles, and the shadow of segregation darkens a few corners. Space forbids tracing all the details, but a few summary observations may serve to show the workings of the congregational process. Beginning in the downtown of the city itself we find a particular collection of clusters of activity. A cluster of governmental buildings occupies the first site of the downtown to such an extent that its relics have largely disappeared and a governmental congregation has arisen that is perhaps exceeded in size only by that in Washington (and possibly Sacramento). Federal, state, county, and city offices shape an office district equal to all but a couple of our urban financial districts. Next to that administrative cluster lies a skid row of fairly impressive scale, adjoined on the west by a congregation of what was once "downtown" shopping but now stands as ethnic— largely black and Hispanic-American—shopping along Broadway. The remaining parts of the Los Angeles central business district are equally places of particular congregation. There is a large cluster of activities related to travel centering on Pershing Square's south side, an attempt to shape a typical urban office district around the beginning of Wilshire Boulevard, and a large and important garment-manufacturing district at the southeast corner of the central area. In each of the components of the central business district there is a striking specialization of interest, and of using population, which differs considerably from the classical view of the downtown. For a variety of reasons the downtown is the best place for the activity, but it is not because all citizens come there, even infrequently.

Instead, most activities in Los Angeles have their respective congregational areas. High class retailing has several class-stratified clusters along Wilshire Boulevard, with the most economically elevated found in Beverly Hills. Not without reason, there is a symbiosis between a large area of Jewish housing in a band extending westward from the outer reaches of downtown to Beverly Hills and West Los Angeles and this street of high fashion and individual customer-serving financial institutions. But this is no ghetto; most of the population here migrated fairly directly, and presumably voluntarily, to this housing congregation from the American East or Europe itself. To think of this as a segregated, rather than a congregated, area is ridiculous. Not so with the black housing district around Watts, which now extends far more widely in the previously industrial towns in the southern part of the basin. In the black areas there was at least initially restriction that forced negroes into an area already "occupied by blacks." This was true segregation: whether all subsequent black towns are equally an imposition from outside would require considerable and careful investigation. Elsewhere in the Los Angeles basin there is a similar clustering of Spanish-Americans. No doubt originally their location was the result of segregation, but in more recent years there may instead have been constructive and voluntary congregation sought by the residents in order to obtain the benefits they perceive in a foreign-speaking "community." Because there is today fairly wide choice in residence for persons of Hispanic origin, it seems far too simplistic to think that clustering of Spanish-Americans comes only, or perhaps even mainly, from segregative rather than congregative processes.

In this brief summary, many other aspects of geographical congregation in the Los Angeles basin might be cited—of industry in war time and postwar suburbs, of retailing in economic-class-divided shopping centers, and of lifestyle components of the population in Venice (oppositional), Marina del Rey ("swingers"), Orange County (conservatives), and Malibu ("the rich")—but only one final point can be made in this short consideration. That is that the residential areas of Los Angeles, despite their often assumed lack of identity and structure, are usually clear congregations. Because the city has such a vast lower middle class and upper working class population, most housing areas seem alike. Still, there are strong contrasts—ethnically, occupationally, and in social attitudes. And quite in contrast to cities wherein transportation policy has called for vastly expensive public undertakings (and the probable public subvention of middle class travel), in Los Angeles the more well-to-do are not found mainly at the city edge and the poor at the center. The mixture of classes is, in broad geographical terms, rather complete. San Marino is near increasingly black Pasadena, Palos Verde near Torrance and Compton, and

other pairings of this sort can be found in all parts of the basin. It would be foolish to hold that there are not very striking contrasts between housing areas; it is equally as foolish to talk about "white flight" in a metropolis where, in those terms, there has been as well "black flight," and several other forms of spread of social groups about the city. They move but they do not do so randomly. Studies have shown that most people take up residence for one or more of three basic concerns: (1) they seek to live in congregation with other persons of similar social attributes, (2) they seek to live near employment that itself shows strong tendencies to congregate in terms of its own type, and (3) they find housing in terms of income and ownership characteristics that permit either single family detached residence, privately owned attached housing, or multiple unit rental housing. With three such variables at work there can be many different expressions of congregation, but in the end it is the clustering of individuals with somewhat common interests that results. For the Spanish speaker, his language needs may be dominant; for the Jewish migrant from the East it may be a cultural "community" that attracts most; for the inmigrant black from the American South it may be the chance of a job in a trade not strangled by union racial discrimination that pulls him to a particular section of the city; and for the well-to-do American lacking an obvious "ethnicity" it may be the chance to live in a generalized native culture that attracts. The ultimate geographical congregation each inhabits will differ, but the process at work in shaping their residential decision will be shared.

CONCLUSIONS

The thoughtful visitor to the great American metropolis seems to share the same overpowering sense of the vast unknown that gripped the pioneers moving across the Appalachians in the years just after our independence. Parts of the city can be understood but the great sweep of urban geography is not any more revealed than was the national geography of the emerging United States in 1776. In both cases a considerable attention to the processes at work in shaping that geography is needed to furnish some idea of the total pattern and its probable evolution. In the twenty monographs that make up this part of the Comparative Metropolitan Analysis Project a vast portrait of diversity is sketched, just as for the nation as a whole, but it is possible to place that seemingly infinite variety of parts in a process model, which may help to reduce the demands of memory that such a wealth seems to force upon us. In addition, it is logical that a concern for the future of those cities depends not merely upon the realities of the present, as given in the vignettes of individual cities, but as well on the processes that will shape those realities that we are viewing 200 years after independence but which those in our third century will be reading about in the past. In essence, facts change but processes evolve, and in that distinction we find the fundamental need for two views of our great cities.

The fundamental processes at work in American cities are those of congregation and segregation, as here discussed in considerable detail. In times of striking change, both are jointly at work so that a new congregation (an active process) leads automatically to a new segregation (a passive process). It is in this distinction that the basic injustice of segregation is to be found. In the past, certain ethnic groups in our society were forced out of the shared national development, surrounded by restrictions, and segregated geographically. The agency of this act assumes great importance because our society must respect the rights of individuals and minorities. It is of considerable importance that the final test of discrimination in our courts has become a geographical one of segregation in space; thus we may argue that spatial patterns assume great importance in our attainment of national goals. But at the same time we must ask whether a static spatial pattern can be viewed in the abstract without any cognizance taken of the process at work in its creation. To be specific on this point, our courts have not found a similar basis for arguing that Germans or Irish in our cities must, by court decree, be "integrated" with other Americans, so we must conclude that in the court's mind there is an implied but unstated pairing with the notion of segregation, which is that where the concentration in space can be assumed to be voluntary, rather than imposed from outside, that congregation stands justified before the law.

Other tests of the legitimacy of congregation exist. We have a strong legal base under the notion of zoning and planning that leads to congregation of land uses and types of structures. There is growing acceptance of the concept of fairly localized "control" of political and social affairs in cities as attested by federal programs aimed at "community control." The arguments of radical reformers and arch conservers of social distinctions tend to converge on control by a distinctive geographical congregation. There seems legal, social, and philosophical justification for considering those congregations the building blocks of our cities both socially and physically. The main qualification that needs be entered is that within the majority component of American society, where ethnic identification is neither practical nor desired, some substitute basis of congregation is required, and it has become, for the morphologic and economic reasons cited, the economic class.

Perhaps the most untested geographical concept at large in our society is this notion of economic congregation. The courts might well argue that as ethnic segregation is illegal, so is economic; and, in fact, there are cases that suggest that the tenor of legal opinion is shifting that way. If the vector of thought in that direction continues, we may well see during the next generation legal contests that seek to "desegregate" the great suburban areas of our metropolises wherein neither ethnicity nor culture provides any basis for what appears a great human need—that of social congregation. If the courts strike down economic congregation on the notion that it discriminates against those not congregated, particularly those of ethnic identification, then the internal social and geographical structure of the great majority of Americans will be destroyed. Such an act should only be undertaken with a clear understanding of its social and psychological implications and of its potentially critical morphological expression.

The first two caveats lie somewhat outside the normal professional interests of geographers, but the last is more particularly our concern than it is of any other professional group. To judge the nature of the potential transformation of the physical fabric of our metropolises we may look back briefly at what has happened during the last fifty years to identify the way the processes of congregation and segregation work. The events may be summarized as showing how one form of community or another provides the physical structure of the city. In earlier years occupation shaped cities, to be succeeded by a time when ethnicity was perhaps most dominant, whereas today economic class stands out, even within ethnic groupings. Marxian analysts have, in their doctrinal concentration on economic determinism, dispatched ethnicity as of no concern at all and focused doggedly on the persistence of economic distinctions. The implication is that such economic distinctions are intolerable in the same way that segregation by race is; thus, ethnics should utterly oppose them. Yet those persons most persistently ethnic—doctrinaire blacks, Spanish speakers, and Jews—now argue strongly for pluralism and against the melting pot society. Is economic class in an economically mobile society less valid? We of the melting pot must respect their individual and minority views even if they are positions unattainable to us. In sum, we seem to be faced with the situation that there are some in our society who crave most strongly to be apart, whereas there are some who do not, and most who cannot except in economic terms. In a democratic nation it seems that we must permit both ethnic and nonethnic congregation or else we tread on the rights of the individual and the minority.

But how do we handle the question of economic congregation, which I sincerely believe is more centrally a national problem than is that of race, in part because we have tried race and income expectation together to such an extent that race relations can never be considered on their own merits. The fundamental justification for the persistence of economic class in America has always been that of economic mobility, that hard work will gain economic elevation for any and all. Clearly this is at best a partial truth; there are groups that encounter great difficulty in gaining economic mobility and there are other groups that become ever more wealthy through no ability of their own, but by the simple adventitious possession of capital. Thus, without entering into a doctrinaire argument about economic class and classlessness, we may hold that the fundamental basis of American class requires at least two reforms—the opening of economic mobility to all groups, and the retrieval of automatic increase in wealth from those who contribute in no personal way to what we may call a society of workers.

The structuring of the vast sweep of American suburbia is somewhat underplayed in the monographs that follow, because our national attention has focused so narrowly on the harrowing problem of race and ethnicity in our central cities. We must not allow the pain of the problem areas so completely to overcome our appraisal of cities that the main body of people and of urban space will be forgotten. If integration is to work, which simply means nonethnic congregation as the main means of organizing our cities, or if separate ethnic congregation is to become a socially acceptable practice, which means affording to the black or Spanish-speaking community economic mobility and the opportunity to move into a mixed, and thereby nonethnic, congregation if individuals from that social grouping so wish, we must maintain some reasonable health in the suburbs. This is the argument for suburbs viewed from the narrowed perspective of the more assertive social activists; viewing it from the perspective of the great majority in our society, the justification is simpler but no less valid: more Americans live in the rather nativist suburbs than anywhere else. And if it might at first seem that those suburbs have such good fortune that their problems are not "real" like proletarian problems, perhaps closing on a brief consideration of the problems facing the residential areas of our great cities may be both worthwhile and soberingly emphasized.

The first quandary that assails us when we turn from the fashionable trouble zone in the city core to a less obvious one in the suburbs is the question here alluded to: Will constitutional thought, and its enunciators in the courts, allow the fundamental geographical structure of the suburbs to stand? Will economic class congregation be found unconstitutional, as involuntary ethnic segregation has been found to be? The enunciation of this question may seem to raise the specter of rigid class distinction in a strivingly mobile society, yet I suspect its real discomfiture attaches to a more basic doubt—whether those persons who are not "disadvantaged" in our society can appeal to the matter of personal decision and viewpoint as a justification for a social action that has a certain self-serving quality. Social thinking currently asserts that, in the communities of the poor, neighborhood action, in distinction to a broader social action, is valid.

Will that principle be extended to the suburbs, particularly the more prosperous ones? If it is, then we will face a real question of responsibility for the problems of society as a general institution rather than its localized expression in the congregation of one particular sort.

This question of responsibility has two attributes—that of governance and that of finance; current social thought asserts the local right to governance but tends to argue the general responsibility for finance. In other words, voluntary social congregations would have the right to form and continue to shape much of their own governance. What is not half so well agreed upon is the matter of who pays for social costs. This is a remarkable geographical question, as also is local governance. At the present, undoubtedly the most valid criticism of the suburbs arises when they seem to represent not merely a case of choosing one's own social congregation but as well avoiding one's proportionate social financial responsibility. But there is a way that this conflict might be resolved: we might accept the real virtue that local governance has in giving a fundamental and vital role to social congregation while at the same time rejecting the notion of a narrow local boundary in finance. The result would tend to dissatisfy both radical social theorists and academic political scientists—the first because they seek a situation in which the proletarian communities determine both their own course (through local governance) and the inexorable financial responsibility of others (through "welfare rights" unmatched by "social rights"); and the second because they wish to experiment with the city, hoping that by reducing local governance they may produce systemic "efficiency" in metropolitan government to force an "improved" government on urban society.

The geographical expression of this compromise would be the continuation, and even enhancement, of local governance, but the creation of major taxing metropolises conterminous with the physical metropolis in a system wherein economic class congregation would not be rewarded by avoidance of broad responsibilities that should be borne by society at large. The tendency has been to treat this geographical conflict in a very doctrinaire way, which completely obscures the real nature of the problem. That problem is how to afford the rights of local congregation to the prosperous as well as to the poor without shifting onto the poor the full responsibility for their own welfare, which is certainly a social problem. To care for the valid interests of both groups, economic class integration is not the answer, however much it appeals to Marxist theorists. Their solution can only work if there is a dictatorship of the proletariate, an economic leveling to the bottom, and the imposition of statism wherein the local group loses virtually all its control over governance. Instead, allowing all economic levels of society to practice congregation assures to individuals—the main building block of our constitutional system in a document that never once, save in the repealed provision on slavery, accepts the collective unit of economic class, ethnic group, or political faction as a valid part of our free existence—the rights that belong to individuals. What it must be tied to is the acceptance by all groups, recipients as well as providers, that social costs will be borne in terms of ability and accepted in terms of societywide, not ethnic and class, decision. In such a context the suburb based on economic class congregation seems as justified as the neighborhood rebuilt and governed in terms of an ethnically exclusive council.

Other problems assail the suburb, perhaps the most geographical of which is the rapidly changing condition of mobility. In our cities it is apparent that the massive urban freeway is an abandoned solution, fought by the environmental activists and the urban poor in an odd but effective harness. Thus we must decide either to locate economic activities in such a way that undue geographical focus of travel is avoided and the existing street system can serve, or else we must work out a general purpose transit system. The first solution is not very likely as it would imply the abandoning of most economies of scale and of automation and mechanization. The second development, that of transit, is probable but rather frightening in terms of recent designs in transit, which have suffered badly from a commuting *idée fixe*. BART in the Bay Area and Philadelphia's Lindenwold line are not useful or desirable national prototypes. In their place we must determine how to provide public transportation to all segments of society rather than merely to the white collar office employee of the downtown area of a large city. Given the rapid recent increases in the cost of gasoline, fairly large components of the urban population need the prospect of public transit in five or ten years when costs may be still higher. Subways and high speed commuter lines to the central city are myopic "solutions" to their problems. Instead we must devise a system that avoids the intolerable quality of spcialization of use with generalization of financial support characteristic of the current systems.

A dangerous trap exists in this search for a solution to urban transit—that of being bemused by technological glitter. Most of the current work on passenger transportation—urban and long distance—is focused on speed and elegance, the two main talking points for BART. Yet if we ask the geographical question, who needs speed, the answer is that group that has built into its lifestyle the greatest consumption of mobility, the rather well-to-do business man or the geographical fidgets of the upper income groups. The poor do not need speed because they cannot afford to go very far; thus, to argue that this is to make their lives less painful is nonsense.

Instead of focusing on technology for the rich—the SST, high speed ground service, personal rapid transit—public effort should turn to the question of continuing the livability of cities, which will find during the next decade that private transport will become increasingly prohibitive in cost for repeating journeys. Its use will become more and more restricted to specific purposes where mobility in place and in time is of greatest individual benefit. As in western Europe today, people will continue to have cars but they will use them for recreation (hopefully an individual undertaking) and pressing personal needs. Those same people will seek to save money by using public transit for daily repeating journeys. Thus, instead of planning for the rapid long distance transport of the upper income businessman, public effort should seek to devise a form of public transportation that will be economically viable in areas of moderately low density housing and be useful for a complexity of quite local transport needs. Economic viability implies forcing some rational form on individual movements (both as to time of the journey and its destination) and seeking to make one system serve as large a group as possible.

A final problem of the suburbs that should be considered is that of the transition from a time of high consumption of energy to one when we will progressively have to improve the productive output of a stable or declining input of energy. At first blush many futurists turn to "technology" and rebuilding our cities to solve this problem, yet any considered evaluation of the energy situation must suggest to us that recourse to high technology is not a solution. Given a situation of undersupply of energy and other nonrenewable resources, high technology ends up consuming more to produce the same or a lesser product. As we have learned during the last few years, speed is an energy glutton, as is excessive attention to personal convenience. At some point it will be necessary to raise a socially based question as to the "right to consume," whatever one's income and position.

It is in such a policy context that these great metropolises, the home of the greatest number of Americans, will have to be reorganized during the next quarter century to consume less energy and other wasting commodities. As the suburbs were built in a time of increasing per capita energy consumption and generally declining relative costs for that power, the impact of the turnaround will be greatest there. We are so conditioned to the notion that the poor all huddle in the central city that we overlook the problem of the outlying poor, for whom the energy crisis has the greatest impact. Already rural people in Appalachia have been badly hit by increases in the cost of gasoline, and it has been necessary to devise assistance programs for people who live in the country but must drive rather long distances to work and to shop. To a lesser degree, this same problem will move into the suburbs of the poorer workers. Jobs are at a distance and usually not in the central city to which public transit normally leads. Thus, costful trips by car or pickup truck become part of earning a modest living. Yet our transportation planning seems blindly focused on glittering "improvements" for the relatively prosperous central city commuters in a suburban world where the greater number of workers have jobs in those dispersed suburbs unserved by public transportation. At some point we will have to begin to analyze how our cities work as geographical structures and begin to question the confident assumption that all urban problems are tied to the central city and all good fortune lies in the suburbs. In an era of increasingly scarce and costly energy the problem of the suburbs can be very real and very widespread.

Futurists have tended to see the solution to any problem in the massive rebuilding of the urban fabric, clustering people into high-rise apartment houses and forcing them into mechanistic solutions of social problems. Paolo Soleri's archologies are merely the symbol of a widespread thinking that holds that if man is to survive he must be denied individuality, privacy, the right to expend inefficient human energy in place of efficient mineral energy, and choice as to lifestyle. Thus the notion is advanced that technology will save us if we will but let it. But technology normally means high consumption of energy, so a rational skeptic must question such solutions; and certainly rebuilding the fabric of our cities will consume more nonrenewable resources than making the present fabric serve in a new urban garment. The argument is normally advanced that we cannot make alterations because they consume so much labor; instead, it is cheaper to cut from fresh cloth. The trouble is that today the resource we have in greatest abundance is labor and it is our one naturally renewing component.

If we accept that to remake rather than rebuild our cities is the wisest and most practical course to follow in the present context of resources, then we must conclude by asking if there is a pattern against which to shape the alteration. The answer is that with so many different urban physiques to fit, no one pattern will serve, but with some understanding of the processes that shape that urban body and the functions it performs, we are fully able to make alterations as needs change. In this introductory essay I have attempted at some length to show the origin and development of a set of inter-related processes that have shaped the morphology and geographical functioning of American cities. With proper attention to the forces of congregation and segregation, it should be possible to retailor our metropolitan areas to meet new jobs, increased stature, greater social equality and justice, continued acceptable levels of privacy for the individual, and choice in lifestyle, as well as more responsible levels of resource use, and yet avoid the disease of involuntary segregation while gaining the strength of voluntary congregation.

Bibliography

Bridenbaugh, Carl. *Cities in the Wilderness.* New York: The Ronald Press, 1938.

Christaller, Walter. *Central Places in Southern Germany.* Translated by Carlisle W. Baskin. Englewood Cliffs, N.J.: Prentice-Hall, 1966.

Dubois, William E.B. *The World and Africa.* New York: The Viking Press, 1947.

Firey, Walter. *Land Use in Central Boston.* Cambridge: Harvard University Press, 1947.

Forbes, Esther. *Paul Revere and the World He Lived In.* Boston: Houghton Mifflin Company, 1942.

Gottmann, Jean. *Megalopolis: The Urbanized Northeastern Seaboard of the United States.* New York: Twentieth Century Fund, 1961.

Hall, Peter, ed. *Van Thünen's Isolated State.* Oxford: Pergamon Press, 1966.

Handlin, Oscar. *The Uprooted: The Epic Story of the Great Migration That Made the American People.* Boston: Little, Brown, 1951.

Harris, Chauncy D., and Ullman, Edward L. "The Nature of Cities." *Annals of the American Academy of Political and Social Science,* 242 (November 1945): 7-17.

Hoyt, Homer. *The Structure and Growth of Residential Neighborhoods in American Cities.* Washington, D.C.: Federal Housing Administration, 1939.

New York Times, May 25, 1974, p. 29.

Park, Robert E.; Burgess, Ernest W.; and MacKenzie, Roderick D. *The City.* Chicago: University of Chicago Press, 1925.

Rischin, Moses. *The American Gospel of Success: Individualism and Beyond.* Chicago: Quandrangle Books, 1965.

Roszak, Theodore. *The Make of a Counter Culture: Reflections on the Technocratic Society and Its Youthful Opposition.* Garden City, N.Y.: Doubleday, 1969.

Soleri, Paolo. *Arcology: The City in the Image of Man.* Cambridge: MIT Press, 1969.

Vance, James E., Jr. *The Merchant's World: The Geography of Wholesaling.* Englewood Cliffs, N.J.: Prentice-Hall, Inc., 1970.

Chapter 2

Boston: A Geographical Portrait

Introduction

Why should I travel when I'm already here?
—Beacon Hill Lady

Boston—the hub of the Solar System.
—Oliver Wendell Holmes

The unique characteristics and qualities of the city are in large part a reflection of the personal perceptions of the observer. The longtime resident, the newly arrived college student, the company-transferred employee, the Portuguese immigrant, and the tourist all see the same city in different ways. Boston is no different in this respect. The features which set Boston apart as a city for one person are the result of those particular experiences that a person has had in Boston which he may or may not share with others.

Outsiders think of Boston as an old city steeped in history—a quality promoted by the Chamber of Commerce. The Boston Tea Party, Paul Revere, the Freedom Trail, the Boston Massacre, Bunker Hill, and Old Ironsides are standard fixtures in the city's heritage. Yet there are virtually no concrete remains of the seventeenth century and precious few from the eighteenth.

Longtime residents know Boston as an historic city, because they know the narrow, winding colonial alleys, the ancient burying grounds, the cobblestoned squares, and the few remaining colonial buildings. For many residents of Boston's lower Roxbury district, however, Boston is dirty streets sparkling with broken glass, boarded-up store windows, and Coca Cola billboards with black faces. For college students Boston is a swinging town, reputed to be "the best" in the country for whatever you want in a college town.

The tourist is surprised to find that Boston is also a new city. Its newly contemporary skyline reminds him of San Francisco and Atlanta. Its airport looks like everyone else's. Its new hotels and convention center are clean, efficient, and accessible. The longtime resident remembers that all this is very new, and there was a day when he wasn't at all sure that Boston would join the rest of the country in postwar change. After all, the Yankee matrons on fashionable Beacon Street were supposed never to throw a hat away. But the newness is a sign of economic well-being; more high-rise office buildings mean more jobs. The Portuguese immigrant quickly finds employment cleaning and polishing the offices, corridors, and restrooms of the forty-fourth floor.

The tourist finds Boston a little out of the way, a bit harder to get to (and *much* harder to find his way around in). Washington, Philadelphia, New York may catch and keep him before he can get to Boston. But the Bostonian sees his city as "the hub of the Solar System." There really is no need for him to go elsewhere. He is already there. For many, Boston is a "livable" city. In spite of its shortcomings, Boston seems to provide an atmosphere of urbanity and civility that sets it apart in the minds of its people. It has an atmosphere which must be experienced personally in order for it to be fully comprehended.

Atmosphere, however, does not begin to convey the real story of what the city is, how it works, what it does for its people, what they do for it, or what it does for the world outside. Cities do not exist simply to excite their inhabitants or rescue them from isolation in dispersed rural environments. Large cities exist to provide goods and services efficiently for vast regional populations of which their own residents form only a small, and sometimes incidental, part. Urban populations themselves become important consumers of these goods and services. But no large city is an island unto itself, independent and self-sufficient. Rather, it is a prominent center of dense human activity in a wide national or international realm from which the city derives a specific and complex role to play. One cannot come to grips with a city merely by walking its streets or sensing its atmosphere. One has to know *what* the city does, and *where* it fits in the regional and national organization of society. These external circumstances do much to identify and account for the internal patterns of daily life and work that give a city its individual character and create its atmosphere.

This essay on Boston begins by placing the metropolis in its broadest geographical context. The focus then narrows to Boston's immediate site conditions—the physical and temporal "milieu" in which the metropolis nestles. Within this, the metropolis itself appears to comprise four basic elements. Without people there would be no city; population forms the obvious cornerstone of the city's inner structure. People work to earn a living, and in so doing help fulfill the city's role in the larger economy. But people with jobs to do need facilities in which to function, and this calls into being a built environment of homes, factories, shops, offices, and transport channels by which to reach them all. Neither people, jobs, nor buildings would function without such civilizing forces as government, health, education, and recreation to organize, maintain, and edify the population brought to the city for economic purposes.

By approaching each of these topics in turn, a working portrait of the Boston metropolitan area should emerge. How this composite picture is perceived by the average resident or the tourist forms the final theme. The image a city projects is important. Whether fully or accurately perceived or not, that image goes a long way in forming people's attitudes and satisfactions about living there. To the extent that large cities have individuality, so the resident gains a valuable sense of belonging to "a" place rather than the limbo of "someplace."

Boston's sheer age, by American standards, sets it apart from newer cities, whatever their size. What are the consequences of maturity for present-day urban problems and possibilities? Does it suggest experience, a corporate ability to solve critical difficulties and rise successfully to new challenges? Or, rather, does it bespeak weariness, an inability to jettison worn-out practices and burned-out leadership? Many of Boston's institutions are new and innovative, while many are old and venerated. What effect do long-established institutions and patterns of life have on the ever-changing social and physical fabric of the city? The long period of economic doldrums have intensified Boston's problems in adjusting to changed conditions of urban life in the twentieth century. How much lost time has Boston had to make up now that things are moving again, and what effect has this also had on the pattern of life in the city? A look at the geographical structure of Boston should provide some answers.

Part I

Time and Place

BOSTON AND THE REST OF THE WORLD

No major metropolitan region of the United States is as peripheral to major national food-producing and mineral source areas as Boston. For this reason Boston and its region is one of the most costly in the nation for family consumer and industrial entrepreneur alike. In ways other than distance, Boston is closer to Europe than to California.

This geographical isolation is only 150 years old, and even so only in relation to the continental area of the United States. In late Colonial times, Boston lay not far from the center of a population apread along the Atlantic coast from Nova Scotia to the Carolinas and backed by the Appalachian Mountains. Trans-Appalachian America was an almost complete wilderness. From an economic viewpoint, the Atlantic colonies were, in fact, the *western* fringe of a Euro-Atlantic culture realm. Thus, Boston's location has been shifting constantly in relation to the changing patterns of human activity on the continent (Figure 1). Since Europeans explored and settled the country from the east, the first cities arose on the East Coast. After serving as footholds on the continent, Boston and its southerly neighbors became middlemen in funneling exports to Europe and imports to the interior. Even today when a much higher proportion of demand for goods is satisfied by manufacture within the country, Boston still functions as an important gateway to

Europe, so that its historical external role has not disappeared altogether.

Nevertheless, it is inescapable that Boston's relative location deteriorated during the last century and a half as the West filled up, and proportionately less of the national demand for manufactured products and luxuries required importation from England. Boston and its hinterland had one asset to counter increasing national isolation—initial advantage. New England quickly industrialized to substitute for European imports with capital from the profits of maritime trade and was thus able to remain important in the national economy. This is, however, a triumph of ingenuity and early timing of innovation over the relentless westward shift of the country's center of gravity. Manufacturing spread to the Great Lakes and Middle Atlantic regions during the nineteenth century, and some new industrial centers in the South and West now claim recognition. Nevertheless, Boston would not be as large and important as it is today were it not for that fortuitous historical circumstance of being first in the field.

If the centrality of Boston's regional location within the nation has diminished somewhat, the situation is not too serious. As the northern pivot of a vast quasi-urban "megalopolis" stretching south to Washington, D.C., Boston has at its doorstep the largest urbanized market in the country. While the city may be far from raw materials, it is very close to the consumer. In this century, urban centers have become dominant factors in the supply of

Figure 1. Boston's geographical context.

goods and services for the nation as a whole. Viewing the distribution of large cities in the United States, Boston's position, while technically peripheral, is a great deal healthier than that of similarly sized metropolises in the country's interior.

Boston may have slipped in national urban rank over the last century, but it remains the dominant regional metropolis for much of New England. The six states east of New York have always constituted a distinctive region in the minds of laymen and expert alike, and Boston is the undeniable center of the region's affairs. Only in southern Connecticut does New York impinge seriously on Boston's influence, and many a study has sought to identify the borderline of indifference between the two cities. Wherever this line lies at any moment, Boston has long been the focus in New England for finance, trade, learning, jobs, and innovations, weaving a web of interrelationships between itself and the region. This role as regional capital of a historically stable hinterland is an important component of Boston's continued influence as a large city. Boston can grow steadily by increasing its manufactures and services to the nation, but its fundamental stability rests upon serving a growing local hinterland.

THE BOSTON "MILIEU"

The Geographical Imprint

The local "milieu" of a city, as evidenced by its topographical site conditions, gives the city its most immediate and unique quality. The configuration of land and water, high places and low, sets the stage upon which the urban creation can unfold. However alive a city is, however clean its streets, beautiful its architecture, humane its citizens, benevolent its government, hardworking its people, or efficient its services, the physical setting is paramount, not only in forming a strong visual urban image, but more importantly in setting limits and creating opportunities for urban life.

Can Boston's geographical setting, then, be described as a help or a hindrance to the city? Boston, like other old metropolitan centers in America, is a sea level city. Lacking the drama of nearby mountainous terrain in places like Rio de Janeiro, San Francisco, or Bergen, Boston cannot excite the eye with the splendor of vertical surroundings. The hills and escarpments that gently ruffle the Boston landscape, important though they are to the local scene, are timid by international standards. What the area misses in the vertical, however, it more than compensates for in the horizontal. To approach Boston by air is to perceive a crazy quilt of visual contrasts—flat peninsulas, rocky peninsulas, estuaries, islands, bridges, tunnels, gridiron streets, crooked streets, woodlots, airstrips, rivers with right angle bends by Nature, rivers with ruler-straight estuarine banks by Man, wide sweeps of smooth dunes, and narrow curves of habor wharves. Boston Bay has for centuries provided the dramatic entrance for the city, and Logan Airport's coastal position opposite the downtown peninsula preserves and heightens the drama of arrival (Figure 2).

Chicago, Los Angeles, Philadelphia, and Detroit, despite their scale, cannot compete, although their sites have hampered their development far less.

The sea has effectively made a 270° city out of Boston, stretching from northeast around to southeast. In perhaps no other large city except San Francisco and New York does the open ocean penetrate so deeply to the urban core. Dock Square, location of the principal town wharf in the seventeenth century, is only a few hundred yards from the Massachusetts State House and a few hundred feet from the Boston City Hall. The deep tidal estuaries are effective barriers to easy movement out of Boston in almost every landward direction. Long traffic delays in the Callahan Tunnel, on the Mystic River Bridge, or even at one of the lesser Charles River bridge crossings are constant reminders to the Bostonian that he has not yet paved over every waterway that runs in from the sea nor built enough bridges or tunnels to satisfy the demands of commuters.

The principal topographic feature of metropolitan Boston (with perhaps the exception of Great Blue Hill, which is simply both easier to see and better known) is a distinct break in topography that delineates an "inner" basin of relatively low elevation and subdued relief from an "outer" rim of higher elevation and considerable relief (Figure 3). The term Boston Basin has long been applied to the inner area, and its boundaries are not difficult to establish on a map or identify in the field. On the northerly side of Boston the basin is bounded by an escarpment that extends in an almost straight line from Waltham on the west to Lynn on the east. The relatively steep slopes of this escarpment, which reaches heights of 350 feet in places, represent, in reality, an ancient fault scarp resulting from movement of the earth's crust. The fault is further accentuated by a dramatic contrast in underlying rock types, with the Boston Basin underlain by soft sedimentary strata while the adjacent upland contains granites, gneisses, gabbros, diorites, and other hard rocks. The distinct topographic break along this northern margin is clearly visible because the lowland surface is relatively flat right up to the edge of the escarpment. With the exception of Interstate 93, all of the major routes entering from the north and west must descend this slope, usually along some erosional break in the escarpment, leaving a magnificent exposure of upland hard rock. The motorist approaching from the north is often afforded a spectacular view out over the city with its cluster of new, high office buildings in the distance.

On the southerly side, extending from Waltham to Quincy, the escarpment is far more difficult to identify on the ground, but its lack of size or vigor is made up by the range of Blue Hills that lies immediately behind it. Faulting along this zone is far more complex, and the border between the Boston Basin and the up-

Figure 3. Basin, bay and Boston.

land is more of a transition zone of gradually increasing elevation and relief. The same change, however, is made from relatively weak silt stones and conglomerates in the basin to the extremely resistant granites of the Blue Hill range.

Tectonic forces were not the only influences upon topography. New England experienced all four of the Pleistocene glaciations, and their legacy strongly modifies the fault-lowered "basin" of ancient rocks and preglacial river valleys. Glaciers that overran the basin partially filled it with sand, gravel, and clays that ob-

Figure 2. Approaching Boston from the east. Bays and estuaries penetrate deeply into metropolitan Boston. Downtown Boston occupies the historic Shawmut Peninsula in center right, with the Charles River Basin behind it to the west. (Courtesy Aerial Photos of New England)

literated the old stream courses and created new ones—today's drainage pattern. The glacial deposits were not enough, however, to obliterate the basin itself—bedrock outcrops frequently in the area—but they did themselves add some new elements to the topography.

The basin is dotted with low, elongated hills with smooth outlines known as drumlins. They owe their origin to the movement of great continental ice sheets thousands of years ago, and for this reason the elongated axis of each hill is parallel to all the others. Orient Heights in East Boston (Figure 4) is only one of more than one hundred such drumlins that characterize the physical texture of the Boston area.

Drumlins were avoided by early settlers because of their very steep slopes, and many of them stood above relatively densely settled villages long after the tide of urbanization had swept past. When the time came in the nine-

teenth century for such urban facilities as water storage tanks, hospitals, and even parks to be sited, the drumlin tops were available and were utilized. In Chelsea, the two principal drumlins bear the Chelsea Naval Hospital and the Old Soldiers Home.

A sense of destiny may well have attended the founding of Boston on the Shawmut Peninsula in 1630, but no human imagination then could have predicted, let alone planned for, the scale of urban expansion during the next three and a half centuries. A look at any of the early maps of Boston Harbor or mariner's charts of that complex maze of channels, islands, shoals, and headlands shows the many fingerlike peninsulas stretching into the harbor. Most of these were relatively low and narrow ridges that lay between the many estuaries in the Boston Basin. In addition to the two major estuaries of the Charles River (tidal all the way to Watertown) and the Mystic River (tidal beyond Medford), there were also numerous smaller tidal creeks that penetrated deep into the coastal zone and impeded easy coastwise movement on land. Miller's Creek in Cambridge, Malden Creek, and Chelsea Creek were three examples of such smaller estuaries on the northern side of the harbor. The peninsula of Old Boston itself was quite irregular, with coves and small creeks on every side.

Early Boston and neighboring villages along the estuaries and inland quickly engrossed the level sites for easy building. Wet, marshy sites, steep slopes with outcropping of rocks, and similar inhospitable areas were avoided and remained unoccupied in many cases until well into the twentieth century. Great amounts of space were needed meanwhile, and it was clear that filling the coves and the principal estuaries would provide an immediate solution. Boston embarked on a landfilling spree that created more dry land for urban uses than in any other North American city (Figure 5).

The first major landfills were made on the main peninsula near the original locus of settlement. Mill Cove and Town Cove were first dammed, then drained in 1804 to make land. Bostonians have been lucky; they have had

Figure 4. Drumlin development. Atlantic Street houses cascade down the Telegraph Hill drumlin in South Boston to reveal the downtown high-rise structures behind the Fort Point Channel warehouse district.

hills they did not want (or at least, care much about) from which material could be cut to make marshes into solid land which they did want. Although the later Back Bay filling (1856–1894) required importation of outside materials, the earlier projects turned upon a simple symmetry of adjacent demand and supply. Thus, central Boston is today much flatter than it was in the eighteenth century; Beacon Hill is a mere shadow of its former eminence, and Fort Hill no longer even exists. Other marsh zones also succumbed to land hunger, and vast areas in Charlestown (1860–1896), East Boston (after 1880), the South End, and South Boston (after 1836) came into being to house railroad yards, factories, docks, parks, and inner suburbs.

All this artificial land is an important element of Boston's geographical "milieu" both for the space it created and also for the limits it imposes on further urban change. Most of the building construction on filled land rests on wooden piles driven into the new "ground." These piles will continue to function only if kept permanently wet (otherwise they will rot), thus making essential the maintenance of a high water table. The configuration of the water table in the Boston Basin verges on the chaotic, given the complex geological structure of glacial and marine sediments resting on undulating preglacial bedrock and alluvium. Add to this the demands of thousands of water wells and the disruptions of highway and highrise construction, and the balance between groundwater inflow and loss or extraction becomes highly precarious. This legacy from Nature sobers Boston engineers in the same way that earthquakes worry San Franciscans. Erection of the new John Hancock Insurance skyscraper in Copley Square has not only dwarfed adjacent Trinity Church but—adding injury to insult, one might say—has caused the church's foundation to teeter and the walls to crack.

The Patina of Age

A city's "milieu" is composed not only of the physical ingredients of its geographical site, but also of the unique people who have created, used, discarded, refurbished, and replaced that urban habitat. This prolonged and complex interaction between dweller and dwelling—a deeply historical process in Boston's case—gives to the present city, however present- or future-oriented its residents may be, a strong

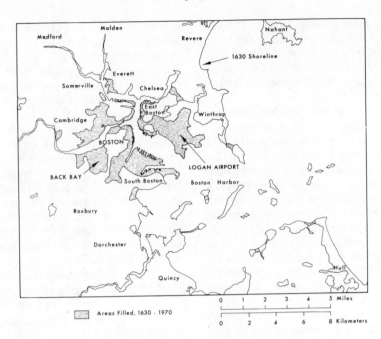

Figure 5. Beating back the sea, 1804–1970. Landfill stretches the urban core. (After MAPC Open Space and Recreation Study)

patina of age. It is impossible to describe and explain the geographical structure or life of the metropolis without a constant sensitivity toward the evolutionary forces that brought it to its present condition. Each phase of growth and change has left its imprint, and the cumulative residue severely restricts what is likely to happen in the future.

There lies a point in Boston's history where general and specific historical forces come together in a particular environment to produce an individual past that finds broad and deep expression in the Boston of today. In sketching the historical contribution to Boston's individuality, it is possible to view the city's development in three major phases. These phases reflect, as they must do, fundamental realignments in the city's economic function and organization, for cities are economic creations first, and only consequently social agglomerations.

Traders' Town (1640–1840). As one of the very oldest metropolitan centers in the United States, Boston has passed through nearly every traditional phase of metropolitan evolution. After its founding in 1630 the town quickly emerged as the premier entrepôt in New Eng-

land. It grew strong in a trading role that outfitted and operated much of the complex Atlantic commerce of the seventeenth and eighteenth centuries and supplied arriving colonists throughout the period. Unlike New York and Philadelphia, Boston did not possess a large hinterland of rich, arable farmland that could produce substantial food surpluses for export. While the city gathered limited supplies of timber and naval stores from the interior and abroad, its chief function was to buy, sell, and process other people's goods. The Massachusetts Bay Colony spread settlement inland by setting up highly independent "towns" that, in the early stages, traded relatively little with Boston. The local trade that existed did pivot, however, on the port.

The post-Revolutionary period hurt Boston's trade, particularly with England, but the city adjusted with an expanded Eastern trade with Russia and China. The harrassment by Britain following the War of 1812 and the general interruptions of European trade during the early nineteenth century, however, had a more lasting effect on spurring the development of infant manufacturing activities in New England. Not all the early factories concentrated in the immediate Boston area, but their location in southern New England was closely linked to Boston capital from the outset.

The trader's town was a modest entity by modern standards. It fitted wholly within the Shawmut Peninsula that helped create a magnificent bay harbor (Figure 5). Downtown consisted of little more than the wharves and warehouses, some public buildings, and the homes of the town's wealthy and respected leadership. The remainder of today's metropolitan area consisted of nucleated village settlements such as Charlestown, Cambridge, and Roxbury, all separated from each other by wide expanses of estuaries, marsh, and broken ground.

This period of Boston's growth has left virtually no buildings in the present central

city. Wood-frame construction and frequent fires have taken care of that. What the Colonial era did bequeath was the street pattern, and this is a relic of surpassing importance to Bostonians, ranging from dedicated antiquarians to frustrated truck drivers (Figure 6). The early colonial "crooked and narrow" street pattern (to use Annie Haven Thwing's phrase) in the historic city core has provided a strong morphological frame that later development faithfully respected for 300 years. Even today, it constitutes with the Boston Common an element of the urban landscape that contributes far more than any physical structure to the historicity of central Boston. Imagine all of Boston's historic buildings arrayed along gridiron streets and their visual impact would be sadly reduced. Conceive

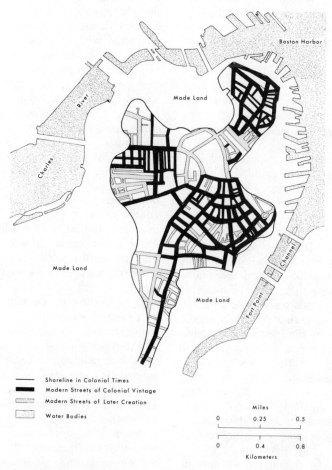

Figure 6. Central Boston's street heritage. The impress of colonial town planning on the morphology of the Hub.

the "crooked and narrow streets of Boston" without their historic buildings and the sense of age would still remain.

Machine Metropolis (1840-1940). The industrialization of New England in the early nineteenth century, in challenging European mercantilist policies that discouraged American industry, was begun in large part by gains from long-standing commercial success. This industrial investment of commercial profits was also to make Boston a powerful financial source for western frontier development throughout the century. The city remained substantially a trading port, while its rural environs industrialized, until the middle of the century. Then, the convergence of increased manufacturing activity and mass immigration produced rapid industrialization of the city. While New York cut Boston off from the nation's interior with early canals and railroads, thus virtually freezing the size of her hinterland, the New England capital quickly married her new unskilled labor to the burgeoning industrial jobs of the textile mills and leather factories. As the century wore on, the Irish immigrants of midcentury were joined by French Canadians and rural Yankees from the marginal areas, and later still by Italians and Russian Jews.

However, the economic pattern was set— only the pace of growth changed. For nearly a century, eastern Massachusetts lived off the mills that had started with waterpower and ready financing. It was an independence that could not last. The change to steam power freed some factories from the river, although the price for that was hauling in coal from Pennsylvania. A coastal location and early railroad network made this an easy adjustment, but it meant dependence on outside areas for basic raw materials. Through the nineteenth century, settlement of the continental interior shifted the center of population westward, and Boston and its region became ever more peripheral in a national economy that grew increasingly independent of European economic intervention. Only the factor of initial advantage kept New England nationally dominant in textiles and footwear well into the present century.

Boston, meanwhile, developed not only in size but in functional complexity as well. As canals and railroads made more and more of

New England accessible to the city, and vice versa, economic and social interaction between city and interior increased. As the general population gained greater financial access to the material accoutrements of nineteenth century civilized life, the city played its role as distributing emporium. Better travel and increased interest in cultural activities combined with economic changes to give Boston a truly metropolitan function within the region as a whole.

Nowhere was this more in evidence than in the emerging downtown district of the city, which evolved, as David Ward has shown, from a core of commercial wharves, public buildings, and superior residences, into a multipurpose central business district with distinct wholesale, financial, retail, governmental, and recreational sectors. Beyond the business district lay the inner residential areas of the North, West, and South ends, becoming more densely populated and built-up each decade. Beyond these, Boston's exploding population competed with growing industry (some of it fleeing the congestion and rising rents of the old commercial core) and the proliferation of new public institutions such as hospitals, museums, and parks, to create a new confusion of suburbs, urban fringe land uses, and industrial zones, pushing the city far beyond the old peninsulas.

By 1880 Boston, like the other major seaboard cities and some interior cities, had become an urban focus of profoundly regional importance, as multifunctional in an American context as were London and Paris in a European one. Indicative of this broadened regional scope is the extent to which Boston reached out into southern New England with her network of passenger services on the railroad (Figure 7). Already in 1870 the zones of influence exerted by Boston and New York almost met in eastern Connecticut. Boston may have enjoyed nominal influence over all New England as the region's recognized capital, but the demand for railroad service to Boston from the surrounding area tells the real story of its day-to-day magnetism. This zone of influence in 1850 had hardly reached beyond the city's suburbs.

From 1880 until World War I the Boston region slowly intensified its economic life by relying upon the old successful formula of manufacturing and trade, although there were missed opportunities in attracting even more

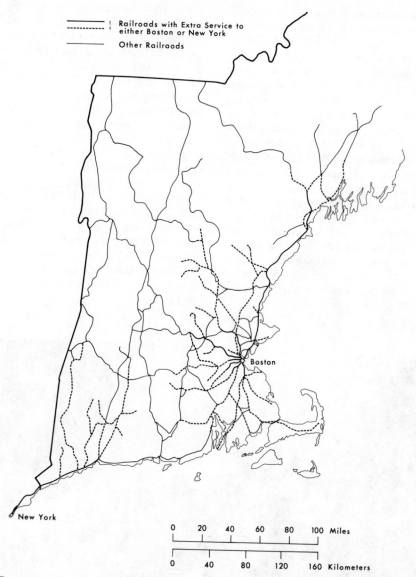

Railroads with Extra Service to
either Boston or New York
Other Railroads

Boston

New York

| 0 | 20 | 40 | 60 | 80 | 100 | Miles |

| 0 | 40 | 80 | 120 | 160 | Kilometers |

Figure 7. Boston's railroad reach into New England, 1870. (After contemporary railroad timetables)

industry than it did. After the war, however, signs appeared that the region's dependence on staple soft goods manufacture would bring trouble. Locational shifts within the textile and footwear industries were occurring that fostered the growth of factories in the Atlantic Piedmont South and elsewhere in the interior. These shifts resulted partly from the changing locus of the national market, and partly from the economics of production which decreed plant sites closer to the raw materials and cheaper labor. In the case of cotton and leather,

their source areas were nowhere near New England. Wool did come in part from the native hill regions, and consequently the wool industry was slower to relocate outside the province. However, the net effect was an outmigration, first of new investment capital and then of actual employment in these industries between the World Wars, exacerbated by the belated rise of the industrial South and, of course, the Great Depression.

The hundred years of urban growth before World War II set the dominant character of much of the central city and its inner suburbs. The impress of this period was achieved in three ways. First, the urban area grew outward by absorbing new land on its fringe, often linking to the continuous built-up area the formerly isolated village nucleations. Second, older parts of the city became replete with infill housing and backyard development, creating a much tighter urban mass with little remaining elbow room. Third, the inner city in particular experienced widespread replacement of single family homes by tenements and apartment blocks, and residential land use by commercial and institutional uses. While nearly all parts of the city exhibit buildings of more than one age, the imprint of these three processes on Boston has bequeathed us today an essentially nineteenth century inner city to look at. The modern intrusions such as the recent high-rise buildings, of course, provide exceptions. The North End, for example, was largely built up in the eighteenth century, but extensive replacement by higher-rent-yielding structures of the 1870–1920 era have changed the district's character out of recognition. Driving through the streetcar suburbs of Roxbury, Dorchester, Brookline, or Brighton, street after street of three-deckers, gable-to-gable frame houses crowding skimpy lots, mock-Tudor school complexes, Scottish-baronial libraries and waterworks attest to the orgy of urban expansion this period generated (Figure 8).

Service City (1940–1970). The Boston region historically has adjusted successfully, if sometimes lethargically, to each major change in the geographical restructuring of the national economy. The decline of textiles and footwear produced another characteristic realignment. A slow diversification of industries that had begun

Figure 8. Boston triple-deckers pioneer the nineteenth century suburbs. Although the streetcar tracks have long gone, these houses on Washington Street still project the classic image of the Boston streetcar suburb.

in the economically dour interwar period accelerated after 1940. World War II gave a brief respite to the cloth and shoe industries on account of military needs, but the new impetus, small at first, came in engineering, particularly with electrical instruments. As traditional industries moved out of the Boston area—indeed the region as a whole—a close alliance began to grow between manufacturing interests and the leading universities of the metropolis to forge new production based on advanced technology. Begun with the war and spurred on by Sputnik, the electronics industry has become a major component of the Greater Boston economy. This time the investment came not from accumulated commercial capital, but from the assembled intellectual capital of institutions like Harvard University and the Massachusetts Institute of Technology.

The marriage of readily available pure research with easily expandable productive capacity was sustained for two important reasons. First, an industry based on high fabricating skill and low raw material quantities stood a good chance of survival in the light of New England's geographically peripheral position, removed as it is from most raw materials. Such labor-intensive concerns could simply absorb much of the labor pool being released by the existing textile and leather companies. In the case of electronics, the substantial female work force of these old industries was felt to be occupationally well suited to tasks of intricate component assembly. Second, the pace of scientific research has built into electrical engineering a high degree of technological obsolescence, thus ensuring that the national market would constantly absorb sustained production of ever-new items. Indeed, the pace of new invention has not only placed a premium on research and development, but has led to a remarkable geographical concentration of this industry dependent on quick access to the latest information. Hence, Boston's ring road (Route 128) developed in the late 1950s and 1960s as an outstanding symbol of this industrial liaison.

For all the changes in manufacturing that Boston has experienced in the last quarter century, the changes in other sectors of its employment structure have been more notable. Relatively speaking, Boston has become more important as a government center and focal point for a wide range of regional services. Among all metropolitan areas in the United States, Boston ranks third in the proportion of its work force engaged in government and service occupations, superseded only by Washington, D.C., and San Francisco (Figure 9). New York is very similar to Boston in its mix of employment activities, retaining a slightly greater proportional emphasis on transport and commerce. Other large metropolitan areas such as Los Angeles and Chicago are characterized by considerably more manufacturing. It appears, therefore, as if Boston, along with some other coastal metropolises, is well on the way toward a new metropolitan specialty—a high degree of specialization in tertiary and quaternary activities based on non-material services and wide-ranging regional decisionmaking activities.

The growth of service employment in modern life has acted to reinforce and further expand the importance of large cities in the national economy. Boston has participated fully in this trend, and since its service function is well above the national average for major metropolitan areas, it serves a "market" much larger than its historical hinterland in New England. All this has created a postwar urban expansion that reaches deep into the eastern Massachusetts countryside. The modern city today is not merely the urban tract—that zone of continuously built-up territory—but rather a region linking a high density core with hundreds of satellite communities through a massive network of crisscross commuting channels.

Repletion and renewal of the urban fabric are constant processes. The dramatic additions of recent times are capped by the new forest of skyscrapers in downtown Boston and the Back Bay. Each phase of city growth produces buildings and city districts worth preserving, both for their intrinsic value and for their unique adaptation to the city's physical site features. The location of major change in Boston frequently coincides with areas of greatest historical individuality. "Manhattanization" is attacking Boston's downtown, which harbors some of the oldest structures in the city (Figure 10). Central Boston's vitality is to be found not in its lethargic docks or fleeing industries, but rather in the rash of new office buildings, epitomizing as they do both the new strength of "service" industries based on paper pushing and also the reasserted strength of banks and insurance companies. The days of prominent railroad stations, retail stores, and massive warehouses in the central city are over.

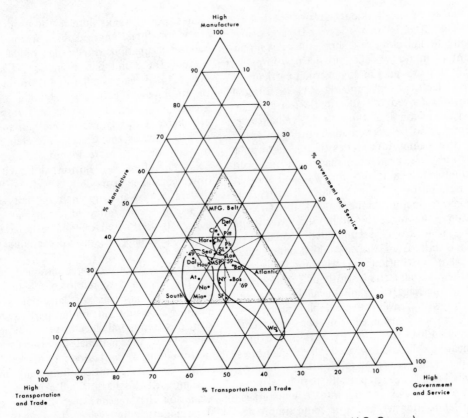

Figure 9.　Metropolitan economic base, 1969. (After the U.S. Census)

Figure 10. Offsetting history: the old state house and new neighbors. Once the centerpiece of State Street, and still the core of the financial district, the historic relic acts in part as a subway entrance.

Part II

A Boston Panorama

THE PEOPLE

How Large the Multitude?

The Boston metropolitan area can be defined in many ways. Over time towns have grown into cities, cities into metropolises—and what will metropolises become? Jean Gottman sees already the urban areas of the eastern seaboard as comprising one huge "Megalopolis" where the fringe of one metropolitan area merges imperceptibly into the next, stretching all the way from Boston to Washington, D.C. For some time, the U.S. Census Bureau has defined Standard Metropolitan Statistical Areas (SMSAs) to include not only central cities but outlying suburbs that belong functionally to the same urban agglomeration. The scale of frequent regional interaction is increasing so much, however, as to warrant defining even larger areas—to be known as Daily Urban Systems (DUS)—in which significant proportions of the local population commute to the established central cities.

The DUS for which Boston is the center includes all New England towns that send daily at least 5 percent of their resident labor force to work in the Boston area (Figure 11). The Boston SMSA is a more accurate representation of Boston's primary area of dominance and coincides fairly well with common recognition of the extent of "Greater Boston." While the SMSA population totals 2,753,700, the city of Boston with a population of 641,071

ranks as one of the smallest central cities in the twenty largest DUSs in the country. The consequences for metropolitan organization are far-reaching and will be discussed frequently in later chapters.

Greater Boston has exhibited some of the slowest decennial growth rates among the nation's largest metropolitan areas. During the period 1960-1970 only 158,000 people were added to its total, representing a modest 6.1 percent increase compared to 16.6 percent for national SMSA growth. Boston has become therefore one of the more important sources of migrants to other parts of the United States, in spite of the fact that the metropolis also serves as a magnet for modest numbers of in-migrants itself.

Most of these migrants come from nearby, primarily from Massachusetts but also from southern New Hampshire (Figure 12). The highly urbanized sections of southwest Connecticut and Rhode Island provide the next largest groups of people moving to Greater Boston. Not all subregions in New England give the same number of migrants to Boston as they receive from it: an index of "net" gains and losses shows considerable variations. In 1960, Boston made net gains from nearly all upland areas in Maine, New Hampshire, Vermont, and western Massachusetts, but gave more migrants than it received to lowland and coastal areas near it and in Connecticut. By 1970, however, the patterns had changed considerably. Re-

Figure 11. The new metropolitanism: DUS, SMSA, and central city, 1970. (After the U.S. Census)

cently, Boston has become increasingly a net "exporter" of migrants to the hill country of the north, while developing new magnetism for migrants from western Massachusetts and Connecticut. Recreational employment in northern New England and the growth of "second homes" (which often become first homes) appear to account for part of this trend, while the increased balance of migration with Connecticut suggests the increasing complexity of internal migration within broad urban regions situated between the northern pivots of Megalopolis, New York and Boston.

Population redistribution within the metropolitan region continues along established lines. Central cities and suburbs lose population absolutely, inner suburbs grow slowly, and outer suburbs and "ex-urbs" post generally large percentage growth rates (Figure 13). Like many other of the nation's older metropolitan areas, Boston's central city population is declining. Boston City, due in part to its small size and in part to the early establish-

ment of competitive settlements nearby, was forced to share the incoming immigrant population.

From the all-time high of 801,444 (1950), the number of residents has now declined to less than 640,000. The causes of this decline in central city population are not unique to Boston. Deterioration, condemnation, and demolition of ancient, substandard housing made a contribution. Moreover, it was a reflection on the postwar housing shortage of Boston that this figure was not higher. Of the 232,000 year round housing units recorded in Boston in 1970, over 200,000 had been built before 1939, and a large percentage of them before 1900. Freeway construction contributed fur-

Figure 12. Boston's migrant "balance of trade" with New England, 1960–1970. Migration data are available only for State Economic Areas, but the Boston SEA is sufficiently similar to the Boston SMSA to make general statements on migration to and from Boston.

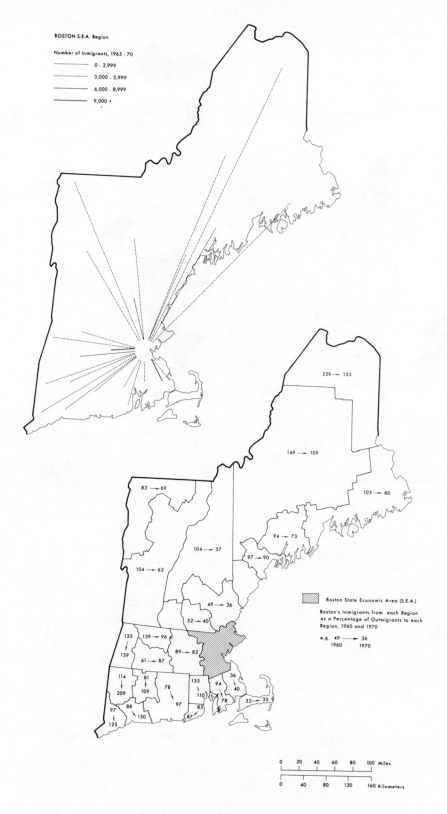

BOSTON S.E.A. Region

Number of Inmigrants, 1965 - 70

- - - - - - - 0 - 2,999
·············· 3,000 - 5,999
——————— 6,000 - 8,999
——————— 9,000 +

Boston State Economic Area (S.E.A.)

Boston's Inmigrants from each Region
as a Percentage of Outmigrants to each
Region, 1960 and 1970

e.g. 49 ——→ 36
      1960   1970

229 → 155

149 → 109

105 → 60

83 → 69

94 → 73

104 → 57

97 → 90

104 → 62

49 → 36

52 → 40

125   139 → 96

139

89 → 82

61 → 87

36

40

114   81   78   135   94

209 109   110   78   52 → 35

97   88   130   97   85

125   87

0   20   40   60   80   100 Miles

0   40   80   120   160 Kilometers

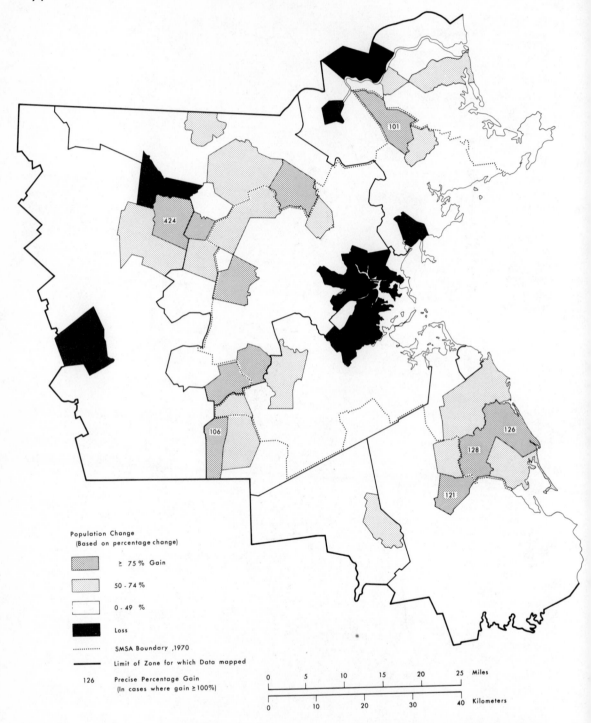

Figure 13. Population shifts in the Boston region, 1960–1970. (After the U.S. Census)

ther to Boston's population decline in the 1950s and 1960s (Figure 14). Losses to highways would have been even greater had two major projected arterials—the Inner Belt and the Southwest Expressway—been completed.

Boston was not the only municipality in the metropolitan area to lose population during the 1960s. Nine other cities and towns experienced population losses in that same period (Figure 13). All but one of these are older inner cities or suburbs and lie within a six mile radius of downtown Boston. The exception is Lynn, a run-down factory town on the North Shore, which had undertaken an ambitious urban renewal program in the 1960s. Six of the other eight communities have much in common with Lynn and Boston—old age, deteriorating housing, urban renewal. Belmont and Newton, however, are metropolitan suburbs of the early and middle 1900s and could hardly be described as deteriorating. Highway construction affected both cities during the 1960s, but the principal factor in each city's population loss was a change in the age structure and family composition of the community. In both cases, aging populations continued to reside in the community, while their children were growing up and moving away. With little land left for further residential expansion, the total population decreased slightly in both municipalities.

The outlying districts of the SMSA show strong growth. The smaller gains tend to be in towns situated astride established major routeways where growth has already pretty well filled up the available space—e.g., Routes 1, 9, 28, and 128. Major growth, then, represents infilling of rural areas midway between major towns. This is being helped by the increasing use made of Interstate 495 by industry and distant commuters. It is clear that if present trends continue, the boundary of the Boston SMSA will become increasingly unrepresentative of the ex-urban population aureole of the metropolis. Extending the boundary to include rapidly growing towns, however, will necessarily require including the Worcester and Brockton areas within the Boston region. Population changes around Boston fit recognized national patterns, but the census convention of defining New England SMSAs on the basis of town rather than county units has resulted in tight clusters of separate metropolitan districts in eastern Massachusetts (Boston, Worcester,

Brockton, Lowell, Lawrence-Haverhill), and they are very close to coalescence.

Ethnic Diversity

And this is good old Boston,
The home of the bean and the cod,
Where the Lowells talk to the Cabots,
And the Cabots talk only with God.

And this is good old Boston,
The home of the bean and the cod,
Where the Caseys talk to the Curleys,
And the Curleys talk with whomever they please.

The nation at large and the cities in particular have long been regarded as a giant melting pot for millions of people with highly diverse ethnic origins. More recently, ethnicity has come to be seen as an enduring cultural trait, much modified by the American experience but no less important than before in defining sociopolitical divisions in society. There is no doubt that Boston has its share, perhaps more than its share, of "unmeltable ethnics." How ethnic is Boston's population, and what consequences does this hold for the structure of metropolitan society and adjustment to the physical arrangements of the metropolis?

Seventeenth century Boston was very much an immigrant city. For many years after 1630, almost every inhabitant of Boston was an Englishman, either as immigrant or descendant. Immigration from England slowed down during the latter half of that century and remained at a low level until well into the nineteenth century. Boston considered anyone of English extraction a "native" and the few residents from France or Jamaica or Germany were the "foreigners." These early Englishmen became the Yankees of today, and an extremely small, select group of them (with a very few foreigners) became the illustrious Boston Brahmins. Few "Proper Bostonians" did not bear good, solid English surnames.

All this changed abruptly in the 1840s with the sudden arrival of thousands of emigrating men, women, and children from Ireland. Boston was the nearest port to the Irish points of embarkation and became, in the matter of a few years, one of the greatest concentrations of Irish outside Dublin. The Irish did not move on in large numbers from Boston to the new

Table 1. Major Foreign and Minority Components of Boston City, 1850–1970

	1850 Number Percent	1880 Number Percent	1910 Number Percent	1940 Number Percent	1970 Number Percent
Total Population	136,881	362,839	670,585	770,816	641,071
Total Foreign-born	46,677	114,796	240,722	180,864	83,988
	34.1	31.6	35.9	23.5	13.1
Blacks	1,999	5,873	13,564	23,679	104,707
	1.5	1.6	2.0	3.1	16.3
Ireland	35,287	64,793	66,038	37,507	12,362
	25.8	17.9	9.8	4.9	1.9
Italy	134	1,277	31,380	31,555	14,990
	0.1	0.4	4.7	4.1	.2.3
Canada	–	23,156	50,658	35,293	10,772
		6.4	7.8	4.6	1.7
Russia	–	345	41,891	28,014	6,012
		0.1	6.3	3.6	0.9
Britain	4,110	11,936	18,978	11,487	3,874
	3.0	3.3	2.8	1.5	0.6
Greece	–	24	1,497	3,141	3,514
			0.2	0.4	0.5
Poland	–	437	n.a.	6,648	3,319
		0.1		0.9	0.5
China and Asia	–	133	1,192	1,068	6,745
			0.2	0.1	1.1
Germany	1,816	7,396	8,700	3,851	1,944
	1.3	2.0	1.3	0.5	0.3
Portugal	–	597	1,225	855	797
		0.2	0.2	0.1	0.1
Sweden	–	1,450	7,122	3,799	564
		0.4	1.1	0.5	0.1

Source: U.S. Census of Population, 1850, 1880, 1910, 1940, 1970.

lands beyond the Appalachians, or even to any great extent into rural New England. Many Irish families did pass through Boston en route to other New England factory towns where the demand for workers had just begun in earnest and to the great canal and railroad projects of the West. Nevertheless, by 1850 there were over 35,000 Irish in Boston and 50,000 by 1855. Other nationalities were represented by very small numbers (Table 1).

The Irish suffered through several generations of poverty and discrimination before making any substantial economic and social progress. Their mass arrival in the city solidified native sentiment against them. The Yan-

Figure 14. Consequences of freeway mania. Cleared land in Roxbury for the vetoed Southwest Expressway. (Courtesy Aerial Photos of New England)

kee community, itself becoming rigidly structured in the strait jacket of commercial wealth from a former era, denied the Irish access to economic power in the city. In frustration, the Irish used their numerical strength to seize political power and, as William Shannon has described, created a buffer to the uncertainties of restricted economic opportunities by greatly expanding the city bureaucracy. From that time to the present, their stamp has been upon the Boston scene—politicians, teachers, priests, policemen, firemen, motormen, and rubbish collectors—nearly all Irish.

By the later nineteenth century, Canadians, Russians (mostly Jews), and Italians had followed the Irish into Boston and formed individually important segments of the total population. More Italians than Irish, however, have continued to migrate to Boston in recent times with the result that the Italians vie with the Irish for first place among the last three generations (Table 1). The Jews came in some numbers from Germany and Poland, but the largest number came from Russia.

As the immigration laws tightened and the quota system changed, and as original immigrants died, the number of foreign-born in Boston dropped. The decrease, however, is much less than might have been anticipated (Table 1). Italians had now taken over first place, closely followed by the Irish and the Canadians, while many Russian (Jewish) families had now left Boston proper for adjacent suburbs. Indeed, the Canadians, Russians, British, and Italians have suburbanized heavily (Table 2), more so proportionately than have the Irish.

In *The Other Bostonians,* a recent study of social mobility in Boston over the last century, Stephan Thernstrom found that the Irish have moved very slowly up the occupational ladder compared with other ethnic groups. In 1890 a full 90 percent of the Irish were still in blue collar jobs, of whom two-thirds were manual laborers. By 1950, first generation Irish were still 82 percent blue collar, while among the second generation the proportion was down to 58 percent. In contrast, however, the Italians who arrived in the city en masse half a century later had equaled the Irish with 82 percent blue collar among their first genera-

tion (69 percent for the second generation). More significant are the Jews, who by 1950 contained only 46 percent blue collar among the first generation, while second generation Jews were merely 25 percent blue collar—three-quarters of them had gained white collar jobs. These figures show that differences exist in the rates of socioeconomic progress among ethnic groups in Boston, although the explanations are complex and not fully understood. They provide a perspective, however, from which to appreciate a common saying about the Irish in Boston, that they are the only oppressed majority in the world. American-born children of Irish fathers have done distinctly better for themselves than their fathers, but a much larger proportion are still blue collar than are Yankees, Britons, and other Western Europeans. Among the later groups, Italians seem to follow somewhat the Irish pattern, and the Jews the British pattern.

One minority that has long felt oppressed is Boston's black community. For a city so prominent in the antislavery movement of the last century, Boston attracted relatively few blacks for many decades, largely because other East Coast cities represented intervening opportunities. Between the Civil War and the First World War, Boston's blacks increased from 2,500 to 13,500, actually not much smaller proportionately to total population than in

Table 2.   Foreign Stock Population of Boston City, 1910 and 1970, and of the Rest of the SMSA, 1970*

	1910 Boston City		1970 Boston City		1970 Rest of SMSA	
	Number	Percent of Total Population	Number	Percent of Total Population	Number	Percent of Total Population
Ireland	154,137	23.0	51,716	8.1	95,608	3.5
Italy	48,691	7.3	44,975	7.0	147,374	5.4
Canada	69,832	10.4	36,333	5.7	179,076	6.5
Russia	63,219	9.4	16,788	2.6	60,178	2.2
Britain	26,488	3.9	12,877	2.0	59,833	2.2
Greece	n.a.		6,165	1.0	16,972	0.6
Poland	n.a.		9,007	1.4	26,809	1.0
China	n.a.		5,598	0.9	4,021	0.2
Germany	19,180	2.9	5,726	0.9	19,435	0.7
Portugal	n.a.		2,517	0.4	11,980	0.4
Sweden	10,676	1.6	2,266	0.4	14,735	0.5

*These data cover first, second, and third generation ethnic group members only (foreign-born and foreign stock census categories). If native-born people with foreign-born grandparents or great-grandparents were included, the figures would naturally be higher. n.a.: not available

Source: U.S. Census of Population, 1910 and 1970.

New York, Chicago, Detroit, and Cleveland. Substantial increases in numbers have come since the Second World War (Table 1).

The present population of blacks in Boston City alone numbers over 104,000 (discounting whatever underenumeration undoubtedly occurred during the 1970 census). One area where progress has been made is employment. From 1890, when only 8 percent of blacks held white collar jobs, to 1940 when they held 11 percent (and 65 percent were laborers and service workers), the blacks made little economic progress. Since World War II, laborers have declined to 27 percent and white collar workers have risen to 30 percent. Except for under-representation in the professions, the changes reflect real gains, independent of the secular shift in Boston's occupational structure. However, the median income of employed black males hardly advances in relation to white income (28 percent below whites in 1950, 23 percent in 1970) because blacks were winning most jobs in occupations that had the greatest racial income gaps.

Blacks in the city of Boston are far from a majority. However, there has been a strong awakening of the black community, which may have been alive earlier, but no one else was bothering to apply the stethoscope. Blacks have entered the political scene with vigor and determination, and blacks have assumed new roles in the arts, business, and some professions. However, with the notable exception of Edward Brooke, blacks have not yet acquired much representation in government. There is no black city councilman, and only a major political row over redistricting finally produced a state senatorial district that is numerically capable of electing a black candidate.

Boston was not a major destination for the large number of Puerto Rican men and women who left that island after World War II in search of opportunity on the mainland. After 1960, however, the pace of arrival of Puerto Ricans in Boston accelerated until, by 1970, there were 11,267 persons of Puerto Rican background in the Boston SMSA. This total made up only 0.25 percent of the total Boston metropolitan population.

The fastest growing population group in Boston is the Chinese. Long a fixture in the Boston landscape, the Chinese have dramatically increased in numbers after radical changes were made in the national immigration regula-tions. From about 2,000 residents in 1950, the Chinese population in Boston alone increased to 7,900 in 1970. Another 5,000 Chinese live within the Boston SMSA, and about 300 new arrivals are currently entering the Boston Chinese community annually.

The ethnic diversity of Boston's population might not be so crucial to an understanding of the metropolis were it not for the contrasts in long term opportunity and economic progress of different groups. Divergent trends have pitted one group against another during most of Boston's history, and cleavages and tensions have produced quite remarkable patterns of residential accommodation and opposition. "Neighborhoods" have come to mean very special entities in the life of Boston, and ethnicity is a strong underlying element in their definition—a theme to be explored later. More immediately, however, this population constitutes the human metropolis, brought together by the presence of jobs. Employment not only provides people with a living, but its character shapes the city's role in the region and the nation.

THE CITY EARNS ITS LIVING

The Job Structure

The total work force of metropolitan Boston between 1951 and 1971 rose from 987,600 to 1,281,200. The trend of growth has been generally steady with moderate growth up to 1964, a slightly heightened growth rate from 1964 to 1969, and a leveling off since then. Manufacturing, long the dominant employer, has declined slowly over the period 1951 to 1971, so that by 1969 it was overtaken by steadily increasing wholesale and retail trade employment and the burgeoning "service" sector, particularly professions and government (Figure 15). Service activities have now become the single largest category of employment. All sectors but manufacturing, transportation, and public utilities emerge as having grown faster between 1951 and 1971 than the general rate. Of these, service shows the most spectacular improvement.

Boston Area Manufacturing

Historically, the entire United States has shifted emphasis from "soft" to "hard" goods manufacture, along with a concurrent trend from processing to fabricating. For a long time

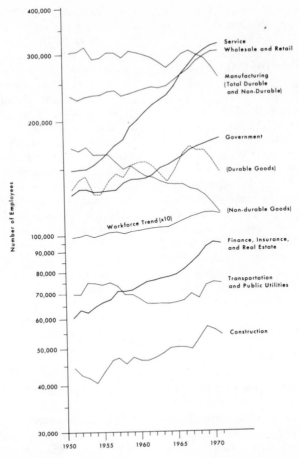

Figure 15. Employment trends, Boston SMSA, 1958–1971. (After the U.S. Census)

the Boston area relied heavily on nondurable production such as textiles and leather and was late in changing toward greater balance between the manufacturing types. This shift has now been made—some might say with a vengeance. The change is significant for several reasons. "Soft" goods manufacture is traditionally less affected by business cycles because it produces most of the daily necessities of life whose purchase cannot be postponed. Therefore, a shift away from such industries means greater vulnerability to short term economic swings. On the other hand, "hard" goods manufacture has generally commanded higher average wages for the work force, and this benefits regional consumer spending, which itself generates more demand. Thus a balance between the two types is held to be desirable. Between 1947 and 1967 employment in "soft" goods in the Boston area dropped from 65.5 to 43.4 percent of the

workforce, while "hard" goods increased from 34.5 to 56.6 percent. The gains among durable industries, however, were not uniform (Table 3).

Between 1963 and the last published Census of Manufactures in 1967, employment increased by over one-fifth in the fields of instruments, transport equipment, and nonelectric machinery.

Among the nondurable goods, there were widespread declines in manpower. With the exception of food and printing, the nondurables represent a rather static component of Boston's industrial scene. Without question, manufacturing in general is not only losing ground proportionately to other types of employment but is steadily shrinking.

Greater Boston has shared a common metropolitan experience of suburban industrialization. Fleeing industries have been one of the

Table 3.   Employment by Major Industry Groups, Boston SMSA, 1963 and 1967, and Percentage Change

	Employment (in thousands)		Percent Change in Employment 1963–1967	Percent of Total Employment 1967
	1963	1967		
Durable Goods Industries	137.9	163.5	+18.6	56.6
Electrical Machinery	47.5	53.4	+12.4	18.4
Nonelectrical Machinery	26.8	32.8	+22.4	11.4
Transport Equipment	16.4	23.5	+43.3	8.1
Instruments	17.1	22.3	+30.4	7.7
Fabricated Metals	17.6	19.6	+11.4	6.8
Primary Metals	4.0	3.7	−7.5	1.3
Furniture	3.5	3.2	−8.6	1.1
Stone, Clay, Glass	3.0	3.1	+3.3	1.1
Lumber	2.0	1.9	−5.0	0.7
Nondurable Goods Industries	128.2	125.4	−2.2	43.4
Printing	23.5	25.2	+7.2	8.7
Food	24.8	22.8	−8.1	7.9
Apparel	21.1	20.4	−3.3	7.1
Rubber and Plastics	17.1	16.8	−1.8	5.8
Leather	18.3	16.7	−8.7	5.8
Paper	10.4	10.1	−2.9	3.5
Chemicals	7.4	7.7	+4.1	2.7
Textiles	4.7	5.1	+8.5	1.8
Petroleum	0.9	0.6	−33.3	0.2
Total	266.1	288.9	+8.57	100.0

Source: U.S. Census of Manufactures, 1963, 1967.

city of Boston's greatest headaches. Although the trend has existed since the late nineteenth century, the problem has been especially acute in the last two decades, since over 45 percent of the city's real estate is tax-exempt. Therefore, the loss of a single factory reduces the tax base still further. An idea of the special character of manufacturing in the central city can be gained from its employment figures (Table 4). While the central city accounts for 25 percent of the metropolitan work force in manufacturing at large, it contains nearly three-quarters of the apparel industry, three-fifths of the printing and publishing activity, and half of the SMSA's food and furniture employment. Of these, it will be remembered, only printing showed healthy overall employment trends. Furthermore, the city's balance between manufacturing sectors shows an employment ratio of 2 to 1 in favor of nondurables compared with the metropolitan region's 5 to 4 in favor of durables production. Altogether, this is not a particularly encouraging situation for the central city, and the well-established historical trend will be hard to counteract. The very industries that could most help stabilize the central city's industrial employment are those forsaking the city for new suburban locations.

Commercial Ties

A city earns its living in many more ways than manufacturing goods for export or local consumption. Economists make a distinction between "city-building" and "city-serving" activity in the urban economy. What the city exports earns the city income, whereas what is produced but not exported—i.e., what is consumed locally—merely sustains the population needed to produce the goods for export. In practice, it is very difficult to calculate exactly what proportion of an industry's output is exported and what retained, but some idea can be gained from the statistics of commerce. Employment in transport services in the Boston SMSA has barely grown since 1951, but wholesale and retail trade employment has increased substantially (Figure 15). That fact indicates that a considerable increase in trade between Boston and the rest of the country has taken place over the period. Since Boston does not produce all its consumer needs, it is intricately tied in with the whole national urban system.

Table 4. Employment by Major Industry Groups, Boston City, 1967

	Employment (in thousands)	Percent of Total Employment in Boston City	Boston City Employment as Percent of SMSA Employment in Category
Durable Goods Industries	22.9	31.6	14.0
Electrical Machinery	6.3	8.7	11.8
Nonelectrical Machinery	5.9	8.1	18.8
Fabricated Metals	5.9	8.1	30.0*
Furniture	1.6	2.2	50.0*
Instruments	1.1	1.5	4.9
Primary Metals	1.1	1.5	29.7*
Transport Equipment	1.0	1.4	4.3
Nondurable Goods Industries	49.5	68.4	39.5
Printing	15.5	21.4	61.5*
Apparel	15.0	20.7	73.5*
Food	11.1	15.3	48.7*
Leather	3.9	5.4	23.4
Paper	1.3	1.8	12.9
Textiles	11.1	1.5	21.6
Rubber and Plastics	0.9	1.2	5.4
Chemicals	0.7	1.0	9.1
Total	72.4	100.0	25.1

*Italicized numbers indicate percentage is above the mean.

Source: U.S. Census of Manufactures, 1967.

Location at the edge of the continent, however, and at the northern extremity of the Atlantic coast, makes Boston's access to the nation worse than all other large metropolises. The average length of haul for goods exported from Boston is 377 miles, compared with 275 miles for Chicago or 302 miles for St. Louis. New York has a higher figure, 408 miles, but only because it supports a far larger distribution function than any urban center on the scale of Boston. Despite this disadvantage, Boston has been expanding its penetration, with 31.5 percent of its shipments by weight traveling more than 500 miles in 1967, compared with 21.9 percent in 1963. According to the last Census of Transportation, about one-fifth of the commercial shipments originating in the Greater Boston region are local—that is, they end within the metropolitan area. One-third move to other major manufacturing regions in the country, and the remainder to nonmetropolitan destinations. Most commodities are now moved by trucks traveling over increasingly longer distances.

The location of specific industries in Boston results in a concentration of deliveries of special products. Chicago is the single largest receiver of electrical machinery produced around Boston (28 percent), and Newark receives 11 percent of Boston's instrument production. Among specialized items many of the area's solid-state semiconductors flow to Dallas, confectioner's candy flows to Los Angeles, cutlery to Houston, rubber footwear to Chicago, and nuts and bolts to Newark. New York receives a quarter of all clothing manufactured around Boston. The remainder of the commodity flows are numerous and small, and diffuse remarkably widely throughout the nation.

One element of Boston's commerce that has declined both relatively and absolutely is its port activity. Historically one of the nation's most important ports, Boston now ranks eleventh in ship arrivals and eighth in customs collections. The harbor has 158 wharves, docks, and piers—enough to handle several times the present traffic—but times have changed. By the late 1950s the port's eccentric location for interior shipments, the high cost of labor, and problems of labor relations combined to edge the port out of major competition. As a result, 93 percent of Boston's port trade was generated within eastern New England—too high a proportion for so small a hinterland—where Boston has a freight rate advantage. Compounding the problem, the port's small export tonnage (7.9 million tons in 1971) has kept away many steamship companies operating containerized vessels which would patronize the port if business were on a larger scale.

The port of Boston handled 7,323,438 tons of imports in 1971, contrasted to 638,254 tons of exports. Three-quarters of the imported tonnage consisted of petroleum products, much of this from Venezuela. Other imports—all raw materials such as sugar cane, gypsum, and salt—were individually small. Among the few exports, iron and steel scrap accounted for 80 percent by weight. While passenger traffic has improved somewhat in recent years owing to the rising popularity of short cruises, the freight traffic through Boston is unlikely to grow dramatically. New York's traffic by value is ten times greater than Boston's, and no improvement in container facilities will be sufficient to wrest the advantage from ports closer to the national market. However, the region's geographic isolation has long extracted a price in higher than average transport charges for materials such as domestic petroleum, and therefore any improvement in port facilities will be sorely needed to stabilize regional differentials in the delivered price of many unprocessed and semiprocessed materials.

Hard by the maritime port is Logan International Airport, the most convenient airport in the whole country for downtown access. Built on landfill out into the bay, the facility symbolizes the paradoxical problem of in-town convenience and massive disturbance to close-in, dense residential districts. Airport expansion has recently been blocked by citizen action that promises to pit neighborhood values against needed capacity for the city to capitalize on its growing popularity as an international departure point for Europe, now that New York's airport congestion is a serious problem for travelers.

Finance, Business, and Services

Ever since the Cabots, Forbes, Gores, Jacksons, and Lowells made their great fortunes from colonial commerce on India Wharf, Boston has been associated with finance. In the nineteenth century, Boston capital underwrote substantial railroad construction, not only in New England but throughout the West. John Murray Forbes put a fortune gained in foreign commerce into the Michigan Central and the companies making up the Chicago, Burlington, and Quincy Railroad. The tradition has survived, and today the metropolitan power of financial institutions is most strikingly advertised in the city's new skyline, in which ten out of seventeen new high-rise buildings have been built by banks and insurance companies.

Throughout the present century, however, there has been a steady decline in Boston's rank as a national money center. In 1900, with nearly 10 percent of the banks around the country maintaining city correspondents there, Boston stood fourth behind New York, Chicago, and St. Louis; by 1965 the percentage had dropped to 4.5, and the city had fallen to tenth rank. Nonetheless, Boston's banking dominance over most of New England except Connecticut has been stable historically, and relative loss of position nationally has only intensified the regional bonds. For example, most of the industrial development along Route 128 was financed by downtown banks in Boston.

The metropolis is not only a significant money center, it is also a major retail concentration. The range of goods for sale in the metropolis varies little in overall complexion. One always needs food, gasoline, hardware, pharmaceutical items, and the like. But changes in the structure of business do occur. In the 1960s there were several trends of great significance for shippers' daily habits. One was the growth of discount stores which accounted for a nearly 37 percent increase in general merchandise group stores between 1963 and 1967. Another was the rise of the planned suburban shopping center, with its acres of parking and one stop shopping appeal that over the years has done so much to threaten the vitality of downtown retail districts.

These changes symbolize a trend toward bigness. While overall retail sales have climbed, most types of stores have declined in number—throughout the SMSA, not simply in the central city. Hardest hit have been hardware and food stores. Not only did they decline an average of 15 percent in numbers, but their sales volumes increased only about 10 percent, far below the 21.8 percent sales rise for all stores. Only furniture stores continued to grow in numbers, suggesting rising family income. With a mere eighteen establishments more than the 1,194 total in 1963, sales volume was up 48.8 percent in 1967 over the earlier year. In general, modest increases in total sales (taking inflation into account) were registered by a slowly decreasing number of stores, meaning that their individual size and turnover has been increasing steadily. The trend toward bigness continues.

Population in Greater Boston is suburbanizing rapidly, as in other large urban agglomerations. This pattern of growing density in the metropolitan fringe and decline in the core runs parallel with steady changes in metropolitan employment. Service jobs multiply as manufacturing jobs diminish. The central city's manufacturing workers are more vulnerable to industry decline and relocation, but their generally somewhat lower wages deprive many of them of the flexibility to move with the trends as easily as workers already in the suburbs. Boston City contains 25.5 percent of the SMSA's manufacturing workers but only 17.6 percent of the manufacturing jobs. At the same time, while it provides 27.6 percent of the jobs in government and public administration in the SMSA, only 17.2 percent of the workers in such jobs live in the central city. With the trend toward more and more service activities in the metropolis, a geographical balance between core and periphery with equal opportunities in employment will become harder and harder to maintain.

The growth of a metropolitan population brought together by jobs requires the simultaneous development of a "built environment" in which to live. Once the dimensions of this physical habitat are explored, the humanizing elements of social regulation and provision can be assessed in greater perspective.

THE BOSTONIAN AT HOME

The Settlement Pattern: City and Suburb

The geographical center of Boston is in Roxbury—at the corner of Westminster and Walnut Avenues, if one cares to be precise. Due north of the center we find the South End. This is not to be confused with South Boston, which lies directly east from the South End. North of South Boston is East Boston and southwest of that is the North End.

—George Weston

Anyone familiar with Boston knows that the geography of Boston's neighborhoods is highly complex. The nomenclature of districts arises from long historical usage. People who live and work in the city do not just live in any residential tract, they live in neighborhoods whose identity is very important to them. The city is, of course, more than a simple mass of residential areas, for it contains zones of commercial, industrial, and institutional land uses, not to mention recreational areas such as parks and beaches (Table 5). These other land uses tend to define the bounds of residential zones either by forming dividing lines between them (such as industrial sectors, railroads) or by uniting them, as commercial areas often do. Human nature being what it is, however, rich and poor, black and white, WASP and Jew do not always live side by side in equal proportions throughout the metropolis. Most large urban areas exhibit distinctive patterns of socioeconomic "terrain" with poorer districts predominant in old, core areas and wealthier districts more prevalent in the outer suburbs.

Boston's settlement pattern is not nearly so simple, and the special relationship between core city and present-day suburb in the Boston region is the singular product of history. This pattern can be likened to an extended city structure in the sense that this term is applied to Nassau County on Long Island or to the Los Angeles Basin. In Boston's case, however, this extended city is not a twentieth century phenomenon associated with the automobile, but a centuries-old framework forged by the unique system of New England towns and the early growth of local manufacturing.

Metropolitan Boston covers less than 1,000 square miles, but it consists of 78 separate cities and towns. There is often little to distinguish a city from a town (except its administrative charter), and population size is one of the *least* useful distinguishing characteristics. Woburn (population 37,406) is a city; Framingham (population 64,048) is a town. The important point, however, is that virtually all of these seventy-eight constituent cities and towns existed as corporate political entities one hundred years ago, and a large majority of them had strong nucleated populations 200 years before that which created focal points of settlement within the broad town areas.

Although Boston was the unquestioned capital of colonial Massachusetts and the primate city of its region in every respect, Boston

Table 5. Land Use Distribution as Percent of Developed Land within Subareas of Greater Boston, 1960

	Core Cities	Inner Suburbs	Outer Suburbs	Outer Cities*	Total Area
Residential Land	56.7	60.9	59.1	64.9	59.6
Commercial Land	6.5	3.3	2.3	3.6	3.4
Industrial	8.2	4.1	2.6	6.0	4.1
Public Utilities	4.0	4.4	3.9	5.4	4.2
Institutions	11.7	10.6	16.0	7.9	13.3
Recreation	12.8	16.7	16.0	12.2	15.5
Total Percent	100.0[+]	100.0	100.0	100.0	100.0

*Lowell, Lawrence-Haverhill, and Brockton SMSAs.

[+]Totals may not be exact due to rounding.

Source: GBESC, *Land Use in Greater Boston in 1960. Land Use Report No. 1* (May 1962).

as a town was granted by the colony only the small peninsula on which it lay plus a few harbor islands. The remainder of the Boston region as we know it today was granted to eleven other groups of settlers. These were in some cases exceedingly large grants, reaching from the vicinity of Boston clear to the New Hampshire or Rhode Island borders. One such grant was Dedham, where, a few miles southwest of Boston, a settlement was made in 1630, the same year that John Winthrop moved his small group of settlers from Charlestown to Boston. Dedham as a village grew and prospered, and over time its lands were divided and subdivided, eventually to form fourteen additional towns. The tiny fraction of the original grant that remained Dedham had a population of 27,000 in 1970. Dedham's story was repeated throughout the Boston region in the lands granted to Dorchester, Cambridge, Lynn, Hingham, etc.

Boston became a city in the decade of the 1820s, just before she reached 100,000 in population. While she had no competitors in terms of size in 1840, Boston was by no means alone in entering the era of manufacturing that was to dominate the century to come. A number of the small interior settlements found themselves fortuitously situated near a potential water power site or, later, on one of the major Boston railroad lines. By 1840, there were many more factories outside Boston city limits than within them. The small town of Waltham, for example, ten miles west of Boston on the Charles River, had developed not one, but three clusters of mills by 1840, although its population was a scant 2,504 in that year. Nevertheless, Waltham had all the municipal infrastructure needed to become a

city—a school system, a police department, a public water supply, a poorhouse. Waltham's population grew by 20,000 during the remainder of the nineteenth century as mills expanded and new industries arrived, and 20,000 more were added in the first four decades of the 1900s.

The Walthams of the Boston region, therefore, were suburbs only by virtue of location, not character. Few of Waltham's 40,000 residents in 1940 worked in Boston, and probably only a relatively small number in adjacent Newton or Watertown. By 1940, the central and southern parts of Waltham were fully occupied by a variety of tenements, carbarns, shops, a few single family homes, and even a few estates. Only the northern third of the city remained an area of farms and woodlands.

The population growth and settlement of post–World War II Waltham is a different story. The farms and woods are gone and in their place are tract housing, shopping centers, apartment complexes, and industrial parks— all the conventional ingredients of the contemporary American suburb. The fact that they are in Waltham is almost coincidental. The municipal infrastructure was, of course, a factor, but the vacant land and the proximity to Route 128 were what counted most. Thus, the 20,000 population increase in Waltham between 1940 and 1970 was more truly "suburban," although it was hardly part of a solidly advancing front of suburban expansion with Boston City as its center.

Metropolitan Boston's outer districts are therefore exceptional suburbs in national perspective. Far from being typical American suburbs, built by developers according to the dictates of speculation and land subdivision lacking in cultural amenities, their long term nature makes them distinctive, independent centers of economic life within the metropolitan area. Many such towns have come to experience social and economic problems certainly equal in nature if not in scale to those of the inner city. Others have preserved some degree of rural character, but above all Boston's suburbs contain a rich historical, social layering that finds expression in the case of Wellesley, as a study by George Lewis has shown, in the fifteen neighborhoods and 143 microsocial areas into which the town could be geographically divided as early as 1950.

Greater Boston gains a large measure of its human scale from this extended city structure. It has meant that there have been good restaurants in the suburbs for half a century, important shopping centers in the centers of outlying towns for decades, and a full range of suburban, if not urban, services for a very long time. Public libraries, good schools, and responsible and effective municipal administration date from the nineteenth century in many of these now suburban towns. The suburbs here were not created as refuges from central city problems, and their population growth was established long before there were enough blacks in the area to have the least bearing on the situation.

Population growth and expansion in metropolitan Boston, therefore, should be seen as a complex set of movements. Boston City accomplished its major suburban thrust in adjacent Roxbury, Dorchester, and Brookline, aided by the expanding surface transit system. Elsewhere in the region, small industrial centers experienced their own population growth and suburban development. In recent decades large scale population growth has been confined to the "outer suburbs," not only because they offered land for large scale tract housing but also because jobs, shops, and restaurants were not concentrated in downtown Boston but scattered throughout the region in a number of old, well-established cities and towns.

This special character of Boston's suburbs has been modified, however, by the postwar decentralization of urban residence. For better or worse, pockets of markedly high or low status that nestle in areas of divergent character do not detract from the broad undulations of the socioeconomic "terrain" of the metrop-

olis. Boston's pattern is neither neat nor regular. It conforms to some degree with generally accepted models of spatial structure, but has wrinkles all its own. Economic status, ethnic background, and stage in the family life cycle are widely regarded as the chief dimensions of social segregation within cities. In metropolitan Boston, as Frank Sweetser's studies of social ecology have shown, the last dimension exhibits the most regular geographical patterns. Family cycle varies in great concentric zones in which increasing distance from the center results generally in younger and larger families and proportionately more single family homes. Economic status, on the other hand, is more sectoral than zonal and merits some discussion. Ethnicity is perhaps Boston's most emphatic social characteristic and has, in conjunction with differences in economic opportunity over the decades, contributed most to the seeming rigidity of Boston's inner neighborhoods.

Defining economic status in terms of per capita income, the metropolis reveals a complex areal distribution (Figure 16). When the population is divided into five income categories, the rich and poor cluster very highly, with those in between filling up the rest of the metropolitan area. The overwhelming majority of the poor find themselves near the downtown core of the city of Boston. Of the sixty-two census tracts in the SMSA in the lowest income group, fifty-one tracts are in the central city alone, and of these forty-one form one continuous zone. The other dispersed low income tracts represent similar locations in other cities contained within the metropolitan area. The rich, on the other hand, while equally concentrated, have managed a much more diverse distribution pattern.

The "Cocktail Belt"

Boston's rich, now too numerous and heterogeneous to deserve the traditional sobriquet "Proper Bostonians," have pioneered a remarkable historical odyssey of residential relocation. In the seventeenth century town of John Winthrop, the wealthy lived on or close to State Street, the center of commerce and government near the harbor wharves. In the eighteenth century, as the settlement grew to cover the whole Shawmut Peninsula, the well-to-do scaled the heights, and Beacon Hill assumed a fashionable character that has lasted to the present day. Other cities have seen the rich appropriate

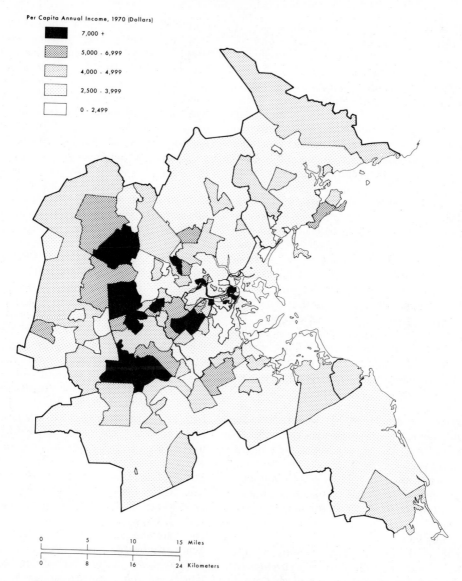

Per Capita Annual Income, 1970 (Dollars)

7,000 +

5,000 - 6,999

4,000 - 4,999

2,500 - 3,999

0 - 2,499

0   5   10   15 Miles

0   8   16   24 Kilometers

Figure 16. Where the rich and poor live, 1970. (After the U.S. Census)

high ground for their elevated living, but few have retained such in-town elite districts in the face of downtown encroachment, neighborhood decay, and immigrant takeover. While sentiment and symbolism, as Walter Firey has suggested, may have kept Beacon Hill the primary prestige district during the nineteenth century, the filling and construction of Back Bay was a conscious—and successful—attempt to extend the high class district westward. Less successful were similar attempts—such as in the South End, which turned solidly middle class, and along Bay State Road and Commonwealth

Avenue west of Kenmore Square, which became a mixed area of automobile dealerships and Boston University. By the turn of the century, the rich had begun to look further out from the central city to towns such as Brookline, Belmont, Newton, and Winchester, a trend that has continued further during the last seventy years, helped by the extension of the intracity transport network.

Today, Boston's "Cocktail Belt," to borrow a term from London's social ecology, is shaped largely in a giant "T," with a stem reaching westward from Brookline to Weston, and a north-south crossbar composed of a tier of towns just to the west of Route 128 (Concord, Lincoln, Weston, Wellesley, and Dedham). Outside this formation are several outliers, such as Milton due south of Boston and coastal Marblehead on the North Shore.

There is a current trend among some of the well-to-do to give the central city a second chance. Urban renewal has removed a number of sleazy neighborhoods from the old residential core around the central business district, as well as replaced industrial wasteland with new multifunctional complexes—e.g., the Prudential Center. Their place has been taken in part by high-rise luxury apartment towers with fine views over the harbor and the "exciting" landscape of the downtown—e.g., Harbor Towers. A high proportion of these residents have no immediate child-rearing worries and, with security guards insulating them and their possessions from the nocturnal danger of the streets, they have traded acreage for accessibility and solitude for city life. Thus, central Boston sports a mixture of affluent residents— those with sentimental attachments who never left, and those with suburban ennui who will give Boston a try. With the current private program of converting the old waterfront warehouses—solid graniteblock and brick buildings— along Atlantic Avenue into a new array of chic town apartments close to all the "action," Boston is making a bold effort to win back some of the social and economic elite—and augment, in the process, its dwindling tax base.

Ethnic Enclaves

The warehouse conversions along Atlantic Avenue form an arc that partially envelops the North End. This area is a classic neighborhood, geographically cohesive, cut off from the CBD first by the early food merchandising area of the Quincy Market and later by the Central Artery (the Fitzgerald Expressway). Historically, the North End stands as a symbol of one of Boston's strongest urban characteristics—the ethnic neighborhood. Ethnic segregation has been a social condition of Boston ever since the Irish arrived in large numbers in the 1840s, and the accommodation of each immigrant group has added to the complexity of Boston's housing market, social tensions, and political climate.

Foreign immigration into large cities in eastern North America has traditionally been conceived in the light of a "ghetto hypothesis." New immigrant groups, arriving poor and in large numbers, move largely into run-down housing at high densities and cheap rents surrounding the old city core. The wealthy and middle class native population, escaping the noise and confusion of a burgeoning downtown for the superior space of new suburbs opened by omnibuses and streetcars, gladly relinquish the aging residential structures on the periphery of the CBD to the newcomers. In Boston, these areas were immediately north and south of the small business district of midcentury, formerly occupied by a mixed native artisan and laboring population (Figure 17).

By 1875 the expansion of CBD land uses threatened these early immigrant quarters, as David Ward has shown, and the Irish moved into adjacent areas in the North End, South Cove, and the South End, remaining close to their major employment opportunities—the CBD and the docks. As the century wore on, both the CBD and the immigrant populations swelled, pushing deep into the remainder of the peninsula. By the 1900s, Italians, Russian Jews, and the growing black community had joined the Irish in competition for inner city space. Many Irish, some of them by now a few rungs further up the income and status ladder than the new ethnic arrivals, moved on to places like South Boston, Charlestown, Roxbury, and Dorchester. The North End switched slowly from being predominantly Irish to being largely Italian. Indeed, today it is extremely difficult to find any physical trace of the Irish occupation. Many of the tenements lived in by the Irish were replaced at the turn of the century by larger and more substantial tenement blocks which have had only Italian residents. Robert Woods' classic study of 1900 actually showed the area in a transition period, with many Jews present. The West End had also been ethnically and racially changing, with Jews and blacks now predominant. The latter had long inhabited the lower back slopes of Beacon Hill while working as domestic servants for elite families on the southern and western slopes of the hill.

Further spread of the CBD in this century and the incipient suburbanization of the better off among most groups resulted in Italian neighborhoods in East Boston and Somerville, and Jewish settlement northward to Chelsea and southward to Roxbury and Brookline (follow-

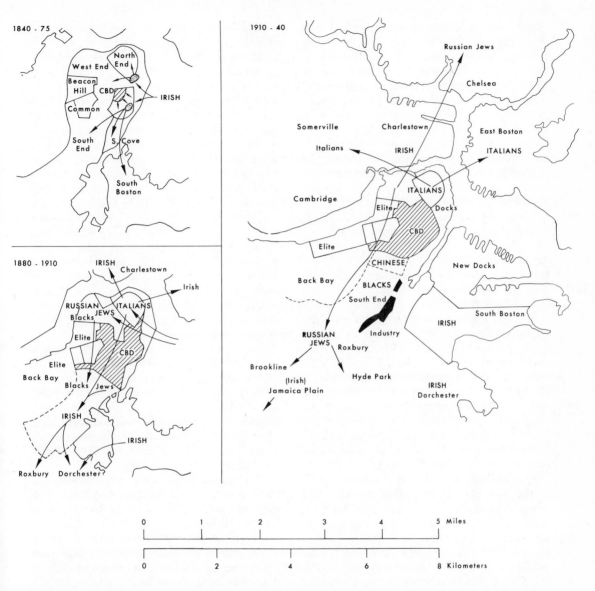

Figure 17. Boston's tribal domains, 1840–1940. (After Ward, Warner, Woods, and U.S. and State Censuses)

ing in part paths trodden by the Irish). Irish residence by then was stabilizing in South Boston, Dorchester, Jamaica Plain, and Hyde Park, while newer generations of Irish stock diffused more widely into other suburbs. The character of in-town Irish neighborhoods, however—with the exception of the South End and Roxbury which they early abandoned—was firmly set (Figure 17). While the population of Irish birth in these areas would decline proportionately through natural attrition and dilution by miscellaneous population, the ethnic stamp on these districts was determined. Jamaica Plain gave the city its most famous Irish mayor, James Michael Curley, and West Roxbury (far to the southwest of present Roxbury proper) the two mayors previous to Kevin White.

Rising land values (especially after World War I), artists, and students drove blacks out of the West End, where efforts to renovate Beacon Hill housing changed the clientele, and at the same time turned the South End near the fringe of the CBD into a deteriorating rooming house district particularly susceptible to black and new Chinese colonization. The Chinese lodged close to the CBD for its general service opportunities, garment firms, laundries, and restaurants. The blacks were undoubtedly drawn to the South End by its proximity to both the Pullman storage yards of the Boston and Albany Railroad (where the Prudential complex now stands) and the South Station yards, not to mention the industry immediately to the east (Figure 17).

From this nucleus grew two distinct ethnic neighborhoods. The first was Chinatown, which nestles compactly between what is today the financial district of the CBD and the blighted "Combat Zone." The area, fully built up since the 1860s, had been occupied successively by Irish, Jews, Italians, and Syrians, before the Chinese (most of them overland migrants from the West) moved in around 1900. Since 1952, when Rhoads Murphey wrote his well-known article on Boston's Chinatown, the area has been steadily eroded by a variety of competing land uses, so that it has suffered a 50 percent reduction in area. At the same time, its population has risen from about 1,600 to 1,900. Chinatown first lost territory to the Central Artery, and the loss would have been even greater but for massive public outcry. Urban renewal, associated in particular with a nearby hospital, made further inroads. And finally, the Massachusetts Turnpike took its toll for a right of way along Chinatown's southern margin. Emigration had taken Chinese to new areas for them like the Castle Square neighborhood (3,000), Allston-Brighton (1,000), and Parker Hill-Fenway (400), but the downtown district still retains a strong vitality.

The second district was the black "ghetto" that had its beginnings in the lower South End and northern Roxbury. The elevated railway that emerged from downtown to run out to Forest Hills traversed this neighborhood, and its associated ugliness and noise were undoubtedly further reasons for the decline of the area's desirability for the Irish and Jews who had most recently dominated the district. The rapid transit line, with several local stops, offered blacks easy access to other parts of the city, especially downtown. In any event, Roxbury soon became the heart of Boston's black community, and by 1930 whites knew this as an area of night clubs, jazz, and illicit whiskey, safe to enter for a night's entertainment.

In the last thirty years, black residential settlement has moved steadily southward from "lower Roxbury." Hemmed in on the northwest by the main line of the New Haven Railroad, a four track, partially depressed line with few cross bridges, and a parallel railroad to the southeast, black residence expanded southward from Dudley Square to Blue Hill Avenue. Franklin Park partially blocked movement to the southwest, causing a bottleneck for further growth between Blue Hill Avenue and the southerly railroad. In general, resistance on the part of established white residents has been strong in predominantly Irish areas and extremely weak in Jewish areas (Figure 18). The route of black residential growth could easily have been predicted by simply determining where heavily Jewish blocks lay adjacent to existing black areas. If one will regard as Jews those persons appearing in the 1970 census as of Russian foreign stock, six key census tracts along Blue Hill Avenue lost 11,848 Jewish residents between 1960 and 1970 (Figure 18). Left behind in the new black neighborhoods were synagogues without congregations; delicatessens and kosher meat markets; and, perhaps most incongruous of all, Jewish homes for the aged, inhabited largely by elderly women.

One notable black outlier was established in the 1960s—a public housing project about three miles east of Dudley Square on the shores of Boston Harbor. Columbia Point became for Boston what Pruitt-Igo became for St. Louis, a cold, cheerless, bleak cluster of orange brick towers set in a sea of emptiness and isolated from the city by a treacherous expressway and assorted industrial harborside uses (Figure 19). Recent events may change this: the new Boston campus of the University of Massachusetts has been built on Columbia Point, and an adjacent site has been reserved for the John F. Kennedy Library.

Blacks are more segregated in Boston than in most other large U.S. metropolitan areas, in the South as well as in the North. Karl and Alma Taeuber devised an index of segregation in 1965 to give a statistical yardstick to the phenomenon of racial segregation. The calculation of the index of segregation for Boston, using 1950 population figures, yields a figure of 91.5 (on a scale of zero to 100, the

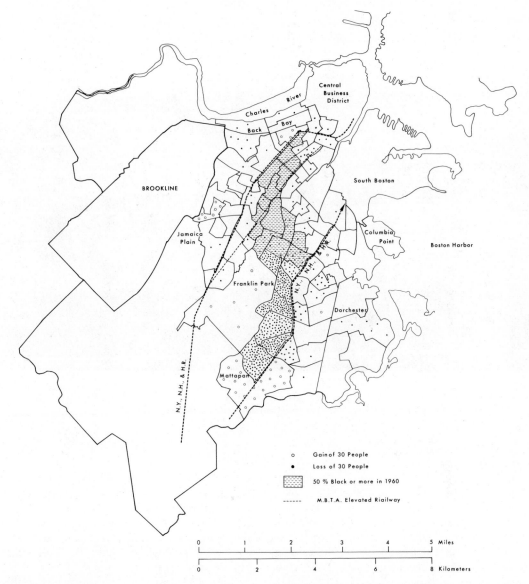

Figure 18. Jewish exodus, 1960–1970. Net gains and losses of population of Russian stock. (After the U.S. Census)

latter figure representing complete racial segregation). Boston's total black population in that year was 40,057. When the same calculation is made using 1970 data, the black population having increased to 104,707, the index is 91.4! The degree of racial segregation in Boston—the home of abolitionists William Lloyd Garrison, Julia Ward Howe, Wendell Phillips, and Lydia Maria Child—decreased by only 0.1 percent during two decades of vigorous civil rights progress in the United States. Another 22,000

blacks lived outside the city of Boston but within the SMSA in 1970. The greatest proportion of these residents—nearly 7,000—lived in Cambridge, and small black neighborhoods existed in Lynn, Medford, and Newton. The remaining black population was scattered throughout the metropolitan area in very small numbers.

Boston's ethnic neighborhoods retain strong identities even as time and family moving thins out the old ethnic stocks. Old Irish neighbor-

Figure 19. Columbia Point housing project. The nadir of public housing design in Boston, looking south toward Quincy and the Blue Hill range. (Courtesy of the Boston Globe)

hoods, for example, are particularly cohesive, and many residents display a real garrison mentality that finds strongest geographic expression in their urban "turf." Peter Schrag has recently described South Boston and Dorchester as not "territories that their upwardly mobile inhabitants recently captured; they are, rather, ancient tribal domains, institutions in their own right. They are artifacts of the city's institutional mind and relics of its restricted economic life." As the Brahmins retreated to the suburbs and busied themselves in a massive array of charitable societies, they transferred as much power as possible to the state legislature, the governor, and metropolitan commissions, abolishing also the ward basis of city council representation. "They simply tried to diversify power," Schrag writes, "to spread it around in little indistinct piles so the Irish would find it hard to gather." The net result of such maneuvers, and of the restricted economic opportunities afforded the Irish, discussed earlier, was to retard their suburbanization, with the consequence that their ethnic areas are tightly demarcated (Figure 20) and contain

much hostility toward blacks and suburban liberals.

The center of metropolitan Boston forms a wheel pattern of ethnic wedges. The broad quadrant extending south and west from downtown was quickly appropriated by the Irish, but Jews were soon able to drive two salients southward through Roxbury, Mattapan, and Milton, and westward through Brookline to Newton. Other wedges to the north of the CBD contain the Italians in the North End, East Boston, and Revere, the Irish in Charlestown, and Jews in Chelsea. Two small neighborhoods existed at the hub of the wheel: Chinatown has remained largely stationary; the black ghetto has expanded to replace almost completely the southern Jewish wedge. Boston residential turnover patterns, as exemplified in a major study of Jews by Morris Axelrod, are predominantly sectoral in direction—a trend that clearly operates to sustain wedge-shaped ethnic districts.

The constant flows of ethnic groups from one part of the growing city to another has produced a social environment fraught with

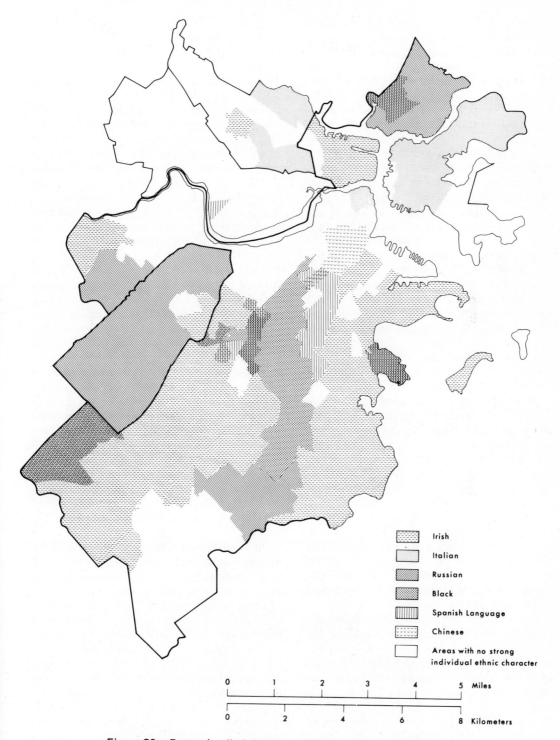

Figure 20. Boston's tribal domains, 1970. (After the U.S. Census)

ethnic tensions. Early locations of ethnic groups were tied to specific employment opportunities and appropriate rents. Subsequent moves have been dictated through the pressure of interethnic competition for housing, relative speed of upward social (and income) mobility, and the city's sector geometry. As some of the established generations suburbanize and mix through intermarriage and residence with the native born in the metropolitan fringe, neighborhood identity tends to lose the strong ethnic dimension of the inner cities. In the heart of the metropolis, however, ethnic divisions are likely to remain strong. As the black population becomes increasingly prominent in Boston proper, for example, old Irish neighborhoods are preparing to resist the seemingly inevitable growth in housing pressure. The extent of recent home improvements in South Boston suggests that neighborhood residents and banks have strong confidence in the continued vitality of the area as presently constituted. However many flee to the suburbs, a great many more will stay and fight.

The Newest Arrivals

Some parts of the metropolitan core, like Back Bay, Cambridge, and parts of Somerville and Brighton, in contrast to the great majority of neighborhoods, do not appear to have prominent ethnic characteristics (Figure 20). These areas contain often high proportions of well-to-do native-born residents belonging either to the old in-town elite groups or the university fraternity. The other areas, surrounding these native-born tracts, appear from the census to act as the major present-day receiving areas for recent immigrants. This suggests a modified hypothesis for the modern-day residential melting pot for new immigrants. First, the principal patterns should be outlined.

Puerto Ricans, as the latest group of any size to arrive, have tended to seek housing at the outer edge of the principal black residential area. In 1970 there were three concentrations of Puerto Ricans in Boston. The largest was located in a district of poor housing being vacated by blacks in the South End-lower Roxbury area (Figure 20), between Tremont and Washington streets just east of Rutland Street. Many of the landscape features common to Puerto Rican neighborhoods are visible in this area—signs in Spanish, small *bodegas,* and storefront *iglesias.*

A second Puerto Rican neighborhood has grown on the southeast side of the black residential area along Cottage and Dudley streets in the general direction of Upham's Corner. This community stops abruptly along a spur track of the Penn Central Railroad that cuts through this area. A third and even smaller neighborhood has developed in front of advancing blacks in the Egleston Square section just north of Franklin Park. The old Puerto Rican core area has relatively few black families intermixed, especially at its center, but the other Puerto Rican neighborhoods contain large numbers of black residents. Friction between these communities has been an increasing part of the Boston social scene since the late 1960s.

Very recent immigrants are difficult to identify by precise nationality since the census provides no such breakdown. Clues, however, can be sought in the predominant ethnic groups occupying the tracts most favored by new immigrants. From such evidence, the Italian North End emerges as a major receiving area—continuing its historic function—with from 13 to 19 percent of its tract populations there being new arrivals. Portuguese census tracts in East Cambridge and Somerville, Canadian tracts in Cambridge, Chinese tracts in the South End near the CBD, and tracts with substantial Cuban representation in Brighton also boast large absolute numbers of recent immigrants. Outside the central area, Italian tracts in Watertown, Canadian tracts in Waltham, and Portuguese tracts in Salem stand out for similar reasons.

In a metropolis far larger than the city of the midnineteenth century, the principle of central receiving areas for immigrants seems to operate even today. These areas do coincide with zones of cheap and dilapidated housing, and most of them are as central to the multinuclear central business districts of Boston and Cambridge as can be expected in an age of rapid downtown land use change. Modern immigration is minute by comparison with earlier epochs, and large homogeneous immigrant ghettoes cannot be expected. The substantial concentration of new immigrants into central tracts within the metropolis, notwithstanding a secondary pattern of dispersed small and medium numbers, does suggest the continuing utility of small areas acting as residential "decompression chambers" in the early stages of adjustment.

Where Is the Poverty?

There is no doubt that the areas of lowest per capita income in Boston are precisely those occupied by the majority of the black population (Figures 16 and 20). In a few instances, however, low income tracts define not black areas but rather student rooming house districts. In this geographical overview of the built environment, a few indicators of living circumstances highlight basic patterns of general adjustment within the city. Since the distribution of low income residence is highly localized within the metropolitan region at large, it is sufficient to focus attention on the central cities of Boston, Brookline, Cambridge, Chelsea, and Somerville.

Substantial areas of Boston and its neighboring inner cities show what might be regarded as undesirable characteristics for the well-being of present residents and the future stability of neighborhoods (Figure 21). Housing is a basic necessity of life, and in general the poor pay a higher proportion of their incomes to secure housing than do the wealthy—leaving proportionately less money available for food, clothing, and other expenses. It is widely accepted that rent for accommodation exceeding one-quarter of a family's monthly income imposes considerable stress on the family budget. Where the percentage of families facing this problem in any census tract is at all high, it can be deduced that housing in that neighborhood poses a real human problem. A generalized zone of "rent pressure" exists in Boston that extends throughout much of the city. Only South Boston, East Dorchester, Roslindale, Hyde Park, and East Mattapan escape inclusion. In addition, lower Brookline and most of Cambridge fall under this rent pressure.

A second problem is high residential turnover which affects upkeep of property and neighborhood stability. Census tracts that have experienced a 75 percent turnover in families in the last two decades also cover a broad section of the metropolitan core, although their extent is not quite as large as that for rent pressure (Figure 21). A third condition is the restricted mobility of families who have no private automobile available and who must therefore rely on public transport or walking to reach jobs and shops. A broad zone in which over 55 percent of all families have no car available includes such areas away from the downtown as Back Bay, Parker Hill, Roxbury, Dorchester, South Boston, Columbia Point, Charlestown, and Chelsea.

These three zones overlap sufficiently well to extend over most parts of the black district, as well as delineating other areas individually. Beyond that, however, large areas of central Boston must rely on public transport to get outside the neighborhood. While car ownership is clearly not so essential where good public transport exists, the added mobility of car ownership is not available to many families. Nowhere in the suburbs does the lack of a car reach such high proportions.

Residential turnover is to be expected in student areas and districts with large proportions of rented property, but it is indicative of a partial stability in the black district that some tracts in the northern section of the district are not characterized by high turnover. These contain some of the oldest settled black families in the black community.

Outside the intensive zone where all three undesirable characteristics are present—the black district, the South End, Back Bay, and downtown—there are areas of special character. East Dorchester and South Boston, both still largely white and Irish, lack many automobiles but do not suffer from acute rent pressure and are residentially fairly stable. The North End, East Boston, Charlestown, and Chelsea show similar characteristics. On the other hand, Cambridge, Allston-Brighton, and lower Brookline show high rates of turnover and rent pressure. The conclusion to draw must be that poverty and poor living conditions in Boston frequently but not always overlap and that remedies must be tailored to the specific needs of individual neighborhoods.

Housing

Metropolitan Boston contains one of the most widely varied stocks of housing in the country. Paul Revere's seventeenth century house still stands, although it is no longer lived in. Beacon Hill and Back Bay contain some of the finest examples in America of Federal and Victorian houses, while the city can also boast its share of industrial tenement blocks and public housing monstrosities. And in nearly every town there is tract housing. Between 1960 and 1970, population in the Boston SMSA grew by 6 percent whereas the housing supply increased over 10 percent. While within the region the central city itself lost population to the tune of

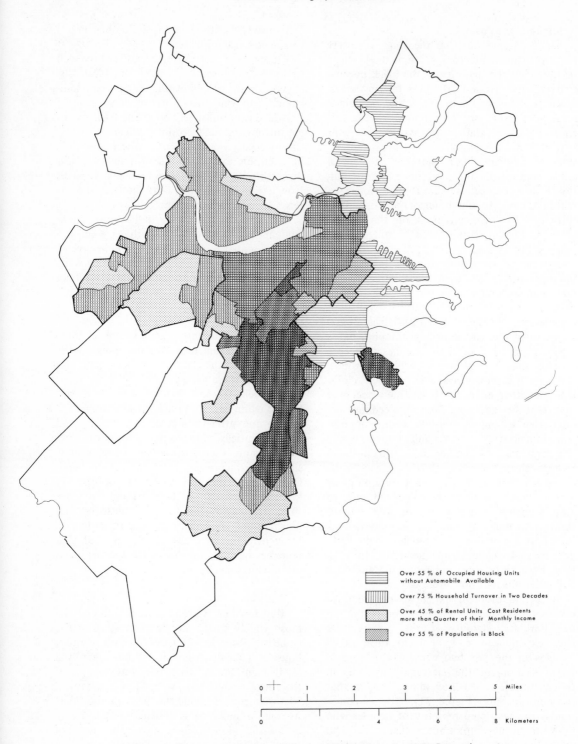

Over 55 % of Occupied Housing Units
without Automobile Available

Over 75 % Household Turnover in Two Decades

Over 45 % of Rental Units Cost Residents
more than Quarter of their Monthly Income

Over 55 % of Population is Black

Figure 21. Selected living conditions, 1970. (After the U.S. Census)

an 8 percent drop, the city's housing declined only 1 percent. These trends reflect both changing demography—smaller family sizes—and partial relief of past overcrowding. One cannot conclude, however, that the housing supply exceeds reasonable demand. In Boston proper, for example, the percentage of housing with more than one person per room actually increased 0.1 percent between 1960 and 1970 (6.7 to 6.8 percent).

The housing stock of any area changes constantly through new construction, demolition, conversions, and other means. During the 1960s Boston proper added 33,400 dwelling units to its stock while losing 36,000 others. In contrast, the rest of the metropolitan region lost only 26,000 while adding 115,400 units. In all, the inner city accounted for 61 percent of demolitions in the SMSA while the other cities and suburbs cornered 83 percent of the new construction. If Boston's neighboring cities of Cambridge, Somerville, Chelsea, and Brookline were included in the core zone, differences between center and periphery would be even more dramatic. Over the period, the rate of loss of existing houses was three times higher in the city of Boston (15 percent) than elsewhere in the metropolis (5 percent).

These patterns are not unique to the Boston SMSA, but are accentuated by the age of the city and its early large size which has bequeathed to the present a particularly large stock of very old housing in its inner zone. This is not a bad

circumstance necessarily, because old houses can be solidly built and aesthetically more pleasing than new ones. Indeed, the current onslaught of renovation along the waterfront, in Back Bay, the South End, Charlestown, Cambridge, and elsewhere testifies to the possibilities of adaptive rehabilitation rather than outright replacement. Nevertheless, these efforts are highly localized and for the most part carried out by and for the middle and upper income groups of the city. A generally old housing stock for low income people spells massive problems of maintenance.

Almost three-quarters of Boston City's housing is rented property; in the remainder of the urban region only one-third of the housing is rented. At 60,500 units, Boston contains only 13.3 percent of the SMSA's owner-occupied housing of nearly 400,000 units. Black property ownership is very slowly increasing as white people leave the central city (Table 6). However, the ratio of owners to renters among blacks (1 to 5) still has a long way to go before reaching the ratio for whites (2 to 5). Among the few black suburbanites, renters outnumber owners almost 2 to 1, whereas among whites, owners outnumber renters by a similar proportion. These figures illustrate the common experience in large cities that blacks encounter great difficulty in becoming homeowners. While black residence in Boston proper between 1960 and 1970 increased by 14,800 units, black ownership increased by only 3,200 units.

Table 6. White and Black Housing Patterns in Boston City and the Rest of the SMSA, 1960–1970

	1960		1970	
	Number	*Percent*	*Number*	*Percent*
Boston City				
White-Owned Housing Units	58,400	25.9	54,600	24.5
White-Rented Housing Units	148,600	65.9	135,100	60.6
Black-Owned Housing Units	2,700	1.2	5,900	2.7
Black-Rented Housing Units	15,700	7.0	27,300	12.2
Total	225,400	100.0	222,900	100.0
Rest of SMSA				
White-Owned Housing Units	334,900	60.8	390,400	61.2
White-Rented Housing Units	211,500	38.4	241,100	37.8
Black-Owned Housing Units	1,400	0.3	2,700	0.4
Black-Rented Housing Units	2,800	0.5	4,000	0.6
Total	550,600	100.0	638,200	100.0

Source: U.S. Housing Census, 1970.

Table 7. "Housing Pressure" in Boston City and the Rest of the SMSA, 1960–1970

	1960	*1970*	*Percent Increase 1960–1970*
"Rent Pressure" Percent of All Rented Homes in			
Boston	36.3	46.7	
Rest of SMSA	31.2	47.1	
"Ownership Pressure"** Percent of All Owner-Occupied Homes in			
Boston	21.3	27.6	
Rest of SMSA	24.8	23.5	
Median Income			
Boston	$ 4,400	$ 6,400	+45.5
Rest of SMSA	$ 5,300	$ 7,700	+45.3
Median Gross Rent per Annum			
Boston	$ 912	$ 1,536	+68.4
Rest of SMSA	$ 1,020	$ 1,692	+65.9
Median Owned-Home Value			
Boston	$13,700	$21,500	+56.9
Rest of SMSA	$16,400	$25,500	+55.5

*Where monthly rent equals or exceeds one-quarter of monthly income.
**Families with 1969 incomes under $5,000 in houses worth over $15,000.
Source: U.S. Housing Census, 1970.

Much of the difficulty stems from the relationship between real estate values and income levels. Earlier, "rent pressure" was introduced as a measure of this interaction. In addition to areas of highly prevalent "rent pressure" (Figure 21), this condition exists for many families all over the metropolitan region. Similar pressure can be identified for homeowners, too, and the patterns over time suggest some overall trends for the metropolis (Table 7). Nine out of every twenty families in Boston who rent their homes experience "rent pressure" today, two families more than a decade before. The suburbs have also witnessed a sharp increase in this problem and, while less than one-third of suburban families suffered pressure in 1960, that proportion has reached nearly half of all families there.

The reason is clear: rents throughout the metropolitan area rose over 65 percent during the 1960s while median income rose only 45 percent. The story is similar for homeowners in Boston proper during the period. Pressure increased as home values rose faster than income. Only in the suburbs did "pressure" affect proportionately fewer families in 1970 than in 1960, but that decline was inconse-

quentially small and likely to be temporary— suburban homes values still rose 10 percent faster than suburban incomes! All this evidence points to increasing problems in the equitable distribution of housing throughout the SMSA. No longer will it be possible to find cheaper housing far from the center of town.

There is, of course, a stratum of metropolitan society for whom discussion of home-ownership is academic. Public housing has rarely if ever drawn enthusiastic public sympathy, and the results of decades of half-hearted attempts at providing such housing in Boston are common to other large metropolises. The Mary Ellen McCormack project (1,016 units) built in 1938 was Boston's first taste of government housing. Begun in the wake of the Depression, it long escaped the social stigma widely attached to project housing in later times, and is generally considered the most successful experiment in Boston. Columbia Point, mentioned earlier, is undoubtedly Boston's worst experiment (Figure 19). Built in 1954, it was originally overwhelmingly white, but during the 1960s high tenant turnover changed its complexion quickly. The Boston Housing Authority (BHA) over the years has shifted new construction from family projects to elderly housing which generate less neighborhood opposition. Since 1957 no new family housing projects have been built. During the 1962-1972 period, 1,777 units for the elderly were erected, but only ninety-four units for family use.

High tenant turnover rates create many vacant apartments that deteriorate rapidly through vandalism. Often, simple repairs take so long to organize that in the meantime vandals have reduced units to shambles. In 1969, 700 housing units stood vacant while 7,000 families languished on the authority's waiting list. It is evident that, regardless of motivation and efficiency, the BHA operates under legislative, fiscal, and social constraints that make it quite unequal to the challenge of providing the city's poor with decent housing.

As it stands, the BHA administers 13,826 housing units, which represent 8.5 percent of the city's 162,400 rented homes. Blacks occupy 16.8 percent of all rental property in Boston, which is close to their proportion of the total population. In public housing, however, blacks account for 38.7 percent of the units. When one considers that blacks dominate the lower levels of the income scale, this small proportion might well seem unfair. But to give blacks priority in all the public housing, of course, would not be politically possible. Public housing is aided by both federal and state funds. Clear patterns of differential preference can be traced in the racial mix of housing subsidized by these two sources. In federally aided projects, whites occupy 55.9 percent of the housing available; in state-aided projects, whites occupy 76.2 percent. Local political pressures do appear to influence public housing patterns.

A major criticism of most public housing projects is the monotony, rigid layout, and dilapidation of their physical structures. Regimented high-rise buildings with little or no greenery, weather-beaten exteriors and peeling interiors, are not conducive to tenant pride and upkeep. After many years, Boston is breaking the architectural mold associated with public housing and offering more humane, informal, and landscaped alternatives. The elderly housing project on Washington Street is a good example (Figure 22). Another innovation is "infill" housing, designed to place small clusters of units or single houses on small vacant lots spread throughout the city that have

passed into city ownership through tax delinquency. The larger clusters, taking sometimes half a block or a large angle parcel between streets, have generated some of the same local opposition that the large scale projects have done. Most successful are frame houses for single families that least disrupt surrounding residential areas. The principle appears sound on a very small scale, but financing for such scattered buildings has proven abortive, and early efforts in Boston are foundering.

If low income families could gain access to the suburbs, the enormous problems facing the central city in dealing with housing provision could at least be shared more equitably around the metropolis. Suburban zoning practices in eastern Massachusetts, as on the fringe of many metropolitan centers, have long been effectively, if not admittedly, employed to maintain their social and economic status by excluding low income housing. Indeed, in many cases, zoning has actually enhanced land values and elevated community prestige. Large lot sizes and costly subdivision regulations have acted to restrict residential builders to the upper ranges of the housing market. Thus such zoning has tended to offer few opportunities to low income, or in some cases even middle income, families to purchase single family houses or to rent apartments (on the unlikely chance that there were any) in many Boston suburbs.

The effect of such discrimination on any minority group, especially blacks, gaining entrance to suburbia (except by cold, hard cash) is obvious. Home rule, especially in matters of zoning, is extraordinarily powerful in Massachusetts, and the requirement of zoning approval (or of zoning amendments) by the attorney general has done little to curb zoning's "snob" effect. The Massachusetts General Court, on the other hand, with a high proportion of its House of Representatives made up of central city men and women, drew up and enacted in 1969 a landmark piece of legislation known as the "antisnob zoning" law as a battering ram against the Green Wall of Suburbia.

The language of the "antisnob zoning" bill requires every city and town in the commonwealth to designate a modest percentage of its total land area for eventual use by low and moderate income housing. Moreover, a developer attempting to construct low or moderate income housing in any municipality may,

Figure 22. Washington Park housing project. Back-tracking to a human scale of design. (Courtesy of the Boston Globe)

if denied necessary permits, take his case through a complex maze of appeals courts. As decisions on the first cases roll out, it appears that the developers are winning hands down. Some developers, however, oblige recalcitrant communities by proposing to exhaust the allotted acreage by constructing housing for the elderly, thus perpetuating the exclusion of low income families from suburban living.

Boston's housing problems are by no means unique, and social attitudes militating against meaningful reform are deeply entrenched. Nevertheless, in a period of sharply reduced federal involvement in solving urban problems, an important theme was revisited recently by the mayor's former chief adviser, quoted in the *Boston Sunday Globe* as saying, "The first thing we need is a helluva lot of money. People underestimate the importance of money. I would like to throw money at all the problems."

THE BOSTONIAN AT WORK

Residential areas form the largest built-up land use in the metropolis, but those who earn a living and run families spend much of their time away from home. What other kinds of land use does the city generate, and how do they affect the structure, functioning, and appearance of the built environment? One out of every thirty acres of the land area of Greater Boston is devoted to stores, warehouses, offices, and other service activities. The core cities devote nearly twice the space to commercial uses as do the suburbs, and the downtown section of Boston itself has over 27 percent of its total area in commercial land use.

This heavy inner city concentration has characterized Boston since World War II. The Boston area has been slow to accept the planned, suburban, highway-oriented shopping center, but the lag has now been overcome. Not only has the retail structure of the region undergone radical decentralization in the past twenty years, but there has also been an office-building boom in the suburbs to rival that of the inner core. Office parks, including several along Route 128, are nearly as common as industrial parks, and frequently the two uses are mixed in a single facility.

Shops

With Boston's history of polynucleated settlement, it is not surprising to find a few large and many small commercial areas scattered throughout the older suburbs. Many of these communities boast a strong, independent, traditional shopping center, only partly weakened by suburban competitors. Such areas are often ringed with municipal parking lots or garages, local responses to the threat of new nearby planned centers. In between these older centers occurs a whole hierarchy of secondary and smaller commercial districts, ending finally with the isolated "Ma and Pa" variety store—or spa, as it is known locally— salvation of the family out of milk or bread on a Sunday in this once-Puritan land.

The planned shopping center of American suburbia was a post-World War II outgrowth of the failure of the old downtown central business districts to provide a new retail model oriented to the automobile and a shifting residential base. First appearing at the outskirts of the expanding city or metropolitan area, the planned shopping center recreated the old CBD in spacious and attractive new facilities, comprehensive in scope and merchandise lines and surrounded by acres of free parking. Later centers were carved out of older neighborhoods, and a hierarchy of center sizes began to emerge.

During the 1950s and early 1960s, Boston's pattern of retailing indicated a keen awareness of the competitive structure of the newly emerging market areas. The first three truly regional centers were properly positioned at the north, west, and south of the city (obviously not the east) at a distance of ten to eighteen miles from the downtown. At almost equal distances in between medium-sized centers sprang up, and so on down the scale. By 1965 Greater Boston possessed eighty planned shopping centers, distributed almost uniformly across the metropolitan landscape. Concentrations were found in areas of rapid suburban population increases (Framingham-Natick:

seven centers; Brockton: four centers), and gaps in the new retail net occurred in communities with low population density where zoning often discouraged large scale commercial development (Lincoln, Dover, Cohasset, Manchester).

The uneven distribution of market opportunities, the restricted number of expressways or upgraded highways, and the relatively small area zoned for commercial use tended to limit the number of first class sites for major new shopping complexes in Greater Boston. Furthermore, shopping center developers were discovering that the best site for a new center might be as close to the competition as possible. This might well be termed the Paramus model—after the first U.S. shopping center agglomeration in northern New Jersey. By 1970 Boston's retail landscape displayed several such concentrations of shopping centers. The traffic congestion and the continuum of brick and asphalt once characteristic of the old downtown appeared in suburbia. On Boston's ancient Worcester Turnpike, the widened and medianed Route 9, no less than five individual shopping complexes lie within a two mile radius. Route 1 to the north of Boston boasts a string of new shopping centers that lie metaphorically within a cash register's throw of one another. Special new traffic lanes and a maze of signal lights try to assist the center-bound shopper to the center of his choice.

Almost without exception, however, the new retail landscape of Boston displays little of regional character. The suburban centers, the centers squeezed into pre-Depression suburbs, all look alike—not only to one another but also when compared to centers on Long Island, in Detroit, or in Kansas City. Only the merchants' names change, and even that is not always the case. Boston was slow to accept the new highway-oriented center, and it has been slow to integrate large scale office and institutional uses into planned shopping centers. Boston offers no unique advances in this particular state of the art, nor examples of aesthetic achievement worthy of emulation elsewhere.

The Office Boom

Boston's downtown has managed to keep a remarkably high proportion of its office jobs, while the retail and wholesale districts have suffered somewhat more at the hands of suburban competition. Retail store and office land uses occupy most of the peninsular Boston, and if other institutional uses such as government facilities, schools, and hospitals are added, the commercial area extends well into adjacent cities and towns. The downtown area has undergone a remarkable physical transformation in recent years. This change may be labeled, inelegantly though accurately, as "Manhattanization." It is only in the last decade or so that Boston's low skyline has been pierced dramatically by a crop of high-rise buildings representing a veritable explosion of office space.

Only one office building was constructed in Boston between 1929 and 1950. A Boston Redevelopment Authority (BRA) survey has estimated that Boston emerged from the Depression with a total of fifteen million square feet in the downtown district, a total which had risen only 1.5 million square feet by 1960. Today, office space is calculated at nearly twenty-eight million square feet, and the additions have come at a sharply accelerating rate, so that half of all Boston's offices are less than fifteen years old. The lack of office construction until very recently is related to the long trend of suburban population growth and declining confidence that the traditional downtown could hold the metropolis together as the latter spread outwards.

However, as shown earlier, jobs in the service sector of the urban economy were rising even during the decade and a half following World War II, and this led to increased office employment. Since investment confidence was lacking, no building initiatives were forthcoming, and office accommodation became more cramped and outdated. Thus, the pressure of pent-up demand for new and upgraded office space increased—spurred on by the continued specialization of the city in service functions for its regional and national hinterland. Finally, the Travelers Insurance Company, the Prudential Insurance Company, and the State Street Bank erected high-rise buildings with extra office space for rent in the late 1950s and early 1960s, and their surplus was readily taken up by other businesses. Helped by massive inner city urban renewal programs initiated by the BRA under Edward J. Logue, and an awakening sense of the need to display their modern image through visual means, large corporations have increasingly taken to office building development. The architectural results are sometimes exhilarating, usually eye-catching, but often monstrous in their impersonal facades and total disregard for human scale.

Boston is unusual among large cities in relying very largely upon institutional developers such as banks and insurance companies for its high-rise office structures. They occupy anywhere between 10 to 90 percent of the space themselves. Purely speculative development is not as common as in New York. The prime example of the Boston pattern is the Prudential Tower building (Figure 23). This venture was of the greatest importance both in inspiring confidence in downtown revitalization in general and also in establishing a new locational pivot within the city (Figure 24). In locating on the site of the former Boston and Albany train yards in Back Bay, the company was expressing renewed faith in an "in-town" site, and at the same time greatly expanding the zone of central commercial land uses.

The Government Center and the West End renewal projects in the old CBD area took up the challenge and sponsored new high-rise buildings in the old commercial core. The financial district to the southeast then also blossomed with new bank and other office buildings. Further construction in the immediate future seems destined to fill in the intervening gap. The Hancock building on Copley Square represents another building block in uniting the Prudential complex with the old downtown area. Of the twenty-five most recent high-rise buildings in inner Boston, four have been developed by major banks and seven by nationwide insurance companies. Among planned additions to the skyline, six will be owned by banks, credit unions, or mutual funds.

The phenomenal expansion of downtown office space in Boston can be explained in large part by the ease of communications in the CBD, general centrality, a ready labor pool, and the prestige of location close to government and big corporations. One recent high-rise complex is advertised as "One Beacon Street: The Finest Address in America." Not all new office buildings are appearing in the increasingly congested CBD, however. Between 1957 and 1973, about ten million square feet of office space appeared in the core, but over six million square feet were constructed in the suburbs. Although widely scattered by comparison, new suburban offices

Figure 23. The Prudential complex. A new commercial-residential redevelopment zone separates Back Bay (lower left) from the South End (top right). Courtesy Aerial Photos of New England)

have tended to seek highway locations similar to those of light industry. In addition to industrial parks, Route 128 is festooned with a growing number of office parks, where the design emphasis is on spaciousness, greenery, and horizontal architecture.

Suburban office complexes can afford generous surroundings. At $1 to 6 per square foot,

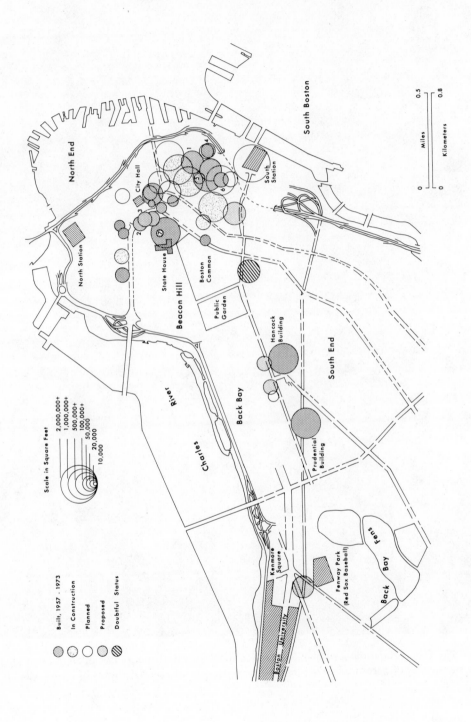

land there is almost a different commodity from its downtown counterpart ($35 to 70 per square foot). In addition, many companies are seeking suburban locations because they draw increasingly for staff on highly educated personnel who are likely to be found in suburban home locations. The desire to avoid daily commutation to the central city is an emerging social preference. The rise of suburban office complexes, in fact, is helping to develop a sizable reverse commuting pattern within the traditional core-periphery structure of the metropolis.

Factories on the Move

Before the industrial revolution manufacturing used to take place in small craft shops and warehouse lofts crowded around the early commercial districts. With the rise of large machinery, the standardization of production, and the consequent growth in scale of operations, manufacturing outgrew the crowded premises of the CBD. Also unable to compete with commercial functions for costly central locations, industry moved out to the nineteenth century fringe of the city. With better access to rail yards and water transportation, Boston's industries quickly formed a well-defined, though interrupted, "fringe belt" around the heart of the then built-up area. This belt forms a discontinuous circle around the old peninsula and its first major residential extensions, and runs clockwise from South Boston through the South End (now partially replaced through renewal—the Boston and Albany yards further west also formed a link in the chain), East Cambridge, Charlestown, and East Boston, back to South Boston. Residential suburbs leapfrogged this zone, only to be themselves partially surrounded by later "fringe belts," of which Allston and the Fresh Pond area of West Cambridge are remnants. Further residential expansion served in turn to lock in these industrial zones within the densely built-up area of the metropolis.

Wedged once again in areas where they could

Figure 24. The office boom. Creating white collar space in downtown core, 1957-1976. Downtown, originally centered in State Street now reaches west to Massachusetts Avenue and south to the Massachusetts Turnpike. (After the Boston Redevelopment Authority)

not easily expand, industry has increasingly moved outwards yet again, and the process is continuing today. Industries move out of central cities for many reasons, but in Boston chief among these are crowded site conditions, old buildings, high taxes, and congested transport channels. As long as the city of Boston must rely primarily upon property taxes to finance city services, it will fight a rearguard action with moving industry. Other large cities face very similar problems, but the restricted area of Boston, with its awkward land areas interrupted by waterways that many industries do not use, makes the situation particularly acute.

Efforts by the BRA are under way to assemble industrial sites of sufficient size and locational convenience within the city to attract either new firms or those due to abandon facilities that have become too small. The attempt is valiant, but the success may be limited. The official emphasis is on retaining blue collar jobs, and certainly a large part of the metropolitan area's lower income families are to be found in the central city, but high taxes and inadaquate intracity transport may keep out all but the smallest employers. Although historical circumstance and geographical limitations reduce the possible remedies, a comprehensive transport policy that separated commercial truck from other types of traffic (either physically or by time schedule) might lessen the problem of accessibility.

One location that contains many of the advantages sought by firms moving from the cities of Boston and Cambridge is the circumferential highway, Route 128, about twelve miles radial distance from downtown Boston. While is was not consciously planned at first as a retreat for industry, the road-based transport accessibility to as yet undeveloped parkland sites available along its fringes quickly proved irresistible for a variety of manufacturers, especially electronics firms (Figure 25). In the last decade the number of companies locating on the expressway has risen to 729, accounting for over 66,000 jobs.

The rise of Route 128 to industrial prominence caught some towns unprepared, and differences in local zoning laws have resulted in varying densities of firms along the road. Nevertheless, the landscape belt bordering the artery is unique in the Boston area for its seemingly endless array of spacious, one or two story plants set in rolling parkland sites

Figure 25. Electronic circuit. Research, development, and manufacturing electronic firms in Greater Boston, 1971. (After the Greater Boston Chamber of Commerce)

with manicured flower gardens and hidden parking lots. Many firms consider this type of locational environment essential for their scientists and engineers—attracted by the verdant "rural" view from their office windows as an aid to creative contemplation and yet within easy truck and car reach of other key points in the metropolis.

Route 128 is regarded as nearing saturation, but the demand for similar sites continues. Interstate 495, an outer belt ringing Greater Boston at twenty-five miles distance

from downtown, is now being prepared consciously as the next "golden arc." A key feature of the new development is the assembly of industrial parks at intersections of the freeway with express arterials from the metropolitan core. The effect of industrial dispersal on journey to work patterns and housing construction in the outer suburbs has already been massive.

The obsolete physical plant of one era is often colonized selectively by the next and nowhere is this more visible than in the Greater

Boston area. Many of the nineteenth and early twentieth century textile mills and leather factories stand today, their bell towers and smoke stacks still in place. But the railroad spurs are largely idle, and many a door within the huge hulks of the mills sports a sign for a small company. Just as some of the old downtown harbor wharves now house fishing tackle stores, architect's offices, and antique shops, so too do old mill buildings house lightbulb companies, paper firms, small engineering outfits, and furniture concerns. Built to carry heavy production machinery, with thick concrete floors and large lighted spaces, many of these relics of an older order serve a renewed purpose and contribute to a striking urban landscape. Inner city replacement industries housed in historic quarters offer strong contrasts to the ultramodern horizontal plants of the garden suburbs.

Respinning the Transport Web

Well let me tell you the story
Of a man named Charlie,
On a dreadful and fateful day,
He put 10 cents in his pocket,
Kissed his wife and family,
Went to ride on the MTA.
Did he ever return?
No, he never returned,
And his fate is still unlearned,
He may ride forever
'Neath the streets of Boston,
He's the man who never returned.
                    The Kingston Trio

Boston's long hegemony as capital of New England has created over the centuries a fine spider's web of roads converging on the metropolis from all directions. Within the half-wheel formed by Interstate 495 there are today over forty radial roads which converge spokelike on the Hub. As railroads were built in the nineteenth century, the initial road pattern was reinforced by major commuter lines. Throughout the nineteenth and early twentieth centuries, thousands of white collar workers poured each morning out of the various railroad terminals that ring the CBD. Today, these great dingy buildings are ghosts of their former selves.

Boston's internal public transportation system evolved out of a large number of smaller local lines built and operated during the later nineteenth century. Many of these merged from

time to time for more efficient (and, it was hoped, profitable) operation. The largest corporation to emerge from this era was the Boston Elevated Railway, a private stock company that created the nucleus as well as the substance of Boston's present rapid transit system.

The Elevated built the first underground lines outward toward Cambridge, Dorchester, Everett, and East Boston, as well as the electrified surface trolley lines in every suburb. The Commonwealth of Massachusetts purchased the Boston Elevated Railway in 1947 and created a Metropolitan Transit Authority (MTA) to run it. The MTA district included Boston and thirteen adjacent communities served by the system. When the MTA was running at a substantial annual deficit, these losses were regularly apportioned among the fourteen member communities. Modest extensions and improvements were undertaken by the new public body.

In 1964 the MTA was dissolved and replaced by a new operating board, the Massachusetts Bay Transportation Authority (MBTA). A prime factor in creating the MBTA was the recognition that public transportation needs now extended far beyond the boundaries of the original fouteen cities and towns. The MBTA district was set up to include Boston and seventy-one other cities and towns, by all odds the largest areawide organization of its type in Massachusetts history.

Boston's subway and rapid transit system is one of the oldest in the United States. The Green Line, the oldest element, is at the very best a quaint affair. Originally a streetcar operation, the lines were put underground in the downtown area by a simple process of cut and cover. The glacial and alluvial ground material offered little resistance. If the geology was cooperative, however, the street alignments were not, and the system has many technical incompatabilities. Nevertheless, in a metropolitan district like Boston with its basic wheel pattern, the trolley cars and later rapid transit cars served the population well enough. Great radial flows rushed back and forth for decades as the core city beckoned its suburban work force daily to their jobs. By 1971 the flows had diminished to 149 million riders annually (from 450 million in 1949). Cars and expressways accounted for the decline.

When freeways blossomed, particularly after 1956, a further etching of the transportation pattern around Boston was set in motion (Figure 26). As the interstate system took shape in New England and as local authorities added some of their own expressways to handle increasing urban traffic, it seemed for a long time as if the Boston region was destined to go the way of Los Angeles and Chicago. Route 128 was transformed into a major circumferential highway with six, and now in parts eight, lanes, followed by Interstate 495 at a radius of twenty-five miles from the center of Boston.

A major transportation study in 1948 set up the master plan for highway construction, and by 1970 much of the plan had been put into effect. Unfortunately, Boston's geography did not fare well at the hands of the planners. Substantial portions of the central city were subjected to road "improvements," the most massive of which was the Central Artery and associated bridges across the Charles River and harbor entrance. These structures, unsightly assemblages of green-painted steel and fluted concrete, unceremoniously fling the roadway alternately high above and then below street level on the edge of the historic city core, as Walter McQuade has said, "like a trail of lava on legs." The more freeways that were built to feed directly into the Central Artery, the greater the congestion became. The process reached a pathetic but comic climax in 1973 when a final link was completed to join Interstate 93 to the Central Artery—but could not be opened to unrestricted traffic flow because of the patent safety hazard. Completion was defended on the grounds that the contracts would have cost more to set aside than to honor.

This outright stupidity well illustrates a highway program run amuck, snowballing at the hands of a highway lobby unrestrained by community sensitivity or basic planning foresight. A major revolution in transportation strategy has now taken place in the Boston area, championed most recently by a moratorium on freeway construction within the Route 128 zone. A thorough policy review has resulted in a complete switch in priorities whereby $1.5 billion will be invested in mass transit facilities over the next fifteen to twenty years. There will be no Inner Belt and no Northeast and Southwest expressways. Instead, rapid transit lines will be extended and upgraded, and commuter railroads will offer improved service.

The latest plans call for an almost total reinvestment of public money in mass transit facilities within the Route 128 ring (Figure 27). The essential element in the design is the MBTA, which will build and operate the enlarged transit system. The automobile will not be completely banned from the central city, and it is realized in any case that the cars of intown residents do not add much to the central congestion. However, the principle has been reasserted that daily central city movements should be primarily by rapid transit. In accordance with this major decision, the ban on in-town freeway construction emerges in perspective as one element of a series of synchronized steps in rationalizing metropolitan transport. The other key elements will consist of major extension and upgrading of rapid transit lines, upgrading and subsidization of some commuter railroads, the construction of gigantic parking facilities along Route 128 and elsewhere at the outer rapid transit terminals, and, as the capstone, a total, absolute freeze on available parking spaces within the central business district and its immediate fringes.

From a long term point of view, these proposals are definitely rational. They take into account human realities in the central city zone and display an unusual sympathy for the overall geographical structure of this historic metropolis. There are serious problems in the short term that will dog the plan's implementation. Foremost among these will be the delicate phasing of the various proposals in order to minimize widespread inconvenience during the twenty-odd years that the reorientation of metropolitan transport is expected to take. Second, there will have to be an unprecedented degree (by Boston standards) of political unanimity on the essential sanity of the measures, and a willingness on the part of local power brokers to expedite the required financing and to aid in educating residents in the general responsibilities of metropolitan residence.

An excellent picture of the status of transportation in the metropolis can be gained from the U.S. Census of Population. An overwhelming proportion of census tracts in the Boston SMSA are characterized by automobile travel as the dominant mode of traveling to work. This is not surprising, and is probably true for all major urban centers. However, Boston may be comparatively unusual in the number of tracts where the largest single

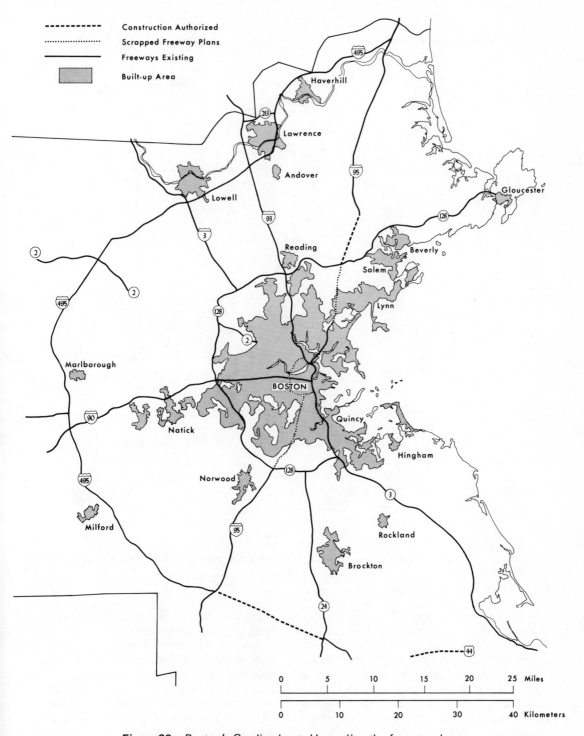

Figure 26. Boston's Gordian knot. Unraveling the freeway plans.

Figure 27. Extending Charlie's ride. Boston's future transit system? (After the Boston Transportation Planning Review)

proportion of their work force commute to work either on foot or by mass transit (Figure 28). Classifying census tracts by only the single most important commuting mode clearly ignores what may be substantial strength in other modes. Nevertheless, the crude pattern is revealing enough as it is, and shows remarkably compact and discrete zones of dominance by different modes.

It is possible that Boston has one of the largest pedestrian districts of any major American central city. By comparison, St. Louis, Missouri, a metropolitan area with a similar population to the Boston SMSA, contains a total of three census tracts in which walking to work is the dominant mode, and only one tract patronizing rapid transit facilities more than any other means of transport (Figure 28, Inset). Boston's pattern obviously reflects the city's small scale, high central density, and the historical proximity of many homes and many jobs within the core. Pedestrian dominance extends in wedge-shaped sectors outward from the downtown district. These sectors reflect the residential area close to the South Boston dockyards, and the student-heavy rooming

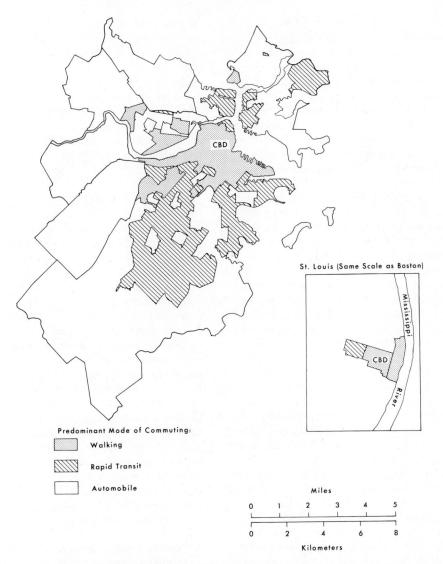

Figure 28. The three cities of Boston. Walking, transit, and auto zones, 1970. (After the U.S. Census)

house districts around Boston University, MIT, and Harvard Square. Equally dramatic is the zone of mass transit dominance, for with few exceptions it delineates heavily ethnic residential concentrations. In the North End, East Boston, and Charlestown, Italian and Irish tracts display compact areas primarily using rapid transit to work. In South Boston, with its longtime Irish elements, there is a second mass transit zone. The largest area of rapid transit dominance, however, is Roxbury-North Dorchester-Roslindale, containing in part the city's major black concentrations.

Apart from the ethnic correlation, the most striking feature of the overall pattern is the degree to which private automobile dominance encroaches on centrally located tracts, especially north of the Charles River in Somerville and East Cambridge and south in the area of Dorchester proper. There is a tendency for mass transit dominance to disappear where trolley lines and rapid transit tracks are absent, which suggests the lower proportional attraction of the bus network to commuters. Most impressive of all, however, is the correlation between what might be labeled "the walking and transit city" and zones of low per capita income within the metropolis as a whole (Figure 16). The correspondence is high between areas of low mean per capita income and extensive use of public transport or personal locomotion. The conclusion is plain. Public transport is utilized heavily, perhaps overwhelmingly, by the lower income strata of the metropolitan population, undoubtedly as much through a lack of economic alternatives as through convenience.

However, the corollary is that, if mass transit is to win over the major portion of the core city's daily commuters, the new patrons it must attract are those traditionally most able to purchase personal convenience and most able to sway the political system toward their preferences. In this context, therefore, the metropolitan transport decisions for the future are very bold. It remains to be seen how many middle and upper class commuters, unused to rubbing shoulders with less affluent fellow citizens, will adjust to a transportation revolution that is designed ultimately to save the physical assets and human quality of the metropolitan area.

The locational characteristics of the proposed changes in mass transit facilities indicate the importance of a general principle. The planned extensions of electric rapid transit are located for the most part through census tract areas with low per capita income. This is particularly true in the case of the Orange Line triple extensions which, if built, will traverse the broad wedge of low and lower middle per capita income areas to the south and southwest of the city center. Also, a badly needed inner belt line will substantially improve the intersectoral urban mobility of people traveling to work from this part of Boston as well as from other directions. Another feature of these extensions will be to tap the commuters from wealthy suburbs at the Route 128 ring. The availability of ready parking there together with speedy electric service downtown would undoubtedly entice the stockbrokers and executives from Boston's Cocktail Belt to patronize the transit system.

In summary, the profound changes planned for Boston's urban transportation system over the next two decades promise to salvage the metropolis from a long, strangling death at the hands of the automobile. The cardinal point about the plan is that it does not set out to ban the automobile across the board in the metro-

politan area—merely to reestablish a balance between the overall carrying capacities and advantages of the various transport modes available for intracity movement. Viewed as a technological problem, urban traffic congestion has long ago been solved (clean electric railcars came in the 1880s). Solving the congestion of today calls for slight adjustments in urban lifestyle rather than further disembowelment of the urban and social fabric of the city's neighborhoods.

CIVILIZING THE CITY

For the traveler, the city is a dot on a map. For the resident, the city is a stretch of ground with hills and hollows, earth and water. It is also a community of people with widely differing backgrounds, incomes, and aspirations. For the economist, the city is a collection of jobs that function to earn the city and its people a living. For the planner, the city is a built environment of physical structures arranged in space. But all these elements are merely the basic building blocks of a city, separate characteristics until they are articulated into a functioning whole by forces of order, direction, and creativity. Government, health care, education, and cultural activity become essential ingredients in civilizing the physical and biological city, in providing a humane environment in which the whole settlement can be not only an economic success, but also a human success in terms of social responsibility, individual satisfactions, and cultural consciousness.

Policing Change: Government and Municipal Services

Few, if any, large cities today are so homogeneous that continued growth and development can proceed without friction between special interests. Local government performs an essential role in mediating disputes among conflicting interests, adopting long term goals for the urban area as a whole, and providing standard services which private enterprise is unwilling or unable to deliver.

The Annexation Century. The legal city of Boston covers forty-six square miles of irregular territory in the center of an SMSA of 997 square miles and an "urbanized area" of 664 square miles. Thus, only a scant 7 percent of the geographical city (and 4.6 percent of the

SMSA) is under the political control of Boston's mayor! Although Boston is among the largest cities in the United States in population, it has one of the smallest land areas. Only San Francisco, of the fifteen largest metropolitan areas, has a central city smaller than Boston. The forty-six square miles that comprise Boston, moreover, are not neatly concentrated into a relatively compact, coherent area but are contained within a highly irregular, indeed a bizarre, set of boundaries (Figure 3). The irregularity of the land area of the city is accentuated by the separation of Boston into several isolated districts, divided by rivers, tidal estuaries, or ocean. "Mainland Boston" is tied to Charlestown by bridge, to East Boston by tunnel, and to Deer Island not at all. There are three other "mainland" peninsulas that are politically a part of Boston.

The original town of Boston was much, much smaller than even its present size (Figure 5). It included at first only the present downtown area on the Shawmut Peninsula. To the south were two other separate, independent municipalities—Roxbury on the southwest and Dorchester on the southeast. The town of Boston claimed two low-lying islands in the northern part of the harbor in 1635 and 1637, but neither of these two areas—Breed's (or Hog) Island and Noddle's Island—became effective urban territory until well into the nineteenth century. Further increases in Boston's territory did not occur until 1804, with the annexation of South Boston (called Dorchester Neck), the peninsula southeast of Boston on whose drumlin height Washington effectively placed cannon during the winter of 1775-1776.

Boston became an incorporated city in 1822, but the real increase in its size had to wait until after the Civil War. Then, in rapid succession, Boston convinced four relatively large neighboring towns to abandon their sovereignty and become part of Boston City. These annexations brought in Roxbury in 1868, Dorchester in 1870, and Brighton and West Roxbury in 1874. During that last year, Boston also added another neighboring peninsula, Charlestown, which lay a short distance beyond the mouth of the Charles River. Therefore, by 1874 Boston has assumed much the size and shape it has today, except for the annexation of Hyde Park in 1911.

Boston was able to prevail upon the residents of these adjacent communities to join her politically through her rapidly developing urban facilities and her apparent destiny as the metropolis of New England. Boston failed, however, to convince two other neighbors, Brookline and Cambridge, to join the annexation parade, and in both cases lands which should "naturally" have become politically united to Boston were not. The Brookline case is the most flagrant, for Brookline literally penetrates into the body of Boston, almost severing it at one point along Commonwealth Avenue. Brookline comes very close to being an enclave within Boston territory. Cambridge presents a somewhat less compelling case. The ownership of Cambridge (at least its easterly half) would have made for a more sensible shape for Boston City and given Boston both sides of the Charles River estuary, but the issue was never pursued as vigorously as with Brookline.

The city of Boston was left, after 1912, with a wide band of contiguous cities and towns, increasingly hostile to Boston as time went on. The historical strength of the New England town system of government, with a long tradition of political independence, coupled with a very weak country system and the increasingly immigrant complexion of Boston, fostered an early unwillingness to merge politically for the efficient provision of municipal services that were becoming increasingly metropolitan in scale. This legacy of highly splintered local government, a fairly general phenomenon among large American cities, led very quickly in Boston's case to problems needing intermunicipal cooperation, and Boston can be credited with some of the earliest experiments in metropolitan planning in the United States.

Innovations in Metropolitan Cooperation.
Boston has an almost century old system of areawide metropolitan services that should, under ordinary circumstances, make her the envy of other large U.S. cities. These services include water supply and sewage disposal, as well as park and recreation facilities. A substantial number of Boston's principal highways are also under metropolitan management with a uniformed traffic force to patrol them. But time has dulled the Bostonian's knowledge of these services, and a series of highly publicized scandals in the 1950s did not raise these metro-

politan organizations in the average Bostonian's esteem.

Boston was perhaps riper than most large metropolitan areas of the late nineteenth century for areawide services because of her very small size with respect to the total urbanized area. After the spate of annexations in 1874, Boston had reached her greatest political potential in terms of land area. That same year, there was considerable agitation for some new form of government to deal with functions at a greater than municipal scale. One proposal that came out of the studies and deliberations that followed 1874 was a suggestion to redraw the confusing and increasingly ineffective county boundary lines of the Boston region. Suffolk County, which contained Boston, was ridiculously small, and the rest of Boston's suburbs were split among Norfolk, Middlesex, and Essex Counties. This plan was never implemented.

Nature, however, overcame politics. The increasing pollution of Boston's rivers with raw sewage, especially the Charles, prompted a series of public health studies that led to the establishment of a Metropolitan Sewerage Board in 1889. This board was to construct an areawide system of sewers and the appropriate discharge, storage, or treatment plants to go with them. Neighboring cities and towns were anxious to be included in the sewerage district because their own separate disposal systems were inadequate or simply lacking.

Three years later the issue of parks and open recreation space raised an areawide problem. The period of establishing large parks and recreation sites (especially modeled after European examples) was in full sway. The legislature responded by establishing a Board of Metropolitan Park Commissioners who set out with speed and determination to provide Boston and the other cities and towns with two very large reservations—the Blue Hills Reservation in the south and the Middlesex Fells in the north—and a number of large beaches were immediately acquired and provided with facilities.

Water supply was next. Boston had already gone well outside her boundaries, even beyond the Boston Basin, to tap distant fresh water sources. Neighboring cities like Brookline were unable to provide water for their rapidly expanding populations, businesses, and factories. The Metropolitan Water District came into existence in 1895 and promptly set forth to build a major new reservoir fifty miles west of Boston and the delivery system needed to assure adequate fresh water at all times to Boston and the other member municipalities of that day. The crowning achievement of the Water District was the completion of the Quabbin Reservoir on tributaries of the Connecticut River in the 1930s, which gave metropolitan Boston the purest and most dependable water supply system in the eastern United States.

These three major functional boards were combined in 1919 into a single Metropolitan District Commission. Since that year, the number of communities serviced with water and sewage facilities has steadily increased. In recent years the MDC has seen the limit being approached in both cases and has stopped accepting new members until facilities are enlarged. The MDC has continued an active program of providing increased park and recreation facilities, ranging all the way from relatively undeveloped "natural" areas to swimming pools, ice skating rinks, and even a floodlit ski slope. Including Boston, the MDC now provides water to thirty-three municipalities and sewerage facilities to forty-three, and its park and recreation facilities in thirty-seven municipalities are naturally open to everyone (Figure 29). In the half century since 1919, only one other function has been raised as an MDC possibility for the future—solid waste disposal.

Boston has had long acquaintance with city and regional planning. Her professional planning schools are nationally famous, and Massachusetts' legislation on land use planning has served frequently as a model for bills introduced in other legislatures across the country. In the 1950s, new areawide studies were carried out, with transportation as a focus, but dealing with metropolitan economic problems as well. In 1963, the legislature established the first permanent areawide planning agency, the Metropolitan Area Planning Council (MAPC). By this time, neighboring cities tended to shun any association with Boston, and frictions existed between many suburbs over such topics as the location of dumps, sites for superhighways, and airport facilities. The mood for cooperation and coordination was far from congenial. The operating guidelines for the MAPC had to be drawn up with the greatest tact, and its responsibilities were set forth with heavy political considerations. Its present area

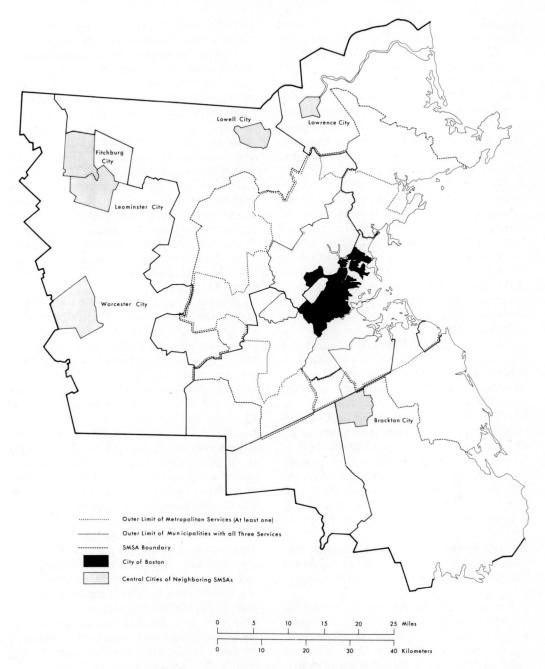

Figure 29. Governmental overlap in Greater Boston.

of responsibility includes eighty-three communities. In spite of the hostile environment of its birth, the MAPC has moved rapidly ahead with a series of thorough areawide studies suggesting a variety of ways in which serious regional problems could be met.

Boston has thus pioneered in the concept of metropolitan government, with the first legally constituted metropolitan district in the country for water, sewage disposal, and recreation. The addition of an areawide public transit authority and official regional planning agency add some further appearance of metropolitan government (Figure 29). These limited advances, however, serve only to accentuate the history of failures and missed opportunities in developing comprehensive planning and government for the entire urban system of Boston, such as the MDC report after 1894, Mayor Peters' proposal in 1919, and the Boston Contest in 1944.

Some signs of grudging enlightenment in the Boston area can be discerned. The major problem throughout the last hundred years has been the suspicion and jealousies of city and town leaders (whose numbers are, of course, legion). A slow reduction of hostile attitudes has occurred as they have found it possible to discuss municipal issues and to agree to cooperate on uniform solutions through membership in such forums as the Massachusetts League of Cities and Towns (1961), the MPAC (1963), and the Advisory Board of the MBTA (1964). The MAPC itself has actively solicited expert discussion of metropolitan governance, but no amount of talk will overcome the council's lack of political power.

Given the Greater Bostonians' sentimental attachment to the historical town as the first level of local government, some form of federated metropolitan council would seem to be the most that is politically feasible in the near future. However, no reorganization will substantially improve metropolitan government in the Boston area without a complete overhaul of the local systems of taxation. Most urgently needed is a coordinated program of public education in metropolitan responsibility, directed mainly to those outside the central city. A variety of plans exist already and have been tried out in other cities, and the voting public needs to be educated to acknowledge the metropolitan scale of urban problems to choose wisely among the already available alternatives.

Where Do All the Taxes Go? No further illustration of the diversity of Greater Boston is needed than the spatial pattern of metropolitan tax rates. Equalized tax rates are much higher in central cities than in suburban towns, but the lowest rates are not uniformly distributed around the metropolitan periphery (Figure 30). The city of Boston taxes its residents as much as four times the rate charged in many suburban communities—such as Wenham, Weston, Dover, and Dedham. In general, nearly all the towns with high per capita income (Figure 16) have low tax rates, although the reverse

is not completely true, for some low-taxed towns contain largely middle income residents.

Property taxes have been rising sharply in recent years. In the Boston area the average rate of increase between 1970 and 1972 was 19 percent. Combining above average equalized tax rates in 1972 with above average percentage rate increases over the previous two years, one finds that areas with heavy tax problems are concentrated almost exclusively in the cities within the metropolitan zone. Only Woburn and Salem show small rate increases, but these are due to already high rates in 1970. Cambridge, with a new tax rate of $92.40 per thousand dollars of property (equalized), experienced the highest increase (37 percent). Boston, however, charges by far the highest rate, $161.30 in 1972, followed by Chelsea with a $119.00 rate.

Differences in tax rates reflect more than governmental efficiency, of course, for there are great variations in the types and amounts of services provided by tax dollars. Indeed, it has long been an argument of central city administrators that their residents must frequently pay for road upkeep, utilities, sanitation, and other services used for the most part by a commuting work force that contributes nothing to their provision. No amount of discussion can detract from this bald fact, and it is the most compelling reason for local tax reform that could shift the load from property ownership to other bases. Boston suffers from this problem to an extreme degree.

A further embarrassment is the so-called "dwindling tax base" of the city of Boston. This decline is composed principally of losses of residential property through outmigration and abandonment, the flight of industry to the suburbs, and the slowly increasing proportion of tax-exempt property within the city. Efforts to halt the first two trends have already been mentioned. The third, tax-exempt property, has become a major political issue.

In 1970 a total of 12,795 acres of Boston's land area valued at $1.9 billion were exempt from taxes. These figures, which exclude streets and sidewalks, represent 43.5 percent of the city's land area and 53.7 percent of its total estimated valuation. New York City by contrast contained only 33.8 percent exempt property (by value) in 1969. The picture in Boston, however, is clouded by overevaluations

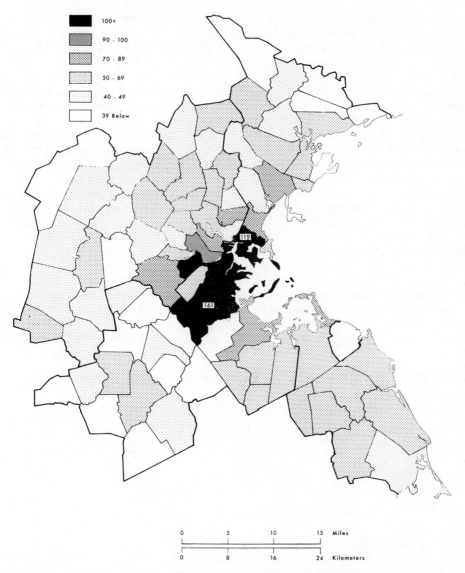

Figure 30. Equalized residential property tax rates, Boston SMSA, 1972. (After the Massachusetts Taxpayers Foundation)

of nontaxable property (for example, the Boston Common is valued at $133 million—maybe not high enough in view of historical sentiment, but definitely not realistic in commercial terms), and underevaluation of taxable property. The charge that colleges, museums, and foundations have been greatly eating into property that was formerly taxable is not accurate. A Massachusetts Taxpayers Foundation study found that the largest gains among tax-exempt property owners have been made in

the public sector, particularly by the Commonwealth of Massachusetts. Colleges have increased their holdings, but largely through more intensive use of land already exempt. On a ward-by-ward basis, there is no strong relation between decreases in the tax base and increases in tax exemption, although some individual cases conform to this link.

There is no consensus on the reasons for the relative decline of Boston's tax base, but the out migration of industry and middle income residents inevitably accounts for much of the problem. In a partial effort to recoup losses, urban renewal has begun to draw back into the city high income professional people willing to pay high rents for central locations, and also to increase massively the office industry within an expanded central business district. The costs of this approach are evident in the barrage of criticism leveled at the city administration for extending the welcome mat to prospective wealthy land users at the expense of middle and lower income groups who have remained in the city all the time.

A rational approach toward improving the financial base of central city services is not to put a stop to all signs of renewal—for Boston has much old property that needs renovation and in some cases replacement—but rather to widen the whole metropolitan tax base of the city. Even here there would be problems of political acceptance. In view of its central city function of providing a wide range of services to thousands living elsewhere in the Boston

daily urban system, Boston would have good reason to collect taxes from the larger metropolitan area (such as the employment tax on commuters to New York City). Such an arrangement, of course, would need to be arrived at through widespread political education in order to forestall parochial retaliation on the part of disgruntled local authorities unable to concede the ultimate fairness of such a plan.

For the time being, Boston labors to supply the traditional services of a large city for all to use largely with property taxes levied upon its beleaguered residents. General revenues amount to $718 per capita, substantially more than the metropolitan average for central cities ($531) but not as high as some cities such as New York (Table 8). A very high proportion of the revenues raised by the city itself—76.7 percent— comes from the property tax. This proportion is significantly higher than the metropolitan average and substantially higher than that of other very large SMSAs. Accordingly, Boston's direct general expenditures are above average

Table 8. Distribution of Central City Per Capita Expenditures among Services, Selected SMSAs, 1970–1971

	Boston 735,190		New York 7,895,563		St. Louis 622,236		Average among 72 Selected SMSAs	
	Dollars	Percent	Dollars	Percent	Dollars	Percent	Dollars	Percent
Total General Revenue	717.6		993.2		497.7		531.4	
Amount and Percent of Above from Own Sources	484.9	67.6	540.1	54.4	387.8	78.0	343.0	64.6
Property Tax Amount and Percent of Own Revenue	371.2	76.7	254.8	47.2	167.2	43.2	218.0	63.7
Direct General Expenditures	607.2	100.0	1076.1	100.0	500.4	100.0	545.6	100.0
Education	174.4	28.7	251.7	23.4	171.1	34.2	227.6	41.8
Highways	20.1	3.3	.26.5	2.5	13.8	2.8	26.0	4.8
Welfare	10.9	1.8	254.0	23.6	3.8	0.8	56.4	10.3
Health	72.8	12.0	127.9	11.9	60.2	12.0	35.0	6.4
Police	61.0	10.0	65.1	6.1	52.6	10.5	30.5	5.6
Fire Protection	39.3	6.5	28.4	2.6	17.6	3.5	15.1	2.8
Sewerage	5.2	0.9	15.9	1.5	39.3	7.9	16.5	3.6
Sanitation	14.5	2.4	26.0	2.4	6.3	1.3	9.9	1.8
Parks and Recreation	14.7	2.4	15.5	1.4	19.4	3.9	15.0	2.7
Administration	6.0	1.0	6.3	0.6	6.3	1.3	6.3	1.2
General Contributions	16.1	2.6	17.2	1.6	11.0	2.2	13.0	2.4
Interest (Debt)	28.9	4.8	36.9	3.4	22.7	4.5	20.3	3.7
Other	143.5	23.6	204.8	19.0	76.5	15.3	74.1	13.6

Source: U.S. Bureau of the Census. *Local Government Finances in Selected Metropolitan Areas and Large Counties: 1970–1971*, Series GF71, no. 6 (Washington, D.C., 1972).

($607 per capita), although within total general revenue. New York and St. Louis face an acute imbalance between revenue and expenses. This is not to imply that Boston runs at a profit, for substantial indirect expenditures push the city's total costs well beyond its annual intake.

While different cities seem to require different per capita amounts of money to run them, a clear sign of local priorities is the percentage distribution among public expenditures (Table 8). Boston spends proportionately far less on education, welfare, and sewerage than the average central city, and far more on health, police, and fire protection. Out of total direct expenditures of $607 per capita, the amount spent on welfare, for example, is only $11, constituting 1.8 percent of the whole, thanks to the state's involvement in the city's welfare provision. Other expenses—such as parks and recreation, sanitation, administration, and financial obligations—are proportionately similar to the metropolitan average. In contrast with Boston, New York places enormous emphasis on welfare payments, but shares Boston's bias toward health and against education. St. Louis, which is similar to Boston in central city size and therefore useful for comparative purposes, gives similar priority to health and police, but is even less concerned with welfare problems and extremely concerned with sewerage.

Bureaucrats and Politicians. At 180,000 strong, Boston's bureaucrats are quantitatively no more dominant in their city than elsewhere, for they make up only 14 percent of the work force and have done so roughly since 1951. Qualitatively, however, they are special. Government in Massachusetts and Greater Boston has long displayed anarchical symptoms of either outmoded methods or under the table political dealings. In many ways the area is well governed, considering the problems, but adjustments in basic structure have been slow to come. A recent census of government listed 147 separate local administrative units within the SMSA, yielding an average area of 6.8 square miles per unit and an average population of 18,733 persons per unit. This contrasts with Baltimore, to choose a random example, which with twenty-nine local governments averages 77.9 square miles and 71,463 persons per unit. Similarly, Boston's eighty-four school systems average 6,560 pupils per system, whereas Baltimore's ten school systems cater to an average of 48,583 pupils each.

The problem of multiplicity of governmental units in metropolitan areas is certainly not unique to Boston, but for Boston it is extremely severe. The prospects for change are clouded not only by the usual fears of giving the central city power structure increased influence, but also by the lingering and quaint Yankee view that no public institution can improve upon the New England town meeting as the ideal form of government. Times change, and this view represents an unfortunate misperception of the role of historical tradition in a modernizing urban world.

Unlike most large American cities, Boston contains the local state capitol. The circumstance has guaranteed a lively political arena of state and city legislators. Picking up the scent of *The Last Hurrah*, the trail leads down the short hill from the gold-domed state house to the fortresslike city hall at Government Center. Designed to symbolize embattled city government serving the people, the building exudes a modernity hardly reflecting the city's approach to solving its mammoth urban problems. The tax base teeters with the erosion of manufacturing plants, and housing policies and mass transportation plans represent too little too late. But for all the city's small scale, which at least keeps its problems within sight, the fact is, as a local political commentator has put it, Boston is a city of "[p]ersonalities instead of parties and controversies instead of issues." Encouraging, however, is the extent to which local community preferences are slowly winning governmental attention. One example is the halting of freeway construction within the Route 128 perimeter discussed earlier.

Boston is experimenting with a bold form of municipal decentralization symbolized by "little city halls." Other large cities are also moving cautiously toward decentralization of their monolithic bureaucracies, but the Boston plan is to date the most innovative and commands most public attention. Responding to charges that city hall has lost contact over the years with ordinary citizens, Mayor Kevin White has instituted a program of establishing neighborhood centers with direct links to the central administrators and departments. So far, there are fourteen "little city halls," housed either in old municipal edifices or in parked trailers, located for the most part in the centers of historically distinct neighborhoods. The assumption was made that the fourteen areas, which average some 50,000–75,000 persons each and which were often independent political units before annexation, have different characteristics of income, ethnicity, and age structure, and that they have individual problems and special concerns that require unique approaches to cope with them.

To respond to the genuine feeling that there were community level values which had been neglected in the city in the past, these little city halls have been established to provide a variety of services. Most important among these are the availability of some standard services such as accepting utility payments, helping with application forms, processing of complaints, and providing information about citizen rights, privileges, and municipal organization. In addition, they have available a variety of locally assigned inspectors for housing, fire hazards, and sanitation, and special programs for voter registration, parking permits, and the like. Located according to market-oriented studies of prime business and shopping activity in each neighborhood, the little city halls are run by managers appointed for their known ability to get things done. Acting as buffers between the citizen and the city bureaucracy, the managers are encouraged to balance divided loyalties. On the one hand, he or she is an ombudsman processing routine complaints and explaining city procedures, but on the other hand, the manager may well support and indeed stimulate local sentiment on large issues. For example, the East Boston manager is credited with leading the fight to limit expansion of Logan International Airport because local opinion was strongly against it.

Little city halls have been controversial since their inception in 1970. Citizens have used the facilities increasingly over time, and the computer-coordinated complaint system is considered to work well in general. It is certainly the first time in the city's history that accurate and detailed information on volume and type of complaints about city services has been made available. At present, for example, complaints about lack of heat and hot water, and garbage and litter on open lots, alone account for nearly one-quarter of all tabulated complaints. It has been shown that in 90 percent of the cases the city is at least technically in a position—i.e., has jurisdiction—to do something about them.

In general, the advantages seem to outweigh the disadvantages, although worries about little city halls without real power just adding one more layer of bureaucracy to a top-heavy system are quite legitimate. Also, it is difficult to keep politics and patronage out of their administration, as in all public affairs in Boston, but a serious attempt at appointing effective managers is being made. Whether little city halls will be the catalysts for the major institutional change that is so greatly needed in Boston is highly doubtful, but there is some experimenting with ways to increase community participation in local government. Withal, this effort only affects the city of Boston. And what of Cambridge, Somerville, Quincy, Chelsea, and others? Brookline, for example, virtually embedded as it is within Boston's territory, is still legally a "town," not even a city, yet its problems are also Boston's problems.

Renewal to Renovation. Government has always played an important role in contributing to the physical landscape of the city. Over time this role has increased its scope. Nineteenth century Boston saw unprecedented plans for city park systems, grand boulevards, and ostentatious neo-Scottish-baronial public buildings emerge from the clutter of small town architecture of early times. The present century has seen even greater scale changes, with skyscrapers and huge slum clearance projects vastly altering major portions of old city centers. For decades in this century, Boston escaped widespread renewal, and only the Depression created some areas of large scale public housing based on slum clearance. Even so, this was low, two or three story development, avoiding high-rise gigantism of the New York variety.

When urban renewal programs got underway in the late 1940s, government in Boston was quick to establish the necessary public mechanisms to promote urban renewal. The various planning, coordinating, and implementation functions were eventually brought together under the Boston Redevelopment Authority in 1957. Soon a dynamic new director, Edward J. Logue, was to be hired and Boston was to be jolted into a far-reaching program. It is important to credit the then new mayor, John F. Collins, anxious to rescue his city from an obvious decline in livability, and a congeries of bankers and financiers, that would prove to be the key movers in Boston's resurrection. Following the partly private Prudential renewal project in the Back Bay, the next impetus came with the Government Center project. This ambitious scheme was proposed for the northern edge of the CBD in an area occupied by run-down commercial and wholesale establishments, all-night movies, burlesque houses, and tattoo parlors. Sailors knew it only as Scollay Square (Figure 31).

The area was condemned and razed, with a few historic buildings preserved. The foci of the center were to be a new city hall, a high-rise federal office building complex, and a state office building (Figure 32). All were to be grouped around a plaza of extraordinary size, especially for a part of Boston characterized by narrow, winding streets. Private commercial and office buildings, parking garages, and the like were to complete the project. Except for the razing of the Old Howard, Boston's oldest and most famous burlesque house, few tears

were shed. The completion of this project, with its great open space and its remarkable new city hall, provided tangible evidence that the city could be changed and, hopefully, revitalized.

A somewhat different story emerged in the first large scale "bulldozer" type of renewal project in the West End. This neighborhood lay on the northwest side of the original Boston peninsula, squeezed between the Massachusetts General Hospital complex on the south and the North Station commercial district on the north. This was a very densely built-up section of the city with narrow, winding cobblestoned streets along which ranged five and six story brick tenements of considerable age. The condition of these buildings was to some extent in the eye of the beholders. To the redevelopment authority it was a "slum"; to the residents it was home and community.

The fever of renewal was rampant in Boston political circles, and the need was felt for a dramatic demonstration project. The West End proposal was tantamount to the complete de-

Figure 31. Scollay Square in 1961 before renewal. (Courtesy of the Boston Redevelopment Authority.

Figure 32. Government Center in 1973 after renewal. This view was taken from the same spot as Figure 31. (Courtesy of the Boston Redevelopment Authority)

truction and reconstruction of the area. It was pushed with vigor and determination against the will of the equally determined but far more vocal local population. The city won. Block after block was razed, until a vast wasteland stretched from the edge of the Charles River to the foot of Beacon Hill. Subsequent developments could easily be predicted. A series of high-rise towers of something less than elegant style rose from the rubble, with rentals ranging from $300 to $500 per month per unit. A small shopping center–office complex followed, as well as appropriate swimming pool and other amenities. A large sign was placed adjacent to the new complex in clear view of the thousands of commuters leaving the city proclaiming—

with both smugness and indisputable correctness—"You'd be home now if you lived here." It *is* a good place to live—handy to the downtown with magnificent views of the harbor and the Charles River—for those with the necessary wealth! By 1970 there were 3,659 such new residents, and little did most of them know of the tragic human drama that had taken place on that site. And the folk who left? With scant assistance from government they scattered themselves all over the city and its adjacent suburbs.

The West End project gained national notoriety as epitomizing the "federal bulldozer," but some BRA officials felt it was needed to demonstrate to middle and upper income families (many of whom had fled to the suburbs) that it was possible to move back to the central city in comfort and safety. A smaller, less famous, but even more brutal story was played out adjacent to the Harvard Business School at the North Harvard Street project.

Elsewhere, urban renewal was used to clear a large area of mixed land uses south of the CBD for a light industrial zone. Opposition to bulldozing was mounting, however, especially where housing was to be demolished, so the urban renewal of the 1960s began to take on much more of a rehabilitation flavor. In particular, neighborhood consultation was sought. When a massive scheme was first proposed for largely run-down Charlestown, it received equally massive resistance, and the whole thrust of the plan was gradually shifted away from "traditional" renewal programs to housing for the elderly, public housing on abandoned industrial land, rehabilitation, and the general upgrading of streets and lighting, new firehouses, libraries, and schools.

In Roxbury, urban renewal concentrated on a number of small housing projects—eventually building over 4,500 new units—and in community facility improvement. The Washington Park project, initiated in 1963 and costing a total of $70 million, provided a wide variety of improvements in what was then the center of the black residential area (Figure 22). A large area of dilapidated housing in adjacent lower Roxbury, razed in the 1960s and designated for a large, campus-style, citywide high school, has remained a wasteland of weeds and broken brick, as Boston's school integration pot simmers and boils over on the political stove.

Such recent renewal thrusts as rehabilitation, Model Cities, and neighborhood development projects have been incorporated into the continuing Boston renewal program. The most active program in the early 1970s centers on the waterfront, where two high-rise luxury apartment buildings—Harbor Towers—have gone up next to Boston's handsome new (private) Aquarium. A thorough renovation and upgrading of the picturesque, historic market district including Faneuil Hall and Quincy Market, and the old produce wholesaling buildings that house the Durgin-Park restaurant, will provide a new focus for tourism.

Urban renewal in Boston's suburbs, like public housing, went on at a very modest scale and at widely scattered sites. Cambridge tried and eventually abandoned formal, federal-type renewal as too hot a political potato. Lynn, Newton, and other cities initiated schemes which were aimed at downtown rejuvenation, general neighborhood upgrading, and industrial sites.

Every age renews some of the urban fabric bequeathed to it by history, but few periods have witnessed such wholesale destruction of viable housing and social organisms as the modern era. Belated realization of the wantonness of massive urban renewal has opened a new era of renovation. This is an auspicious trend if mortgage and rehabilitation funds are provided by government on a sufficient scale to enable middle and lower income groups to participate in the renovation process. This will be a sterling test of government's social responsibility towards all taxpayers in the metropolitan area.

Teaching and Healing

The twin areas of education and health illustrate more emphatically than anything else a supreme irony about Boston. The metropolis houses some of the very finest universities and medical institutions on the continent, and yet major aspects of education and health provision for the bulk of the population are seriously inadequate. Thanks to the property base of school taxation, some suburbs, such as Newton and Lincoln, have exemplary primary and secondary school systems, while others and the central city limp along with insufficient facilities and outmoded methods. The city of Boston, for example, has produced some of the lowest big city reading scores in the nation, and control of the School Committee has been such as to precipitate withholding of federal aid to schools on account of entrenched racial prejudice. Despite the considerable effort by the city to erect new buildings in the last three years, basic improvements in the *quality* of local education are unlikely to come without more involvement from local universities and colleges on the one hand, and a major depoliticization of the school system hierarchy on the other. This latter need is not likely to receive urgent attention.

The most critical aspect of Boston's educational environment is the high degree of racial segregation in its schools, in which blacks are in a majority of over two-thirds. Although blacks comprise only 16 percent of the city's total population, their children constitute 36 percent of the public school population, and 68 percent of these children attend the highly segregated schools. This situation arises from the unusually high proportion of white children who in Boston attend church-run schools. The closing of many parochial schools owing to financial stringencies in recent years and changing residence patterns have served to increase the pressures on the public school system.

Massachusetts has prohibited racial discrimination in its public schools since 1855, but the most recent cause for conflict has been the racial imbalance law of 1965, which forbids the continuance of individual schools with largely black or white pupils. This law has aroused the ire of all social groups within the city of Boston. Whites resent legislation that was created largely with the support of suburban liberals salving their consciences, whose own towns' zoning ordinances effectively shielded them from minority neighbors. Thus, immune themselves, the suburbanites were thrusting compliance with the law largely upon the predominantly ethnic, lower income whites of the inner city. Blacks in the city feel equally unhappy with the situation because extensive busing to achieve balance seems cumbersome, and because redistribution of power to blacks in teaching and administrative positions would help much more than busing children around the city.

As a result, the law has failed to work, and while forty-five schools were said to be racially imbalanced in 1965, the figure had risen by 1973 to sixty-seven schools. Much of the responsibility for this situation rests with the elected five man Boston School Committee. Its members are all lawyers except one, and all of them are simultaneously Democrats, politicians, Irish, Roman Catholic, and unswervingly "antibusing." The committee has responded to, and in some ways encouraged, public uproars over school integration, and in the process so hindered implementation of the imbalance law that both state and federal aid to education in the city has been stopped. Immense litigation has ensued, and clearly the withholding of essential operating funds cannot be borne for long.

There is widespread recognition now that the racial imbalance law was an oversimplistic attack on a complex problem. Boston can be proud of some of its schools, like the two Latin schools, but the bulk of its ethnic and low in-

come population has received a poor education. Local reformers see this tradition of inadequate schooling, coupled with the timidity of a church that has failed to work effectively for race relations, as largely responsible for a "fearful population." While this may be true, however, the lack of a substantial middle class in Boston has brought low income white into conflict with low income black. City officials now believe that desegregation by class is far more imperative than by race.

If the picture of recent public education is one of persistent failure on the racial issue, there have been some experiments and successes. New schools have been built. Only five new schools were constructed between 1945 and 1965; in the decade since 1965, thirty-seven schools have been added to the system. Buildings and facilities, however, may not be as important in improving the learning environment as changes in teacher attitudes and the social and cultural isolation of the children. In this connection, considerable success in voluntary city-suburb cooperation has been gained by the Metropolitan Council for Educational Opportunity (METCO) in its small program of placing 1,650 black youngsters in schools in twenty-nine suburban towns. The scheme reaches only 5 percent of the inner city black school population, however, and is thus no ultimate solution at its present scale.

At the root of the problem lies the basic antagonism between city and suburb. The mayor may or may not succeed in his bid to abolish the School Committee and transfer its responsibilities to a regular city department, but the crucial battle will come in amalgamating a city and suburban school district. It has become a travesty of justice that eighteenth and nineteenth century political boundaries should allow those who earn a good living from and benefit by the social and cultural attractions of the city to escape responsibility for its problems merely by moving just beyond its technical limits.

At the university level, Greater Boston fairly staggers under the weight of concentrated intellectual talent. Within twenty miles of the state house there are fifty-six degree-granting institutions of higher learning enrolling just under 170,000 students and releasing annually 30,000 graduates of whom one-third have higher degrees. The figures are coincidentally intriguing—for virtually every bureaucrat in the region there is a student! By size, the most significant institution is Northeastern University with 41,700 students, well over half of whom are part time, and nearly all of whom commute. More representative an institution is Boston University with 25,100 students, mostly resident. In terms of national prestige, the undoubted jewels of metropolitan Boston's educational crown are Harvard University and the Massachusetts Institute of Technology with 19,000 and 8,000 students respectively. Other nationally known centers include Boston College, Brandeis University, Tufts University, and Wellesley College.

The reputation of the Boston area is not lost on students around the country. One out of every forty students in the United States attends college in Greater Boston. It has been estimated that there are more books in college libraries in the area than in the combined public libraries of Chicago, Los Angeles, Detroit, Philadelphia, and San Francisco. A survey was made by David Buerle recently to determine the extent to which the cultural influences of Boston and New York overlapped in their common hinterland in southern New England. Interviewees were polled as to their preferences for equivalent colleges in the two cities, and the patterns that emerge are revealing. Boston University consistently drew preferences from 30 to 55 percent of the people when compared with New York University which drew 5 to 25 percent preferences. Distance from each city had some effect on preference levels throughout the interview area, but the attraction lay clearly with the Boston institutions. A comparison of Boston College and Fordham University in New York produced a similar result.

The consequences of this concentration of colleges and universities in the Boston region are many, but two principal effects must be acknowledged. First, the 170,000-odd students residing in the metropolis impart to it a young, active, involved, and exciting personality. Students simultaneously are attracted by and contribute to an extraordinarily high level of cultural activity that has drawn large numbers of other young people not attending school. For many students this town is definitely "The Hub"; and even for the jaded New Yorker, forced by the prospect of a first-class education in Boston to leave the only city that ever existed, there is the grudging concession that for a town in the sticks Boston

has indeed a lot of life in it. The second consequence has been commented upon already—namely, that a unique liaison has grown up between the university community in Boston and the world of industry, business, and government.

Another area of contact, between universities and the health industry, is perhaps even more characteristic because so much research and teaching is shared by colleges and hospitals that their independent identities are often blurred. Boston is undoubtedly one of the chief medical meccas in America, and the health industry in the area benefits accordingly. It is correct to refer to the health field in Boston as an industry (some have even called it a "cottage industry") because much of its activity is legally private enterprise. Only in recent years has concern become widespread for the dissemination of health care as a general "delivery system" to all parts of the city and all sectors of the population. Acceptance of the view that easy access to health care is a human right, not a privilege to be dearly bought, has been as slow in Boston as elsewhere.

For those with easy access, Boston medicine is superlative. In addition to the world-renowned Massachusetts General Hospital, the area boasts Tufts New England Medical Center, Peter Bent Brigham Hospital, Beth Israel Hospital, and fine medical schools at Harvard University, Boston University, and Tufts University. An extensive amount of research is carried out at these facilities, and major developments are being made in the application of computer technology to medical diagnosis. For those with money, and for those with exotic ailments, the medical machine is ready to roll whenever called upon. Routine health care requirements, however, are another matter.

Boston has 197 physicians for every 100,000 inhabitants, which compares favorably with the national average of 123. But out of the 197 total, there are only sixty-eight "primary care" physicians available for each 100,000 people on a daily basis, and even these are highly concentrated in the suburbs—and the wealthier ones at that. While only 35 percent of the physicians handle primary care, it is estimated that 80 percent of the population's health needs in manpower fall into this category. Another way of looking at the metropolitan health picture is to view the proportions of psychiatrists and pediatricians available. There are 725 practicing psychiatrists serving a clientele drawn largely from the ranks of upper middle class adults, whereas only 425 pediatricians exist to service 1,200,000 children and dependent youths.

The decline of general practitioners has been tremendous since World War II. In 1940 there were 132 such "primary care" physicians available in the general community per 100,000 persons. By 1961 the ratio had fallen to sixty-seven physicians. Much more serious, however, has been the geographical inequalities to providing local care. Because physicians have tended increasingly to locate their residence and practices in wealthier neighborhoods of the city, according to J.L. Dorsey, the urban poor have been losing access to physicians at an alarming rate (Table 9). While both the wealthy and the poor have lost general practitioners in their districts, there continues to be a differential between the groups. Intermediate care facilities actually increased between 1940 and 1961 for wealthy neighborhoods, whereas they remained at the exceptionally low rate of eight per 100,000 persons in poor districts. The general practitioner has been disappearing in all parts of the city, and a shift to hospital care

Table 9. Access to Physicians in Boston and Brookline, for Different Social Classes, 1940–1961

Socioeconomic Class*	Doctors per 100,000 Population	
	1940	*1961*
Primary[+]		
Uppermost 40 percent of social scale	218	86
Lowest 40 percent of social scale	96	53
Intermediate[++]		
Uppermost 40 percent of social scale	94	116
Lowest 40 percent of social scale	8	8

*Based on median values relating to income, education, and occupation, calculated by individual census tracts.

[+]Primary physicians: general practitioners.

[++]Intermediate physicians: pediatricians, gynecologists, etc.

Source: J.L. Dorsey, "Physician Distribution in Boston and Brookline, 1940 and 1961," *Medical Care* (November-December 1969): 429–440.

has taken up the "slack." This trend, however, can more easily be borne by the well-to-do who can afford expensive health insurance and are not inconvenienced in reaching appropriate hospitals.

The general image of Boston medicine may be high and widespread, but the problem is an embarrassment of riches poorly apportioned. Some steps are leading in the right direction. The Harvard Community Health Plan is a case in point, but its clients hardly form a community, for it represents an amalgam of employee groups dispersed throughout the metropolitan area. The problem will not be ameliorated until *area* health care is widespread and efficient. The few neighborhood clinics that now operate in the face of budget stringencies and hospital indifference or opposition collectively cast a considerable shadow over the social responsibility of the Greater Boston medical world and dim the lustre of its genuine excellence.

Entertainment and Edification

A great deal can be written about Boston's rich cultural life which, in the eastern United States, is widely considered second only to that of New York. The danger lies in encyclopaedism. In almost every field of endeavor—music, drama, visual arts, libraries, historical associations, mass communications, sports, and recreation—Boston has its luminaries. Even the shortest list of cultural phenomena must include the Boston Symphony Orchestra, the Boston "Pops," the Opera Company of Boston, the Boston Ballet Company, the New England Conservatory of Music, the Boston University Celebrity Series, the Boston Public LIbrary, the Boston Atheneum, the Bostonian Society, the Boston Globe, Boston After Dark, WGBH-TV (public television), the Aquarium, the Boston Bruins, the Red Sox, and New England Patriots, the Boston Celtics, Chinatown, the Massachusetts State Lottery, and organized crime.

A concomitant of the university presence in Boston is the extremely varied roster of college theater, music, and fine arts available in the region. In addition, many highly specialized cultural institutions have located in Boston, often on account of the intellectual threshold that exists in this metropolis and few others. Many reflect a long continuity of location within the city since the nineteenth century. There must be few cities that can equal the extra-ordinary menu of public lectures in and out of the university arena. A few singular Boston institutions or cultural "conditions" need emphasis.

First, the historical heritage dies very hard. Thus, for all the "invasions" of Celts, Latins, and Russians during the last century, many of Boston's institutions maintain an "Englishness" that sets the metropolis apart from any other in the United States. This manifests itself not only in legacies from the past—such as after-noon tea at the Boston Atheneum, sadly, discontinued of late—but in a perceptible An-glophilia, detectable especially among some academics. It causes little wonder, therefore, to discover the existence of the Longwood Cricket Club. This cultural strain is perforce muted in Boston, drowned out often by the heady vigor of more raucous cultures and pervasive Ameri-canization. But where else in the United States can a Briton say "tom-ar'-toe" and be under-stood?

A second condition is the sports fever around town. One local commentator has called it Boston's "unending love affair, that's what it is." Hockey, basketball, baseball, football, tennis, soccer, and lacrosse all have major league teams in the metropolitan area. The arch-rival is usually New York, a complement gen-erally returned. Boston fans exert themselves not only at the games, but also on the tele-phone to a clutch of highly successful radio sports talk shows. Local newspapers carry some of the most extensive sports coverage in the whole country. And in the sports capital of the U.S.A. they also have such relatively eso-teric activities as the internationally famous annual Boston Marathon and frequent rowing contests during the summer drawing much strength from the many colleges at water's edge.

A final theme that applies to Boston's cul-tural health is the vigor of its communications media. *The Boston Globe* may not rank with *The New York Times,* but it is not too far be-hind. The metropolis is also home for the *Christian Science Monitor* and the *Atlantic Monthly,* as well as numerous cultural publica-tions with a more regional emphasis. Book publishing is a particular strength of the region. The electronic media, although suffocating un-der a network load of inane programming and asphyxiating commercials, manage to air some excellent locally produced material. Chief among these is WGBH-TV, the major of two public television channels in Boston and a very early establishment in public broadcasting, which is responsible for, among other things, "The Advocates," "The French Chef," "Eve-ning at Pops," "ZOOM," "NOVA," and the importation of "Masterpiece Theater," all of which are syndicated throughout much of the national public television system. There is lit-tle doubt that the outstanding quality of this type of programming derives in part from the deep reservoir of artistic talent available in the cultural life of the New England metropolis.

What, then, is Boston? It is a place, a city, a metropolis, with its own geography and its own history. One can dissect and describe it from many perspectives, to present an objec-tive picture of its place in the larger scheme of things and people's place in it. But Boston's structure, functions, people, and fabric to-gether create a special blend of metropolitan living that challenges objective portrayal. In the end, one is tempted to ask, What does it feel like to be in Boston, and what kind of city do people perceive it to be? The city's image becomes important not only for external prestige, but for the levels of satisfaction that it affords its citizens. What, then, are the criti-cal components of this image?

Part III

The Image Is the City

URBAN VIEWPOINTS

> The principal difference between Harvard
> and Yale is Boston, and the principal distinc-
> tion of Boston is that it is totally unlike any-
> thing in Illinois, and the chief difference
> between anything in Illinois—say, Chicago—
> and Boston is that Boston has citizens who
> wear the kind of felt hat you can still see
> on the hooks at the Tavern Club.
>
> —Archibald MacLeish

Boston, like any large metropolis, looks different from the outside than from inside. Visitors see it differently from residents, and those
who visit or live in it by desire may receive
other impressions from those compelled by
business or employment to be there. Almost
inevitably, images of the metropolis are derived from its center, that small nexus of peak
activity and densest environment that most
plainly exhibits the city's depth of history and
unique development of site.

A canvass of periodical writing and scholarly study on the question of Boston's image produces a composite picture that can best be
grasped by delineating two intersecting dimensions. The first dimension contrasts the out-
sider with the insider. Insiders' everyday
images of the city naturally differ from the
more episodic but more widely diffused views
of those who live elsewhere or those whose
cosmopolitan travel adds an external perspective to the city's local character. The second
dimension contrasts the dual elements of environmental fabric with human atmosphere.
Bricks and mortar, streets and parks provide a
powerful physical framework for structuring
the urban image, but the imaginative lubri-
cant that breathes life into the picture is, of
course, the essence of the social scene.

View from Outside

Above all, outsiders see Boston as a compact place—green, manageable, and relatively
small. The old town is seen as crowded, with
narrow and crooked streets—definitely a place
to walk rather than drive in or take a cab
through. As if retaliating for the legacy of a
seventeenth century street system, Boston
drivers impress visitors as positively demonic.
The customary shock of downtown's laby-
rinthine street pattern totally blinds the out-
of-towner to the great expanses of gridiron
roads that exist beyond the peninsula's tip
if, indeed, he ever ventures there. History is
writ large on Boston's image with plentiful
reminders of the Revolution such as Paul
Revere's House, The Old North Church, Bunker
Hill, and Faneuil Hall (food downstairs and
ideas upstairs).

Outsiders see Boston as a center of education and finance, a mecca for the young, and a
rich fountain of cultural life, particularly of the
cerebral kind. Boston is also regarded as the
most European of American cities. Its history
is viewed in terms not only of old buildings, but
also of early institutions. The city had the first
bank, the first public school, and the first newspaper in the land. Apart from the Boston Massacre and the Boston Tea Party, the city's history

is widely known for its Puritan past, which many outsiders believe still affects its social climate. Many books and plays have been banned in Boston over the years, and as for serious night life—forget it!

Nevertheless, Boston draws good marks for entertainment. Its restaurants are highly regarded, particularly for seafood, and afterward there are the Boston Pops concerts, or evening games of hockey and basketball, or a pre-Broadway theatrical show. For the bargain hunter, Filene's Basement enjoys a national reputation.

The city's literary stature seems well established. The intellectual home of Emerson, Hawthorne, Lowell, Longfellow, Holmes, Whittier, and Thoreau, Boston is constantly tapped by national publishers and broadcasters for its creative talent. But for all the fame of the Brahmin culture, an engaging balance is maintained for the outside world with the city's perpetual brand of "rousing" politics. And out of this caldron have come the likes of Henry Cabot Lodge, the Kennedys, Leverett Saltonstall, John McCormick, James Michael Curley, Kevin White, Louise Day Hicks, Edward Brooke, and Eliot Richardson. Perhaps in no other American city over the decades has an old, established elite mingled so thoroughly in the urban arena with the more recent generations of ethnic politicians.

Most outside assessments of Boston constantly fuse references to its social atmosphere with references to its physical characteristics. For non-Bostonians, Boston's people and life "fit" with their urban environment unusually snugly. The city's history has at once produced interesting people and an interesting landscape —not all big city images display such unity.

For all the plaudits, Boston's "fan club" around the nation is somewhat select. In a national poll of city preferences conducted by the Gallup Organization in 1969, people across the country failed to place Boston among the top ten cities in which they would most choose to live. Cities that ranked considerably higher than Boston included San Francisco, Los Angeles, Miami, Denver, New York, Phoenix, San Diego, Chicago, Honolulu, and Portland, Oregon. Boston achieved some commendation for its food and degree of interest and special character, but even here it was outshone consistently by New York, San Francisco, Los Angeles (!), and New Orleans.

One conclusion that might be drawn from the divergent assessments of literati and average home-owning Americans is that Boston has to be visited to be appreciated. The city's peripheral geographic position, combined with its northern latitude, certainly cause it to lose out in the mass tourist market. There is, for example, no Disney World near Boston to suck in the summer trade. But then, Boston has resisted the incursions of the "Big Mac" and Kentucky Fried Chicken more than most places, which adds precisely to its charm.

View from Inside

However useful or prestigious it is for a city to be well liked by outsiders, the image it has among its own residents is ultimately more important, for it is they who must experience it every day and share its advantages and shortcomings. Inevitably, too, the resident has a vastly more intensive image of the city than the visitor, etched from constant experience of its pleasures and frustrations.

Bostonians have a clear sense of living in an "old" environment, steeped in history. The fact that a row of apartment houses now stands where clipper ships once were berthed persuades one that history is part of the working, living city. To residents—even more so than to visitors—Boston is a walking city (at least its center is), carved from hills and harbors and, as architect Benjamin Thompson has said, "scaled to the six-foot man and the three-foot child."

Not so long ago, Boston seemed Americanized but not plasticized. Now, the urban core is threatened with a loss of identity. "Glaring at each other in mute isolation," writes Joseph Eldredge, are "buildings that seem to dare the city to absorb them into its 18th Century fabric ... structures conceived in the 19th Century Manhattan economic matrix that condemned that island to an eternity of roaring canyons filled with predatory taxi-cabs." Boston has lost its low skyline for good, and many people exult that the new visual profile seems better equipped to mirror the excitement of a big city.

People's attitudes toward urban form have rarely and only with great difficulty been subjected to objective measurement of any sort. Some years ago, Kevin Lynch set out to characterize the image that central Boston created in the consciousness of its residents. Conceptualizing the townscape as a congeries of paths, edges, nodes, districts, and individual landmarks, he first mapped the city center according to an "objective" field survey and then interviewed sample residents in depth to reconstruct mental maps from verbal descriptions and sketches. On the basis of frequency of recognition, a derivative map of the "distinctive elements" of Boston emerged (Figure 33). Even in a dense, downtown environment, it is clear that not all visual arrangements of streets and buildings leave lasting impressions on people's minds. Some districts, some shopping streets and boulevards, some intersections, and one or two "edges," like waterfronts, serve important mental functions of articulating the inner city's geography—the rest lapses into limbo, to be recognized only by incidental travel.

However, spare this urban imagery of central Boston is, Lynch describes Boston as unique among American cities, "being both vivid in form and full of locational difficulties." The survey was conducted in the late 1950s, and recent urban renewal would certainly alter the mental maps. Government Center, for example, has replaced Scollay Square and undoubtedly forms a distinctive node in today's scene. The new high-rise towers likewise create individual landmarks that might fill out the mental map. Boston's vividness, nevertheless, can be assessed in roughly quantitative terms. Using identical survey methods, a contrasting picture of Los Angeles' downtown area displays far fewer distinctive elements in the minds of that city's residents (Figure 34). Boston can boast more distinctive (mentally recorded) paths, edges, nodes, and districts, trailing Los Angeles only in individual landmarks.

Boston is, according to Lynch's subjects, "a dirty city, of red-brick buildings, symbolized by the open space of the Boston Common, the State House with its gold dome, and the view across the Charles River from the Cambridge side ... an old, historical place, full of worn-out buildings ... bay windows, iron fences, [and] brownstone fronts." Although the five-sided Common and irregular streets make orientation difficult, the townscape creates a strong, and paradoxically quite well-structured, visual impression.

David Lowenthal in a recent study has attempted to gauge judgmental attitudes toward the complete urban environment in selected locales in central Boston and Cambridge. Interviewing subjects after they had completed a series of half-mile prescribed walks through each core district, Lowenthal was able to construct composite pictures of general emotive reactions to the area. Groups of Boy Scouts, secretaries, architects, medical technicians, students, housewives, and Golden Agers were used to create standard images based on sophisticated semantic scales. Downtown Boston emerges as "dense, dirty, bounded, old, peopled, and devoted to business." In common with New York (also studied), Boston appears "vertical, urban, vivid, moving, poor," and in general "exciting, historic, atmospheric."

Cambridge, on the other hand, has the characteristics of a "real big city," but it strikes some observers as odd that it should indeed be a city. This connection between legal city status and expected atmosphere is indicative of the dual role that Cambridge plays in metropolitan Boston. The seat of its two most famous universities, Cambridge is a special-function district within the metropolis; but, as with any functional suburb, central or peripheral, it cannot create or duplicate the environment of the true central business district.

Images of the city, however, are composed of more than feelings gained from walking the streets. In addition to the physical dimension of the city, the insider has a strong sense of the human consciousness of the area. Gleanings from the urban journalism of Boston suggest that residents, as well as outsiders, see the city as a mecca for the young. But the context is richer: Bostonians sense a paradoxical dualism in the social fabric. On the one hand, there is a strong continuity of generations in the city— each generation passes the neighborhood down to the next from era to era. On the other hand, however, there is the anxiety whether current trends are not depleting the city of its traditional population, the backbone of its past, tending toward less diversity and more polarity. The city has extended a special invitation to the affluent to return to the inner city (the West End, Harbor Towers), and the indigenous population feels great pressure in the housing market from the young professionals eager to buy and renovate aging structures.

For all that, Bostonians feel that their city is, in this age of escalating urban dilemmas, one of the nation's most "savable" cities. Rules

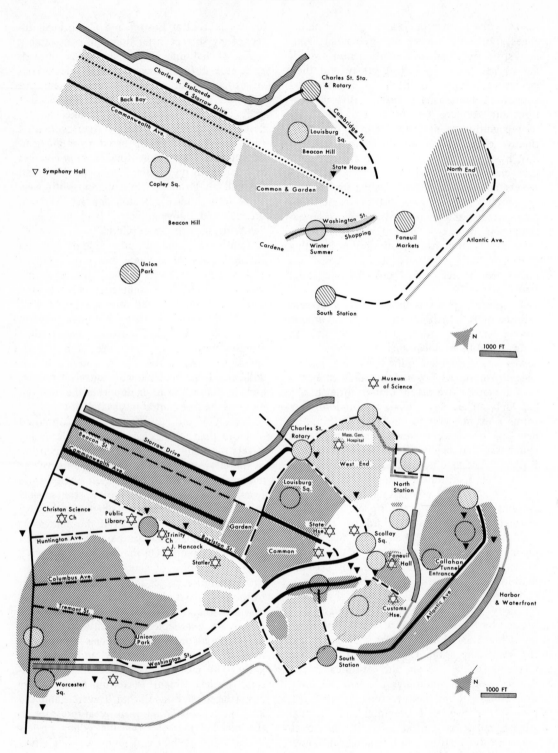

Figure 33.   The distinctive elements of Boston. (After Lynch)

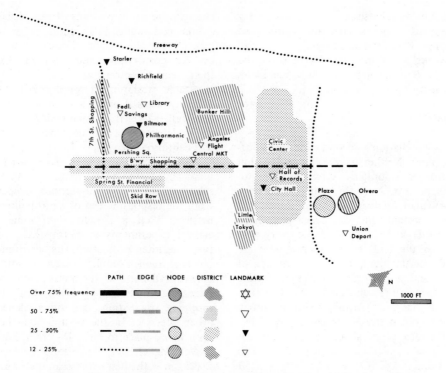

Figure 34. The distinctive elements of Los Angeles. (After Lynch)

are forged and bent, things change, but the pattern persists. This has always been a very good city for those who can afford it, and it will continue so. For the poor it is less so, but if the neighborhoods can remain vital social organisms rather than becoming boundless tracts, and if the upgrading of poor city services can actually be accomplished rather than merely talked about, Boston could keep what humanity and diversity it has. Thus are image and imagination intertwined.

But Boston is more than the sum of mundane ingredients for urban living. There is a sparkle that adds the uncommon touch to the public atmosphere of Boston and its satellite communities, and this sparkle, keenly felt by many a Bostonian, is well captured in the writing of George Frazier:

Our folkways are old and established and infinitely charming. The Boston Marathon. The carolers in Louisburg Square on Christmas Eve. The fragrance in the Ritz elevators. The L Street Brownies. The Symphony on Friday afternoon. The Latin Oration at Harvard Commencement. The tangy smell of leather goods in Winship's. . . . And then,

too, there is the remembrance of captains and kings long since departed. . . . How many summer days since Ted Williams strode in that loose-limbed way up to bat for the first time? How many since he departed in that unforgettable moment immortalized by Updike? And how many summer evenings since Fiedler first conducted the Pops? . . . How many wintry nights since Eddie Shore retired? How long since Joe Cronin made his final pinch hit? But it doesn't much matter, for the more this city changes, the more it seems the same. Now on weekends, there are women in the men's grill at Locke-Ober's, but the Lobster Savannah, the Anchovies Winter Place, and the Sweetbreads Eugene are as they were in the gilded time when Lucius Beebe and his fellow members of the Michael Mullins Chowder & Marching Society used to turn up in their pearl grey toppers and frock coats.

For many, Boston is the "Athens of America." It is not a resort, but it is far more than a commercial center. San Francisco is a Shangri-La, a land of lotus eaters. New York is the Big Apple, candied on the outside but poisoned at the core. Los Angeles searches for itself among its freeways. Chicago is gaunt and windy. And Philadelphia? Philadelphia is where second prize is two weeks' vacation there. But Boston, the Hub of the Solar System, on the other hand, exacts a heavy toll of affection.

RETROSPECT

Boston is the nation's second oldest city, after New York. Neither its age nor its location have burdened it unfairly in its progress toward the present. Nor, for that matter, have they particularly helped it either. Renewal is the only constant. But for every generation that succeeds to the city and for every new addition to the built environment, there are inherited social values, customary modes of behavior, and a bequeathed physical setting of streets, buildings, and land uses. The cityscape and the spatial arrangement of urban activities record much of the cumulative interaction between physical and social processes as they have molded the metropolis through its evolution.

Boston's employment outlook is dominated by increasing orientation toward "services." Manufacturing, while slowly declining in relative importance, is stabilizing its future with a shift toward a better balance between soft and hard goods. "Services" promise more emphasis on bureaucracy and higher levels of educational attainment. The colleges in the area are well prepared for this, but some of the high school systems are less so. If equality of opportunity is to prevail in the highly trained job market of the future, inner city education must drastically improve, and metropolitan inequalities in taxation and access will need to be radically diminished. The history of Greater Boston's political development, as expressed in the geographical pattern of legal boundaries, reflects deep divisions in urban and suburban society inherited from past conflicts over distribution of economic opportunity. The scars of this struggle live on in patterns of residential segregation compounded by ethnicity as well as class. "Save the neighborhoods" is a rallying cry for conservative and reformer alike, but their real objectives are clouded by almost inevitable escalation of social conflict. Boston in many ways is arriving at some urban problems rather later than other major cities, thanks to its depressed economic progress in the last half century.

Suburbs have long been places for the economically fortunate to retreat to. In Boston, suburbs have enjoyed a glorious independence from the responsibilities of metropolitan membership. What a paradox that some of the earliest experiments in metropolitan cooperation flourished in Boston! The age of megalopolis is at hand. Complex patterns of interaction between all parts of the metropolitan area are increasing in terms of commuting, finance, shopping, recreation, and other elements of urban lifestyle. In the Boston area there will soon be no place to hide: Haverhill, Lawrence, Lowell, Manchester, Worcester, Providence, and Brockton with their own urban systems all hem the central metropolis in. Spatial coalescence and political administrative streamlining are inevitable at present rates of growth.

While the Boston region faces problems of accommodating growth common to all large metropolitan areas in the nation, the image of the place is critical in coloring local views of Boston's future progress. The city's historicity is increasingly recognized as an invaluable asset not only to the Chamber of Commerce, but to the very quality of life of all metropolitan residents. Sheer urban age does not bestow a license on the population for smugness or idleness toward urban problems, but it does infuse many aspects of metropolitan life with a sense of continuity and variety. Greater Boston possesses great human, institutional, and physical variety which constitute a rich resource, if wisely integrated, for coping with future challenges.

Bibliography

Amory, Cleveland. *The Proper Bostonians*. New York: E.P. Dutton & Co., 1947.

"A Travel Guide to the No. 1 City of the Young." *Life,* July 7, 1971, pp. 69ff.

Axelrod, Morris, et al. *A Community Survey for Long Range Planning: A Study of the Jewish Population of Greater Boston.* Boston: Combined Jewish Philanthropies of Greater Boston, 1967.

Baedeker, Karl, ed. *The United States, With an Excursion Into Mexico: A Handbook for Travellers, 1893.* New York: Da Capo Press, 1971, Reprint.

Baltzell, E. Digby. *Philadelphia Gentlemen: The Making of a National Upper Class.* Chicago: Quadrangle Books, 1971.

Bearse, Ray, ed. *Massachusetts: A Guide to the Pilgrim State.* Rev. 2nd ed. Boston: Houghton Mifflin Co., 1971.

"Boston: Exciting City With a Past." *Today's Health,* July, 1966, pp. 36–41.

Boston Housing Authority. *Data Sheet of Managers and Projects.* Boston, 1973.

———. *Report of Non-White Occupancy As of January 1973.* Boston, 1973.

Boston Redevelopment Authority. *1965/ 1975 General Plan for the City of Boston, March 1965.* Boston, 1965.

Boston Redevelopment Authority Planning Department. *Preliminary Analysis of Industrial Land Use in the City of Boston.* Boston, January 1972.

———. *The Office Industry.* Preliminary Draft. Boston, September 1973.

"Boston Sets the Pace for Livability." *Business Week,* November 13, 1971, pp. 150ff.

"Boston: The Livable City." Special Supplement. *Boston Sunday Globe,* June 24, 1973.

Boston Transportation Planning Review. *Regional Systems.* Prepared for the Commonwealth of Massachusetts, Executive Office of Transportation and Construction, Department of Public Works, Massachusetts Bay Transportation Authority. Boston, 1972.

Buerle, D.E. "Some Measures of Boston and New York City Social Influence on Their Common Hinterland." Ph.D. Dissertation, Clark University, 1965.

Bushee, Frederick A. *Ethnic Factors in the Population of Boston.* Published for the American Economic Association. New York: The Macmillan Company, 1903.

Butwin, David, ed. "Back to the Hub." *Saturday Review,* December 20, 1969, pp. 43–45.

Deardorff, Robert. "Step by Step Through Boston." *Travel,* September 1968, pp. 39–43.

de Roos, Robert. "Massachusetts Builds for Tomorrow." *National Geographic* 130, 6 (December 1966): 790–843.

Dorsey, J.L. "Physician Distribution in Boston and Brookline, 1940 and 1961." *Medical Care* 7, 6 (November-December 1969): 429–40.

Duncan, Beverly, and Lieberson, Stanley. *Metropolis and Region in Transition.* Beverly Hills, Cal.: Sage Publications, 1970.

Eldredge, Joseph L. "A Few Have Succeeded." *The Boston Globe,* July 7, 1973, p. 8.

Estall, R.C. *New England: A Study in Industrial Adjustment.* New York: Frederick A. Praeger, 1966.

"Executive's Guide to Boston." *Business Week,* October 5, 1958, pp. 147–48.

Farquhar, O.C., ed. *Economic Geology in Massachusetts.* Proceedings of a conference in January 1966. Graduate School, University of Massachusetts, 1967.

Federal Writers' Project. *Massachusetts: A Guide to its Places and People.* Boston: Houghton Mifflin Co., 1937.

Firey, Walter. *Land Use in Central Boston.* Cambridge, Mass.: Harvard University Press, 1947.

Gallup International, Inc. *Gallup Opinion Index.* Report no. 53. November 1969.

Gans, Herbert. *The Urban Villagers.* Glencoe, Ill.: Free Press, 1962.

Gottmann, Jean. *Megalopolis The Urbanized Northeastern Seaboard of the United States.* New York: The Twentieth Century Fund, 1961.

Greater Boston Chamber of Commerce. *Greater Boston Directory of Electronics.* Boston, 1970.

Greater Boston Economic Study Committee. *Land Use in Greater Boston in 1960. Land Use Report 1.* Boston, 1962.

Handlin, Oscar. *Boston's Immigrants: A Study in Acculturation.* Cambridge, Mass.: The Belknap Press of Harvard University Press, 1959.

Hartman, Chester. "The Housing of Relocated Families." *Journal of the American Institute of Planners* 30, 4 (November 1964): 266–86.

Holmes, Oliver Wendell. *The Autocrat of the Breakfast Table.* Boston: The Jefferson Press, 1858.

Knights, Peter. *The Plain People of Boston, 1830–1860: A Study in City Growth.* New York: Oxford University Press, 1971.

LaBlanc, Robert G. *Location of Manufacturing in New England in the 19th Century.* Geography Publications at Dartmouth, 7. Hanover, N.H.: Dartmouth College, 1969.

Levin, Dr. Melvin R., et al. *The Boston Regional Survey.* Prepared for the Massachusetts Transportation Commission. Cambridge, Mass.: Commonwealth of Massachusetts, 1963.

Lewis, George K. "A Technique in Social Geography for the Delimitation of Urban Residential Subregions." Ph.D. dissertation, Harvard University, 1956.

Linscott, Robert N., ed. *State of Mind: A Boston Reader.* New York: Farrar, Straus & Co., 1948.

Little, Arthur D., Inc. *A Quality of Life: An Assessment of Massachusetts.* Prepared for the Commonwealth of Massachusetts. Boston, n.d. [circa 1972].

Lowenthal, David. *Environmental Assessment: A Comparative Analysis of Four Cities.* Publications in Environmental Perception no. 5. New York: American Geographical Society, 1972.

Lupo, Alan; Colcord, Frank; and Fowler, Edmund P. *Rites of Way: The Politics of Transportation in Boston and the U.S. City.* Boston: Little, Brown & Co., 1971.

Lynch, Kevin. *The Image of the City.* Cambridge, Mass.: The MIT Press, 1960.

Malony, Dr. Joseph F. *Mass Transportation in Massachusetts.* Final Report on a Mass Transportation Demonstration Project. Prepared for the Mass Transportation Commission. Commonwealth of Massachusetts, 1964.

Massachusetts Department of Commerce and Development. *Massachusetts Industrial Directory, 1971.* Boston, 1971.

——. *Mass Market Data Book.* Boston, n.d.

Massachusetts Taxpayers Foundation, Inc. *Institutional Property Tax Exemptions in Massachusetts.* Boston, November 1971.

——. *Tax Rates/1972: Actual and Full Value.* Boston, December 1972.

Massachusetts Transportation Authority. *Eighth Annual Report.* Boston, 1972.

McCaffrey, George H. "The Political Disintegration and Reintegration of Metropolitan Boston." a Dissertation submitted in the Division of History, Government, and Economics, Harvard University, March 1937.

McCrosky, Theodore T.; Blessing, Charles A.; and McKeever, J. Ross. *Surging Cities: A Secondary School Textbook in Two Parts.* Boston: Greater Boston Development Commission, 1948.

McQuade, Walter, "Urban Renewal in Boston." In James Q. Wilson, ed., *Urban Renewal: The Record and the Controversy.* Cambridge, Mass.: the MIT Press, 1966.

Metropolitan Area Planning Council. *Economic Base and Population Study.* Vol. I. *Historical Analysis.* Eastern Massachusetts Regional Planning Project. Boston, n.d. [circa 1963].

—— *Governmental Development of the*

Metropolitan Boston Area 1629-1972. Boston, November 1972.

Morison, Samuel Eliot. *The Maritime History of Massachusetts, 1783-1860*. Cambridge, Mass.: Sentry Edition, 1961.

Murphey, Rhoads. "Boston's Chinatown." *Economic Geography* 28 (July 1952): 244-55.

National Railway Publication Company. *Facsimile of the June 1870 Traveller's Official Railway Guide*. Ann Arbor, Mich.: Edwards Brothers, Inc., 1971.

Rand, Christopher. *Cambridge, U.S.A.: Hub of a New World*. New York: Oxford University Press, 1964.

Reinhold, Robert. "More Segregated than Ever." *The New York Times Magazine*, September 30, 1973.

Sargent, Governor Francis N. "Policy Statement on Transportation in the Boston Region." Mimeographed. Boston, November 30, 1972.

Schrag, Peter. *Village School Downtown: Politics and Education—A Boston Report*. Boston: Beacon Press, 1967.

Shannon, William V. *The American Irish*. New York: The Macmillan Company, 1963.

Shurtleff, Nathaniel H. *A Topographical and Historical Description of Boston*. 3rd ed. Boston: Rockwell and Churchill, 1891.

Sullivan, Charles, and Hatch, Kathlyn. *The Chinese in Boston, 1970*. Boston: Action for Boston Community Development, 1970.

Sweetser, Frank L. *The Social Ecology of Metropolitan Boston 1960*. Boston: Massachusetts Department of Mental Health, Division of Mental Hygiene, 1962.

——. *Patterns of Change in the Social Ecology of Metropolitan Boston 1950-1960*. Boston: Massachusetts Department of Mental Health, Division of Mental Hygiene, 1962.

Taeuber, Karl T., and Taeuber, Alma F. *Negroes in Cities: The Measurement of Residential Segregation*. Chicago: Aldine Publishing Co., 1965.

Thernstrom, Stephan. *Poverty, Planning, and Politics in the New Boston: The Origins of ABCD*. New York: Basic Books, 1969.

——. *The Other Bostonians: Poverty and Progress in the American Metropolis, 1880-1970*. Cambridge, Mass.: Harvard University Press, 1973.

Thompson, Benjamin. "A City of Lovely Variety." *The Boston Globe*, July 7, 1973, p. 8.

Thwing, Annie Haven. *The Crooked and Narrow Streets of The Town of Boston 1630-1822*. Boston: Marshall Jones Co., 1920.

Ulrich, Laurel. *A Beginner's Boston*. n.p., 1970.

United Community Services and Action for Boston Community Development. *Five Ethnic Groups in Boston: Blacks, Irish, Italians, Greeks, and Puerto Ricans*. Boston, 1972.

U.S. Bureau of the Census. *1967 Census of Business*. Vol. II. *Retail Trade Area Statistics*. Pt. 2. *Iowa–North Carolina*.

——. *1967 Census of Governments*. Vol. I.

——. *1967 Census of Manufactures*. Vol. III. *Area Statistics*. Pt. 1. *Alabama–Montana*.

——. *1967 Census of Transportation*. Vol. II. *Commodity Transportation Survey*. Pt. 2. *Production Areas and Selected States*.

——. *1970 Census of Population. Detailed Characteristics. Massachusetts*.

——. *1970 Census of Population and Housing. Census Tracts. Boston, Massachusetts*.

U.S. Department of Labor, Bureau of Labor Statistics. *Employment and Earnings: States and Areas 1939-1969*. Bulletin 1370-7. 1970.

Vance, James E., Jr. "The Growth of Suburbanism West of Boston: A Geographic Study of Transportation-Settlement Relationships." Ph.D. dissertation, Clark University, 1952.

Ward, David. "The Emergence of Central Immigrant Ghettoes in American Cities: 1840-1920." *Annals of the Association of American Geographers* 58 (June 1968): 343-59.

Warner, Sam B., Jr. *Streetcar Suburbs: The Process of Growth in Boston, 1870-1900*. Cambridge, Mass.: Harvard University Press, 1962.

Washnis, George J. *Municipal Decentralization and Neighborhood Resources: Case Studies of Twelve Cities*. New York: Praeger Special Studies in U.S. Economic and Social Development, 1972.

Whitehill, Walter Muir. *Boston: A Topographical History*. Cambridge, Mass.: Belknap Press, 1968.

Wolfe, Albert Benedict. *The Lodging House Problem in Boston*. Cambridge, Mass.: Harvard University Press, 1913.

Woods, Robert ed. *Americans in Process: A Settlement Study*. Boston: Houghton Mifflin Co., 1902.

Woods, Robert A., and Kennedy, Albert J. *The Zone of Emergence: Observations of the Lower Middle and Upper Working Class Communities of Boston, 1905-1914*. Cambridge, Mass.: The MIT Press, 1962.

Wright, John K., ed. *New England's Prospect: 1933.* Special Publication no. 16. New York: American Geographical Society, 1933.

Zimmerman, Joseph P. "Governing Metropolitan Boston." Prepared for the Metropolitan Area Planning Council's Technical Advisory Committee on Regional Organization. Mimeographed. Boston, November 1972.

Chapter 3

A Vignette of the New York-New Jersey Metropolitan Region

Preface

In preparing this study for the Comparative Metropolitan Analysis Project, I have tried to present a regional description of the urbanized core of the New York–New Jersey metropolis in a manner which avoids the penalties of scholarly writing as much as possible, and which anchors itself in field experience as much as possible. Since all of the ideas in this monograph did not spring full blown from my brow, I wish to call attention to the bibliographical notes at the conclusion in which those publications to which I am chiefly indebted are listed.

Paramount among these sources are the two great New York Metropolitan Regional Studies sponsored by the Regional Plan Association—one of the 1930s and the other of the 1950s. Indispensable to the serious field trip devotee in the region are the Hagstrom Company's maps and atlases, the WPA *New York City Guide* of 1930s, and the AIA Guide to New York City of the 1960s.

In the area of New York City and Newark housing policy, my colleagues at Rutgers—George Sternlieb and Jim Hughes—are sources of information of the highest order. I owe many of my insights in the area of environmental quality to my teacher, colleague, and friend Leonard Zobler, of Barnard College, Columbia University, and to my Rutger associates Michael Greenberg and Robert Hordon.

My eyes were opened to the landscape of Paterson, New Jersey, when Sally Gibson of the Paterson Museum took me on a walking tour which is the basis for much of the Paterson section of this study and which was developed by the Great Falls Development Corporation.

Many acute observers have accompanied me on various field trips which I have led in the region. They have enriched my understanding more than they, perhaps, realize: Maurice Yeates, Barry Garner, David Lowenthal, Peirce Lewis, Mike Woldenberg, Art Getis, Robert Harper, Ted Schmudde, Briavel Holcomb, and most of the Rutgers geographers come to mind. Their material is reflected in both the text and photographs.

Many thanks to John S. Adams and Ron Abler who made it possible for me to participate in the project. Ron Foresta, who served as a research aide when the pressures got tough, deserves my appreciation, as do my other colleagues, friends, and students in the Urban Studies subculture at Rutgers. I look back on this task with misgivings and unease at the audacity implicit in presuming to prepare a study of such a metropolitan giant in so few pages.

And so I emphasize that all of the overgeneralizations, gaffes, and canards which may be found in this work are mine alone.

Tappan, New York 1974

An Overview of the Region

The area known as the New York Metropolitan Region (NYMR) extends over those portions of three states which adjoin where the waters of the Hudson and the Raritan rivers mingle with those of the Atlantic Ocean, Long Island Sound, and the numerous bays, channels, and kills of the port of New York and New Jersey (Figure 1). Connecticut on the mainland to the East; New York in the center, extending over the vast expanse of Long Island; and New Jersey on the mainland to the west are the major political jurisdictions.

Twenty-two counties are roughly included within this metropolitan giant—one in Connecticut, nine in New Jersey, twelve in New York. The focal point of the region is New York City, located upon a group of islands at the junction of the principal bodies of water. Of the five counties in New York City only one—the Bronx—is principally on the mainland. Kings County (Brooklyn) and Queens County are on the western end of Long Island, Richmond County is on Staten Island, and most of New York County is on Manhattan Island.

As the map reveals, the rolling terrain of the coastal plain covers most of New York City, but the mainland to the northwest is quite broken. The "mountains" alluded to rarely exceed 800 feet in elevation, but the relief is usually sharply defined and numerous cliff faces and escarpments are present which have slowed urbanization to the northwest and channeled it to the northeast, east, and southwest.

To some extent areas such as the Ramapo and Putnam mountains will remain permanent-

ly undeveloped. Harriman State Park, Bear Mountain State Park, and the United States Military Reservation at West Point are all located in the Ramapo subregion, while major portions of Putnam County are held in forested watershed lands.

Nevertheless, major arteries have penetrated these barriers and Orange County in the trans-Ramapo area is in development as is Dutchess County to the north of the Putname Mountains. The New York State Thruway found its way from New York City upstate through the pass at Suffern on the Ramapo River that had formerly been used by Indian trails, corduroy roads, railroads, and U.S. Route 17. Major routes like U.S. 9 and the Taconic State Parkway have sliced northward through the difficult terrain of the Putnam Mountains to Dutchess County, incorporating the environs of Poughkeepsie in the metropolitan system.

In New Jersey to the west, core cities like Elizabeth, Newark, and Jersey City lie in the zone between the Watchung Mountains and the tidewater. Paterson, New Jersey, another old core city, lies at the fall line where the Passaic River drops over the Watchungs in Passaic Falls. Railroads and highways have bypassed or cut through the Watchungs. The land behind them is in middevelopment today.

It was not until the 1930s when the beautiful George Washington Bridge was completed spanning the Hudson River between Manhattan and New Jersey that the barrier of the Palisades was effectively breached. Since then, the area between back slopes of the cliffs and the Ram-

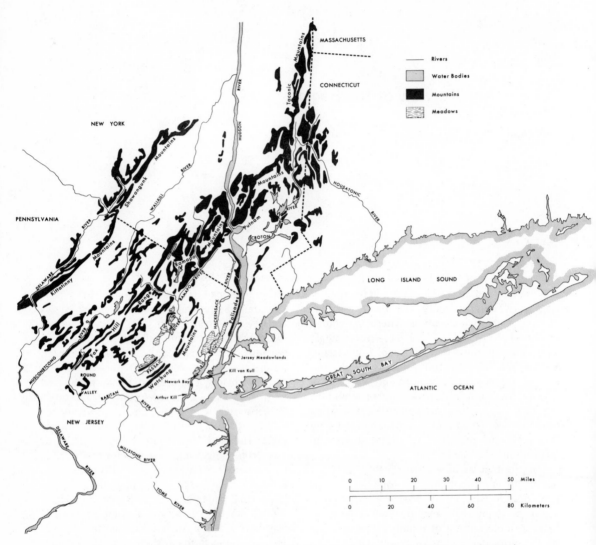

Figure 1.   Major Natural Features of the New York Metropolitan Region (NYMR)

apo River has become extensively urbanized. Bergen County, New Jersey, and Rockland County, New York lie within this zone. The Rockland County portion, which lagged in development at first, has experienced extremely rapid growth since the New York State Thruway Bridge provided a Hudson River crossing in the 1950s. It penetrates the Palisades at Nyack.

To the East, in Connecticut, the region has grown up around other old core cities on the coastal plain like Bridgeport. The easy terrain in this direction and also to the Southwest has led to the development of a corridor of trans-

portation facilities which reaches from Boston to the national capital, with the NYMR roughly at the center.

The still easier terrain of Long Island, to the East, has provided even less impediment to development. The remarkable photograph in Figure 2 presents a vista along the entire 120 mile length of this suburb. Brooklyn and Queens, on the near tip of the island, are the heart of New York City. Beyond, the heavily urbanized zone of Nassau County blends into the outer reaches of Suffolk County where suburbs, rural spaces, and a seashore resort industry coexist in an unstable relationship.

Figure 2. NYMR as Seen from 35,000 Feet. New Jersey is to the far left. Manhattan lies left of center. Brooklyn and Queens lie at the near end of Long Island. The far end of Long Island is 120 miles away. Source: Aero Service.

Over the past quarter century the impetus to growth has been so great in the NYMR that almost all barriers have fallen to expansion. One of the last major undeveloped tracts remaining in the heart of the region is the marshy meadowland in the tidewater location where the Passaic and Hackensack rivers meet. Major portions of the Hackensack Meadows have been the subject of landfill operations since the 1950s, and industrial and warehousing activities have been located there. Related to this, of course, is the fact that the transportation corridor alluded to above traverses this area, placing it in an enviable position from shipping considerations.

A large fraction of the NYMR is actually made or reclaimed land. Vast areas of wetland have been filled to provide level sites for urban development. Many acres of the New York Metropolitan Region of the 1970s lie upon the wastes and midden of previous centuries. Drainage and pollution problems thus engendered have become serious in some localities. Plague and pestilence which ravaged Southeastern Manhattan in the mid-1840s came about from contaminated wells sunk through layers of ordure to the water beneath. Today, the unstable hydraulic properties of the soil in the same area makes building construction costly and difficult.

Making geographical sense out of a region this vast, complex, and dynamic in the compass of a few short pages is a challenging task. To some extent it is made even more difficult by the fact that New York City is an entity with a world image. Almost everyone has formed impressions of this well-publicized city from the media, from visits, or from stays of various durations. In a manner of speaking, it is like the elephant of the fable that numerous people have sensed partly, but fewer people have come to know well.

Thus, insofar as any short treatment of the subject will probably leave many readers feeling that the essence of the region which *they* have perceived is inadequately treated, the following statements reflect some of the premises from which this work proceeds.

First of all, Manhattan is not identical with New York City, and New York City is only one portion of the NYMR. Whoever wishes to understand how people live in New York City must concentrate upon Brooklyn and Queens more than upon Manhattan (Figure 3).

Second, within the NYMR, waves of suburban development have spread out far from the core in all directions. They have been restrained and deflected by natural barriers, but not blocked. Economic activity has been decentralizing as rapidly as population since 1950.

Between 1953 and 1970 New York City experienced an absolute decline in manufacturing and wholesaling employment while barely holding its own in retailing jobs, a fact which actually reveals a relative decline of the city with respect to the region. On the other hand, New York City had a 32 percent expansion in total jobs. This expansion is in finance-related, white collar office and corporate headquarters jobs. These comprise what Gottmann called quarternary activities. A similar trend prevails in the New Jersey core city counties in manufacturing, although wholesaling and retailing continue to show growth.

The process of displacement of other than quarternary activities to the suburbs is already well advanced. Consider the band of manufacturing, wholesaling, and retailing activity which lies across Long Island in Nassau and Western Suffolk counties. Growth in Nassau and Suffolk has provided a total of 158,000 manufacturing jobs, 39,000 wholesaling jobs, and 147,000 retailing jobs outside of New York City. Adding to all other jobs, more than half a million jobs now exist on Long Island between the easternmost suburbs and the city boundary.

Growth on the western side of the Hudson River was equally dramatic. In Bergen County (New Jersey) and adjoining Rockland County (New York) overall employment growth rates reached 92 percent and 135 percent. The New York State Thruway Bridge and the George Washington Bridge, which provide links between these areas and New York City, now have busy flows in both directions during rush hour.

Even in those sectors with which the image of Manhattan is heavily identified, the outlook is less than sanguine. In finance, insurance, and real estate, and in business and personal services—the traditional growth strengths of Manhattan and the New York City core—suburbanization of employment may be observed. The core city areas of New York and New Jersey continue to show strong growth in these sectors, but their growth in the perimeter is extraordinary. Finance, insurance, real estate, and services are booming in Nassau and Suffolk counties. In the New Jersey perimeter, Bergen County employment is strong across the board while Essex (Newark), a traditional location for banking and insurance activities, lags.

Passaic County, New Jersey, and Fairfield County, Connecticut, are remarkable among the perimeter counties in that they lag their neighbors markedly in manufacturing employment. This is because they contain two old core cities—Paterson and Bridgeport, respectively—which share in central city losses of manufacturing. Thus minipatterns of employment suburbanization which resemble the broad

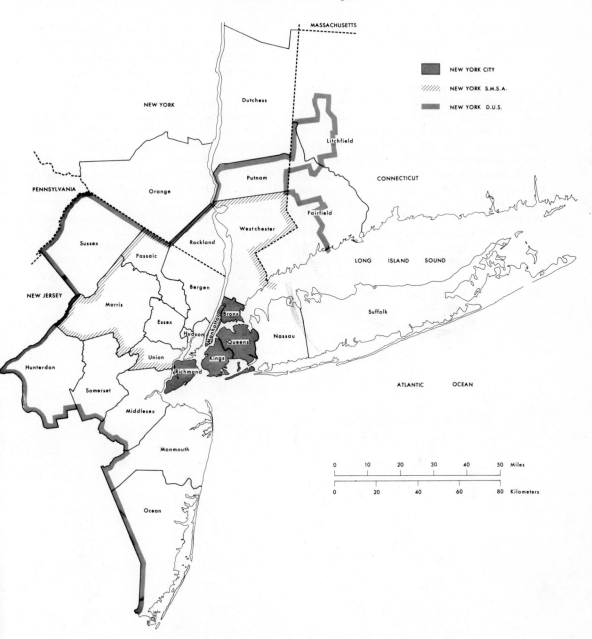

Figure 3. New York Metropolitan Region Counties.

regional patterns which we have been discussing provide minor eddies around these nuclei.

Many suburban residents make a daily journey to work in the suburbs rather than the central city. Moreover, increasing numbers of core city residents are journeying to work in the suburbs rather than the city. Thus, in order to understand the location of economic activity in the NYMR, we must understand something of the industrial parks, office buildings, warehousing facilities, wholesaling centers, and retailing hubs in the suburbs as well as the center city. Port Newark-Elizabeth and Paramus in New Jersey, and Nassau and Dutchess (headquarters for IBM operations) counties in

New York assume their importance alongside Manhattan.

Finally, in those portions of this study which do concentrate upon New York City, the prognosis will be mixed. Even with respect to activities which retain some vitality there, standardized operations which are routine and require a large labor force are suburbanizing. These fields include advertising and the media, central office functions of major coporations, the fashion industry, publishing, finance and insurance, the securities industry, international trade, and rare and specialized forms of retailing which command a far-flung market. It seems likely that the Manhattan office building boom of the past twenty-five years has come to a close. Many vacancies go unfilled in the towers of Wall Street as a result of what has probably been an overbuilding of office space. To a certain extent government has stepped in as a kind of "tenant of last resort." Major state and federal bureaus and departments have located in Wall Street space, helping to stabilize it. But clearly even in the areas of finance, insurance, real estate, and business services, New York City is no longer the whole story. Indeed, even within New York City, the undeniably great strength still left in these sectors lies concentrated in Manhattan south of 70th Street. Secondary centers like Brooklyn and Newark are eroding.

In line with this discussion, this overview of the NYMR will possibly be more decentralized from a focus on Manhattan than the reader may anticipate. Yet from the standpoint of what some writers are calling a massive economic "disinvestment" in the core city counties it may well prove to be not suburbanized enough.

The New York Metropolitan Region—Process, Form, and Control

PROCESS

The essence of the New York Metropolitan Region (NYMR) is that its hinterland of reference is the world. Jean Gottmann has pointed out that the NYMR and its contiguous urbanized area—more than any other American city region—serves as a hinge between the United States and the rest of the world—the vital junction between the variegated commodity and service flows which originate within the immense productive network formed by United States industry and comparably scaled foreign productive behemoths such as the European Economic Community and Japan, among others.

American society depends for its existence upon the flow of goods and services from the cities where they are produced to the destinations where they are consumed. An elaborate socioeconomic system has developed whereby, for instance, primary materials flow from mines, farmlands, forests, and oceans to staging points where they are converted into intermediate or final products for consumption. At these staging points—by other routes—energy, labor, and capital resources are accumulated to facilitate the process of production and ancillary activities arise to sustain the lifestyle of the population who are there engaged in the complex human relationships of production.

The multibranched network of rivers, roads, railroads, pipelines, shipping lanes, power lines, telephone and telegraph cables, airline routes, and other channels over which this immense complexity of flow passes constitutes the veritable circulatory and nervous system of our society. The staging points, or sites of production, which lie at the major nodes where these channels intersect are critical elements of human settlements—villages, towns, cities, metropolises.

Some small towns and cities serve as productive and distributive nodes for the limited area which constitutes their hinterland. These are smaller in scale than their larger siblings which relate to regions which are national or subnational in scope.

William Warntz has worked out an elaborate statistical measurement which he calls "income potential," measuring the intensity of personal income at various points on the earth's surface (Figure 4). Dumbell-shaped contours of enormous income potential ring the NYMR, on the one hand, and the Rhine delta seaports of the European Economic Community, on the other. If we imagine these points to resemble magnetic poles, and if we were able on a world scale to duplicate the high school physics experiment of sprinkling iron filings on the earth's surface between the magnetic poles, it becomes possible to image the discipline with which the filings would slowly flow toward these poles as the map is tapped. If each filing were a ship, the metaphor would be complete.

The visitor to New York has only to stand on the eastern shore of Staten Island, in Van Briesen Park, on a sunny Wednesday (when visibility is good, and the midweek maritime traffic is at its peak) to see the magnet meta-

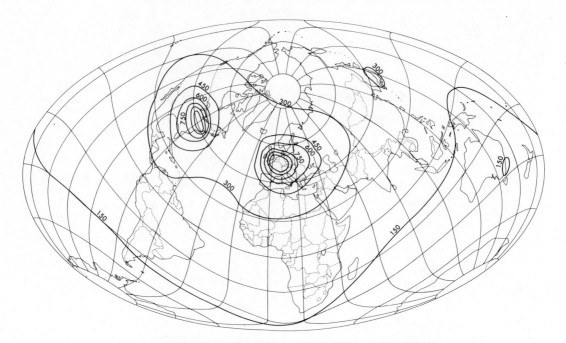

Figure 4. World Income Potentials about 1960. Source: William Warntz.

phor made concrete in the flow of container ships into and out of the harbor. And for each container ship (with perhaps 900 containers) a host of invisible flows—of messages, information, orders, insurance and financial arrangements—passes through the air or through cables invisible to the eye to and from the port.

The essence of the NYMR is that it is the prime United States node for worldwide flows. But, at the regional or local scale, the resident has a more limited vision and his existence expresses itself in a small life space within the regional system. We face a challenging task—to come to grips with the grand scale of the major processes in the region, and yet to understand their relationship in numerous localities with the people who inhabit it and who view it with the perspective of the ant in a lawn. What is orderly at one scale, appears a chaotic thicket at another.

FORM

If the NYMR represents the node where important flows which sustain our society—and other societies—converge, this fact has a profound effect on the physical form which the

social organization of the region assumes. A parcel of land in a city is valuable depending upon that to which it gives access. If it is so located that it gives its user access to the array of goods, services, and opportunities passing through the NYMR, it will be more valuable than one remote from the metropolitan center. Since locations in the NYMR supply users with immediate access to more than 400 out of the 450 broad categories of American economic activity, and since the remaining fifty or so are easily available to the region, it follows that some of the region's real estate will be among the most valuable in the world.

This is true particularly at the traditional heart of the region—the island of Manhattan. This central subarea of the primate nodal region in the United States serves as the epitome of the city as conceived by Karl Deutsch:

Any metropolis can be thought of as a huge engine of communication, a device to enlarge the range and reduce the cost of individual and social choices. In the familiar telephone switchboard, the choices consist of many different lines. Plugging in the wires to connect any two lines is an act of commitment, since it implies foregoing the making of other connections. The concentration of available outlets on the switchboard permits a wider range of alternative choices than would prevail under any more dispersed arrangement. The limits of the potentially useful size of a switchboard are fixed by the capacity of the type of switching and control equipment available.... The facilities of the metropolis for transport and communication are the equivalent of the switchboard (p. 96).

To amplify and enrich Deutsch's metaphor, consider a clay contoured model of the New York-New Jersey-Connecticut urbanized area, the height of which at any point is proportional to the intensity of business activity carried forward at that location (Figure 5). The towering twin peaks emerge on Manhattan, near the center of the pattern. The southernmost lies at the Wall Street financial complex. A saddle surface sags to a "pass" of relatively lower business activity near Canal Street. From there the surface climbs to the midtown Manhattan peak near 42nd Street, where a vast amount of central business office and retailing activities thrive in the shadow of the United Nations on the East River. On the sloping flanks of these peaks—northward into Harlem, across the East River in Brooklyn and Queens, and across the Harlem River into the Bronx—lie acre after acre of land devoted to apartment houses of varying age, condition, tenantry, and ownership.

Business intensity can also be represented by employment per acre in the NYMR (Figure 6). Yet as one gets farther from the intense activity of the Manhattan center, uses other than commercial may successfully bid for the cheaper land. In Brooklyn, for example, the high "ridge" along Atlantic and Fifth avenues in the west—a privileged position of access to Manhattan by six subway tunnels, one vehicular tunnel, three bridges, and four vertically superimposed layers of roadway running along the shore—rapidly slopes off into the vast residential areas of Bedford Stuyvesant, Bushwick, Flatbush, Williamsburg, and Brownsville. Since most of the 600,000-plus housing units for Brooklyn's more than two million people were built since 1901, this area represents one of the greatest construction efforts in human history. It was an effort which was fueled by the nineteenth century explosion of economic activity at the Manhattan center and which fed on the housing needs of the millions who were drawn to the city to provide labor, each wave of im-

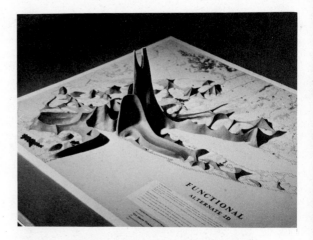

Figure 5. Activity Model, New York Metropolitan Region. The height of the clay above the map conceptualizes human activities. The two-pronged summit is Manhattan (Wall Street and Midtown). Lower crests are Brooklyn (nearer) and urban New Jersey (farther). Source: Reproduced by permission of Thomas J. Thomas, who prepared the model for the Tri-State Transportation Commission.

migrant labor destined to dwell in tenement houses built by its predecessors.

As time has passed, seaport activity has shifted to New Jersey. In that segment of the NYMR major rail, airport, road, and pipeline facilities adjoin one another. Since large acreages of marshland lie between the transportation axis and Newark Bay, landfill efforts have been undertaken which have led to container port construction. This setting has been conducive to the design of facilities which are capable of transferring cargoes from one transportation mode to another with ease and despatch. So the greatness of New York as a seaport resides in Port Newark and Port Elizabeth—both in the state of New Jersey—while many of the once vaunted dock areas of Brooklyn and Manhattan rot into a rich flotsam which defies the efforts of the Coast Guard to clear it from the estuary.

The growth of this urban region has obviously long since spilled over the political boundaries of New York City, to engulf portions of three states, numerous counties, municipalities, and various other jurisdictions. Wood, in writing of this confusion of governmental complexity which defies rational planning and con-

Figure 6.   Employment, Manhattan CBD. The height of the paper forms is proportional to employment density in Manhattan circa 1969. Each quadrant is forty acres. The total volume of jobs is two million. Source: Reproduced by permission of Ernst Hacker who prepared the model for the New York City Planning Commission.

trol in the region, entitled his book *1400 Governments* for good reason.

THE PROBLEM OF REGIONAL CONTROL— AN OUTLINE

At one extreme of scale in the NYMR are tiny, semiautonomous fire, sewer, and school tax districts whose boundaries do not always coincide with those of the municipalities which they serve. At the intermediate range of scale we find municipalities, towns, counties, and the five boroughs into which New York City is divided. At the other extreme of scale are the metropolitan giants—the Port of New York Authority, the Tri-State Planning Commission, and the Metropolitan Transportation Authority —whose functions overarch portions of three states. Finally, like the icing on the multilayered cake of political regulation and planning, federal regional agencies span the region.

Obviously the vast segmentation, overlapping of functions, and, indeed, competition for resources and territorial privilege among these more than 1,400 entities suggests the difficulty of securing the goal of rational planning in the NYMR. In some spheres of sensitive public interest such as the design of social services, housing, and educational programs, the situation borders on chaos.

Despite the fragmentation of governance, the well-integrated functioning of the American economic system as it affects the metropolitan land market has impressed a rough order on the region. The high access inner core predictably manifests an array of variegated and complex interrelated activities which are sensitive to communications in the metropolitan market—the commodity and stock markets; the fashion industry; the publishing industry; the media and advertising; a highly specialized medical care industry; retailing of high value commodities and specialty goods; and the numerous ancillary financial, legal, and consultative services upon which these industries depend. Vast residential areas, equally diversified, ring this core, from high density and highrise luxury neighborhoods, to high density neighborhoods of poverty and disintegration, to low density communities of wealthy estates matched by low density poverty areas in desolute suburban pockets of despair. As residences have been developed farther out in the suburbs, economic activity has suburbanized as well. An outer zone of transportation, industry, and

warehousing has developed on the flatlands of New Jersey, on Long Island, and along the Connecticut shore.

But again, the rough order imposed by the economic system cuts across the patchwork of jurisdictions which are charged with controlling, planning, and managing the region for the benefit of the citizenry. In the jurisdictions most desperate for public services, the tax yield per capita is often low despite enormous local tax effort. An older municipality housing poor blue collar workers simply lacks the resource base of an affluent suburb like Princeton, New Jersey, where there is a concentration of wealth.

In a sense, the core and the peripheral industrial ring act in tandem as wealth-producing and wealth-distributing regions. The proceeds from this wealth are zones unequally divided among workers, management, and professional elites. Small trickles of income are carried by working class breadwinners to numerous lower middle class and poor neighborhoods close in around the core. More substantial dollar flows course to centers of affluence in the portfolios of the income elite. Since the major political decision-making boundary for many crucial service functions—like education, police, and welfare—is not drawn around the entire region, many small municipalities of poor people must make their decisions separated in economic benefit from the affluent municipalities of the rich. Income inequality is thus rigidified into inequality of municipal service consumption by the political fragmentation of the region, in contrast to its economic integration on the producing and distributing side. Now that state and federal controls are slowly smoothing out some services like education, planning efforts may gradually move the system toward greater equity in government services.

The fragmentation of the region raises control problems resembling what Paul Samuelson has suggested can lead to "the fallacy of composition." A person watching a soccer game and wanting a better view may stand on his seat. This strategy is a good one only if no one else follows it. What is good for an individual may not be good for the group. There are many public programs, development opportunities, and policies which to a community seem highly desirable. Yet if each community adopts such a program, disaster may ensue for the region. It seems splendid for a community to foster the development of an industrial park, which will bring in tax ratables, while at the same time enacting ordinances aimed at excluding school age population, perhaps by fostering the construction of two bedroom garden apartments and homes for the elderly and by expanding the lot requirements for private houses. Let the workers with families in the industrial park settle elsewhere—along with the educational burden of their children.

Of course, the neighboring communities adopt the same strategy. A housing crisis results for workers with families, employment problems develop for the firms, and a crushing commuting burden is imposed on the region as workers find themselves living far from their jobs.

Again, perhaps an upstream community on the Raritan or Hudson rivers decides to mini-mize costs on waste treatment by pouring sewage into the water course: after all there is plenty of dissolved oxygen in the river to dissipate its waste load. Yet if all communities make the same decision, downstream reaches of these rivers run septic in the summer months, and portions of the New York-New Jersey estuarial system become dead seas, like the notorious Arthur Kill between Staten Island and New Jersey. Our society in general, and the NYMR in particular, has yet to learn how to cope with this class of problem.

With these preparatory comments about process, form, and control in mind, we now turn to the urban geography of specific sectors of the NYMR chosen to be representative of the more crucial aspects of these issues.

Commercial and Industrial Activities

There are four categories of goods and services production within the NYMR—manufacturing produces goods; retailing and wholesaling exchange goods at intermediate or final points of consumption; transportation and communication move goods and information from node to node within the system; and energy production and distribution drive the entire process.

MANUFACTURING INDUSTRY

The location of manufacturing industry within the NYMR changes constantly. At the turn of the century much of it would have been found at the cores of the cities of the region—New York, Newark, Paterson, Bridgeport, for example. Today, a centrifugal movement is well under way from the impetus of strong outward or centrifugal forces. The inward-directed, centripetal forces are by no means negligible, however, and we shall see through some industry examples how a variety of industrial activities are "centrifuged" outward, or remain at the core according to their intrinsic characteristics of land and labor requirements, marketing and financing attributes, and technological change, always coupled with the operation of chance and externalities.

Petrochemicals

The enormous market of the NYMR, coupled with its excellent seaport access to world sources of petroleum, virtually assured that a major petrochemical industry would arise to serve it. The labor requirements of this kind of industry are less pressing than those of more labor-intensive industries like garment manufacturing, and so, while access to residential areas attractive to skilled personnel is important, the number of journeys to work generated are insufficient to require a plant to relocate near the terminus of a major urban mass transportation system.

At the same time, the technology of the industry requires large, inexpensive allotments of land to such facilities as storage tank farms, cracking towers, processing complexes, and all of the space-consuming plumbing supporting the petrochemical industry. Access to rail, waterborne, truck, and pipeline modes of transportation are of great importance in combining the enormous tons of input materials and in marketing the final product.

In the more central and heavily urbanized areas of the region, not only are real estate values prohibitively high for the development of this kind of enterprise, but the parcels of land are very small. Even if an industry were willing and able to purchase a central tract for a plant, the negotiation for parcel acquisition in the tract can be extrordinarily difficult and expensive. In the end, a small number of hold out owners can imperil an entire scheme.

The preponderance of these factors argues for a peripheral rather than a central location for the petrochemical industry. Certain other industries which are oriented to a highly sensitive and changeable market (the New York Stock Exchange and the fashion industry come to mind) need speedy communication between customer, buyer, broker, producer, and financier on a day-to-day basis. Sometimes moment-to-moment information can be so crucial to survival that access to the center of the metropolitan switchboard overrides every consideration.

In the case of petroleum products, there are few differences among brands of gasoline, oil, and other petroleum and chemical products. There is thus little impetus for the firm to be located in the high cost metropolitan center. Indeed, since the differences among many of these products are largely imaginary, and fashions and fads in their consumption are produced not by manufacturing variations but by the imagination of advertising agencies, we do find a major concentration of advertising agencies in a high communications center on Madison Avenue in Midtown Manhattan.

In petrochemical manufacture, facilities cluster in massive complexes because the outputs of one set of plants are the inputs for others. Chemicals produced at basic refining complexes form the raw materials for other plants which produce paints, plastic, solvents, and other synthetic materials. Thus, the preponderance of locational influences tend to make the industry assume a perimeter rather than a core location, while technological considerations produce clustering. The industry is not spread out on the urban perimeter.

In the New Jersey coastal plain area to the south of Port Newark–Port Elizabeth, along the Arthur Kill which separates Staten Island from the mainland, we find all of the conditions discussed here fulfilled. Adjacent to the giant petrochemical installations of Exxon, Texaco, Hess, Reichold Chemical, and many others may be found the main line of the Jersey Central and the Penn Central, the New Jersey Turnpike, the natural gas pipeline from Texas nicknamed "the Big Inch," the two giant container ports, Newark Airport providing convenient air freight and management access, and tanker berths all along the Arthur Kill. Some of the companies are interconnected with each other by pipes, so that direct delivery of a product manufactured by one plant and required by another is accomplished with a minimum of transportation cost and with direct billing through an automatic metering system.

But metropolitan expansion has engulfed this complex of petrochemical plumbing. Once at the fringe of the urbanized core, urbaniza-

tion has leapfrogged over this industrial area deep into New Jersey, hemming it in so that large tracts of open land for expansion are no longer easily acquired. Other plants have become obsolete and may be phased out, as in the case of Hess. The development of supertankers and the competitive economics which attend their use have made the Arthur Kill obsolete as a tanker port, for not only is the thirty-five foot deep channel inadequate for the largest modern vessels, but also the turning radii from New York Bay into the Kill van Kull (north of Staten Island) and thence into the Arthur Kill are far too sharp to accommodate them.

The external diseconomies of the petroleum complex to the region have been great. The industries of the NYMR contribute to the largest air and water pollution problem in the nation. Waste discharges, oil spills, and tanker traffic have played a part in rendering the waters of the Arthur Kill and part of the Kill van Kull septic for part of the year. These waters are so polluted that they could not even be purified by massive distillation. The boiling points of some of the complex chemical pollutants are the same as that of water.

One hundred years ago these waters were the pride of a flourishing oyster and shellfish industry. Today there are reaches which are so contaminated that even sewage bacteria cannot survive in them. The effects of this kind of pollution of the marine ecology of an important estuarial and offshore environment are poorly understood, but, coupled with garbage scow dumping and the unsatisfactory treatment of sewage waste effluent introduced in these waters, an extensive "dead sea" has developed in the New Jersey–New York Bight between the Raritan and Hudson rivers. Since seashore recreation is a major industry on the New Jersey Atlantic shore the inhabitants there are understandably skeptical about the development of a deep-water port and offshore oil drilling in their vicinity, with its attendant dangers of spillage and pollution.

Will the petrochemical industry on which the NYMR market depends find the means to grow and modernize in the midst of a public increasingly sensitive to issues involving environmental degradation? What are the alternatives? Relocation of the industry within the crowded region with its incredible fixed investment in plant seems impossible. Limitation of its growth could possibly put a brake on regional growth in industries which depend on cheap petroleum products. These industries are key elements for regional employment patterns. Yet, the price to be paid by the region for continued growth to meet demand might very well be ecologically disastrous for the estuarial environment and the air quality over many urbanized portions of the region. There does not really exist a planning mechanism by which these dilemmas may be rigorously attacked.

The Garment Industry

The garment district of Manhattan, located on the west side of the island in the numerous industrial lofts extending through streets north of 34th Street and focused on Seventh Avenue, has become a part of American folklore. It represents an industry which is strongly agglomerated like petrochemicals, but centrally rather than peripherally located.

The casual visitor strolling around the district during the peak period of its operation may well wonder how any business can possibly survive in the midst of the incredible traffic congestion and human clamor which fills the streets during working hours. The visible negative externalities would seem to choke and stifle any enterprise located here. How does it survive?

The core of the industry is the manufacture of women's and misses' ready to wear garments. Traditionally, this industry has been highly sensitive to the dictates of fashion and intensive in its use of skilled labor, with numerous small and sometimes ephemeral firms and unusual seasonal financing and capital requirements, and is highly seasonal in its operation.

These observations may be summed up by noting that in regard to the requirements of loft space, labor capital, marketing, and finance, it is an extraordinarily nonstandardized industry. Whereas the differences between one brand of gasoline and another may be insignificant, the differences between a "hot number" and a dud in the garment trade spells the difference between success and failure.

These considerations have led to the development of a remarkable and subtle supporting infrastructure of positive externalities in the district. The area is centrally accessible to labor residing all over the region by means of the highly developed West Side subway facilities of Manhattan, the Port Authority bus terminal at 42nd Street which connects with most of the northern New Jersey suburbs, and the Pennsylvania Railroad Station which immediately adjoins the district. These facilities serve a population of more than ten million people. In addition, the needle trades unions maintain hiring facilities in the district.

An extensive market in loft space also exists in the district, with rental arrangements tailored to the highly variable nature of the industry. Closely related to this is a highly developed capital goods market (sewing machines, cutting equipment, and so forth) enabling failing firms to turn over assets quickly to the benefit of the newly established firm. In a similar fashion certain banks and financial institutions such as the Chemical Bank of New York have developed a specialization in the unusual short term types of financing required by garment district firms.

Certain processing firms provide manufacturing services in everything from embroidering to button making. This enables a dress firm to avoid the expense of establishing its own embroidery department for a special style which may have only a short fashion run.

The successful manufacturer not only possesses a top designing staff, but also has a finger on the pulse of the very best deal available in securing his loft space, labor, capital, financing, and subcontracting. A good cutter in his labor force can so arrange the cutting of the basic cloth to the required pattern that wastage is minimized in production. Access to good quality used equipment and the saving of a point or two of interest in financing may mean survival.

There is a highly interconnected garment manufacturing subculture which is extremely interdependent. The central persons in the communications network of this subculture have the edge on being successful in an extraordinarily competitive field.

Our emphasis on the external economies available to the production end of the business should not obscure similar conditions which prevail on the sales end of the business. The chief customers of the garment center manufacturing firms are major department stores throughout not only the NYMR, but also the country. The agglomeration of so many of these firms into the Seventh Avenue district has led to the development of a highly organized fashion market. Buyers from all over the country flock to the district for the purpose of securing new seasonal fashion lines for the stores which they represent. The manufacturing firms are poised for this event by having the best of their newly designed fashion apparel available for showings. Contingency plans have been made to take on the necessary additional equipment, labor, financing, material, and ancillary services should a big order ensue.

The buyers' season results in spin-off demand for other business services in Midtown Manhattan, ranging from cinema and legitimate theater entertainment, night clubs, and restaurant and hotel services, to illicit services in the immediate vicinity of Seventh Avenue.

Access to this market, and to the buyers' annual visits, is the sine qua non of the successful garment entrepreneur. The year's profits depend on the comparative advantage of the firm's line in this brief span of time.

Recently, some garment manufacturers have become sufficiently large and diversified that they have enough business volume to generate their own specialized ancillary departments, year round labor force, and long term capital and financial arrangements. Such large scale firms can afford to separate themselves from the external economies of production in the garment district and move elsewhere—to the South, for example, where labor and materials may be cheaper. Even these firms, however, tend to retain showroom space where some of their designers may remain in close contact with fashion trends.

Nevertheless, there has been erosion in New York's garment district. Lines of garments such as uniforms and undergarments which are made in long runs and are less sensitive to fashion have long since begun to move away from Seventh Avenue to lower cost locations in the hinterlands. The flag industry—a finished textile industry, although not a garment industry— moved all the way to Puerto Rico.

Finally, major fashion markets have arisen in the South and West following changes in consumer preference for clothing—casual over formal, western style over eastern, and the vogue for jeans and levis. These shifts have undercut Seventh Avenue's prosperity, relative importance, and employment, causing great concern in the New York City government.

All of these factors add up to a loss of manufacturing jobs in Manhattan. The fashion-sensitive functions of the portion of the industry remaining in the NYMR will probably continue to be aggregated and centrally located, at least in the short run, but the industry as a whole is gravely weakened.

THE FINANCIAL INDUSTRY

The Manhattan yellow pages list four full four column pages of stock and bond brokers. One estimates well above 1,000 listings, of which only a handful are outside of the triangular district of lower Manhattan known as Wall Street. In the securities industry and its financial auxiliaries, *information* is the quintessential commodity about which all else revolves. In the precise concretization of the switchboard metaphor of Deutsch, the stock exchange established itself as closely as possible to the seaport message source, with its roots going back informally to 1792, and formally to 1817. Ship lookouts with telescopes on the roofs of buildings, ship-to-office couriers, fire signalmen on Staten Island, and privilege riders in pilot boats all played a part in the nineteenth century marketing of information. Today, the Wall Street district is a maze of information exchange mechanisms.

A system of swift bonded couriers are used for the transfer of special financial paper. They know the shortest point-to-point routings in the area, using basement tunnels and sequestered alleyways in some cases. They are assisted by firms providing armed guards and armored trucks for important financial shipments. Five such firms operate in and near the financial district, including one which specializes in air courier service. The usual media—telephone, telegraph, stock ticker—are supplemented by elaborate computer-data-processing connections. One major bank in the district built a second multifloor building only a few blocks away on some of the highest priced real estate on earth to house its mammoth data-processing functions.

Despite a recent major upgrading of the data-processing system of the New York Stock Exchange, it has outgrown its classic 1903 building at Broad and Wall streets and plans have been made to move it to a landfill site at the Fulton Fish Market location on the East River near Wall Street.

As with brokerage houses, so with banks. Most of the major commercial banks in the world have a substantial commitment in office space in the Wall Street district. From "Algemene Bank Nederland, N.V." to "Wells Fargo Bank International Corp.," there are well over one hundred bank headquarters in the Wall Street area, representing American giants like Chase Manhattan, First National City, and Marine Midland as well as American headquarters for numerous foreign banking firms.

Among the institutional fixtures of the district are the New York Customs House; Federal Reserve Bank of New York; Federal Deposit Insurance Corporation; Securities and Exchange Commission; Federal Home Loan Mortgage Corporation; the Cocoa, Coffee, Sugar, Commodity, Cotton, Wool, and Produce Exchanges, the New York Clearing House; and the World Trade Center. This complex of finance, brokerage, exchange, insurance, and ancillary services is unparalleled in the western hemisphere and has the world as its region.

As a measure of the vigor which still attaches to Wall Street, it may be pointed out that in the boom years of 1925–1933, 138 buildings with an aggregate floor area of 30.4 million square feet were built in all of Manhattan including Wall Street. In the years 1967–1972 alone, for the downtown office area only, seventeen buildings with an aggregate footage of 214 million were built or nearing completion, including the ten million square foot World Trade Center. Thus, seventeen buildings in the late 1960s and early 1970s provide two-thirds the square footage, in the financial district alone, that the entire "Roaring Twenties" provided for all of Manhattan.

Since 1972, however, stagnation has increasingly affected the development of even this traditional Manhattan activity. Suburbanization and regional decentralization is occurring in the securities industry.

ADVERTISING

What Wall Street is to finance, the East midtown area (from the Forties north and centered on Madison Avenue) is to advertising. Well over 1,000 advertising agencies and counselors are listed, the greatest concentration of which are found in and near the Madison Avenue district. Surrounding and permeating this district is the midtown Manhattan concentration of banking and financial institutions. Two of the great Wall Street banks (Manufacturers Hanover, First National City) have established a "dual head-quarters" structure, dividing midtown and downtown operations. The banking facilities available in midtown are second only to the Wall Street district.

One of the reasons for the dual center is the migration and concentration of headquarters functions of major American corporations into the midtown area. By 1970, about 120 of the 500 largest industrial concerns in the nation (almost 25 percent) and about forty of the 250 largest nonindustrial concerns (16 percent) had established their headquarters in New York. Virtually all of the others maintain major regional offices there. Banks are drawn to the center of such corporate concentration.

In addition, to the west of Madison Avenue lies Rockefeller Center and the focus of entertainment and radio and TV activities—especially theater and television. To the east lies the United Nations district, abounding with national trade missions and consulates with public relations problems. Downtown, along Park Avenue South, lies a district rich in technical specialists in all aspects of the design, graphics, and photographic trades.

Madison Avenue enjoys the distinction of being within a pleasant walk of more potential corporate customers than, perhaps, anywhere else in the Western Hemisphere. Once their media needs are established, the theatrical district and the graphic arts firms supply the personnel and technical help. Television and other media are immediately at hand to diffuse the product; and—if the client is recalcitrant—some of the best restaurants, shops, and theater in the world lie within a few blocks to soften moods.

The result of Manhattan's attractiveness for such functions as corporate headquarters, advertising, finance, and related activities may be gauged by the fact that, since 1947, some 212 major buildings which aggregate to more than 94,910,000 square feet of office space have been built there. Most of this construction has spread out from the UN nucleus on 42nd Street and the East River. The other major growth center has been Wall Street.

While the spurt of development which has followed the demolition and subsequent replacement of a run-down warehouse and factory district by the beautiful architecture and carefully landscaped center of a world organization is a textbook case of the spillover effect of an urban amenity upon neighboring space, there was strong evidence by the mid-1970s that the offices were overbuilt. A tendency for major firms to move headquarters functions to the suburbs of the NYMR is now viewed with concern by the city's administration. If central office functions suburbanize—like manufacturing, wholesaling, retailing, and shipping—the essence of Manhattan's viability as an economic entity will have been undermined.

PUBLISHING AND PRINTING

More than 600 book publishers or branch offices of publishers are listed in Manhattan. A few are giants—McGraw-Hill, John Wiley, Charles Scribner, Simon and Schuster, and Random House, for example. Many more are tiny specialized firms catering to a limited market. Most are located in midtown Manhattan; the largest close to 42nd Street on the East Side near the UN, the smaller ones stretching to the south and north.

Aside from the obvious advantages of Midtown Manhattan for book publishing—access to publicity and the media, access to an enormous pool of skilled and professional workers by means of the metropolitan mass transit systems which converge at midtown, and access to the worldwide network of financial institutions which have long experience in the needs of activities like publishing—there are special local advantages external to the firm which favor Manhattan.

The presence of the New York intellectual community is extremely important from the standpoint of book criticism, manuscript evaluation, and the generation of publishable manuscripts themselves. Located at 42nd Street and Fifth Avenue is a great literary resource, the New York Public Library. Moreover, in the side streets of East midtown numerous small specialized libraries provide collections unduplicated elsewhere—the Morgan Library, the Mercantile Library Association, the Library of the Regional Plan Association, and libraries which belong to universities or to professional organizations of architects, engineers, and unions, not to mention the UN.

In a manner analogous to the garment center, there has been a tendency for activities related to manufacturing—like book printing and warehousing—to move out of the intellectual, media, and entertainment center of New York, but few enterprises have followed the lead of Prentice-Hall or Pergamon Press in establishing themselves in the suburbs. More typical is Oxford University Press, which maintains editorial and executive offices on Madison Avenue, while keeping its customer service functions in a suburban location in Fair Lawn, New Jersey. But even the New Jersey office has a direct tie New York City telephone number.

Book publishing remains concentrated in New York State (Table 1). A slight fall-off in percentage contribution in all of the states in the list was matched by an increase in Massachusetts. Since New York State really emphasizes the NYMR, and Massachusetts means largely the Boston Metropolitan Region, it seems that the areas richest in support services needed by publishers are also strongest in book publishing. By contrast, whereas the New York SMSA had 21 percent of

Table 1. Book Publishing by Leading States

| | Establishments | | Number Employed | | | |
| | | | 1954 | | 1967 | |
	1954	1967	(1,000s)	Percent	(1,000s)	Percent
U.S. Total	814	1022	34.7	100	51.8	100
New York State	333	349	15.9	46	21.4	41
Illinois	88	112	5.9	17	8.0	15
Wisconsin	15	19	2.1	6	–	–
Pennsylvania	39	47	1.7	5	1.8	3
Minnesota	23	19	1.5	4	2.4	5
Massachusetts	39	57	1.4	4	5.5	11

Source: W. Eric Gustafson "Printing and Publishing," in Max Hall, ed., *Made in New York*, ch. 2 (Cambridge, Mass.: Harvard University Press, 1959); and U.S. Census.

United States book production workers in 1954 (as against publishing,) by 1967 it had dropped to 15 percent.

The printing establishments in the city (in contrast to publishing) cluster in areas in which the demand for their services is substantial. At City Hall Plaza, where city and state bureaucracies and court functions are to be found, there is a massive assortment of law offices, bail bondsmen, and printers serving the city's legal trade. Other printing shops are found along the edges of midtown, in the upper floors of office and loft buildings, holding on to the coattails of the advertising and media worlds. All of these functions respond more to centripetal than to centrifugal forces, while petrochemicals and certain lines of retail and wholesale merchandising have been "centrifuged"outward.

A key is the role played by nearby supportive services available to the firm. These are called "external economies." Publishing depends on such external economies as are found in midtown Manhattan. Printing shops collectively form one of these external economies and, in turn, depend on publishing houses for their own trade. They are two terms in a symbiotic equation.

RETAILING AND WHOLESALING

The specialized activities that have as their aim the distribution of goods and services to the general population must strike a careful balance between central and perimeter location. Pulling wholesaling to the center, for example, is access by way of the shortest route to the largest market. Major components of this market are restaurants, caterers, and food retailing establishments which have traditionally had a core city location. Other things being equal, the optimum location for wholesaling activities would lie at the transportation nodes closest to the center of metropolitan population—that is, Manhattan Island. And, indeed, for many more than a hundred years, the various wholesaling districts for produce, butter and eggs, fish and meats, to name a few responded to this rule and could be found in stable locations in Manhattan. They could thus distribute to both core and outer rim markets by efficient transportation connections.

But today, "other things are not equal," and some wholesaling functions are being drawn outward from the core. The first and possibly the most important factor is demographic. Inner regions of the city like Manhattan and Brooklyn lose their residential popularity as business uses multiply and the population that remains is diminishing in density. Instead of a densely occupied central city tapering off to more rarified suburbs, it is convenient to imagine a "doughnut" of population with a small but growing central "hole" occupied largely by commercial uses, surrounded by suburbs of thinner densities.

Pulled out to doughnut locations have been restaurant, catering, and retailing establishments that serve the suburbs. As time goes on, the hole is growing and the doughnut increasing in overall diameter. The time has come when certain types of wholesaling—of foods and perishable items in particular—are more effectively done from a "doughnut" location (in terms of efficient access to retailers) than a "hole" location.

This tendency has been reinforced by the development of circumferential regional transportation routes and by the clogging up of central radial routes by traffic overloads. The availability of land for more spacious perimeter terminal facilities also contrasts with the cramped facilities and limited expansion possibilities at the city center.

Since New York City is located on a set of islands, rail connection with all of New York except the Bronx is largely accomplished by carfloat, railferry, and a few intermittently opening bridges. The logic of these conditions of site difficulty, when coupled with the demographic growth imperative of the city, has drawn wholesaling and warehousing activity into more peripheral locations. The food and produce markets of lower Manhattan are relocating. Wholesaling has moved, in these cases, to the giant new Hunt's Point terminal in the Bronx—a location which maximizes truck access to inner and outer ring population and retailing centers of the region by means of circumferential routes, while retaining the delivery capability to retailers at the core by radial ones.

To the west, in the New Jersey meadowlands, especially in the region roughly extending between Newark and Hackensack, an immense amount of light manufacturing, warehousing, and terminal activity has sprung up, partly on landfill. This location, on its inner flank, adjoins the New Jersey Turnpike, major circumferential highways, the Central of New Jersey and Penn Central classification yards, the ports of Newark and Elizabeth, and the Newark Airport. On its outer flank is found the major concentration of residential suburbs in northern New Jersey.

If wholesale activity is responding to the impulse for centrifugal movement, retailing is even more strongly suburbanizing. Major outlying shopping centers have sprung up in a ring throughout the demographic "doughnut" where major radial and circumferential access routes cross. In this sense, New York does not differ from other metropolitan regions where economic activity is suburbanizing.

In New York, however, the central business district retains great vitality. While residential population no longer exists in such great abundance in Manhattan, the diurnal working population is enormous. Furthermore, the range and diversification of goods which may be purchased in just a few square blocks of midtown Manhattan is perhaps unparalleled on the globe. One major bank (the Drydock Savings Bank) has used this theme in advertising in order to persuade its customers to "bank in Drydock Country, where everything is."

Two kinds of retailing continue to show great vigor in Manhattan. The first is the specialty good or service, for which Manhattan is the center of a regional or even worldwide network of buyers. Art galleries, tapestries, antiques, fine furniture, opera, theater, concerts, and jewelry are but a few. The *range* or distance which customers will travel in person or through agents to make a purchase is large, and the *threshold* or gross dollar volume of business which the firm must do in order to break even is large. These firms find it worthwhile to bear the large operating costs of prestigious Manhattan locations such as Fifth Avenue, Madison Avenue, or, in the case of entertainment enterprises, Broadway or Lincoln Center.

The second type of retailing which is vigorous in Manhattan is that which serves either the diurnal working population (novelty, notions, drug, cosmetic, restaurant, and haberdashery establishments, for instance) or the places where they work. Office furniture and equipment, commercial linen services, and window washing firms provide one type of example. Specialized music-retailing firms which serve the opera and concert world; art appraisal firms; and the firms of the diamond center which buy and sell, cut, and set stones are other examples of firms which have other basic businesses as their customers.

The medical industry, which retails health services extensively in the region, is a useful example. A number of major medical facilities of worldwide repute catering to highly specialized needs and health problems are concentrated along the East River, both north and south of the midtown business district. Auxiliary activities ranging from laboratories and medical supply firms to major research institutes provide services directly to this complex of health care facilities. By virtue of the enormous *range* (people come from the antipodes to avail themselves of the services) and the high *threshold* (occasioned by the cost of equipment, plant, and medical labor), this service-retailing industry occupies a central Manhattan location.

In contrast, other kinds of medical retailing (the general practitioner and the small group) have tended to follow population and purchasing power to the suburbs. And so, as in the case of merchandise retailing, where convenience goods and standard lines of widely purchased durable goods have moved to suburban shopping centers while highly specialized retailing functions remain in the city, major medical functions remain in the city and more common branches of practice have moved to the suburbs. Thus, in the suburbs, one can buy reproductions of paintings suitable for framing (but not an original Braque), or standard kinds of medical service (but not treatment for a rare and complex ailment).

Such movement and relocation tends to leave on the inside rim of the doughnut an area of poor tenement neighborhoods badly served both by retailers in the process of closing and moving out and, especially, by medical practitioners who are retiring or moving away with no replacements in sight.

The overall pattern set forth here is complicated by topography and the configuration of waterways, which, in turn, are reflected in the pattern of transportation routes, and by the occurrence of state, city, and municipal boundaries that separate regions of differing sales, income, and business tax regulations. Occasionally retailing activity is thinner on the more highly sales-taxed New York City side than on the Nassau County side, for example, of the boundary of western Queens. The major new shopping centers on Long Island are all in Nassau County rather than Queens. Gasoline stations often thin out sharply as one drives north from New Jersey into New York state.

But withal, the density of purchasing power in the outer band of the expanding population "doughnut" coupled with the growing central commercial "hole" in which jobs are intensively concentrated is driving a process of functional separation and redistribution of both wholesaling and retailing activity in the region.

TRANSPORTATION

That transportation feature in the New York metropolitan region that sets it off from most other metropolitan regions is its general cargo container port. Its counterpart is found in the Rhine Delta container port area, since New York's container port and that of the Rhine Delta are really simply two stations on an intercontinental conveyor belt.

The port of New York has undergone a series of transformations during its 300 years, with the container ports as the logical latest stage. The cramped finger piers and canals built along the East River side of Manhattan south of Wall Street by the Dutch gave way to the expansion of the East River and, later, the Hudson River waterfronts. Already bustling by the midnineteenth century, port facilities spilled across the East River to Brooklyn and beyond the Hudson River to Hoboken.

Ever pressed by the squeeze of congestion and costs of delay on the landward side combined with development pressures raising Manhattan real estate values, the Manhattan seaport was already doomed by World War I. Brooklyn had assumed the dominant shipping role by then. But, inexorably, the technological and managerial revolution which has dominated general cargo handling since World War II eventually led to the obsolescence of the great expanse of Brooklyn dock area and the concomitant development of Port Newark–Port Elizabeth as the center of life in the port of New York and New Jersey. It is now appropriate to recognize the addition of the term "New Jersey" to the title of that entity.

To illustrate today's port operations let us consider what happens when a freight shipment is consigned at an inland location like Schenectady, New York, for delivery at, say, Dusseldorf in West Germany (Figure 7).

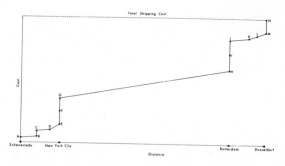

Figure 7. Shipping Costs before Containerization.

- The first increment to the shipping cost (A) represents initial loading costs on a truck or railroad car.
- The rise in cost between A and B represents shipping costs into the New York City area.
- The vertical line between B and C represents the cost of a traffic jam, dead cost of driver salary, and stationary vehicle.
- Shipment resumes between C and D.
- Costs rise to E as shipment slows getting to the dock.
- Unloading costs at the dockside, plus pilferage and insurance, or both, bring charges to F.
- Slowness of loading means a longer turnaround time in port. Part of cost of maintaining the vessel in port is borne by the shipper, raising charges to G.
- Costs of shipment to Rotterdam bring the aggregate cost to H.
- Unloading, pilferage, and insurance in Rotterdam raise costs to I.
- A portion of the vessel turnaround costs related to slow unloading by stevedore gangs jacks the shipping cost to J.
- Movement inland by truck adds cost between J and K.
- Increased costs of congestion between K and L upon nearing the Rhur district.
- Dusseldorf destination is reached at M.
- Final unloading costs raise the total shipping bill to N.

This sequence of events is a simplified version of the traditional shipping process. At Port Newark–Port Elizabeth, however, landward and waterward means of transportation are drawn together in an unprecedented fashion. Thirty-six deepwater berths are available along two thirty-five foot deep channels constructed in filled land along the western shore of Newark Bay. The landward extension of the facilities covers more than 1,400 acres and provides for wide aprons, ample warehousing space, and more than four million square feet of paved upland area. Already, by 1973, this port was handling more than 20 percent of the general cargo of the metropolitan region—the largest general cargo handling port in the nation.

Gantry cranes stand ready at the dockside to load trailer truck boxes, railroad car boxes, lighters, or standardized containers (depending on the nature of the vessel and the company concerned) on shipboard in a matter of minutes per container, cutting port turnaround time to a minimum. Many vessels can now arrive in port, unload, reload, and sail the next day. Thus, vessels with a capacity of more than 1,000 trailer truck boxes can be almost continuously in use.

Furthermore, pilferage is inhibited because the shipper seals his cargo into a container which is not opened again until it reaches its ultimate destination. Thus, insurance costs drop. In 1973, a record year, only one container load was stolen.

Immediately adjacent to Port Newark-Port Elizabeth are the New Jersey Turnpike, Newark Airport, and the main lines of four major railroads, including the Jersey Central and Penn Central lines. All have connections with complexes of wharfside cargo distribution buildings. The Penn Central International Container Terminal at Port Newark is capable of handling trainloads of up to sixty cars. Under these circumstances, the facilities are within overnight, second morning or third morning delivery to over one hundred million people in the United States (Figure 8).

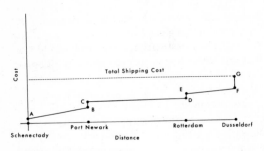

Figure 8. Shipping Costs after Containerization.

With traffic delays, turnaround delays, and pilferage controlled, and with fast motorship transportation provided, the total cost is cut greatly. Automated terminals have been developed in this great port complex to handle frozen goods such as meat, bananas, wine (by pipeline from tank ships), lumber, and general cargo.

In addition, there are two on site commercial bank branches serving Port Newark-Port Elizabeth. In a manner comparable to the technology which has smoothed the seams in goods transportation between the water mode and the land modes, information transmission systems have been developed that send invoices, manifests, and commercial paper parallel to the goods shipment so that dockside and customer clearances may be expedited.

The location of the container ports at Newark Bay is part and parcel of a pattern of centripetal movement in shipping facilities which has gone on in the port of New York for a long time. For more than 400 years urbanization has pushed seaport acitivites progressively further from the downtown city center. By the 1850s the seaport had migrated north along Manhattan's East River shore nearby to the newly created landfill area beyond the present location of the Williamsburg Bridge. A small but tightly knit colony of Norwegians engaged in the maritime trade worked near the docks and lived in a portion of the lower East Side.

By 1870, port activity was pushed to Brooklyn across the river near Furman Street. From 1870-1910 the Norwegians, following their livelihood, resided in adjoining areas of Brooklyn, today a hopelessly obsolescent site despite Port Authority efforts to modernize the area. At a cost of $94 million, a two mile long system of twelve modern steel and concrete piers with twenty-seven berths and a capacity of 3.5 million tons of cargo per year have been installed. At its heyday, 4,300 jobs were provided here, but, despite all efforts, landward connections are unsatisfactory, cramped by the cliff of Brooklyn Heights. The railroad line located here is only two miles long and offers no landward connection to any mainline. Remembering that Brooklyn is part of an island, like most of New York City, rail connections are few (Figure 9).

In other cities, rail junctions bring ocean freight inland to a spider web of radial and circumferential railroad lines by which goods may

Figure 9. Brooklyn Waterfront Cramped between the East River and the Foot of Montague Street. Note tugboat in float bridge slip at left.

be switched inland and laterally to a variety of sidings and yards. Chicago is usually taken as typical. The port of New York–New Jersey lacks the complete development of circumferential belt lines, so carfloats, lighters, and barges perform this circumferential transfer function. The vast marshaling yards on the New Jersey mainland and the yards at Sunnyside–Long Island City in Queens serve this ferrying operation by means of float bridges, such as the one which serves the Furman Street facility.

Overloaded even by the 1890s, the Brooklyn waterfront pushed to the still more decentralized location at the Bush Terminals. In the 1890s, as the North Brooklyn docks were feeling pressure, Irving Bush began to develop this terminal district based upon the concept of coordinating landward and seaward transportation with industrial processes through a site plan which brings railroad sidings from piers into the center of factory blocks. Located on the side of his father's oil business, it covers 200 acres, comprises eighteen piers with three

berths on each side, 150 six to twelve story building units, and its own railroad (the Bush Terminal Railroad), unconnected directly with any main line. At its peak, its industries employed 30,000 workers (Figure 10).

Today it is obsolescent as a port facility. Vertical loft buildings are unsatisfactory for many kinds of manufacturing. Inadequate landward transportation connections by road and rail are a handicap. Instead of a flow of materials to factory and goods to market over the integrated transportation arrangements, the toymaking, textile, garment, and novelty firms in the lofts today have little need for rail and ship transportation. Conversely, the palletized and containerized ship operations nearby serve the general urban region rather than chiefly the Bush Terminals.

When port expansion was dictated by the shipping needs of World War I, a less central location was again developed immediately to the south of the Bush terminals. In 1917, in response to the shipping pressure in World War I,

(A)

(B)

Figure 10. (**A**) Bush Terminal Buildings, Brooklyn. To the left is the waterfront and a dockside railroad. To the right, surface roads connect with Brooklyn. Rail sidings penetrate the interior bays of the buildings. (**B**) Bush Terminal Buildings, Brooklyn. Interior bay showing railroad sidings.

Irving Bush was made chairman of the War Board of New York. The Brooklyn Army Base was built, with 3.8 million square feet of storage space and sidings for 450 railroad cars. It is connected by land with the marshaling yards at the Penn Central in Queens. At its peak, it has had 60,000 jobs. In World War II, half of the troops and one-third of the supplies sent overseas from the United States went through this terminal.

In adjoining Sunset Park and Bay Ridge, the Norwegian colony which we remarked in Brooklyn by 1879 was present by 1910, corresponding to shifts in maritime trades activity. Vestiges of this colony can still be seen, suggesting how the suburbanizing of the maritime trades and its working force have gone hand in hand.

The latest stage in the process of port decentralization is Port Newark–Port Elizabeth, close to railroad, thruway, and airport. On the northern side of the Newark Channel is the Auto Port where specialized carriers of European and Japanese cars unload. Container ship facilities are located on the south side. Also located in this zone is a palletized lumber port and an automated wine terminal. An overhead pipeline brings wine from tanker ships to a bottling and distribution facility (Figure 11).

On the north side of the Elizabeth Channel is the scrap steel port, facing the container ports on the south side. The massive cranes which serve the port cost more than $1 million each and roll along 5,000 feet of bulkhead by railroad track. These cranes can accommodate twenty, twenty-four, thirty-five, and forty foot containers. They illustrate how heavily capitalized the modern port is. Large areas of land for storage terminals and truck marshaling, along with the intensive use of machinery, substitute for labor.

THE LANDSCAPE OF ENERGY

The functions of the metropolis which we have so far discussed in this study—manufacturing, retailing, wholesaling, and transportation—are driven by energy. Driving to New York City by way of the New Jersey Turnpike, one cannot help noticing the landscape of energy which develops north of Carteret. To the left are the gas and petroleum pipelines which serve the metropolis. To the right, beside the Arthur Kill separating New Jersey from Staten Island, are oilport facilities, tank farms, and petrochemical complexes. At the northern end of the turnpike is a giant thermal electric plant of the Public Service Gas and Electric Company of New Jersey. This region is one of the giant engines that drives the metropolis. What is the significance of this scene? Five sources of energy—coal, oil, gas, hydraulic flow, and nuclear fission—drive a series of electric generation plants, which are linked together into a system affording electricity to the metropolitan power market. Additionally, some coal, oil, and gas pass directly to metropolitan consumers without going through the intervening step of electric conversion.

If the metropolitan power market exercised a steady, unchanging demand it would be possible, theoretically at least, to bring the entire flow system into such nice balance that the fuel imports, conversion rates, and power outputs would be exactly in equilibrium, with no need for system adjustments to varying supplies or demands. Such is not the case, however, and there exist great fluctuations in the demand for power in the metropolitan region on a regular diurnal, weekly, and seasonal basis. Additionally, there is an annual trend for power demands to increase.

The above implies that due to daily, weekly, seasonally, and annually fluctuating demands (and failures of supply as well), storage and back-up capacity must be available at all times. This is provided by coal yards, oil tanks, and gas tanks which maintain surplus capacity to fill sudden needs. The Consolidated Edison Company of New York has also proposed a special pump storage facility atop the highlands overlooking the Hudson River at Cornwall, north of the city. This facility would comprise a reservoir and a pumping and generating station. During periods of surplus power, water would be pumped up out of the Hudson River to the reservoir, while during periods of power shortage, the water would be released to fall back to the river, driving turbogenerators on the way, and thus reconverting the potential energy of the raised water into needed electrical energy.

Within the context of this discussion, one can envision energy in the form of coal from Appalachia; electricity from the hydroelectric stations on the Canadian frontier; oil and gas from the South and from overseas; fission fuel from Oak Ridge, Tennessee, destined for

(A)

(B)

Figure 11. Port Newark-Elizabeth: **(A)** Scrap steel port. Ship being loaded with electromagnet cranes. **(B)** Trailer-truck-sized container being loaded on a container ship by a gantry crane.

(C)

(D)

(C) Imported Japanese automobiles await shipment inland. **(D)** Palletized lumber bundles await shipment inland.

the Indian Point fission electric plant on the Hudson River, all converging by every conceivable means on the metropolis, and especially on northeastern New Jersey, to be transformed into the power needs of America's primate metropolitan area.

The effects of this metropolitan power landscape are great; refinery storage tank areas, coal yards, railway yards, pipelines, wharf facilities, transmission lines, generating plants, and relay stations are all part of it.

Residential Space

THE BASIC HOUSING STOCK

Most residents of the metropolitan region live in multiple dwellings. In 1970 in New York City, 2.2 million out of 2.9 million units were rental units. In the New York City portion of the region, this housing stock can be subdivided into the following categories:

- Pre-1867 multiple dwellings
- "Old Law tenements" built between 1867 and 1901
- "New Law tenements" built between 1901 and 1929
- Post-1929 structures
- Rented one or two family houses (Table 2)

Table 2. Renter-Occupied Housing Units by Structure Type, New York City, 1970

Structure Type	Units (1,000s)	Percent
Old Law	248	12
New Law	756	36
Post-1929	616	30
Others	169	8
Rented Houses	265	13
Total	2,024	100
Unaccounted for	143	–

Source: George Sternlieb and James W. Hughes, *Housing and People in New York City* (New York: The Housing and Development Administration of the City of New York, Department of Rent and Housing Maintenance, 1973).

The rented houses tend to be located in newer areas on the perimeter of the non-Manhattan boroughs. The bulk of the housing in Manhattan and the inner areas of Brooklyn, the Bronx, and Queens was built before 1929, and a substantial amount prior to 1901. This observation is reinforced when we consider that many residences in the "other" category consist of nineteenth century (or earlier) townhouses which have been subdivided, flats constructed prior to the Old Tenement Law of 1867, or vintage buildings originally constructed for nonresidential purposes. In Greenwich Village (Manhattan) and Brooklyn Heights (Brooklyn) there are numerous carriage houses located on eighteenth and nineteenth century mews which have been converted to residential use. In the cast iron building section—south of Houston Street in Manhattan; called the SoHo district locally—there are likewise numerous factory lofts dating from the 1870s which have been illegally converted to residential use. Table 3 presents a breakdown by borough.

More than half of Manhattan's 613,000 rented units were built before 1929. Brooklyn and the Bronx reveal comparable patterns. Only partly suburban Queens and Staten Island deviate from this pattern. This is not to say that age inexorably implies decrepitude. A small percentage of Old Law and New Law tenements command high rentals, while some post-1929 dwellings and rental houses eke out very small rentals. In any era there is shoddy as well as sound construction, and some early structures, by virtue of their careful construction, quality

Table 3.   Rental Housing in New York City, by Type, by Borough, 1970 (percent)

Structure Type	Bronx	Brooklyn	Manhattan	Queens	Staten Island
Old Law	4	12	25	1	1
New Law	59	36	30	22	4
Post-1929	29	24	30	45	33
Others	3	8	14	4	4
Rented Houses	6	19	1	28	57
Total	100	100	100	100	100
Units (1,000s)	406	622	613	354	28

Source: George Sternlieb and James W. Hughes, *Housing and People in New York City* (New York: The Housing and Development Administration of the City of New York, Department of Rent and Housing Maintenance, 1973).

materials, and neighborhood amenities have beckoned to the rehabilitation process. In turn, some newer structures—for instance in the crisis area of Brownsville in Brooklyn—began to deteriorate almost as soon as they were constructed in the 1940s. They are now abandoned or burned out shells.

A trip from southern Manhattan outward through the surrounding boroughs to the suburban counties is, to a large measure, a trip through time. At the point on the Lower East Side of Manhattan near the Chinese district of Chatham Square we find vestiges of what used to be numerous streets of Old Law tenements in the 1870s. Earlier housing tended to lack light and ventilation in interior rooms. The Tenement Act of 1867 required the plan of the tenement to be dumbell shaped, in order to provide airshafts at the waist of the building. Many of these structures still exist along Madison, Catherine, and Henry streets in the Lower East Side. Because late nineteenth century subway construction proceeded northward in Manhattan and eastward through Brooklyn, districts of Old Law tenements to this day are scattered along the rights of way of several branches of the Interborough Rapid Transit (IRT) and Brooklyn and Manhattan Transit (BMT).

By 1904 transit had reached northward into Harlem and its extension in the Bronx and Brooklyn was well under way. Thus northern Manhattan, especially the Broadway line of the IRT, and portions of the South Bronx become the *loci classici* of the New Law tenement. These structures are usually larger than the Old Law tenements and have more front footage. Rooms are more spacious and they were required to be designed to higher sanitary stan-

dards. Decorative touches such as white stone corner quoins against a red brick base and matching stone treatment of window lintels and sills, sometimes with egg and dart embellishments, are frequently found. The best of these buildings are valued as residences, especially in the neighborhood of Columbia University, owing to the excellent interior plaster work and fireplaces. Many have, of course, fallen into desuetude, as have the bulk of the Old Laws.

Most of the post-1929, yet pre–World War II buildings are concentrated in the more outlying reaches of the older boroughs and in Queens and Staten Island. Since World War II, however, the profitability of high-rise, high rental apartments of few rooms catering to singles or childless couples has led to a renewal cycle of inner city construction. Especially along the East Side of Manhattan, north of the midtown office district, new construction appears among the Old and New Law structures of York, First, and Second avenues, breaking up the integrity of the old German-American Yorkville area. Development south of midtown, already starting, is triggered to explode if and when the new Second Avenue subway is further along in construction, an eventuality which has recently been cast into doubt since work was indefinitely suspended as a result of the 1975 city fiscal crisis.

TENANTRY

The black population of New York is quite heterogeneous. Many recent black immigrants are persons of urban American origin, whereas earlier migrants came from the rural South. There are enclaves of West Indian blacks in Har-

Table 4.   New York City Household Heads, by Race and Ethnic Group, 1970 (percent)

Borough	Non-Puerto Rician White	Negro	Puerto Rican	Other	Total	Total Households (1,000s)
Bronx	55	21	14	10	100	497
Brooklyn	66	21	7	6	100	876
Manhattan	65	19	8	8	100	687
Queens	81	10	1	8	100	690
Richmond	90	4	1	4	100	86
All Households	68	17	7	8	100	2,837

Source: U.S. Bureau of the Census, 1970 Census of Population.

lem and elsewhere that lend additional diversity to the scene—the blocks to the west of Mount Morris Park (with St. Martin's Episcopal Church as a cultural focus) contain many middle class blacks of West Indian origin, areas in Queens are inhabited by French-speaking Haitians, and there is a Cape Verdean League in Harlem. The census category "black" in the New York case implies much more ethnic and cultural diversity compared to other American cities.

What holds true for blacks is also true of "Puerto Ricans." The visitor to the Chelsea district of Manhattan (West Side in the teens and twenties) may discover that some of the persons of Spanish surname who are sometimes labeled "Puerto Rican" are republican refugees from the Spanish Civil War, who sometimes entered the U.S. via Puerto Rico. Dominicans, Cubans, and many other persons of Hispanic origin form mixed families with Puerto Ricans and are sometimes misclassified. As a result, the significance of the term "Puerto Rican" is somewhat doubtful.

Queens and Richmond are the whitest (and most suburban) of the boroughs (Table 4). About 20 percent of the population of Manhattan, the Bronx, and Brooklyn are black (Figure 12). The Harlem concentration in central Manhattan is the best known of the black areas nationally. Central Brooklyn (Bedford-Stuyvesant) and its adjacent areas are even more extensive regions of concentrated black residency, however. That part of the South and East Bronx connected to the Harlem area by bridges across the Harlem River also contains a marked concentration of black residents.

Areas of Puerto Rican residence often lie between black areas and predominantly white ones (Figure 13). Thus, the Barrio (the East

Harlem Puerto Rican neighborhood) lies between Harlem and fashionable Park Avenue to the south. Between Bedford-Stuyvesant in Central Brooklyn, and white residential areas like the region from Flatlands to Bay Ridge to the south, there are Puerto Rican districts. A similar phenomenon is to be found in the Bronx, where Puerto Rican population concentrations in the Hunt's Point area lie between whites to the north and blacks to the southwest.

Insofar as tendencies may legitimately be observed among New York City's renters, blacks and Puerto Ricans tend to have larger, younger, and poorer families than whites. Black, Puerto Rican, and white families in descending order tend to have families with a female head (43.4, 33, and 31.3 percent, respectively).

In 1970, about 36 percent of white renter households had incomes below $6,000, while 39 percent had incomes above $10,000. For blacks, 52 percent of renter households had income below $6,000, while only about 19 percent had incomes in excess of $10,000. In the case of Puerto Ricans, 61 percent of renter households fell below $6,000, while only about 13 percent earned in excess of $10,000.

New York renters requiring the most in services, housing space, and access to mass transit inhabit the regions in Manhattan, the Bronx, and Brooklyn with the oldest housing stock (New and Old Law tenements). These houses are the costliest to maintain and renovate and possess the most obsolescent sanitary, electrical, plumbing, and heating systems. Moreover, there is a shortage of housing for the poor, since construction of low income housing has been far outstripped by demolition in favor

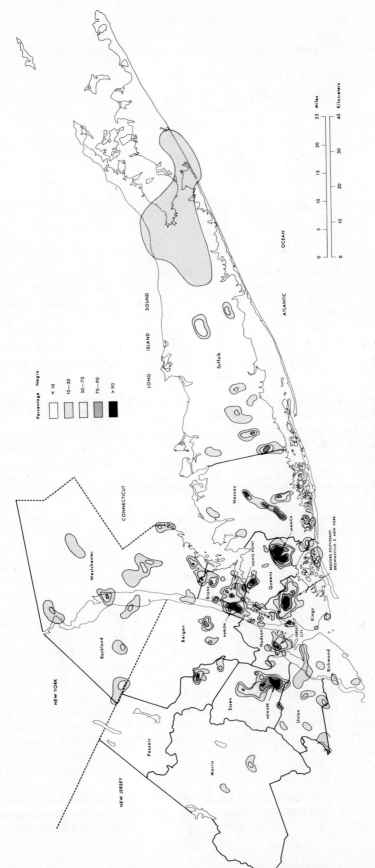

Figure 12. Map of Percentage Black.

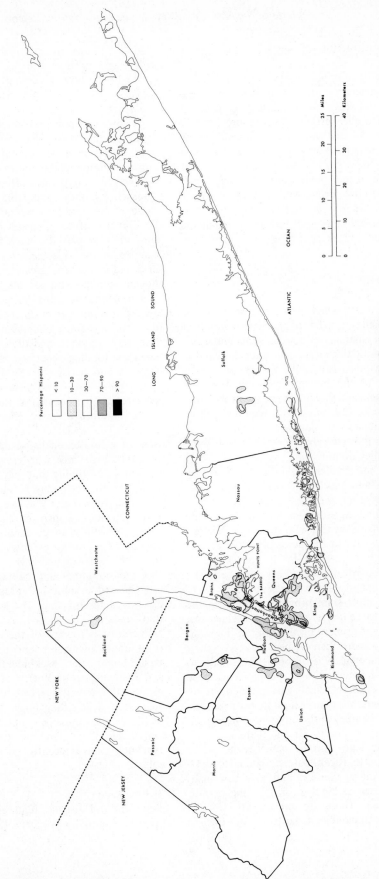

Figure 13. Map of Persons of Spanish Surname.

of the construction of high-rise, high rental units.

Recipients of public assistance live in housing badly in need of public or private rehabilitation, but for which no such assistance is forthcoming. Sternlieb estimates that more than 20 percent of Old Law and intermediate-sized New Law structures have over 20 percent of their tenants on welfare. The result is the kind of disaster which the reader who tours Brooklyn will witness in the Brownsville-East New York area—acres of rubble and demolished shells of hopeless buildings with blocks of tenements interspersed and an agonizing lag in new construction.

OWNERSHIP

There is a myth which pervades discussions of urban housing. It is that of the vicious slumlord whose vast domains of squalid tenements provide him with the means for squeezing profits out of the poor. From this follows an instant resolution of the housing problem: Let the slumlord be made to pay for the solution of the housing crisis. That imperative would be a fine policy statement if slumlords existed. Sadly enough—in the sense that it would simplify the solution—they do not.

Among the smaller Old Law and New Law tenements—housing New York's poorest tenants and creating the most acute problems in the city's housing stock—nearly 40 percent are in the hands of owners who own no other real estate. Only 16 to 20 percent of these categories are estimated to be in the hands of owners who own more than seven parcels. The large slumlord appears to be a myth.

In fact, most slum property owners in the city tend to follow a profession besides real estate as their primary occupation. In the poorest housing, more than 50 percent report their property income as a minor supplement to their regular income. These people tend to be craftsmen, workers, small businessmen, or retired people rather than real estate professionals or lawyers. In areas of the city where the tenantry is black or Puerto Rican, there is a concomitant tendency for the parcel owner to be black or Puerto Rican. An estimated 15 to 16 percent of the smaller Old and New Law tenements are owned by Spanish-speaking or non white owners. These are concentrated in districts of comparable tenancy. The owners tend to be newcomers to real estate ownership. This suggests that the least profitable real estate in the city is coming into the hands of inexperienced minority group ownership. The problems are obvious.

It is well to point out another form of ownership at this point—the city itself. In earlier days, when renewal or redevelopment of an area was contemplated, speculators would rush in and buy up parcels. Then, through paper transactions, they would bid up the apparent value of the parcel considerably, reaping windfall profits after condemnation. To correct this, the city passed "quick take" laws which can freeze the titles and status of all parcels in a redevelopment area, transferring title to the city and blocking speculative activity.

Unfortunately, this leaves the city as the owner of a number of decrepit buildings. Since the lag between condemnation and demolition may be years, and the city has not developed the funding necessary for adequate maintenance and service of these properties, and since there are few residential alternatives available to the occupants, the city finds itself as the landlord of these doomed and hopeless parcels. The social consequences to the children of a household living on a marginal level of public assistance who grow up in a squalid submarginal building that they perceive as being owned by the city may be imagined. They are prone to view the city as the oppressor that is forcing them to live in squalor, fear, and misery. Hostility to the landlord is transferred to the city and by extension to the political process. Alienation and anger are the result.

Condominiums and cooperatives are now put forward as solutions at least to the middle class need for housing. The more cynical note that transforming a multiple dwelling into a cooperative is a way for the owner to get out from under ownership and to pass on to the tenant-buyer the backbreaking maintenance and financing arrangements of the building. In return, the tenants receive ownership of an apartment which they might never be able to resell. Under these circumstances it is not remarkable that sales and transfers of coop apartments have recently become quite difficult.

Financing
A landlord usually requires mortgaging in order to acquire his property. His future success

depends on resale value and the potential for remortgaging. Equity in the property is meaningless unless it can be recovered in cash. Remortgaging is one way of doing this. As a mortgage is paid off, the owner's wealth is held in real estate instead of cash. In an upward market, the owner may want to remortgage and translate his wealth into cash. Sale of the property is another way of doing this. Remortgaging in an upward market is analogous to sale to oneself using bank financing.

Sternlieb's study showed that 54 percent of owners of all the buildings considered in his research (including post-1929s) felt that if they could get institutional mortgage money on their properties (and many Old and New Law owners felt that they could not under any circumstances), they would have to supplement it with money out of their own resources. Sternlieb's conclusion: "In sum, many buildings have fallen out of the effective scope of the institutional money market" (p. 385). In other words, financial institutions had laid down a policy against lending on Old and New Law buildings regardless of condition. Furthermore, for the small Old and New Law tenements which form the heart of the poverty housing problem, the key reason for mortgage unavailability is their location. Insurance coverage is also difficult to get for these buildings. The mortgage and insurance company policies reinforce each other and present both the landlord and tenant with an impasse.

Under these circumstances, owner and tenant alike are ruined. How is the owner to maintain his obsolescent parcel in livable condition in the absence of financial incentives and in a neighborhood where the charging of higher rent is impossible? Tenants and prospective tenants cannot pay more either because of poverty or public assistance rigidities. Diverting any income at all to his personal benefit implies deterioration of his property and a decline in the quality of his tenancy. The point is often reached where the property is a drain on the owner. When efforts to sell are fruitless, abandonment starts to spread into the worst of these older borough areas.

Rent control is often blamed for the problem. Without a doubt the rigidities imposed by rent control upon the ability of rents to move upward affect the economics of many housing areas in the city. But, with respect to the question of poverty housing, abandonment, and the decay of neighborhoods that is so poignant in those areas inhabited by a young, minority, and public assistance clientele, it is doubtful whether rent control has much effect. After all, within the New York–New Jersey metropolitan region lies the major city of Newark, lacking rent control but acutely manifesting the same syndrome noticeable in the housing market of New York City. The hapless landlord, caught outside the mainstream of the real estate market, is rendered impotent by the deterioration of the neighborhood around him, mounting costs, and a limited flow of cash.

REHABILITATION—THE CLOGGING UP OF FILTERING DOWN

But let us renovate and rehabilitate the declining structures and thus upgrade the basic housing stock. Or else, let us build for the rich in confidence that an improved housing stock will "filter down" to the poor.

Brooklyn Heights stands as a splendid example of rehabilitation. Some areas of the city have intrinsic amenities—a well-scaled street plan, a noble view of a park or of the harbor; a supply of old and decaying yet architecturally distinctive brownstone townhouses which are cheap, subdivided, downgraded, but salvageable; access to centers of employment and shopping. Brooklyn Heights has them all. To a lesser degree, so do the nearby districts of Cobble Hill, Boerum Heights, Park Slope, and Fort Greene. A process begins in such a neighborhood which in New York City is called "brownstoning." People of means purchase and renovate the old brownstone townhouses, usually reserving one or two floors for themselves and developing flats on other floors for rental, at a good price. As the stroller through Brooklyn Heights will appreciate, the outcome is a charming, attractive neighborhood in which the essence of all that is best in a city is embodied.

The effect, however, is to displace a poor population (largely Syrian and Puerto Rican in the case of Cobble Hill, now in the midst of the process south of Brooklyn Heights) and to convert poor residences into wealthy ones. The "filtering" here is up, not down. Simultaneously, other poor neighborhoods are being "renewed."

Renewal generally involves the demolition of blocks which are suitable for "brownstoning" or renovation. Replacement is usually by high-rise buildings with small apartments at substantial rentals. Fifty or sixty years from now, if these buildings filter down, they will become instant slums if the poor tend to have families too large to be easily accommodated by the small apartments, as they do now. The immediate effect in renewal areas is to reduce the stock of housing for the poor. Tomkins Square, in the East Village, is at the center of an area which will be subject to demolition and rebuilding if the Second Avenue Subway is finished.

And then there are "cities within a city" or planned unit developments (PUDs). A PUD underway on Welfare Island in the East River includes 1,050 units, of which 20 percent are earmarked for low income families—a drop in the bucket.

The PUDs which are under construction in the NYMR will provide only a miniscule number of low income housing units in relation to the need revealed in the Brownsville and East New York area of demolition and condemnation. None of these solutions to the problems of urban housing is anywhere near to dealing with the scale of low income housing need.

Public low income housing developments have been slow in developing since federal funds have become less available and many critics have condemned them as unsatisfactory. New York City has still to devise a way to house the inhabitants of slums of despair such as those in these desolate areas of central Brooklyn.

Urban Landscapes and Social Processes

The history of European settlement of the New York Metropolitan Region spans the years from 1625 to the present. During those years, the landscape has been progressively transformed from a wooded archipelago inhabited by American Indians residing at low densities to an urbanized area in which great expanses of land have been paved over, filled in, and converted into a landscape of human artifice. In this landscape vestiges from earlier times may often be noted, and the nature of social processes related to their placement and use may be clarified. As the geologist reads events relating to the history of the earth from layers of sediment deposited in earlier eras, the artifacts present in an urban neighborhood can help us recreate social processes of bygone days. There are several such in the New York Metropolitan Region.

THE WALL STREET-BATTERY AREA OF SOUTHERN MANHATTAN

Little remains of the Dutch and early English colonial eras in New York City, although there are some early Dutch farmhouses in New Jersey, a few old houses on Long Island, and one schoolhouse from the seventeenth century in Staten Island. The street layout of the Wall Street area, however, is from the past. Broad Street and Beaver Street, at the core of the financial district, were canals in the Dutch days. Many streets carry the name "slip" (Coenties Slip, Rutgers Slip, Peck Slip). A slip was the channel of water between two finger

piers. In effect these streets were originally water channels along which the Dutch and English merchants did their business, for southern Manhattan was originally a group of islands in a maze of marshy channels.

The present shoreline of the East River has been extended several hundred feet from the original shoreline which lay near Water Street (now far inland). Part of the shoreline extension has to do with the fact that sanitary wastes, offal, and refuse were commonly dumped into the slips until navigation was impossible. Then landfill was added and new finger piers were built farther out into the river. The process then began again.

Fraunces Tavern is a much renovated 1719 building still standing in the area. Famous as the site of Washington's farewell address, it serves to make a useful social point. The proprietor, Black Sam Fraunces, was Washington's victualer, and became a member of the free black community in the city after the Revolution. Much of the restaurant, catering, and related industries in Manhattan during the first half of the nineteenth century was carried on by free Negro entrepreneurs. This was not atypical. W.E.B. DuBois, in his 1899 study, *The Philadelphia Negro,* alludes to the League of Negro Caterers as an established organization in eastern cities.

The great fire of 1835 devastated the Wall Street area, and what conflagration failed to do, real estate development accomplished, so that only a couple of blocks of 1811-1850 buildings are left in the South Street Seaport Restora-

Figure 14.   Schermerhorn Row. These buildings date variously from 1811 to 1850.

tion area (Figure 14). These do, however, indicate that until the midnineteenth century, and during the heyday of the clipper ship, it was the East River side of lower Manhattan which was the seaport and not the Hudson River side. A glance at a regional map will show that the East River communicates not only with lower New York Bay, the Atlantic Ocean, and southern coastal routes, but also with New England via Long Island Sound. India House, a stately 1854 building was a center for midcentury commercial activity (Figure 15).

The northern boundary of the district on the East Side is the stately Brooklyn Bridge (1883) built by the Roeblings. Its location and date are also of some significance. By 1883, both Brooklyn (then a separate city) and New York were rapidly urbanizing and interdependent entities. The ward of New York north of the bridge had a density exceeding 300,000 per square mile. When technology developed to the point where a bridge was feasible, it was so located as to link the City Hall of New York with its Brooklyn counterpart.

CHATHAM SQUARE

The Chatham Square region, to the north of the Brooklyn Bridge, is an extremely rich and complex one. Owing to the convergence of a number of streets into a square, which was once called "Paradise Square," it has also been called the "Five Points."

The earliest artifact in this area is the Congregation Shearith Israel burying ground (1682), located on the Bowery, which was then a rural farm-to-market road (Figure 16). Note the land level of the cemetery in relation to the surroundings as an indication of landscape change.

By 1820, the area had passed from rural to suburban (Figure 17). By 1840 many squalid pre-Old Law tenements had been built signaling the transition of the area to a poor core city slum inhabited largely by Irish immigrants. Demolition and intensive building occurred

Figure 15. India House on Hanover Square, an 1854 commercial building located near where Captain Kidd (a distinguished vestryman of Trinity Church) had his residence earlier.

Figure 16. Shearith Israel Burying Ground (1682) which reveals the early land level near Chatham Square.

Figure 17. Early townhouses built during the urbanization of the Chatham Square-Five Points Area, circa 1822.

during the 1870s and 1880s, resulting in block after block of Old Law tenements housing the poor Italian and Jewish immigrants who labored in the city's growing garment trades and construction trades (Figure 18).

The modern American can have little grasp of what it was like to live in this district in the nineteenth century. Until 1842, the poor New Yorker had to depend on well water (the first aqueduct brought fresh water to the city only in 1842). In the Chatham Square area a marshy site called the Collect Pond, which had originally been a small lake before it became choked with refuse, was the principal source. Now completely filled in and converted into the site of the Criminal Courts Buildings and a park, it was then highly polluted. Typhus, typhoid, yellow fever, and cholera periodically ravaged the district. Matter from a nearby potter's field leached into the groundwater after mass burials until 1827 when burials south of Grand Street were prohibited. In 1840 one person in four died in this area, yet the plague of 1849 was reputed to have been more serious.

We are now in a position to note that the suburban phase (Georgian and Greek Revival townhouses), gave way to the old Five Points phase (pre-1867 tenements) and thence to the Old Law tenement phase, and finally to the Chinese district of today.

Corresponding to the first phase were "old Knickerbocker" family groups. After the Napoleonic Wars and the distress in English industrial districts which led to the Peterloo Massacre of 1819, the fringes of the area were occupied by poor English immigrants. Notorious and vicious gangs which included English youths ravaged the Five Points. These gave way, in turn, to the Irish and German migrants of the 1840s and 1850s. The "Dead Rabbits," Roach Guards, and Kerryownians terrorized New York until the 1860s when gang activity peaked in connection with the draft riots of 1863.

Corresponding to the Old Law tenement phase was the development of the Jewish and Italian Lower East Side pattern. Between the Bowery and the East River was Jewish turf (centered upon East Broadway). West of the

Figure 18. Old Law Tenement in Chatham Square District. Notice the indentations on the side which, together with matching ones on an adjoining building, provided an airshaft for fenestration. The adjoining building predates the Old Tenement Law of 1867.

Bowery was Italian turf (centered upon Mulberry Street). The Bowery was no man's land—a dark and dangerous place covered by an elevated rapid transit railroad. The song "The Bowery," with its refrain, "I'll never go there any more," sums it up.

Not until the years immediately preceding the First World War did the Chinese move into the area as still later occupants of the shabby and variegated housing stock of the area. Again crime flared up briefly. The Hip Sing and On Leong tongs fought for control of the district along Mott and Pell streets and in the "bloody angle" of Doyer Street.

Vestiges of the Italian period may still be seen on Mulberry Street, in the form of funeral parlors with Italian names which are still available to cater to the needs of the last of the previous population wave. Manhattan Bridge, however, and its landward extension, Canal Street, have become the rough boundary of the Chinese area to the south and the Italian and formerly Jewish, but now largely Hispanic, areas to the north.

In the early part of the nineteenth century, the workers from the Irish slums walked south to the old East River waterfront to work. By the Old Law tenement phase, jobs were located to the northwest in Manhattan's interior where the Cast Iron District was being built to house the growing needle trades industries of the city.

THE LOWER EAST SIDE

North of Canal Street and west of the Bowery lies the old Italian Lower East Side, which preserves much of its ethnic identity to this day, while the Jewish Lower East Side, east of the Bowery, has changed substantially. In the Italian district, Italian tricolor streamers and painted fire hydrants in red, white, and green are noted everywhere. Even when the younger generation of Italian-American families moves to a suburban residence, it is often a matter of routine for them to return regularly to the old Italian East Side to visit with relatives. On such occasions as the feast of San Gennaro, during the week of September 19, the streets are packed with vendors selling delicacies and throngs of revelers.

Grand Street, in the northern portion of the Italian district, is still noted for fine Italian needlework (Figure 19). A declining bridal gown industry is still located there. Italian-American citizens concerned with preservation are now mounting an effort to preserve this ethnic neighborhood as an historic area.

In contrast, there has been much change in the Jewish Lower East Side. Demolition of the Old Law stock has been extensive, as more modern housing has been underwritten by the activities of such unions as the International Ladies Garment Workers' Union. This has led to the establishment of a well-housed population with dependable purchasing power in the area (Figure 20). Symptomatic of this, there has been some commercial improvement in areas near the union housing.

A social landmark in the area is the Henry Street Settlement. Established by Lillian Wald in 1893, it is famous in the annals of social reform (Figure 21). It occupies beautiful restored Greek revival townhouses of the 1827–34 period. To the south of the settlement, however, lies its problem and a challenge. Signs with Hebrew characters confront streets with Hispanic pedestrians.

This is an area in which an aging and declining Jewish population is being replaced by a young, predominantly Catholic Puerto Rican population. The settlement houses are left without the population to serve for which they were intended. The newcomers, badly in need of service, have not found the avenue by which assistance might flow to them from the agencies. It is a dilemma of neighborhood change.

Yet there is still one landscape element left which evokes the old Jewish Lower East Side most forcefully. On Sunday, the outdoor market on Orchard Street still teems with activity and with bargainseekers from all over the metropolis (Figure 22).

THE CAST IRON DISTRICT

The heart of the city's early garment industry, toward which many of the inhabitants of Five Points and the Lower East Side turned for employment in the 1870s and 1880s, is also an architectural treasure. South of Houston Street (always pronounced How-stun in New York) lies the district called SoHo. Along such thoroughfares as Greene Street lie some of the finest examples of the cast iron factory loft style of construction which the city possesses (Figure 23). Following the renown of such efforts as the Crystal Palace in London (1851) which employed cast iron, New York designers such as

Figure 19. Bridal Goods Shop on Grand Street near the Bowery.

Figure 20. The Sidney Hillman Homes (1926-1930). Financed by the Amalgamated Clothing Workers, these houses replaced primarily Old Law and pre-Old Law dwellings.

Figure 21. The fine old 1827–1834 townhouses occupied by the Henry Street Settlement, the principal of which is shown here, have been carefully preserved and restored.

Bogardus, Gaynor, Thomas, Fernback, and Snook developed a style in which entire facades were cast in units which were decorated in classical ornaments.

Today, the person standing on Greene Street and Grand looking north can recapture the 1870 factory loft cityscape to a great degree, for the entire district is still nearly intact. Obsolescent for factory use, these lofts have attracted attention as workplace-residences. In fact, near Houston Street it is noticeable how many of the cast iron lofts are being lived in.

Strictly speaking, such occupancy is illegal in New York. If, however, a person claims that he is operating a residence-workshop in an activity which requires loft space, he can be permitted to do so. Many artists have taken advantage of this provision and an art-oriented neighborhood is developing there. This is quite in conformity with the tradition of Greenwich Village, immediately north of Houston Street.

In 1875, the workers in a SoHo loft would walk westward to their jobs from the Lower East Side. Some of the affluent owners and

Figure 22. The rich and diversified ethnic mix of the Lower East Side is manifested in this Sunday photograph of the Orchard Street Market.

managers of lofts would journey south to their places of business from their fashionable Greenwich Village or Chelsea townhouses. The pattern is not unlike that in which, today, core city workers are separated in residence from the suburban white collar and professional classes by a perimeter factory belt.

Yet, as the lovely tree-shaded streets of Greenwich Village declined at the end of the nineteenth century, it became a poor neighborhood of tenements and cheap rooming houses carved out of declining townhouses (Figure 24). After World War I, artists popularized residence here. These "bohemians" alerted the otherwise insensitive public to the intrinsic worth of the Village as an attractive cityscape. Redevelopment drove out the artists as land values boomed.

Moving due east, toward the river, artists next invaded the East Village. In the years after World War II, the cycle repeated itself. Now the commercialized bohemia of the East Village has again priced them out of the market. In lieu of

moving directly into the river, the next shift was to SoHo. As the reader may already have guessed, cast iron loft space is rapidly getting priced out of sight. Thus, the poor artist creates the very condition which drives him from the district which he has had the vision to renew.

THE BARRIO

Park Avenue is a synonym for wealth. From 42nd Street to 96th Street along this boulevard lie fifty blocks of housing for the wealthy. Yet at 96th Street a remarkable transition occurs (Figure 25). A sharp downslope in the road grade results in the Penn Central tracks emerging above ground upon an embankment. Immediately the landscape changes to one of poverty. Within only one block, comfortable, well-kept New Law structures give way to decaying Old Law tenements, run-down townhouses, and public housing developments. This

Figure 23. The Haughwout Building (1857) at Broome Street and Broadway. Its cast iron exterior by J. P. Gaynor, early date of construction, and pioneering interior elevator by E. G. Otis make it a landmark. Most of its cast iron neighbors in this portion of the district, however, are later in date (1870–1890).

Figure 24. An Urban Miniature Landscape. Barrow Street townhouses, circa 1826–1828, in Greenwich Village.

is the Barrio. It is a powerful demonstration of how landform influences cityscape.

To the right of the "Chinese Wall" of the railroad rampart lies the vast tract which James Delano sold to the city in 1825 for $25,000. The completion of subway lines such as the Lenox Avenue (1904) during the turn of the century period opened up Harlem to settlement.

The area now known as Spanish Harlem was at first Italian. Suburban central Harlem was the subject of extensive fashionable townhouse development in the 1880s and 1890s. The poorer Italians were crammed into the East Harlem fringes. By the 1920s, however, there were also some good blocks of well-to-do Italians mixed in with the tenement dwellers. Slowly in the 1940s, and then rapidly following the Second World War, as the younger generations of Italians left for the suburbs, poor young Puerto Rican families began to fill in the vacancies. Today, the area has become Hispanic.

A central institution in Spanish Harlem is La Marqueta, the Spanish Market, which occupies space under the Penn Central railroad tracks along Park Avenue from 112th to 116th streets. Inside the shed buildings of the market, the ambience of shopping crowds, odors, sights of tropical vegetable products, and spoken Spanish is unforgettable. Prices are good, and since it is a New York City market, quality is supervised. One may purchase avocados, mangos, bananas, plantains, yautia, ñames, sofrito, and achiote seed among other things. So attractive is the market to business, that along 116th Street and Park Avenue it has spilled over into sidewalk stalls.

HARLEM

The suburbanization of the rural fringe village of Harlem dates from the 1880s, when townhouses were constructed there. But the suburban phase did not last long, as a depression combined with a softening of the real estate

(A)

(B)

Figure 25. **(A)** Park Avenue and 96th Street Looking South. A landscaped median mall contributes to the scale of the apartment buildings of the wealthy. **(B)** Same Location Looking North. The emergence of the New York Central tracks blights a landscape of Old and New Law tenements and public housing projects.

market to produce a condition of overbuilding in Harlem (Figure 26). These circumstances, combined with the destruction of an earlier site of the black community for the purpose of building Pennsylvania Station led to the entrance of blacks into the portions of Harlem north of 130th Street.

Until about 1930, Harlem south of 125th Street and west of Fifth Avenue was Jewish (Figure 27). In fact, Italian Harlem and Jewish Harlem existed side by side as the turfs of the two groups had in the Lower East Side, except that now the Italians were nearer the river.

Change occurred swiftly in the 1930s, however, and black Harlem now extends all the way to Central Park. One can still notice signs of former times on the Mount Olivet Baptist Church at Lenox Avenue near 125th Street (Figure 28). Originally the Temple Israel, it still has the Star of David on the windows. It now lies near the Muslim Mosque at which Malcolm X preached (Figure 29).

Two neighborhoods of Harlem will serve to dispel the myth that this complex residential area is an undifferentiated black slum. Mount Morris Park near St. Martin's Church represents an area inhabited by many West Indian blacks who have preserved a middle class atmosphere to the west of the park where in the summer events of the Harlem Cultural Festival take place.

The second neighborhood lies around 135th Street and Lenox Avenue. The landscape here includes Harlem Hospital, several developments of black cooperative high quality housing, and the Shomburg Branch of the New York Public Library renowned for its collection of American black historical documents.

One Hundred Thirty-Fifth Street is close to being a central focus of intellectual life in Harlem (Figure 30). Nearby are the Harlem YMCA and the Abyssinian Baptist Church, central cultural institutions. Most of the apartment buildings here were built after the New Tenement Law of 1901 (Figure 31).

Between 138th and 139th streets and Seventh and Eighth avenues is a New York historical landmark—the block of houses along 138th

Figure 26. Harlem Brownstone Townhouses circa 1890 Flank St. Martin's Church (1888). The church serves a West Indian congregation, many of whom live nearby.

Figure 27. Astor Row. Downgraded townhouses circa 1890 on West 130th near Lenox Avenue. The amiable young man asked whether I would take his picture as he took mine!

and 139th streets some of which were designed by Stamford White and built by McKim, Mead and White in 1903. A walk along the row on 139th Street especially gives one a sense of the quiet scale and quality of these buildings. Here, as well as in the Mount Morris area and elsewhere in Harlem, black families of means have "brownstoned" and retored many of the houses, as whites have done in Brooklyn.

The Paul Lawrence Dunbar Apartments (1928), nearby, were designed by Andrew J. Thomas, a prize-winning effort. The landscaped inner court is a pleasant and peaceful place to walk through. From the outset, designed as a residence for blacks, many of the present cultural and political leaders of Harlem have lived there.

Visitors to Harlem will appreciate the complex texture of the area. Some good and much poor housing exist close together. Poverty areas adjoin neighborhoods which manifest means and taste. The ethnic diversity of the population is reflected in their cultural and religious institutions. It does not lend itself to facile stereotype.

BROOKLYN HEIGHTS

Like Greenwich Village, Brooklyn Heights is a community where site, situation, and development history have combined to produce an urban district rich in amenities. One need only walk along the Esplanade (completed in 1950–1951) at the foot of Montague Street to realize that nowhere else in the NYMR is there a better view of the towers of Wall Street, the old harbor area, and the Brooklyn Bridge. (Figure 32). As early as the 1830s, sail and steam ferries made commutation between this location and lower New York feasible and pleasant, while the shopping center and city hall area of the city of Brooklyn was developing only a few blocks inland.

Figure 28. Mount Olivet Baptist Church, Lenox Avenue, Harlem (1907). The Star of David may be distinguished in the upper arch of the windows recalling its previous role as the Temple Israel of Harlem.

Whole blocks of the suburbs of 1830 to 1850 remain in this charming tree-lined locale. The portion of the Heights nearest to the Esplanade was developed as a splendid pedestrian court lined with townhouses (Montague Terrace and Pierrepoint Place, 1857–1886) in which Abiel Low and his son Seth Low lived (Figure 33). Seth Low was one of the first mayors of the combined city of New York and Brooklyn under the consolidation of 1898.

While, in the course of time, outlying streets at some remove from this central point became run down and subdivided into rooming houses, the Montague Terrace location retained its urbane charm and quiet luster. Yet even some of the tenements built at the outskirts of the Heights were distinctive. The Tower and Home Apartments (1878–1879) were built as model tenements for the poor with the aid of philanthropist Alfred Tredway (Figure 34).

Considering that they were contemporary with the Old Law tenements of Manhattan,

they are a constructive innovation, embodying better ventilation. There is an open yard behind the apartments which provides through ventilation. Warren Place, a few steps to the east, is a gem (Figure 35). A walk through this charming court invites one to inspect the workmen's cottages built as a part of the same development. The *AIA Guide* by Norval White and Elliot Wilensky tells us that these six-room cottages rented for $18 per month. The four room apartments in the tenement rented for $1.93 per week. This was one of the first low rent "projects" in New York which was much emulated in Northern Europe, if not in the United States. Are the most recent ones much of an improvement?

With the decline of the southern and eastern fringes of the Heights in the early twentieth century, a Near Eastern population came to occupy many of the old houses. One can still see an occasional Syrian shop along Atlantic Avenue (Figure 36). More recently, a Hispanic

Figure 29. This Muslim Mosque near Lenox Avenue and 117th Street has become the focus for Muslim-related social activities. Malcom X was its most distinguished founder. It typifies the diversity and complex texture of Harlem.

Figure 30. This Harlem cooperative, with integrated shopping, has replaced older structures at Lenox and 135th Street. Across the street from Harlem Hospital and near cultural centers, it is a sought-after residential complex.

population of predominantly Puerto Rican origin has established residence in the downgraded townhouses of the Heights and adjoining Cobble Hill.

But a countervailing tendency has manifested itself. The intrinsic amenities of the Heights, sharpened by housing shortages, has led people with means and with a taste for urban life to purchase downgraded old townhouses with their stately brownstone facades, interior fireplaces, high ceilings, and fine plaster work. The poor residents are evicted and the places rehabilitated into spacious, floor through apartments, with the proud owner living in a ground floor duplex with a backyard garden. This process, called "brownstoning," amounts to the replacement of a dense, poor population with a less dense affluent one.

Almost all of the Heights north of Atlantic Avenue has been thus "unslummed" (Jane Jacobs' striking term). The process is now spreading to the southeast, displacing Syrian and Puerto Rican families. The net result is to erode further the number of housing units available to the poor, as described in the preceding section.

BROWNSVILLE-EAST NEW YORK

There is a neighborhood in Brooklyn known as Brownsville and East New York which, until the end of World War II, was largely composed of Jewish lower middle class residents. Today, this population has mostly been replaced by an extremely poor population, largely on public assistance, composed primarily of minority groups. The neighborhood change was facilitated by the entrance of the Bedford-Stuyvesant and Bushwick populations from the north and west, and by the location of major highrise low income housing projects in the heart of Brownsville.

In the midst of a neighborhood diminishing in economic status and purchasing power, com-

Figure 31. A New Law tenement (post-1901) on the corner with Beaux-Arts-style trim and characteristic ground floor shops. The white building adjoining is the Shomburg Library (1905). Harlem: Lenox Avenue and 135th Street.

Figure 32. Lower Manhattan from the Montague Street Esplanade, Brooklyn Heights. The East River is in the foreground. Out of the picture, to the left, lie Upper and Lower New York Bay, and the harbor entrance.

Figure 33. The Low House, Brooklyn Heights. A townhouse row in the background. To the right, a fine Beaux-Arts-style New Law building.

mercial blight and business property vacancies abound. The 1970 mean family income here was about $6,500, with much public assistance. Maintenance and operative costs have risen, accompanied by the decline of income and purchasing power in the neighborhood. The result is a region of desperation. The landlord and tenant, usually of different racial and ethnic origin, become pitted against one another. The landlord sees his property investment vanishing. The tenant sees the rapid erosion of quality in his residence. The hostility between the two, nurtured by the economic crunch, leads to abandonment on the part of the landlord, and squatting and rent strikes on the part of the tenants.

The city has entered the Brownsville-East New York area with a major Model Cities program. Construction under the program has failed to keep pace with demolitions, however, and some families have been temporarily placed in trailers, while others live in condemned houses awaiting demolition and owned by the city (Figure 37). The scope of the problem,

when measured against the efficacy of available solutions, presents a gloomy picture (Figure 38).

THE PATERSON-FAIR LAWN, NEW JERSEY, REGION*

Paterson, New Jersey, was one of the cradles of the American industrial revolution. The mill district clustered around the Great Falls contains valuable archeological remnants of early industrial buildings and hydraulic works. The Great Falls Development Corporation, a non-profit, public membership organization, has set for itself the commendable task of working to

*The author is indebted to the Great Falls Development Corporation and the Society for Industrial Archaeology, both of Paterson, for much of the information contained in this section, which has been made available to me through their kind cooperation. Materials on the Riverside District in Paterson may be secured by writing to Great Falls Development Corporation, Maple Street, Great Falls Park, Paterson, New Jersey 07502.

Figure 34. The Tower and Home Apartments, Brooklyn.

Figure 35. Warren Place, Next Door to the Tower and Home. These cottages, originally built for the poor, are now much in demand. Will modern model low income housing of today be in demand in 2075?

Figure 36. Near Eastern Shops on Atlantic Avenue, Brooklyn. Notice the Arabic lettering on the sign at the left. The buildings are nineteenth century townhouses, renovated. Note the Arabic characters displayed in a residential window in the upper left.

Figure 37. Temporary prefabricated trailer structures housing some of the families displaced by demolition, Brownsville, Brooklyn. In the background, the middle income developments have balconies, the lower income ones don't.

preserve this area as an historic urban industrial park.

The Great Falls area of Paterson was selected by Alexander Hamilton at the behest of our First Congress as a site where power, markets, labor, and raw materials could converge into a national manufactory. The Society for Establishing Useful Manufacture (SUM) was created to administer and promote its development. Pierre L'Enfant, of Washington, D.C., fame, was engaged to plan the district, but his grandoise design came to naught save the middle hydraulic race (Figure 39).

Peter Colt of Connecticut, one of a succession of Colts prominent in the district, assumed prominence in 1792 when he established a cotton-spinning mill. By 1816, protected by the tariff, Paterson grew rapidly in cotton textiles. Machine repair and foundry industries grew alongside the cotton mills.

The end of the 1830s saw the beginning of the silk boom, while the metalworking industries matured into locomotive manufacture.

The predominantly male labor force in locomotives and foundries was thus the complement to the female labor force in textiles. By the time of the Civil War, Paterson was America's leading locomotive producer.

Even though obsolescence and industrial strife in the shape of the tragic Silk Strike of 1913 took its toll on the district in the twentieth century, there continues to be a residue of textile manufacture in the old mills (Figure 40).

Adjoining Paterson on the opposite bank of the Passaic River is the suburb of Fair Lawn. A portion of Fair Lawn, called Radburn, is the location of a celebrated planned development by Henry Wright and Clarence Stein, distinguished "new town" planners of the pre–World War II era.

The houses in Radburn are developed on small plots clustered around cul-de-sac driveways which are arranged around the perimeter of large "superblocks." Thus, while neighbors are close together, and their driveways give

Figure 38. Demolition, Abandonment, and Condemnation in Brownsville, Brooklyn. All of the buildings to the right and center are empty. Some are burned out by vagrant fires. Most of the buildings at the right were built in the 1930s. Elsewhere in the city there are buildings of this style which remain in good condition. In the center background can be seen a middle income structure which will not solve the housing problems of the poor displaced in large numbers from demolished tenements. To the left, in the background, is part of a low income public housing project. Loss of low income housing has so far exceeded replacement in this area. There are literally acres of Brownsville which have resembled this photograph for more than five years.

auto access at the rear of the house, the front of the house faces upon the beautifully landscaped common parkland of the block interiors. A walk through the paths which penetrate the commons will show a variety of interesting touches. Sandboxes for children have been placed at frequent intervals. An occasional gazebo will be seen. The circulation pattern, emulating the pioneering work of Olmsted and Vaux in Central and Prospect parks, separates vehicular and pedestrian traffic completely (Figure 41). Where a path crosses a road, there is a tunnel for pedestrians. A common recreational facility including a pool and tennis courts has been built into the plan, as has an elementary school.

Originally conceived as a complete "garden city," the original plan provided for four times the area actually developed, and intended to allocate space for commercial and industrial use so that workplace and residence might be brought together. Unfortunately, the stock market crash of 1929 and the ensuing disaster in the real estate industry aborted the scheme.

Yet, partially developed or not, these houses, which sold (more than forty years ago) at prices in the $10,000 range, have appreciated in value more than four times. The development's common land and facilities, which are managed by the nonprofit Radburn Corporation, are kept as a vital external amenity for the resident. The purchaser of a house automatically becomes a voting member of the corporation and agrees to pay an assessment (which has averaged less than $200 per year recently) to cover common expenses. Upon selling, the

Figure 39. The Upper Race which diverted water from the Upper Passaic River to the Mill District, Patterson. Designed by Pierre L'Enfant.

sale passes through the corporation which maintains a listing of prospective buyers.

At first—although racial and religious restrictions were imposed—it was considered a goal to have a broad cross-section of economic classes represented among Radburn residents. As time went on, however, marginal owners were wiped out by the Depression, while property values appreciated. As a result, today Radburn is somewhat more skewed toward the higher socioeconomic categories than the founders intended. Developments like Radburn and Sunnyside should be studied carefully today, as PUDs and enterprises like Reston, Virginia, and Columbia, Maryland, are conceived to foster social goals in the mid-1970s similar to those the earlier developments intended to serve in 1927-1932, in the teeth of the processes of the land market. As in the case of Brooklyn Heights, we may wonder whether intrinsic good physical design may

not serve to defeat goals of socioeconomic heterogeneity as the price of scarce good physical design gets bid upward.

It is fascinating to notice how little influence Radburn has had upon its surroundings. If one were to leave Radburn along streets named for such pioneering planners as Ebenezer Howard, the boundary is sharp; one would see that typical suburban development houses cluster right upon its doorstep. The reason may also be partly understood in terms of our economic system.

Radburn was somewhat more expensive to build than neighboring areas of Fair Lawn and East Paterson (Figure 42). Since (under the concept of a limited profit development corporation) the house selling prices were to be kept competitive with these areas while fewer units were built per acre, at best, when sold, the Radburn houses would be less profitable to the builder than the others. Yet, if

Figure 40. Paterson Mill Building. The water flows through the lower race beneath the building. It used to be used for water wheels which provided factory power through a vertical arrangement of belts and pulleys. Textiles are still made in this building, using electric power.

(A)

(B)

Figure 41. Radburn. **(A)** Houses are clustered around automobile access cul-de-sacs. This frees the large block interiors for landscaping. **(B)** On the opposite side of the same houses, pedestrian walks communicate to the landscaped block interior. Pedestrian walkways are kept separate from automobile roads as an important design feature.

Figure 42. Radburn. **(A)** A pedestrian path avoids contact with an automobile road by means of an underpass. **(B)** Landscaped block interior with gazebo.

(C)

Figure 42, continued. Radburn. (C) Communal pool and children's recreation area in block interior.

total cost to society over the years is considered, many of the $10,000, 1929 Paterson bungalows are now valueless slums.

Profits of housing development are reaped by the seller at the time of the sale. Costs of shoddy layout and construction are paid by the buyer (or by society after downgrading and abandonment) long after the sale. In the short run shoddy practice yields higher individual profits to the builder, but in the long run greater social costs result. Except for the occasional idealist like Clarence Stein or Henry Wright there seems to be little profit incentive to create Radburns. Thus good design remains scarce, and gets bid up in price and taken out of the reach of the working class and poor family as the slum-generating and slum-concentrating processes of our economic system continue to operate, leaving interstitial oases of good design for the affluent.

The Urban Environment—The Pollution Feedback

Since the metropolis is a junction in the organization of our society at which energy, materials, people, and land are combined in the productive and distributive processes by which our needs are met, it follows that the metropolis is likewise the place at which the waste products from these processes are concentrated. Let us consider the ecological process which imposes stress upon the vital components of the NYMR environment—the land, water, and air. Metropolitan population growth stimulates in a complex way activities such as industry, retailing, and local service provision which are directed toward local consumption, as well as export and import activities which cross the region's boundary. The population growth occurs partly through natural increase and partly through inmigration related to employment expansion.

During expansion of economic activity and population, the demand for space in the metropolis intensifies, inducing environmental change. Direct demand for land and water is affected as waste generation leads to landfill on the one hand and pollution of water on the other. Scarce water reserves lead to the inundation and reduction of the land area supply in the form of reservoirs and storage facilities, while sanitary landfill shapes the growth of some parts of the region.

Eventually, environmental stress can lead to a brake on growth. High costs and few amenities pressure individuals into leaving. The affluent have the most options and tend to leave, while the weak and the poor, those with the least choice, will stay. Environmental stress has reached the New York metropolitan region.

WATER QUALITY AND THE NEW YORK–NEW JERSEY BIGHT

In the late nineteenth century, oyster fisheries were a principal industry in upper New York Bay, the Kill van Kull north of Staten Island, the Arthur Kill west of Staten Island, and Newark Bay (Figure 43). Today, the bottom of these waterways is simply dead muck filled with oyster shells. Water samples taken from the Kill van Kull have indicated that even coliform (intestinal) bacteria cannot survive in it. During the months of July and August, reaches of the Arthur Kill run septic, completely lacking in dissolved oxygen, it all having been consumed oxidizing organic waste. The impact of the petrochemical and other industries, and the sewage effluent generated by the New York–New Jersey metropolitan region, have been catastrophic.

Fortunately, while the estuary remains a disaster, progress has been made in cleaning up the Hudson River. As a result of the combined efforts of public enforcement agencies and conservation and sportsmen's groups, the Hudson River has sufficiently recovered in quality so that the annual shad migration north of the city has returned in force.

But other rivers are not so fortunate. The Passaic, flowing through Paterson, Passaic, and Newark, is indescribably contaminated, as is the lower Hackensack where it empties into the

Figure 43. Howland's Hook, Staten Island, New York. The Arthur Kill (middle distance) frequently runs septic (no dissolved oxygen) in the summer owing to pollution. Dump in the foreground, petroleum-based chemical industry in New Jersey (background). The air, water, and solid waste pollution problem flows across state lines.

tidal marshes across which the New Jersey Turnpike wends its way to New York City (Figure 44). In Dutch days these two rivers so abounded with salmon that the good burghers passed an ordinance forbidding landlords from relying exclusively on that fish to feed their indentured servants. As late as the turn of the twentieth century, the now foul tidal marsh area was a noted fishing, hunting, and trapping summer resort for the cities nearby.

But the pollution has not stopped at the estuary. Sewage sludge and other waste has for years been barged out into the Atlantic Ocean and dumped south of the Narrows (the passage between Brooklyn and Staten Island) producing a contaminated "dead sea." The shoreward movement of this waste now threatens the Atlantic beaches along Long Island and Staten Island with contamination and closure. Also threatened, by way of the long shore currents, is the multimillion dollar resort industry of the New Jersey shore north of Atlantic City.

AIR POLLUTION

If New York is threatening the pollution of the New Jersey shore by water, New Jersey is striking back by air. The prevailing westerly winds bring the pollutants from refineries, chemical plants, industries, and cities like Newark and Jersey City over the Hudson River to mingle with the pollution dome generated by New York. The result is a pollution layer which is unmatched by any other major American metropolitan region.

Fundamentally, there are two kinds of pollution—oxidizing and reducing. The reducing type was typical of the nineteenth century industrial city. The burning of fossil fuels often releases into the air chemicals such as sulphur dioxide which, upon contact with atmospheric moisture, become acidic—in this case, sulfuric acid. The chemical action of such materials is searing, burning, and irritating to exposed tissue surfaces. The oxidizing type of pollution—also

Figure 44. Tidal Marshland, New Jersey Meadowlands. Grading and bulldozing (foreground), salt hay meadows (middle distance), light industrial–warehousing complex (background). Pollution destroyed much of the fishing-hunting-recreational ecology which prevailed in this area at the turn of the century. Landfill and development is proceeding on the carcass.

called photochemical smog—results when a complex of petroleum-derived organic chemicals mixes in the air in the presence of sunlight. The end product of these reactions is chemical ozone, which also has a corrosive effect on tissues. Vapors from burning gasoline and the New Jersey refineries are rich sources of these chemicals.

The two types of pollution are antagonistic to each other. Thus, when reducing pollution dominates, the photochemical reactions are arrested and oxidizing pollution disappears. New York has both.

In the winter, the New Yorker may experience old fashioned reducing pollution arising from the burning of fossil fuels for power and heat. In the summer, when these sources subside, photochemical smog takes over to assail the lungs and nostrils of the public. On a clear day in spring or summer, the dust dome over the region is clearly visible from the New Jersey Turnpike as the traveler looks toward the New York City skyline.

SOLID WASTE DISPOSAL—LANDFILL AND THE GROWTH OF NEW YORK

New York City is no stranger to the landfill process. About one-third of Manhattan is filled or reclaimed land. As long ago as the seventeenth and eighteenth centuries, a more or less spontaneous fill process was underway. Water Street—several blocks inland in southern Manhattan—once approximately marked the shoreline. Piers projected into the East River, and sewage poured down gutter trenches into the slips which lay between the piers. As a slip filled in above the low tide line, the foul odors prompted the residents to lay dirt above it, filling in the slip, and then extending new piers out still further. It is a matter inviting ironic reflection that some of the most expensive land in the world (near Wall Street) is basically formed of antique sanitary wastes. Also, every street west of Tenth Avenue and south of 59th Street is composed of landfill. More recently, projects have been initiated in the downtown area to develop landfill sites to accommodate a new home for the Stock Exchange, and to develop a PUD "new town in town" near Battery Park overlooking the harbor vista.

Landfill has also accounted for the development of Port Newark–Port Elizabeth, and many an unsuspecting city resident lives upon a tract which was once a garbage dump. But landfill sites are now scarce. Barging incinerated wastes out to the New York Bight sludge area is becoming more and more common as an alternative to the incredible landscape of trash in northwestern Staten Island.

Almost every major city has an area of automobile graveyards, scrapyards, and the like, often along blighted water courses where barge traffic is available or in poorly drained land where normal development has been slow. The tidal marsh area known as the Jersey Meadows northeast of Newark is typical. To a certain extent they serve a useful purpose as dumps, especially for wrecked automobiles, which formerly were widely abandoned in the streets of many cities until scrap prices rose high enough to pay for their collection.

As garbage and refuse disposal becomes an increasing need in metropolitan areas, sites suitable for these uses become scarcer and open incineration becomes prevalent. Since open dumping provides an optimum breeding environment for rats and other vermin, sanitary landfill dumps are often sought, where every day's load of refuse has some six inches of dirt bulldozed over it. Unfortunately this method, which is relatively inexpensive $4.50 to $5 per ton, 1974 prices), is an extensive user of land. On the average, one acre of land is required for each 10,000 people, and may only be used for about five years. Clearly, a city of a million would need one hundred acres every five years, and between the growth in urban demand and the decreasing supply of land, this method is most suited to the relatively less densely settled suburb, and even there is of limited use. By 1963, several Westchester towns were trucking garbage sixty miles to landfill sites, while the same suburban New York county in 1967 was considering exporting its garbage 200 miles upstate at night by rail, since the nearer landfill sites were exhausted. At the same time, San Francisco was considering a 450 mile rail haul for its garbage.

Tragically, the potential of composting, recycling, and other constructive alternatives to sanitary landfill methods have barely been considered in the region. At Howland's Hook in northern Staten Island, looking across the land polluted with garbage toward the septic Arthur Kill and the Kill van Kull, where the sediment washed from the garbage flats into the water is deposited along with the material from the outfalls from the New Jersey chemical plants, one can easily see the industrial smoke stacks poisoning the air. It is a domain of seagulls and rats.

Conclusion

Like many other American metropolitan areas, the NYMR is experiencing the suburbanization of human activities. Jobs in manufacturing, transportation, wholesaling, retailing, and various services (including some like finance, insurance, and real estate which traditionally have been centralized) have migrated out into the suburban perimeters of the old core cities like New York, Newark, Paterson, Jersey City, and Bridgeport. Of course, it has been even more true that the recent past has witnessed the strong decentralization of residence in the region.

Economically, what this amounts to is a disinvestment in the city accompanied by investment in perimeter areas. Hughes and James have reviewed some of the forces which are driving this process forward in the NYMR. Space needs have generated a demand for large-sized building lots for modern plants which are difficult to secure in core city locations where land values are high and land parcels are small. Related to this are the increased needs for loading and unloading aprons for trucks and railcars, along with warehousing facility needs.

Simultaneously, innovations in transportation and communications technology have freed many factories from a dependence upon rail or water access. Furthermore, within many firms it is no longer necessary for head office functions to be located at the site of production, since data-processing systems and communications links allow control to be exercised from some distance.

The classic economic raison de'etre for the existence of a city—the economic gain which may be realized by using the nearby independent business and financial services which abound in the city external to the firm itself—is now increasingly neutralized by the fact that suburbanization of enterprise has made these external economies available in the suburbs.

Trends in automation and technological development tend to shift hiring needs of firms from many unskilled workers to fewer skilled workers. The imperative to locate the plant near a massive manpower pool is thus eased, while the weakness of unions in the NYMR suburbs (as compared to the city) may be attractive to some firms. The suburbs also provide a strengthening white collar labor pool compared to the city.

The prestige and image of a firm is related to its location. As the prestigious New York City address is perceived as tarnished by the negative attributes which have become identified with old core cities (often unjustly, as figures on violent crime in New York City compared with other cities and with suburban crime increases show), the firm's image may be buttressed by a more sylvan location, preferably visible from a parkway.

But in addition to all of these points, Hughes and James suggest that a very important consideration in the decision to locate in the suburbs is tied to the upbringing of today's young executives. A generation of young corporate managers was reared in the suburbs. Unlike preceding generations of executives who might recall with fondness their city childhood, these young adults have had little or no exposure to the city, except as a location from which their family fled. For them, the suburb is the norm, the city terra incognita.

All these forces have helped to decentralize NYMR business and residential activity, while the balkanization of political jurisdiction in the region has been incapable of resisting the tide. Perhaps as the 1970s advance and ominous trends toward a continuing energy crisis and recession in the building and construction trades mature, the time will ripen for the reestablishment of city life which remains relatively more economical of materials and energy than the suburban-style single family house cum automobile. In my opinion, however, this time is still relatively remote, at least in the NYMR.

The newest suburbs around the old cities of the NYMR tend to be developed as complete and relatively efficient land use packages rather than the stereotype of a single purpose residential subdivision. Shopping center, office tower, industrial park, multiple dwelling, and single family residence are all woven into the fabric. Even the shopping center, which has been stigmatized by some as the destroyer of the urban texture provided by the central business district, has been broadening its functional base to include some of those amenities as the functional bases of many downtowns have been eroding. In some suburban malls in the NYMR, noncommercial activities like churches and community meeting halls have been incorporated, extending both the social utility and the use time of the mall into evening and weekend activities and thus improving its efficiency.

The social function of the suburban activity center has spilled over from a narrow retailing purpose into broader social purposes. Senior citizens frequent the enclosed malls, taking advantage of controlled climates and safety-patrolled corridors. Teenagers come to the malls for dating and social life. In fact, the *paseo* characteristic of the central square of a Latin American small town, a time of ritualized strolling on the part of young men and women for the purpose of socializing, resembles the social pattern of the suburban shopping center. In the one case the town hall and the church are the two ceremonial terminals of the interaction space, while in the other case they are two major retailing institutions. In both cases

the sides of the space tend to be lined by shops, and the central space public, well lighted, well patrolled, and safe.

In our opinion these suburban activity foci of the NYMR are evolving toward the form of an enclosed minicity in which social functions proceed in an atmosphere of relaxation, comfort, and safety. They are now well on the way to becoming the critical points of intersection of a growing suburban public transportation system.

And what of the central cities? Mayor Kenneth Gibson of Newark is supposed to have remarked that while he didn't know where American cities were going, he believed that Newark would get there first. The comment must be interpreted with some pessimism since, in fact, those with the financial options seem to be vacating Newark as fast as they can. Prime, modern office towers in a downtown area that is still regionally second only to Manhattan in terms of financial institutions are plagued with unfillable vacancies as the city struggles against decline. The central ward, afflicted with a poverty population and declining housing stock, manifests high abandonment rates and high municipal service needs.

As Newark becomes a city of municipal services provided to a poor population without an adequate tax base, the Newark worker is faced with the rising costs of commuting to the perimeter suburban factory belt coupled with a rising tax rate. In the case of Newark (and perhaps elsewhere) these tendencies cut across racial and ethnic groups. The middle class Newark black is moving to the suburbs along with middle class whites. The residuum in the city includes the poor of all groups. Of course, owing to the discriminatory practices of our economic system, blacks and Hispanics are disproportionately represented among Newark's poor, but the central city–suburban dichotomy is becoming more class based and less based on race or ethnicity as time goes on.

What we are suggesting here is that the benefits and costs of the NYMR are increasingly concentrating in geographically separated areas. Benefits, and the principal beneficiaries, are concentrating around the suburban "minicities" which are thought of as safe and of a desirable human scale, while social costs and the residences of the poor are cordoned off into central city "cost sinks." In some instances, as economic functions vacate central city office structures, government offices become "renters of last resort." Much of the World Trade Center and many other downtown office sites in Manhattan are thus increasingly occupied by state and federal functions. In Norton Long's metaphor, the city becomes a reservation for the poor and public sector institutions to which service-providing custodians commute. The urban enrichment of the circumcity zone accompanies the impoverishment of the center.

It is our view that, in the short term, there seems little prospect that these trends will alter in the NYMR. As political power follows economic power to the numerous small suburban jurisdictions it seems unlikely that they will act in a way to force the redistribution of resources on an intra-state basis to the few large central city jurisdictions, most especially in a national climate of receding economic indicators. Similarly, a national government which has turned away from the concept of strong federal intervention in local affairs on behalf of the cities is unlikely to force a redistribution of resources to central cities equal to the task of deflecting these tendencies, even if its political constituency would tolerate it. Insofar as court decisions can achieve resource redistribution, recent judicial actions have indeed forced piecemeal, spotty remedies for inequitable funding of public programs—in housing, public sanitation, and education, for example. But it is not within the court's power to initiate the kind of massive effort that the renewal of Newark would require.

Finally, it must be observed that the "mini-city" lifestyle which is developing in the suburban reaches of the NYMR is probably preferred by the overwhelming majority of regional residents including, and even especially, those who are trapped in the old cities. To a great extent, the regret of many of them seems to be less that the center city is declining than that they lack the means to leave it, and are forced to reside in a landscape of despair.

Bilbiography

※

Bibliography

Albion, Robert G. *The Rise of New York Port: 1815-1860.* New York, 1939.

Asbury, Herbert. *The Gangs of New York.* New York, 1927.

Bryson, R.A., and J.E. Kutzbach. *Air Pollution.* Resource Paper no. 2. Washington, D.C.: Association of American Geographers, Commission on College Geography, 1968.

Burchell, Robert W., with James W. Hughes. *Planned Units Development.* Rutgers University, New Brunswick, N.J.: Center for Urban Policy Research, 1973.

Carey, George W.; Leonard Zobler; Michael R. Greenberg; and Robert M. Hordon. *Urbanization, Water Pollution, and Public Policy.* New Brunswick, N.J.: Rutgers University, Center for Urban Policy Research, 1973.

Deutsch, Karl W. "On Social Communication and the Metropolis." *General Systems Yearbook* VI (1961): 95-100.

Dubois, W.E.B. *The Philadelphia Negro.* New York: Shocken Books, originally published 1899.

Duffy, J. *A History of Public Health in New York City, 1625-1866.* New York: Russell Sage Foundation, 1968.

Gottmann, Jean. *Megalopolis: The Urbanized Northeastern Seaboard of the U.S.* New York, 1961.

Gustafson, W. Eric. "Printing and Publishing." In Max Hall, ed., *Made in New York,* ch. 2. Cambridge, Mass.: Harvard University Press, 1959.

Hall, Max, ed. *Made in New York.* New York Metropolitan Regional Study. Cambridge, Mass.: Harvard University Press, 1959.

Handlin, Oscar. *The Newcomers.* New York Metropolitan Regional Study. Cambridge, Mass.: Harvard University Press, 1959.

Helfgott, Roy B. "Women's and Children's Apparel." In Max Hall, ed., *Made in New York,* ch. 1. Cambridge, Mass.: Harvard University Press, 1959.

Hoover, Edgar M., and Raymond Vernon. *Anatomy of a Metropolis,* Cambridge, Mass.: Harvard University Press, 1959.

Hughes, James, and Franklin J. James. "Suburbanization Dynamics and the Transportation Dillimma." In James Hughes and Franklin J. James, eds., *Suburbanization Dynamics and the Future of the City,* pp. 19-42. New Brunswick, N.J.: Rutgers University, Center for Urban Policy Research, 1974.

Huxtable, Ada Louise. *Classic New York.* New York: Doubleday and Company, Anchor Books 1964.

Jacobs, Jane, *The Death and Life of Great American Cities,* Vintage Books, Random House, N.Y., 1961, page 270 ff.

Jonassen, Christen T. "Cultural Variables in the Ecology of an Ethnic Group." *American Sociological Review* 14 (February, 1949): 32-41.

Kenyon, James B. *Industrial Location and Metropolitan Growth, the Paterson-Passaic District.* Chicago: University of Chicago Department of Geography, Research Paper no. 67, 1960.

Long, Norton. "The City as Reservation." *The Public Interest* 25 (Fall 1971): 3-14.

McDermott, W. "Air Pollution and Public Health." *Scientific American,* October 1961.

Osofsky, Gilbert. *Harlem: The Making of a Ghetto*. New York: Harper and Row, 1966.

Port Authority of New York and New Jersey. *Port Authority Handbook*. New York, 1973.

Regional Plan Association. *Regional Survey of New York and its Environs*. New York, 1929.

Riis, Jacob A. *How the Other Half Lives: Studies Among the Tenements of New York, 1919*. New York, 1919. Reprinted Harvard U. Press 1970.

Rischin, Moses. *The Promised City: New York's Jews, 1870–1914*. Cambridge, 1962.

Robbins, Sidney M., and Nestor E. Terleckyj. *Money Metropolis*. New York Metropolitan Regional Study. Cambridge, Mass.: Harvard University Press, 1960.

Samuelson, Paul. *Economics*. 7th ed., pp. 12 and 13. New York: McGraw-Hill, 1965.

Sternlieb, George. *The Tenement Landlord*. New Brunswick, N.J.: Rutgers University Press, 1969.

——. *The Urban Housing Dilemma*. New York: The Housing and Development Administration of the City of New York, Department of Rent and Housing Maintenance, Office of Rent Control, 1972.

Sternlieb, George, and Robert W. Burchell. *Residential Abandonment, the Tenement Landlord Revisited*. Center for Urban Policy Research, New Brunswick, N.J.: Rutgers University, 1973.

Sternlieb, George, and James W. Hughes. *Housing and People in New York City*. New York: The Housing and Development Administration of the City of New York, Department of Rent and Housing Maintenance, 1973.

U.S. Department of Commerce. *The Automobile and Air Pollution: A Program for Progress*. Report of the Panel on Electrically Powered Vehicles. Washington, D.C., 1967.

Ware, Caroline F. *Greenwich Village: 1920–1930*. Boston, 1935.

Warntz, William. *Macrogeography and Income Fronts*. Regional Science Research Institute Monograph 3. Philadelphia, 1965.

Weber, Adna F. *The Growth of Cities in the Nineteenth Century*. Vol. XI, Columbia University Studies in History, Economics, and Public Law. 1899.

White, Norval, and Elliot Wilensky. *The American Institute of Architects (AIA) Guide to New York City*. New York: MacMillan Company, 1968.

Wood, Robert. *1400 Governments*. Cambridge, Mass: Harvard Univ. Press. 1961.

Works Progress Administration, Federal Workers' Project. *New York City Guide*. New York: Random House, 1939.

Chapter 4

Metropolitan Philadelphia: Study of Conflicts and Social Cleavages

Introduction

There is a great difference between what Philadelphia is and what Philadelphia could or should be. A city with its rich history, civic and cultural resources, and ethnic variety could be an exciting place to live, but the contemporary Philadelphian's inability to cope with social heterogeneity makes the city a battleground for different interest groups. It has been said that Philadelphia is 200 small towns in search of a city—a statement which underscores the extent of fragmentation found within the political unit. Similarly, the enormous suburban complex of the Delaware Valley, covering most of southeastern Pennsylvania and southern New Jersey and extending into northern Delaware, is beset by divisions. These cleavages are at the root of the serious metropolitan problems which face our society in the 1970s, and their geographical expressions are the organizing theme of this study.

Philadelphia is a deeply rifted city in many ways, and the rifts among various groups create and reinforce conflicts and tensions among them. Distinct groups are aligned according to ethnicity, economic status, and age, as well as according to behavior traits such as preference for different lifestyles, occupations, consumer durables, forms of entertainment, and other interests. The geographical manifestation of these cleavages is spatial segregation. Thus, within the metropolitan area there are communities of racial homogeneity; distinctive ethnic neighborhoods which refuse to disappear; areas of poverty and areas of wealth; districts inhabited by families; areas for the old and for the young. Moreover, flows of consumer traffic, commuter traffic, and social traffic such as the visiting of friends, as well as the spatial behavior of people seeking a variety of other activities, mirror existing urban cleavages.

There is nothing unusual in people differing in socioeconomic background and in preference for different lifestyles, or in the translation of these differences into patterns of geographical segregation. Every city has its mixture of people who often cluster into homogeneous concentrations. However, with the exception of New York City, Philadelphia is probably the most socially heterogeneous city in the United States. It has a long tradition of immigrant settlement, and a diversified economy that attracted a diverse population. Moreover, because it is more a city of single family homes than New York, the Philadelphian has more control over physical distance between himself and others, thereby increasing the possibilities of rigid separation of supposedly incompatible groups.

Thus, the translation of social differences and insecure social status into spatial segregation patterns may be accomplished by choice, as when an ethnic group chooses voluntary residential segregation in maintaining a cohesive, homogeneous neighborhood over several generations. In other cases, segregation is largely a function of discrimination, when restrictions imposed and enforced by others dictate where members of a certain group may live, work, shop, or be entertained.

The fragmentation of society prohibits defining and working toward common goals. Each group remains ignorant of the problems of the others, or becomes so immersed in its own concerns that it never learns that their problems might be related. Unless cooperation among these groups develops, "every man for himself" becomes the norm in an environment of seemingly insurmountable urban problems.

The translation of social distinctions into geographical separation discourages cooperation because physical distance between social groups perpetuates misunderstandings, stereotypes, and even hatreds. "Every man for himself" becomes "every neighborhood for itself" or "every ethnic group for itself." Thus, common metropolitan goals for public transportation, schools, taxes, or the elimination of visual blight become impossible to anticipate.

Furthermore, a two way cause and effect relationship develops between the geographical cleavages and the pervasive feeling of personal insecurity in Philadelphia. Residents fear threats to their safety and security; and many of their fears, real or imagined, are directed at specific ethnic groups, individual economic classes, or certain parts of town. These anxieties elicit unfortunate behavioral responses which only intensify the problems and create new ones. Many live in fear, withdrawing from social circulation within the city and leaving home only when necessary. In the performance of necessary activities such as shopping, working, riding the bus, or fueling the car, the Philadelphian comes in contact with many diverse people, but as sociologist Louis Wirth has pointed out, such contacts are frequently "impersonal, segmented, superficial, transitory, and often predatory in nature," making the urban resident somewhat anonymous and isolated. Such withdrawal only intensifies the difficulty of intergroup contact and cooperation.

Perhaps such an evaluation of life in the city is too pessimistic, particularly since not all urban residents are anxiety-stricken, and many enjoy the opportunities offered by crowded, heterogeneous environments. But it is undeniably true that city living today is seldom carefree living. Many residents of Philadelphia feel constrained in their behavior. Recent letters to the editors of Philadelphia's newspapers express strong anxieties. A reader complained to the *Daily News:* "Freedom from mugging is a human right. . . . We have been made prisoners in our own home. What happened to our freedom?" A letter to the *Philadelphia Inquirer* stated that: "The parents have to worry about sending their children to school. They worry if they will come home all right after walking through changing neighborhoods." Another letter to the same newspaper echoed: "The kids coming out of school are faced with these situations which have come out of control here. You can't walk the streets without someone hitting you over the head; you're not even safe in your own home."

Is it that some of the things which are basic to the style of life in cities are self-defeating? Have the choices we have made concerning where in the city and near whom to live, where to work and how to get there, where to shop and where to be entertained worked against us? Answers to these questions are critical in diagnosing and solving Philadelphia's intensifying dilemma. For too many people the city is dead or dying, and those who seek life in a city such as Philadelphia are, unfortunately, too few in number. However, many people have high hopes, and in order to realize them we must understand the nature and causes of the illnesses afflicting America's Philadelphias.

A Tour of the Philadelphia Region

A visitor touring the Philadelphia area would probably wind up rather confused. The Delaware Valley is extremely diverse socially, architecturally, and in the use of land. The seemingly incompatible juxtapositions of varied land uses prevent the visitor from devising an ordered mental image of the city's spatial structure, and the existence of numerous nearby smaller urban centers such as Camden and Trenton, New Jersey; Chester, Pennsylvania; or Wilmington, Delaware, complicate the image of the region around Philadelphia. The short term visitor nevertheless obtains an image of the city and region including distinctive features as well as those which contradict popular images of the metropolis.

Walking through downtown or Center City Philadelphia the visitor would express surprise at seeing so much new construction of skyscrapers amidst recently completed ones. Many cities are experiencing building booms; but Philadelphia has had such a bad image. Why would anyone invest here? What's more, why would anyone want to live downtown in new apartment buildings or condominium towers (Figure 1)?

Our visitor would also note that there is some greenery in the downtown area, and would remember Rittenhouse Square as a very human, intimate park squeezed in among surrounding tall buildings. Some planners must have remembered people in their designs. And surely the designer of the Benjamin Franklin Parkway had the Champs Elysées in mind. For nearly one mile this broad boulevard suc-

cessfully moves a heavy volume of traffic past a mixture of greenery and impressive public buildings, statues, and fountains.

The residential areas encircling Center City would also leave an impression. The prevailing row house architecture, with the exception of Baltimore, is quite different from anything found in other major American cities. Rows of identical housing units share walls from one end of the block to the other. Each unit presents an identical red brick facade, the same number of windows in the same places, and identical doors and stoops. There are differences from street to street, but within any block one finds a monotonous, rather drab sameness. The sense of monotony is fortified by the city's topographical flatness, the absence of trees or lawns in many residential areas, and by the endless grid street pattern. Only after becoming accustomed to seeing such a residential landscape does the visitor begin to suspect that the Philadelphian must be sensitive to minor variations such as window shutters, new doors, flower pots on the window sills, or fresh coats of exterior paint, all of which help relieve the monotony and give each house a distinctive appearance (Figure 2).

One row house neighborhood stands out among the rest: Society Hill, located in the city's historic area just southeast of Center City near the Delaware River, contains some of the oldest homes on the continent, and yet it seems to complement the modern high-rise apartment towers nearby. It is an area of rela-

Figure 1. Center city with high-rise construction.

Figure 2.   Row houses in Philadelphia.

tively recent renovation from slum status in the mid-1950s to one of the highest income areas in Philadelphia today. Where old homes were not salvageable, they were replaced by new townhouses designed to reflect colonial building styles. Society Hill mixes new and tastefully renewed old structures in a setting of brick sidewalks, narrow residential alleyways, tree-lined streets, small parklets, and walkways (Figure 3).

Society Hill startles visitors because interior city neighborhoods are supposed to be for the poor, not the rich. The parts of Society Hill bordered by a decaying slum neighborhood with dilapidated homes, countless vacant and boarded-up shells of homes and stores, and huge quantities of litter and evidence of vandalism are all the more confusing because rich and poor neighborhoods are seldom found side by side. Further reflection suggests some sort of linkage between the population of Society Hill, the occupants of Center City high rises, and the apparent health of downtown Philadelphia. Some visitors might go a step further

Figure 3. A street scene in Society Hill.

and wonder if the poor, located just beyond the zone of prosperity, are a necessary ingredient of this evidence of economic vitality.

The social divisions within Philadelphia come into focus. The visitor recalls that the row house neighborhoods were either black or white. Segregation occurs in every city, but it always makes an impression no matter what the visitor's race. In one area street signs were Chinese and in another they were Spanish. Advertisements in store windows elsewhere were in Polish. In a different neighborhood Cyrillic script was used, and Greek was common in still another area. Italian names mark South Philadelphia's businesses, and the open-air Italian market takes on a meaning within the context of Philadelphia's society. Scattered about the central portion of Philadelphia in such a way that the visitor will have trouble finding them again, the city's ethnic communities collectively present a cosmopolitan image but individually reflect a highly fragmented city.

These are Philadelphia's poor and working class communities. Scattered between blocks of residences are the remaining old factories which comprise a large part of Philadelphia's declining industrial economy, places which provide jobs for the residents of the row houses and require the services of the managers, lawyers, and financial wizards with offices and residences in Center City.

No single industry dominates the city to the extent that steel dominates Pittsburgh, automobiles Detroit, or aircraft Seattle; and no single factory is so large that it stands out among Philadelphia's other employers. Philadelphia's is a mixed economy—refining oil, baking bread, making steel, manufacturing machinery, loading and unloading ships at the port, brewing beer, and making men's suits. Because the city's factories are small and declining in number, most are scattered, and the visitor could identify only stretches along the Delaware River as exclusively industrial areas.

Continuing beyond the central zone, the visitor notes other contrasts. Traveling in the direction of what is called the Northeast, he notices a transition from row houses to semi-detached units resembling row houses and finally to detached homes like those he has seen in many other places (Figure 4). As elsewhere, such construction stretches for miles beyond the central city limits. The products of the construction booms of the 1950s and 1960s are basically the same everywhere: hurriedly built housing for white middle class families, interspersed with shopping centers, gasoline stations, and new employment concentrations.

Satisfied that he has seen what there is to see, the visitor takes another route out of central Philadelphia. This time he pays the bridge toll and crosses the Delaware River into New Jersey. A high rent apartment complex sits at the Camden end of the Ben Franklin Bridge, and the visitor notes its convenient location with respect to Philadelphia's Center City. But the rest of Camden is home to lower income groups. Black and Puerto Rican neighborhoods sit amidst factories, relict commercial districts, and blocks razed by urban renewal. Camden is old, but traveling outward the visitor moves quickly into newer suburban developments reminiscent of Philadelphia's Pennsylvania suburbs. Billboards give directions to new, planned condominium communities. The south Jersey segment of the region is a major area of suburban growth. At least one hour's driving time to Philadelphia, the visitor thinks while returning across the bridge, but, recalling what he has seen so far, he understands why thousands of people pay high prices to live and increasingly work in the outer suburban city.

Exploring still another directional sector northwest of Center City, the visitor discovers Germantown, an old formerly independent city within Philadelphia's limits. Here are still other apparently incompatible juxtapositions. Blocks of row houses are interspersed with blocks containing large Victorian homes, some of which rate mansion status (Figure 5). The larger homes tend to be white-occupied, but some blocks in Germantown and its bordering community of Mount Airy are racially mixed. Many Philadelphians consider this area of higher ground, tree-lined blocks of historic homes, and convenient public transportation attractive and buy homes according to their incomes with less regard for the race of their neighbors. There are instances where whites have "busted" blocks which had been totally black-occupied for decades. A similar process is under way in West Philadelphia near the University of Pennsylvania.

Beyond Germantown is Chestnut Hill, and not far from there beyond the city limits to the

Figure 4. Semidetached housing in Northeast Philadelphia.

Figure 5. A house in Germantown.

west, are the "Main Line" communities. Seeing mansion after mansion, some with separate servant quarters, the visitor recalls another image of Philadelphia, that of a stodgy, status-conscious town with its own published social register.

Much of the city is poor—perhaps one of the grittiest cities in the country, with dirty streets, graffiti-saturated walls, abandoned cars, and dilapidated neighborhoods. Yet so near such misery a visitor sees great wealth, both in Center City and at the fringes. The social hierarchy of the city is no different from elsewhere in America, but it is more visible in Philadelphia because of the city's scale and because of its mixed population. In Manhattan the contrast is between those who live in the fortified, luxury high-rise apartment buildings and the residents of the island's tenements. Westchester County seems far away. Smaller cities tend to have more gradations between varied neighborhoods, but Philadelphia is somewhat diferent, as old inner city neighborhoods sometimes house the affluent as well as the poor. The built-up area around Philadelphia is so extensive that space accessible to the city's downtown CBD is valuable for residential purposes. The wealthy outbid the poor for their old homes and improve them to suit their own tastes. Furthermore, Philadelphia's ethnic mix dictates a checkerboard of relatively homogeneous neighborhoods competing for space with residents of adjacent but socially different squares. It is a most interesting city.

Social Heterogeneity in Philadelphia

The social heterogeneity of Philadelphia comes largely from the city's long history of immigration of ethnically varied groups. Swedish and Dutch traders were the first Europeans to contact the Indians near the confluence of the Delaware and Schuylkill rivers in the 1630s and 1640s. William Penn's Quakers, who arrived in 1682 on the aptly named ship *Welcome*, were the first permanent European settlers. They founded the "City of Brotherly Love," and welcomed migrants from a variety of backgrounds.

The largest immigrant groups during the colonial period were English Protestants and Germans. The latter founded the independent community of Germantown six miles northwest of the city, and by the late seventeenth century Germans were quite conspicuous in the Philadelphia area. The mid-19th century potato famine in Ireland brought large numbers of Catholics to Philadelphia, and by 1870 half of all the foreign born in Philadelphia were Irish. Despite continued immigration of the Irish after 1870, their proportion declined with the new wave of immigration during the late nineteenth and early twentieth centuries as large numbers of Italians, Jews, and Poles came to Philadelphia. In addition, numerous smaller groups—including Greeks, Ukrainians, Hungarians, Lebanese, Syrians, and Chinese—settled in Philadelphia. Because they tended to cluster in tight neighborhoods and dominate certain occupations, their presence was strongly felt despite their small numbers.

While Philadelphia's population was ethnically diverse during the early twentieth century and had large numbers of foreign-born residents, the city's proportion of foreign born (less than 25 percent) was lower than that of other northeastern cities. For example, more than a third of the residents of Boston, Chicago, Detroit, Cleveland, Milwaukee, and New York were foreign born at this time. One reason for the smaller proportion in Philadelphia was the attraction of the city for large numbers of southern blacks. There was a substantial black population in Philadelphia late in the 18th century, and during the 19th century the city was an important destination on the underground railroad. While the black population in other major northern cities never exceeded 2 percent during the 1870–1920 period, Philadelphia was more than 5 percent black. Its proximity to the Mason-Dixon line made it a convenient destination for the northward migration stream of freed men after the Civil War. This black influx provided Philadelphia with a relatively large supply of cheap, unskilled labor, a social condition which may have diminished the city's attractiveness for unskilled European immigrants.

Immigration from overseas declined after 1920, but picked up again after World War II when displaced persons from Central and Eastern Europe came to Philadelphia and other large cities. This mixed wave of immigrants revived the city's ethnic enclaves and organizations. Most recently, migrations of Puerto Ricans have seasoned the city. Taken cumulatively, these various infusions have given Philadelphia a rich multiethnic flavor, a social kaleidoscope matched only by a small handful of cities on the North American continent.

Ethnicity remains very important in Philadelphia today. Today's observer is constantly impressed by the diversity of the city's population. The pages of the Philadelphia telephone directory list an admixture of surnames as varied as can be imagined. Names on shops throughout the city, the foreign-language newspapers in corner stores, the medley of languages heard on city streets, the foreign flag decals on auto bumpers all portray vivid images of an intricate ethnic mosaic. Local names in the news further reflect this diversity. In 1976 the mayor was Italian, the police commissioner Irish, the city council president Jewish, and the leader of the Democratic party a Polish Protestant. In addition, recent mayoral candidates have included an Irishman, a black, a Jew, and an Anglo-Saxon Protestant, as well as the Italian victor. Even those who report the news on radio and television reflect the city's population mix.

Another aspect of life in the city which distinguishes Philadelphia from other cities is the proliferation and use of proper names for its neighborhoods. The city is almost 300 years old and has undergone a complex social history through many periods of growth and development. The result has been a fragmentation of urban space into scores of named units with popularly recognized locations and boundaries. With City Hall at the CBD focus of the city's grid street system as a reference, Philadelphia is subdivided into North Philadelphia, West Philadelphia, and South Philadelphia (Figure 6). Each section is subdivided further. For example, North Philadelphia, which increasingly refers only to the inner city of north central Philadelphia, has two major appendages—one to the northwest in the direction of Germantown and Chestnut Hill, and the other to the northeast reaching toward the Far Northeast, the name given to the outer reaches of this suburblike extension of Philadelphia. This nested hierarchical regionalization continues. Germantown, for example, is subdivided into, among others, Pulaskitown, Beggarstown, and Dogtown.

The toponymy or place name geography of Philadelphia is colorful and is a vivid reminder of the diverse cultural influences which have affected the Delaware Valley. British names are dominant, but other early settlers have left their mark. The Dutch are responsible for the name "Schuylkill." Indian names are quite common: "Moyamensing" (meaning "dung heap") is but one colorful contribution to the city's map. Beyond the city limits other influences are observed. Reference to things Swedish are found downstream from the city on both banks of the Delaware. The western suburbs, particularly the famous "Main Line," contain the largest cluster of Welsh place names in the United States, including such jaw breakers as Cynwyd, Uwchlan, and Bryn Mawr; other Main Line town names are of Irish (Ardmore), Italian (Paoli), and even Spanish (Villanova) origin. As we will see, such devices have given rise to a certain provincialism or chauvinism at the local scale within the metropolis. Nathaniel Burt, a well-known local writer, has even described Philadelphia as the "largest provincial city in the world."

POPULATION

As a result of its immigrant infusions and natural increases, Philadelphia's population grew from an estimated 13,000 in 1744 and 42,520 in 1790 (the year of the first United States census) to a maximum of 2,071,605 in 1950. Philadelphia has consistently ranked among the ten largest cities in the country; the 1970 census reported that 1,948,609 people live in Philadelphia, making it the fourth largest city in the nation. The Philadelphia SMSA, which includes Bucks, Chester, Delaware, Montgomery, and Philadelphia counties in Pennsylvania, and Burlington, Camden, and Gloucester counties in New Jersey, ranks as the fourth largest metropolitan area with a 1970 population of 4,817,914. Only the Depression decade of the 1930s and the present postwar suburban era have seen population losses for the city, losses which both reflect and intensify much of what is now wrong with Philadelphia. The satellite cities of Chester, Wilmington, Trenton, and Camden are also experiencing population losses for many of the same reasons as Philadelphia, and with similar consequences.

Figure 6. Philadelphia's neighborhoods. Adapted from Richard Saul Wurman and John Andrew Gallery, *Man-Made Philadelphia: A Guide to Its Physical and Cultural Environment* (Cambridge, Mass.: MIT Press, 1972), p. 70.

Philadelphia's suburbs, on the other hand, have continually gained population (Figure 7). Some suburban communities have recently grown at an extraordinary pace between 1960 and 1970: Willingboro Township (formerly Levittown) in New Jersey grew from 12,000 to 43,000; nearby Cherry Hill Township more than doubled its population from 32,000 to 64,000; and East Goshen Township in Chester County more than tripled in size from 1,700 to 5,100. These patterns of population change reflect an accelerated deconcentration trend of people moving out of the central cities to suburban communities and new housing develop- ments on the fringes of the metropolitan region. Philadelphia lost 69,000 people during the decade following the peak population year of 1950, 54,000 during the 1960-1970 census period, and at least another 65,000 since. Were it not for the excess of births over deaths, reinforced by high nonwhite natality rates during the period since 1950, the city's population would be lower still because outmigration totals for the past quarter century are much higher than population loss totals. Thus, Philadelphia had a net migration loss of nearly 285,000 between 1950 and 1960, and nearly 210,000 between 1960 and 1970.

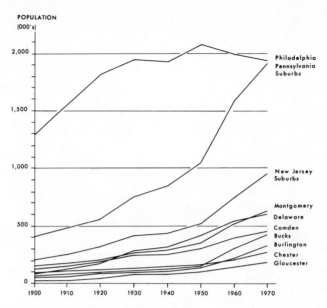

Figure 7. Population change by county, 1900–1970. Source: Philadelphia City Planning Commission.

SOCIAL CLEAVAGES

The distribution and composition of population within the metropolis, particularly according to such social distinctions as race, ethnicity, and economic class, are central to this study. There is considerable geographical segregation along these lines, and many see metropolitan problems as being closely tied to such social partitioning. Some people flee areas occupied by social groups of lower status, or else attempt to completely insulate themselves within the city. Devices abound for diverting the diffusion of urban problems and the social groups seen to be associated with them. In many cases, these mechanisms include restrictions upon the movement of the poor and minority populations, particularly blacks and Puerto Ricans.

Minorities

In 1970, one-third of Philadelphia's population was black and an additional 1.4 percent Puerto Rican. These figures are increases over the 1960 figures of 23.3 percent and 0.7 percent, respectively (Figures 8 and 9). In 1950 blacks comprised 18.2 percent of the city's population and in 1940 the figure was 13.1 percent; Puerto Rican population before the late 1950s was insignificant. Similar social changes have occurred in the region's satellite

central cities, while the suburban parts of the metropolitan area have remained overwhelmingly white throughout these decades (Figures 10 and 28).

The relocation of whites from increasingly black neighborhoods promotes the continued segregation of Philadelphia's black population in racially homogeneous ghettoes. Four such black concentrations are found in Philadelphia: North Philadelphia; Germantown-Mount Airy; West Philadelphia; and South Philadelphia (Figure 8). In part this segregation is related to income differences between the races. The poorer black population (median family income in 1969 for blacks in the Philadelphia SMSA was $7,522) is confined to the older, lower rent housing in the inner city, while the generally higher economic status of whites (median family income for all population in 1969 was $10,783) gives them more options in the selection of housing. The differential in income levels between blacks and whites in Philadelphia helps to perpetuate patterns of residential segregation by race. The fact that the median family income increased by $4,350 between 1959 and 1969 for the total SMSA

Figure 8. The four major black ghetto clusters in the city of Philadelphia. Source: Philadelphia City Planning Commission.

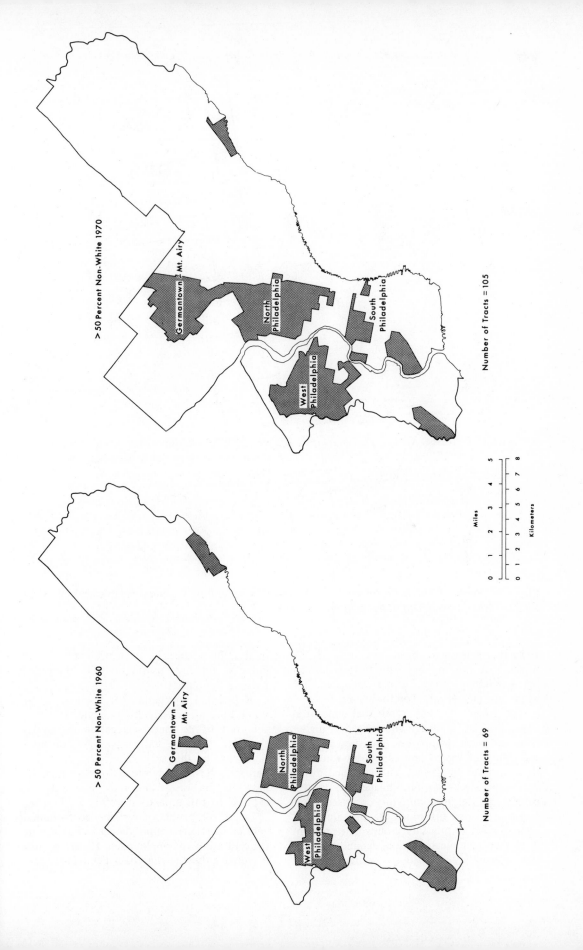

> 50 Percent Non-White 1970

Germantown—Mt. Airy

North
Philadelphia

South
Philadelphia

West
Philadelphia

Number of Tracts = 105

> 50 Percent Non-White 1960

Germantown—
Mt. Airy

North
Philadelphia

South
Philadelphia

West
Philadelphia

Number of Tracts = 69

Miles
0 1 2 3 4 5

Kilometers
0 1 2 3 4 5 6 7 8

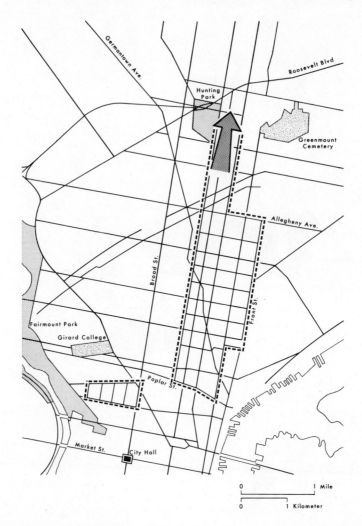

Figure 9. Puerto Rican concentrations in Philadelphia, indicating a general northward movement. Adapted from the *Evening Bulletin*, June 13, 1971.

while the increase for blacks was only $3,231 means that housing opportunities as defined by purchasing power alone increased for whites at a greater rate than for blacks.

The growth of black residential concentrations in the city is further encouraged by higher rates of black population increase and the availability of vacant houses left by whites in their outward migration. The confined distribution of blacks within Philadelphia is also perpetuated by discriminatory practices that effectively close off much of the local real estate market to minority groups. The problem is further complicated when lending institutions usually refuse loans to white buyers in

or near black areas (a practice known as "redlining"), thereby insuring racially segregated patterns in housing.

Residential segregation has implications beyond housing considerations alone. It lies at the root of de facto segregation in schools, shopping districts, and many places of entertainment. In this way such segregation perpetuates the limited interaction which occurs between the races; the only important exception to this separation occurs at the place of work for people of certain occupations in certain locations within the city, but the deconcentration of employment to the suburbs is reducing these few interracial contacts.

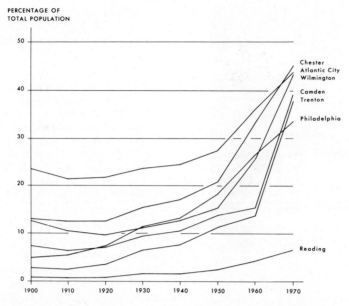

Figure 10. Nonwhite population change in Philadelphia and its satellite cities, 1900–1970. Data source: U.S. Census.

Limited contact among social groups breeds suspicions, stereotypes, and misconceptions that are often unfounded in fact. Such feelings among whites concerning blacks are so strong that flight from black neighbors proceeds on a block-by-block basis. Those nearest the edge of an expanding black neighborhood are most likely to move, often after shady real estate operators have fomented fears through block-busting, while those slightly farther away move later after the blocks bordering them have experienced racial change (Figure 11). It is in this manner that black neighborhoods expand in territorial extent, the rate of expansion in any direction varying according to the differential resistance of white populations as determined by such criteria as differing economic class, tenant versus homeowner status, and different levels of social cohesiveness. Thus there are stable racial boundaries in parts of South Philadelphia which abut on a working class Italian neighborhood, and another in North Philadelphia where the Irish and Poles of Kensington and Fishtown live alongside, but do not interact with, neighboring blacks to the west. There are several white ethnic enclaves sprinkled throughout the black concentrations, such as an Italian area in the heart of black North Philadelphia, a Polish commu-

nity centered around a church a bit further north, and the Ukrainian community to the southeast known locally as "Franklin." University areas such as those around the University of Pennsylvania and Temple are also white islands—the latter particularly by day, amidst almost exclusively black concentrations.

The reasons for whites' reluctance to share residential space with blacks are complex, but many can be summarized in a single word—fear. Important here are fears of becoming a crime victim and anxieties about the decline of real estate values in racially changing neighborhoods.

Apprehensions about race and real estate values are somewhat understandable, but are frequently based on misconceptions. If property values drop in a racially changing area, it is because the supply of available housing has exceeded the demand, creating a buyers' market. Where mass flight occurs because of anticipated declines in real estate values, a surplus of vacant housing is created and property values actually do decline, thereby fulfilling the prophecy of the sellers. However, as demand catches up to supply, property values rise again. Thus, one sees areas in Philadelphia where whites are selling large homes at greatly

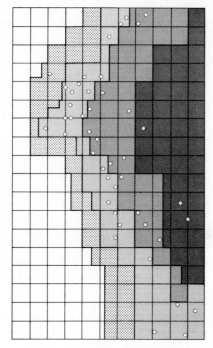

○ Street Fronts with First Sales to Black Households, 1955

	% Black	Sales to Whites	% of Total Sales
Area 1	32	8	3.9
Area 2	16	26	4.3
Area 3	5	65	40.6
Area 4	1	72	98.7
Area 5	1	112	100.0

Figure 11. The distribution of house purchases by blacks on the edge of the West Philadelphia ghetto, showing initial entries onto streets in 1955. A stylized map adapted from Chester Rapkin and William G. Grigsby, *The Demand for Housing in Racially Mixed Areas* (Berkeley: University of California Press, 1960), p. 76.

deflated prices, and then putting down payments on smaller and probably overpriced tract houses located much farther from the core of the city. Professional landlords may buy these hastily disposed of houses, convert them to multiple occupancy, and then make a tidy profit renting to blacks.

Occasionally, racial stability in white neighborhoods is maintained by force. Not only is there outright discrimination in the transfer of housing, but sometimes white response to black residents is nothing less than ugly. The mother of the first black family to settle on a block in

one of the several white enclaves in the inner city explained to a *Philadelphia Tribune* reporter why she and her children moved out after a short stay:

> People just can't live like this. I can't have visitors, play the record player or have parties. If I do, then one of these people [her white neighbors] calls the cops and tells them I have a disorderly house and they come banging on the door. My children have to run back and forth to the store. They have been threatened, stabbed, and ... burned. This is a hell of a place.

As elsewhere in the United States, truly integrated neighborhoods are rare in Philadelphia. Occasionally one hears that parts of Germantown, West Mount Airy, and Logan in North Philadelphia, or the Wynnefield-Overbrook section of West Philadelphia, are racially mixed areas. Closer inspection, however, shows that any racial mixture is probably only temporary. Housing turnover might be slower in such areas of fine homes, but the fact remains that relatively few whites have tried to obtain the homes put up for sale in these neighborhoods. As a result, these areas have been becoming extensions of existing black concentrations.

A *Philadelphia Inquirer* article evaluating the racial situation in several of these neighborhoods concluded that Wynnefield has been losing its racial "balance" because "in the end, many more blacks wanted houses in Wynnefield than whites did." In another article of the series, a Logan resident was quoted as saying: "[Y]ou have to just keep saying 'changing,' you can't say 'integrated.' It will constantly keep changing to an all-black neighborhood." If any neighborhood can be called integrated, it is West Mount Airy where an active neighborhood group, the Northwest Community Housing Association, has worked hard at maintaining racial balance. Community leaders take prospective home buyers, both black and white, on tours of the area, and advertisements for new homeowners are placed in such national magazines as *New Republic*.

Ethnicity

Race, however, is but one of the cleavages in Philadelphia society. Ethnic identification is also important. While Philadelphia's tradition of European immigration has produced a colorful street atmosphere, it has long contributed to what has been called an "environment of fear." One author, writing about interethnic relations in the late eighteenth century, refers to Philadelphia as the "City of Brotherly Fear," and recounts incidents of conflicts among immigrant groups, each fearing that newer waves of immigrants would compete for their jobs in an often fragile economy. Appeals to "proper Philadelphians" for charity for poor immigrants distinguished between the "industrious poor" and the "vicious poor," the latter being seen as "worthless and vagabond types and as 'Drunken, Rioting, Sulking, Lazy fellow[s]'." The city's ethnic history is full of such conflict: Irish Catholics and Irish Protestants battled one another on the streets of South Philadelphia in the midnineteenth century; Catholics were forced to defend their homes and churches against violence in the Native-American riots of 1844; and street gangs of various ethnic affiliations, going under names such as the Killers, Blood Tubs, Molly Maguires, Rats, and Death-Fetchers, opposed each other throughout Philadelphia's period of rapid European immigration from the 1850s to the 1920s.

Tensions among ethnic groups have always festered, and still do today. Philadelphia recently elected an Italian-American mayor—some say because he best represented the interests of frightened whites. A map of the 1971 mayoral election returns (closely replicated in the re-election campaign of 1975) very clearly approximates the racial distribution of the city: Frank Rizzo won in white areas, and his opponents (Thacher Longstreth in 1971; Charles Bowser and Thomas Foglietta in 1975) carried most of the black wards (Figure 12). However, some of the mayor's subsequent political appointments have pitted a number of his supporters against what some people feel are "favored Italians." Jewish and gentile teenagers do battle in the high schools and streets of the Northeast in what is locally termed "The Holy War," and the militant Jewish Defense League is active in the city. The widening of a freeway corridor in Center City has antagonized the Chinese-American community which lives in its path, and many residents interpret these plans as a direct threat to Chinese life and cultural unity in Philadelphia. The editorial pages of the *Evening Bulletin* have carried a prolonged debate between the

city's Poles and Germans over the question of the nationality of Copernicus. And all sorts of people are down on the Irish, who are seen to "drink too much." The letters-to-the-editor pages of the city's newspapers frequently publish ethnic sentiments. Consider, for example, the following letter which "White Observer" sent to the *Daily News:*

> Why have all our black American trash collectors been replaced with Puerto Ricans? This is most unfair. I resent looking at signboards printed in Spanish. This is America. If they don't speak the language, why don't they go back to Puerto Rico?

Some of these conflicts can be associated with a long history of spatial segregation and therefore limited contact among groups. When immigrants first came to Philadelphia, they formed, and remained in, tight ethnic enclaves near Center City. For example, Italians first settled in South Philadelphia east of Broad Street; Jews settled near them in an area called Southwark; the first Irish concentration was in South Philadelphia west of Broad Street; German immigrants settled in a number of North Philadelphia districts; and Poles settled northeast of Center City in Kensington and Frankford. With time there has been a breakdown of these well-defined social areas, particularly those of European groups which have been in Philadelphia the longest. But, with the exception of areas in which there has been massive racial change, traces of ethnic identification remain, with some neighborhoods still possessing strong cultural cohesiveness.

In 1860 the population of Philadelphia was 30 percent foreign born, including some 95,000 Irish and 44,000 Germans, but by 1920 the pattern of ethnic settlement had stabilized. Although the foreign-born population has greatly declined since the 1920s as a result of immigration quotas and shifts of white ethnic groups into the suburbs, much of the early twentieth century pattern is still in evidence. More than 80 percent of all foreign born in the city in 1920 could be traced to six national origin groups—English, Irish, German, Russian (which includes many Russian-born Jews), Italian, and Polish. Despite a substantial drop in the foreign-born population in the past fifty years (from 22.0 percent in 1920 to 6.5 percent in 1970), these same six groups continue to

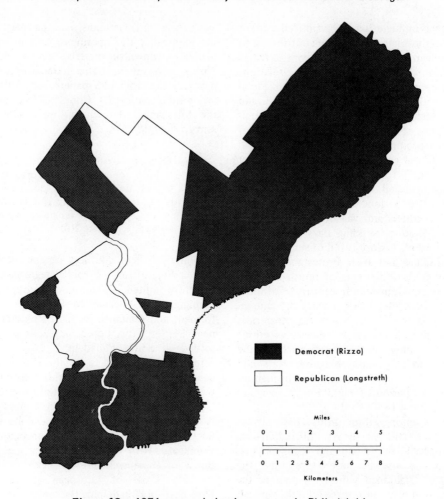

Figure 12. 1971 mayoral election returns in Philadelphia.

dominate the ethnic population; in 1970 these groups accounted for more than three-fourths of the foreign stock (foreign born and their children) of the city.

Ethnic neighborhoods tend to be located in the older inner sections of the city (Figure 13). Historically, the pattern has been one of succeeding waves of immigrants moving into aging inner city housing vacated by earlier immigrants, with the latter moving outward along public transit routes to newer less crowded housing after establishing an economic foothold in the city. Some of these neighborhood successions involved a single ethnic group. For example, recent Italian immigrants have occupied a number of dwellings left vacant by other Italians in South Philadelphia; Poles

have done the same thing in parts of North Philadelphia; and post–World War II Ukrainian immigrants have moved into Fairmount where they made use of Ukrainian community facilities established by their countrymen who had migrated to Philadelphia at the beginning of the century. Other successions involved two or more different ethnic groups, resulting in complex ethnic mixtures in certain neighborhoods. On the other hand, in areas where blacks and Puerto Ricans were the succeeding populations, a virtually complete ethnic turnover occurred.

Figure 13. The largest ethnic groups in the city of Philadelphia, 1970. Data source: U.S. Census.

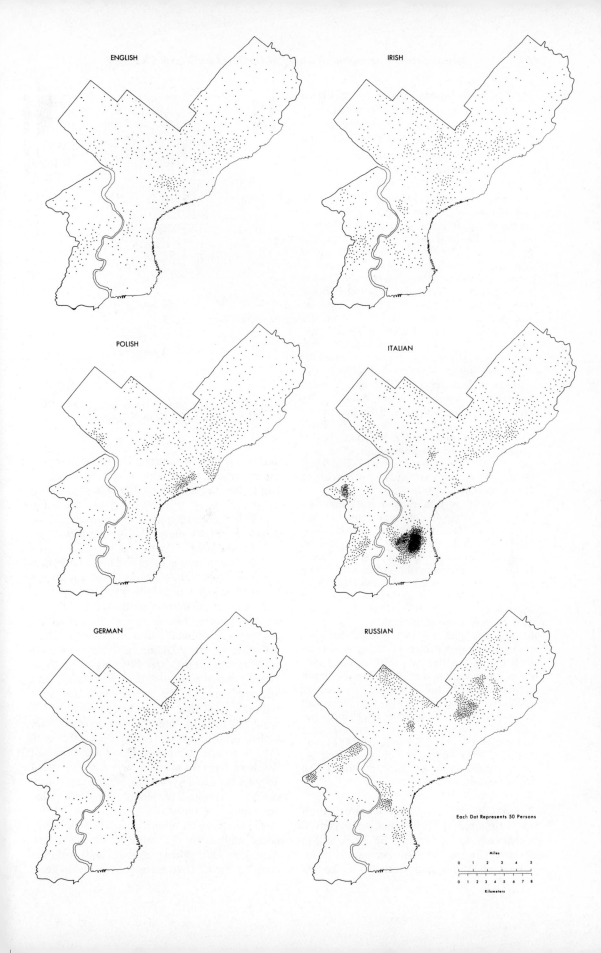

ENGLISH

IRISH

POLISH

ITALIAN

GERMAN

RUSSIAN

Each Dot Represents 50 Persons

Miles
0   1   2   3   4   5

0 1 2 3 4 5 6 7 8
Kilometers

Many neighborhoods, which in tabulated statistics appear to be ethnically mixed, have traditionally been strongly segregated at the block level. According to Caroline Golab, the Northern Liberties section northeast of Center City in the late nineteenth century

> ... was a virtual crazy-quilt of nationalities. No one was unrepresented. Every imaginable group of Slavic nomenclature, as well as handfulls [sic] of Italians, Greeks and Syrians, could be found here. There were at least a half dozen varieties of Jews, not to mention pockets of Irish, Germans, English and native-Americans, both Black and White. Such endless diversity resulted in splendid isolation for everyone. The city's first Slovak settlement was located at Fourth and Brown Streets. The intersections of Mascher and Master Streets was the center of Philadelphia's "Little Hungary." The first Ukrainians settled between Sixth and Seventh Streets, just south of Girard Avenue. The majority of the orthodox Russians settled near Third and Fairmount Streets, Fifth and Poplar, and Hancock and Oxford Streets in southern Kensington. The Serbian center was Girard Avenue and Hancock Street; the Albanians settled along Girard Avenue.

The lower portion of the Northern Liberties was originally populated by German Jews. In the 1880s, however, Front, New Market, Second, Third and Fourth Streets, from Arch to Girard Avenue, began to house Lithuanian, Russian and Polish Jews. The great influx of the 1890s caused the Jews to spread as far west as Eighth Street and sometimes as far north as Lehigh Avenue. The endless number of little streets hiding behind the larger thoroughfares between Front and Eighth Streets were soon crowded with the new settlers. As early as the 1880s Poles from Poznan and West Prussia began competing with the Jews for space along Delaware Avenue. By 1915 the Poles had extended their settlement over into the adjacent Kensington section of the city. Indeed, Front, Second and Third Streets between Fairmount and Lehigh Avenue became long, narrow columns of Polish and Slavic settlement.

A recent study of a nearby inner neighborhood (Fairmount) has documented a continuing tendency for segregation by block within small areas (Figure 14). The circulation of information about housing vacancies as well as

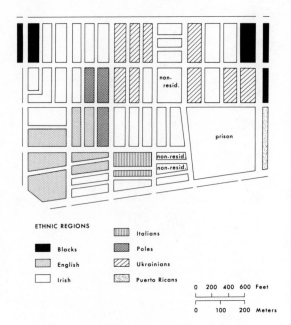

Figure 14. Segregation by blocks in the Fairmount neighborhood of Philadelphia.

active searches for housing is confined to each ethnic group. More than 50 percent—and for some ethnic groups up to 70 percent—of apartment rentals in this neighborhood are intra-ethnic in nature—despite the fact that no ethnic group comprises more than a quarter of the area's population.

Even where ethnic neighborhoods have broken down, their former residents do not always scatter in all directions within the metropolitan area, but often move together to a different neighborhood or neighborhoods located within a specific directional sector of the city. Thus, for example, many Ukrainians from Fairmount and Franklin near Center City moved north to Logan, and then northeast to Fox Chase and adjacent communities across the city line. Suburbs bordering on heavily Italian southwest Philadelphia and Camden tend to have higher percentages of Italians than other suburbs, a frontierlike phenomenon also observed for Jews from Wynnefield who have migrated across City Line Avenue to Merion and other nearby communities along the Main Line stretching to the west.

Dispersal of an ethnic population does not necessarily mean the breaking of social ties. Americans are highly mobile and maintain contacts across large metropolitan areas. Visits from suburbs to old neighbors in the city are common, and crosstown trips to ethnic churches, stores, and organizations are made regularly. Such patterns are difficult to document because of the lack of appropriate data, but consider the following surrogate information. One of the possible outcomes of social interaction is marriage, and analysis of data concerning who marries whom in terms of ethnicity and place of residence can be used as a revealing measure of social interaction patterns in the city. An analysis of marriage patterns by residents of the ethnically mixed Fairmount neighborhood showed that ethnicity is in fact associated with the selection of mates—despite the fact that most partners are second and third generation Americans. Distance is also important: nearly one-half of all marriages involved cases in which the previous addresses of both husband and wife were within this small neighborhood. Marriages involving longer distances, with one partner from outside the neighborhood, tended to be as frequent as intracommunity marriages. Evidently certain aspects of the American "melting pot" are mythical. Ethnic identity perpetuates heterogeneity in urban society.

Economic Class Polarization

The changing distributional patterns of ethnic and racial groups have resulted in segregation according to economic status within the metropolis. Generally, the poor and low income groups concentrate in the inner areas of central cities where overcrowded housing is old and in poor condition. A gradation of rising incomes can be observed with increasing distance from the inner city, with migrants to the suburbs being wealthier than those who remain in town. The city can thus be generalized into a concentric arrangement of economic class categories, a spatial structuring that has led one geographer, William Bunge, to describe the "typical" American city as having three zones— an "inner city of death" marked by poverty; a "middle zone of need" where people survive on tightly budgeted incomes; and an "outer zone of superfluity" or concentrated affluence.

A recent change in this concentric zonation of Philadelphia is the increasing concentration of wealth in and immediately adjacent to downtown, a phenomenon referred to locally as the "renaissance" of Center City. Many former suburbanites have decided that the lengthy and formerly fashionable commute over crowded expressways is a senseless waste of time and have returned to live in the city. Many young, successful whites, perhaps bred in the suburbs, prefer the increasingly fashionable center city and currently have no intentions of living in suburbia. Old row houses, some dating back to the colonial period, have been extensively remodeled in prestigious areas such as Society Hill, in the vicinity of Independence Hall, where these restored single family antiques frequently have a market value in excess of $100,000.

Other areas of Center City restoration for the wealthy are found in the southwestern quadrant around Rittenhouse Square, and to the northwest along the Benjamin Franklin Parkway leading from city hall to the Philadelphia Museum of Art. Other affluent downtowners live in high-rise apartment buildings and condominiums which border high amenity Society Hill, Rittenhouse Square, and the Parkway (Figure 15), and the early seventies saw a building boom of these housing units in Center City.

Not unexpectedly, the 1970 census showed a big jump over 1959 median incomes for downtown: from $6,314 to $12,273, or from 109 percent of the city's 1959 average to 131 percent of its 1969 average, making Center City the highest income district in Philadelphia after wealthy Chestnut Hill in the city's far northwest corner. The revised model can be referred to as the "urban doughnut." The wealthy live and work in the center, which is surrounded by a "gray zone" of the inner city where the urban poor are concentrated; beyond, we find a gradation of increasing wealth until the limits of the built-up urban area are reached in the outer suburbs.

Conflicts and Social Cleavages

Given this "urban doughnut" distribution of social and economic classes and the directional expansion of its various elements, we can say something about the nature and location of stress and conflict in the city. The poor move outward as their houses deteriorate beyond liveability and as urban renewal and expressway construction bulldoze away entire city blocks, thus creating conflicts with the working and middle class populations occupying the encircling zone. When those advancing are poor blacks, one observes the city's highest out-migration rates as white residents respond

Figure 15. Rittenhouse Square high-rise housing.

Figure 16. Redevelopment and blight side by side.

quickly by moving farther away. In the meantime, redevelopment of central areas for the well-to-do is frequently carried on at the expense of the poor. Thus, Society Hill grows southward block by block, so that one side of the street may be extensively redeveloped and occupied by middle and upper income households, while the other side is largely vacant and in a deteriorated condition, with its few occupied dwellings housing the poor until they too are displaced (Figure 16). A similar process occurs in the northwestern quadrant of Center City, where a redeveloped zone becoming known as the Fairmount Art Museum Area is expanding almost literally house by house in one direction into a Puerto Rican enclave, and in another direction into a white working class area, displacing tenants and stimulating property tax increases for homeowners.

When white working class neighborhoods like the Art Museum Area of Queen Village south of Society Hill see themselves threatened by racial change, their residents frequently undertake extensive home remodeling projects themselves in an effort to quickly upgrade their blocks and send rents and property values soaring out of the reach of low income blacks. Thus, an alliance is struck between the two white populations against blacks: the poorer whites benefit in that any change in their neighborhood is "positive" white change, while the wealthier element takes comfort in maintaining a buffer population between itself and blacks. Concerning the buffer zone of Fairmount, one journalist, Mike Mallowe, wrote: "Rich Parkway types in their plush high rise sleep sounder at night, safe in the knowledge that their buffer zone against black North Philly is secure." This social buffer area concept is important. In several instances when a wealthy white community expands directly into a black or Puerto Rican area, a buffer population—composed of white college students and other young not so wealthy types—has settled at the front. Thus we have the South Street "Bohemian" community located along part of the border between Society Hill and the South Philadelphia black community, and a substantial student population in Fairmount which rents apartments in the transitional zone between the Art Museum Area and the nearby Puerto Rican community.

Where redevelopment for the rich necessitates the removal of established residents, conflicts result. A case in point is Franklin Town (Figure 17), a $400 million office and highrise housing complex for those who can afford its high rents. It is to be located in a mixed residential-commercial-light industrial section above the Parkway in northwest Center City and its construction requires the clearing of fifty acres. This plan is bitterly opposed by local residents, many of whom have lived in the area for more than twenty years. Initial protest against this privately funded project was carried out by those threatened with displacement, but apprehensions about Franklin Town soon diffused to other communities in the area. Residents foresaw increased pressures on schools, streets, and other public facilities, and the threat of property tax increases in the vicinity of this luxury complex.

Tensions at the boundary between expanding neighborhoods of wealthy whites and less affluent communities are subtly manifested in a number of ways. Different lifestyles are involved. The wealthy people are indoor oriented, entertaining guests with cocktail parties or traveling outside the neighborhood to dine out, visit friends, and attend movies, plays, and concerts. Working class people make much more use of the streets and sidewalks. Their children play outdoors, visiting inside homes is infrequent except among relatives, and in good weather much time is spent socializing at doorstoops in front of their homes. Hence, outdoor space takes on different meaning for each group. For the affluent, streets and sidewalks are used as a means of getting to places, but for the working class sidewalks tend to become functional extensions of living quarters—space for rest, relaxation, play, and conversation with friends. These different perceptions and uses of space occasionally bring about conflicts between populations. Childless, indoor-oriented people complain about active, noisy streets, failing to understand why neighbors do not "control their children," and frowning upon the "distasteful" practice of adult streetcorner lounging. Outdoor-oriented people, on the other hand, are repeatedly offended by dog litter on their sidewalks, which piles up as the wealthier element frequently walks its canine "burglar alarms" along their neighbors' outdoor meeting grounds (Figure 18). And on occasion one might also hear a working class resident grumble about the bearded or braless bicyclists who

Figure 17. Franklin Town planned urban development.

"tour the neighborhood gawking at the people."

Much of the city consists of "defended space," as dozens of distinct communities, some with ethnic identities and others without, inspire strong personal attachments to Philadelphia's neighborhoods. This is expressed in a number of ways. Graffiti on walls, fences, and other surfaces frequently proclaim local loyalties to certain neighborhoods. Thus, one reads "Fishtown" or "Fairmount Rules" in those communities. Teenagers in Manayunk, an old industrial community on the Schuylkill River, wear T-shirts reading "YUNK." Front license plates on cars in other communities read "I Like Mt. Airy" or "I Like Oak Lane." A study

of an Irish neighborhood in South Philadelphia by John W. Anderson offers some insights into this theme of neighborhood cohesiveness. One informant said: "This is a clannish neighborhood, family and working people, and we take care of our own. A man couldn't spit here without hitting a cousin; and you cross one guy, you answer to everybody." Another informant described the neighborhood in this manner: "This place is like a fort, and we're the pioneers who go outside the walls to work and get what we need and then shut the gate at night around our families to hold off the renegades." As a final example of neighborhood loyalty, consider the following letter to a newspaper written by a proud resident of Kensington,

Figure 18. Exercising the burglar alarm.

a staunchly white working class community. Here, the writer defines the boundaries of his neighborhood to exclude the location where a crime was committed: "... reporting a hold-up that happened on the 4500 block of Frankford Avenue and calling it Kensington is indeed an injustice to our area.... In future reporting, make certain that the following boundaries are adhered to: Lehigh Avenue to the south; Torresdale or Erie Avenue to the north; Richmond Street to the east, and Front Street to the west. This is Greater Kensington as we know it."

Many Philadelphians are proud of their communities and feel reasonably secure therein. They care about their neighborhood's physical and social environment. However, too frequently these feelings can be translated into conflicts with other neighborhoods, particularly in those parts of the city which are undergoing social change. Gestures of local chauvinism then become manifestations of an identity crisis, and proclamations such as "Fairmount Rules" are reactions against social change; in this particular instance, white residents feel threatened by the presence of blacks at the fringes of their community, and slogans such as these, others reading "White Power" (Figure 19), and more obscene racial epithets are concentrated on those walls where racial change is perceived to be most imminent. Conflicts concerning the defense of communities are very common in the city. The Chinatown protest mentioned earlier is an example. Others include reactions against public housing projects by residents of communities in South Philadelphia, where the opening of the Tasker Homes produced weeks of violence in a white working class area; Society Hill, where the issue of public housing had divided the residents of this wealthy inner city district; and Tioga, a black neighborhood in North Philadelphia whose residents bemoan

the fact that urban renewal and institutional expansion to the south have displaced a lower class element which in turn has been invading their own formerly middle and lower income community.

A letter to the *Philadelphia Inquirer* from a resident of Fishtown, an old industrial community near the Delaware River northeast of Center City, reflects still another interneighborhood conflict in the city. The writer complains that the construction of Interstate 95 displaced working class Fishtown residents, while the wealthy and politically more powerful residents of Society Hill, located along the Delaware River south of Fishtown, were able to alter plans for the expressway near them so that no residents would be displaced.

I hope the people who are opposed to I-95 ramps in the Society Hill area do not use I-95. Maybe the people in Fishtown and Lower Kensington [an adjacent working class community] should picket at the Frankford Avenue ramps. We have homes

Figure 19. Philadelphia's walls frequently portray social sentiments.

here that are over 100 years old. Don't these people think we would like our neighborhood to stay residential? If they don't want the ramps in their neighborhood, then they shouldn't ride on I-95 through ours.

Many inner city neighborhoods are subdivided into gang turfs. It is impossible to estimate the number of street gangs in the city, because it is difficult to define just what a street gang is, and because many are only intermittently active. But various sources quote figures such as eighty, 200, or simply "hundreds." Each gang claims a block or a small number of blocks as its territory and defends this turf, sometimes violently, against rival gangs. Philadelphia's gangs commonly use the initials of street intersections as their names, and mark off their turfs with wall graffiti using these initials. Thus, inner city walls read "15-V," "23-A," or "28-Ox," representing gangs whose turfs are centered around the intersections of 15th and Venango Streets, 23rd and Atlantic Streets, and 28th and Oxford Streets, respectively. A small percentage of the gangs use nongeographical names such as Zulu Nation, Moroccans, or the Clang Gang, but these groups are place-specific as well. Occasionally, several neighboring gangs will form alliances, such as North Philadelphia's Valley Gang, in order to protect a neighborhood from more distant gangs.

The implications of the city's gang structure are enormous. During 1971 there were forty-three deaths and countless other injuries directly attributed to gang warfare. In 1972, thirty-nine people died as a result of gang fights, and the 1973 toll was forty-four. Residents of gang-controlled areas frequently respect turf boundaries between rival gangs; certain turfs are "closed off" to people living beyond their limits, even though these people might not identify with any gang at all. Geographer David Ley demonstrated that pedestrians in Philadelphia's inner city frequently take circuitous routes to reach their destinations in order to avoid certain locations. He discovered that students who must walk through gang-controlled territory on their way to and from school are more frequently absent from classes than those whose paths are safer. A recent interview of a black West Oak Lane family by the *Philadelphia Tribune* under-

scored this relationship, as a mother explains why three of her children have not been to school in four months:

> It's like living in a prison. Not only do the kids not go to school: they hardly ever go out for any reason. If we do, it may be the last time we ever go anywhere. [Her seventeen year old daughter adds:] It's the Clang Gang. They told me if they catch me coming home from school, they'd kill me. One boy was killed just last week on the next block, so we know they mean business.

The fear of violence pervades the city, and everywhere one sees defenses being set up—metal grates over windows; new locks and doors; and burglar alarms, both electrical and canine. The statement "you just can't go anywhere anymore" is typical, and reflects the fact that people have been locking themselves up. The streets become more and more deserted as increasingly higher proportions of their users travel in "automobile shelters," reinforcing the existence of vacuous spaces at the expense of community life. Except during office and retailing hours, downtown streets become vacuums, as have many of the city's parks and playgrounds. The results have been disastrous. The fact that legitimate users of city space have withdrawn has made it easier for illegitimate users—muggers, rapists, vandals, and dope peddlers—to score successes in their activities. In this way a vicious cycle is formed: withdrawal offers the opportunity for more crime, which then causes further lock-up, or, alternatively, more flight from the city. Because fear of crime extends beyond high crime zones, the area of extensive lock-up and withdrawal is larger than the high crime area, creating a potential for the further spread of crime. It is in this way that crime and the pervasive fear of it have diffused from the low income areas of the inner city throughout the metropolitan region, such that some suburban communities now have crime problems as serious as Philadelphia's.

CONSEQUENCES OF CLEAVAGES AND CONFLICTS

Those who fled Philadelphia for the suburbs have brought about numerous other negative human consequences in the city. Because these emigrants tend to be wealthier and more politically powerful then residual city residents, there is an uneven distribution of community services and facilities within the metropolis, so that suburbanites are better provided for than Philadelphians. Where there is wealth, one finds better schools and better maintenance of parks, playgrounds, and streets. And, as inner city community leaders continuously argue, better police protection as well.

On the other hand, the quality of Philadelphia's public services has been declining in recent years as tax revenues become increasingly insufficient to finance demanded services. The school system is a mess—many graduates can barely read—and there are persistent rumors of cutbacks in education programs and even of a total shutdown of the system. A recent strike by teachers, the longest in the United States up to 1973, closed public schools for nearly three months. Adequate money is not available for the construction of housing for the poor, for the rehabilitation of slum dwellings, for the cleanup of littered lots, or for the maintenance of city streets. Tens of thousands of housing units in the city lie abandoned and boarded up, and most have heavy tax liens against them (Figures 20 and 21). Buyers are difficult to find, as mortgages are hard to obtain for homes in inner city neighborhoods. Countless small businesses have shut down in the face of competition from larger chains, and the small Mom and Pop stores, once so common on Philadelphia's street corners, are facing virtual extinction in many parts of the city as old customers move to suburbia while storeowner fears rise as the neighborhood begins to undergo rapid social change and crime rates increase. Because buying power is now heavily concentrated in the suburbs, many of the better stores have opened larger branches in outlying shopping centers. Recent years have seen the steady suburban migration of large employers, with concomitant damage to Philadelphia's economy, tax base, unemployment rate, and the cross-social interaction which traditionally occurs at the urban workplace.

On top of all this, many people have given up and are no longer willing to sacrifice money and effort for the sake of Philadelphia. "Let the other guy do it" is an increasingly common attitude, and the growing restlessness of taxpayers dictates that less money should be spent on the poor. A city resident writing to a newspaper complained: "Why do the people in the 2700 block of South Sheridan and 2700 South 7th think the city should clean their alleyways? The people living there made the mess, so why don't they get out and clean it themselves." Another letter reiterated: "The amount of money the city spent on rat control is ridiculous. Why can't the people catch their own rats?" A former Philadelphia resident summarized his feelings about the city this way: "I've been out here in the suburbs five years now, and I don't care what the niggers are doing to each other. I want to know what's happening around the corner from my home. I'm sick of hearing about the city."

It is largely because of polarization resulting from these problems that added tensions exist between urban and suburban residents of the metropolitan region. Some people are very emotional about this problem. Mike Mallowe, writing in *Philadelphia Magazine* about his personal antisuburbia crusade stated:

> Bitter people insist that the cities died because black and brown minorities invaded by the hundreds of thousands, bringing with them poverty and crime and rending forever the social fabric of city life. But this explanation is too slick—too sick. Nonwhite Philadelphians did not turn this city into the sad, leprous hulk that it is today. The people who killed this city are the whites who fled at the first sign of a black face. They let neighborhoods die where three and four generations of their own families had lived and grown. They fouled their own nests when they ran like ignorant, helpless cattle, reverting to the basest instinct of the herd. They deflowered my virgin city and that is why I hate them.

These are strong sentiments, representing one of several interpretations of Philadelphia's plight. This view also argues that not only was the city abandoned by hundreds of thousands for the suburbs, but these ex-Philadelphians also slammed the doors behind them as they entered their new residences. Because these suburbanites include a high proportion of the

Figure 20. One of the thousands of vacant houses in the city.

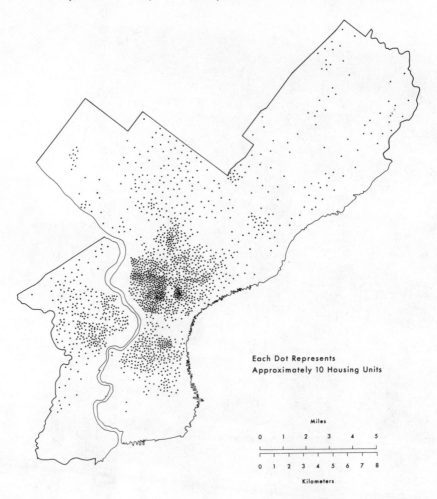

Each Dot Represents
Approximately 10 Housing Units

Miles

0   1   2   3   4   5

0 1 2 3 4 5 6 7 8

Kilometers

Figure 21. Vacant available housing units in 1970. From a map prepared by the Philadelphia City Planning Commission.

region's wealthy, talented, and well-connected people, the city suffers all the more as such people's attentions shift from Philadelphia to local residential communities. Many Philadelphians contend that solutions to the city's problems are "hiding" in the suburbs, and that efforts to better integrate city and suburban needs are necessary. Mutual derision between city and suburbs—like the Mallowe diatribe—helps little toward this goal.

Another view argues that the suburbanization trend was a *response* to Philadelphia's plight by those who could afford a "nicer" environment, not the *cause* of that plight. Peo-

ple left the city because its housing was old, small, and tightly packed; because schools were failing to educate children; and because the streets were becoming unsafe. Any exacerbation of Philadelphia's situation was an unintended consequence of mass middle class outmigration which Philadelphia's leaders either failed to foresee or failed to come to grips with. One might argue that large scale suburbanization was necessary to accommodate the region's population growth in this century. Without a step up in rates of suburban population increase in the last several decades, Philadelphia's 1970 population would have been something on the order of 3.3 million. One wonders about the city's potential to handle such large numbers, no matter how talented the residents and their leaders.

Nevertheless, the urbanization of the suburbs has drastically reshaped the metropolitan structure of the Delaware Valley. These changes are crucial for understanding the spatial organization of the Philadelphia region in the 1970s, and we now shift our attention to this outer ring of the metropolis.

Suburban Delaware Valley

The origin and continued growth of suburbia is in large part due to the lure of such advantages as low density living, clean air, and modern schools, residential amenities which increasing numbers of Americans are able to afford. However, high rates of suburbanization in the last two decades are not only responses to these "pulls," but are also associated with "push" factors related to the increasing stresses of central city living. These include the physical decay of the city, deterioration of municipal services, and social tensions. In order that the problems of the central city do not become the problems of suburban communities, most of suburbia has become defended space in much the same way as many outer city neighborhoods have withdrawn into a partial seclusion from other parts of Philadelphia. As the settlement pattern of the suburbs has emerged, residents of similar social status and lifestyle have tended to cluster. This sorting process, which is closely related to the prices and rentals of housing, has produced an intricate geographical partitioning of the population so that each part of suburbia caters to a specific type of household and is basically off limits to others. The result is that geographical polarization within the suburbs is hardly less pronounced than in Philadelphia. The pervasive form of segregation in suburban Delaware Valley is *economic:* its main cleavages and conflicts exist among income groups of different levels. Over the past two decades, the whole fabric of suburban land use has increasingly emphasized this economic polarization as zoning practices have produced a dispersed and highly compartmentalized spatial pattern of residential and nonresidential activities.

Mortgaged to the hilt, the wary new suburbanite fiercely protects his investment by fortifying his home and locality against those conditions which encouraged him to desert Philadelphia. Vigorously supported local zoning laws and land use controls dictate that new housing command prices and rents high enough to exclude lower income groups and the poor; any efforts at introducing plans for low income housing set off widespread protests. Such exclusionary practices, of course, not only perpetuate tight racial segregation in the suburbs, but also foster separation between young and old, families and unmarrieds, educated and uneducated, and auto owners and public transportation users.

These zoning practices are justified by local officials in several ways. Most often, public accountability takes the form of pleading the necessity of maintaining only high tax ratables in order to keep the tax burden fair, and that zoning for large lot single residential uses is essential to keep areas from becoming "overcrowded." A more subtle practice, which is common in more than a few Philadelphia suburbs, is to tolerate a small poverty pocket, almost always hemmed in on "the wrong side of the tracks" or in some obscure corner of the municipality. Critics of race segregation may then be disarmed by local spokesmen who can claim a "balanced" total mix of population, which appears to exist when demographic statistics for the entire township or borough are displayed.

The suburban experience in the Delaware Valley has been translated into a number of sharply contrasting lifestyles, generally comparable to the income levels of various groups of residents. Rather than surveying a large number of communities, a sequence of four vignettes of typical suburban lifestyles in the region is presented—the Main Line, a string of high income suburbs stretching west-northwest from the city line for about ten miles; the area around Echelon Mall in central Camden County, New Jersey, a planned unit development of upper middle class young families; Levittown, Pennsylvania, a largely blue collar and lower middle income suburb located along U.S. Route 1 beyond Philadelphia's northeastern boundary; and the Northeast portion of Philadelphia itself, an inner de facto suburb containing separate large middle and working class populations.

LIFESTYLES IN SUBURBAN DELAWARE VALLEY

The Main Line

Philadelphia's Main Line is one of the nation's wealthiest residential enclaves. The area was originally developed in the 1830s as a series of commuter suburbs along the main line

of the Pennsylvania Railroad west from Philadelphia. Because transportation was limited to rails, each station formed the core of a compact community, the extent of which was limited to a few minutes' walking distance from the railhead. The resultant pattern was a line of small settlements, approximately one mile apart, strung out like beads on a chain. The contemporary Main Line, thanks to the automobile, has expanded laterally, but the railroad and its parallel highway—Lancaster Pike—still function as the twin axes of the region.

From its beginning, the wealthy and socially prominent elite of the Philadelphia area first vacationed and then permanently concentrated along the Main Line, spurred on initially by the railroad's upper crust executives who viewed the area as their private stamping ground. To a great extent this is still true, and until recently all but those with the right social credentials were discouraged from living in the most prestigious sections of the Main Line. As an enclave of the rich, the somewhat anachronistic Main Line lifestyle is built upon the cornerstones of high status and prestige. Accordingly, the delimitation of the region is accomplished largely by mental map—everyone "knows" just which communities are Main Line and which are not (Figure 22). Within the region itself, the reputation of individual communities and streets is crucial. The best addresses in Bryn Mawr,

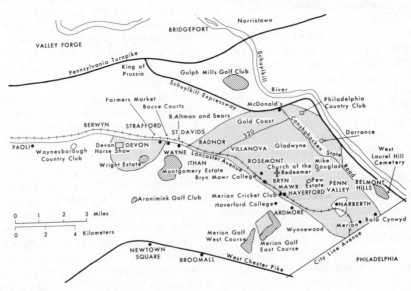

Figure 22. Philadelphia's suburban "Main Line." Shaded areas are perceived to have the highest prestige. Source: *Philadelphia Magazine*, June 1973, p. 117.

Villanova, and Rosemont are highly prized for their prestige, and some residents of communities below the uppermost echelon have been known to rent post office boxes in more glamorous towns in order to receive mail at the proper place. The trappings of Main Line wealth are highly visible throughout the region —breathtakingly beautiful estates; hunt, cricket, and tennis clubs; and fleets of expensive foreign automobiles (Figure 23).

For well over a century, the Main Line has staunchly defended its exclusiveness. By the late 1960s, however, signs of change began to appear as the influx of the middle class increased rapidly with an apartment building boom, particularly on the southern side of the

Penn Central tracks. In 1972, a ruling by Pennsylvania's Supreme Court upheld a liberal new fair housing law. For the Main Line this means that all vacant house listings must be made available to any licensed broker, rather than to a select group of local realtors who had consistently worked to maintain the status quo. Conceivably, anyone who can afford the housing is now free to enter the Main Line, though it should be mentioned that some barriers had already been slowly coming down: wealthy Jews, for example, are now quietly accepted. Devious practices, however, continue to be used on occasion; apart from such usual ploys as not posting "For Sale" signs, some uglier incidents have been reported. In

Figure 23. Main Line house. Courtesy of Ellen R. Sager.

one case, a college professor sold his Main Line home to a high income black family, and, in the few days' interim between occupancies, vandals attacked the property, rendered it unlivable, and forced the blacks to withdraw. Short of outright criminal acts, other ways of skirting the new law have appeared. For example, it is reported that more than half of the Main Line house turnovers in 1972 were effected without any official involvement of a real estate broker.

Lately, the traditional Main Line lifestyle has begun to show signs of breaking down. A shortage of domestic servants makes mansion living increasingly burdensome. The pressure of suburban development on all sides greatly increases the financial maintenance and tax burden of estates, and one reads almost weekly that some large property has been sold to a developer for subdivision and high density development. Traditional shopping areas—such as Ardmore's Suburban Square, one of the nation's oldest suburban shopping centers, which began drawing customers via Main Line trains in the late twenties—are hard pressed to keep up with nearby regional malls. Finally, there is growing talk of moving to new wealthy enclaves in exurbia, which undoubtedly are becoming attractive alternatives for the elite who wish above all else to maintain their social distance from the other economic classes of the suburban outer city.

Echelon Mall Area

Echelon Mall and its vicinity, located at the urban frontier in South Jersey some twelve miles southeast of Center City, is a good example of the type of community popular with today's young upper middle income familes. Increasingly dissatisfied with single houses on quarter acre lots and their relatively high prices, young couples today seem to prefer environments offering variety. The Rouse Corporation, one of the most successful suburban developers in the northeastern United States and builder of the well-known "new town" of Columbia, Maryland, has provided just such a community; this planned residential development surrounding Rouse's new regional mall at the site of an old airfield has only been in business since late 1970, but it is proving to be one of the most successful community innovations in the Delaware Valley since World War II. The formula is simple: around a tastefully designed large shopping center, supply a variety of high quality services and employers (office parks are made to order); surround this core with a well-planned residential ring which offers single family dwellings, townhouses, and garden apartments for purchase or rental; and complete the complex by attracting educational, cultural, and other communal facilities.

The Echelon lifestyle in every way signals the arrival of the South Jersey suburbs. The development trend began in the early 1960s at Cherry Hill, a few miles north of Echelon, and is now much in evidence in the corridor stretching southeast from Camden to Lindenwold (Figure 24). One reason is the success of a new rapid transit line—the ultramodern Lindenwold Speedline, opened in 1969, a single route forerunner of the BART system of the San Francisco-Oakland region. As a result, downtown Philadelphia and the region's highest paying jobs can be reached in under twenty minutes from the station which serves Echelon, an important initial location factor for the new community.

The popularity of South Jersey is growing rapidly. For years the region's leaders across the Delaware viewed the area as "boondocks," passively awaiting development as a Philadelphia suburb. During the late 1960s, however, as more and more people and especially jobs left the city for South Jersey, the area's image rose steadily, helped along greatly by its burgeoning reputation as the "in" place for entertainment in a metropolitan area dominated, so the cliche went, by a "stodgy" city in which the "sidewalks were rolled up at 5:00 P.M." Belatedly, influential Philadelphians have begun to acknowledge the emergence of South Jersey as the Delaware Valley's most glamorous growth area. As with other upwardly mobile income groups—the same kind of lifestyle is also being sought by upper middle class young marrieds in the outer Pennsylvania suburbs— the Echelonite and his neighbors are growing increasingly status conscious. For years residents of South Jersey have anticipated the rising prestige of the area. To reflect the new image, communities are given classy sounding place names like Wexford Leas and Locust Grove. Renaming localities is also common. Levittown, New Jersey, voted to switch back to its pre-1950s name of Willingboro; Delaware Township was changed to Cherry Hill after its successful regional mall opened in 1961; and

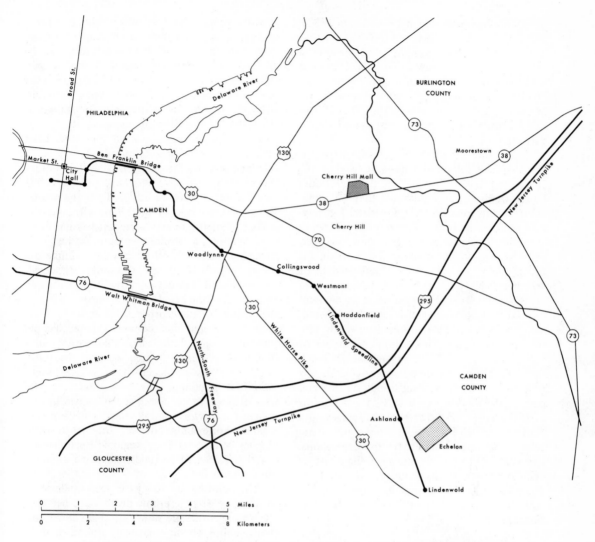

Figure 24. The Lindenwold Speedline Corridor in Camden County, New Jersey.

there is now much talk about rechristening Voorhees Township in central Camden County in honor of its new core—Echelon.

Levittown

Levittown, put simply, was the Echelon of the early 1950s. However, in sharp contrast to the opportunities for varied and sophisticated contemporary suburban living, Levittown offered only the chance to escape living in the city. It seems hard to believe twenty years later, but developers really had to push their projects hard in order to lure people in, and Levitt and Sons offered such typical inducements as financing by $100 down and $60 per month. Not

unexpectedly, the people they attracted were of modest means, and nearly all were war veteran families, young couples with a child or two who were ready for the move from overcrowded apartment to house. Interestingly, more than half of Levittown's first residents did not come from the Philadelphia area; rather, they came in large numbers from poverty stricken areas all over the northeast United States, particularly from the coalfields around Pittsburgh, Wilkes-Barre/Scranton, and the "hell's kitchen" neighborhoods of Manhattan and the South Bronx in New York City. The primary attraction of Levittown in the early 1950s was its proximity to the U.S. Steel Company's Fairless integrated mill (opened in 1952), then the world's largest steelmaking facility. The manufacturing complex did include a satellite · company town—Fairless Hills—but many steelworkers shunned its rigidity and architectural austerity and chose instead to live in the Cape Cods of neighboring Levittown, which must have looked quite pleasant by comparison.

After more than twenty years Levittown is thriving. The community has not become the conformist failure its critics predicted it would be. However, while adults say they are quite content with their lifestyle, a widening generation gap appears to be polarizing the young; in a recent interview a college-bound teenager, who claimed to be speaking for many of his peers, loudly decried what he perceived to be the superficiality of daily life, personal non-identity, and lack of a local sense of community. Although its blue collar image has adhered, many residents of Levittown are upwardly mobile middle income, and a limited number of black families (heavily segregated at the block level) have been accepted recently. The surrounding commercial landscape, an integral part of the local scene, is still as unsightly as ever—the strips of greasy spoons, garages, and auto rows which line U.S. Routes 1 and 13 are among the most unaesthetic in Megalopolis. Nevertheless, Levittown sits near the heart of booming lower Bucks County, and its local shopping center continues to prosper in the face of growing competition from newer regional malls.

Northeast Philadelphia

Philadelphia's Northeast has already been identified as a de facto suburb within the city limits. A sort of citified Levittown in lifestyle, though not in the source of its residents, the Northeast's enormous population (ca. 600,000) is a solid expression of the remainder of prewar white ethnic Philadelphia; Maury Levy has written that the Northeast is "a way of life that brought the life's savings out of South Philly and West Philly and Kensington ... and set them down in a little corner of heaven in Oxford Circle or Mayfair or Frankford [neighborhoods of the Northeast] ."

The area has created a surprising amount of its own local color since its development began in the late 1940s. The Northeast grew in two distinct stages. The first, lasting through the end of the 1950s, saw the continuous high

density development of inexpensive brick row homes as far northeast as Cottman Avenue. Ethnically, the "Near" Northeast succumbed to the realtor's pitch to settle with "your own kind," and to this day one finds the segregation of Jews northwest of Roosevelt Boulevard (Route 1 again—the central spine of the whole Northeast), and Roman Catholic ethnics on the southeastern side toward the river. Levy claims that these neighborhoods can easily be distinguished by the most casual visitor—Catholic areas have a tavern on each block, while Jews seem to prefer beauty parlors! The second stage of expansion in the 1960s witnessed the filling in of the "Far" Northeast beyond Cottman Avenue, a development process just now reaching the northeastern city line. Unlike the inner "Near" Northeast, the outer half developed around a series of growth points along Roosevelt Boulevard where large factories belonging to such corporations as Budd, Yale and Towne, and Nabisco were situated. People tended to spread themselves outward around these focal points, though again at the fairly high densities produced by row and semi-detached dwellings. The late 1960s saw the rest of the area occupied, spurred again by the expansion of local employment and shopping centers. For example, the new Internal Revenue Service Middle Atlantic Regional Headquarters on the Boulevard at Haldeman alone employs more than 5,000.

The Northeast today is overwhelmingly white. The original ethnic distinctions between Jews and gentiles are slowly breaking down, and both groups are now strongly united in their desire to preserve the social *status quo,* even if this may mean keeping blacks out of this section of Philadelphia. A whole repertory of exclusionary techniques is supported by residents, with the most common involving the practices of local realtors (such as "steering" whites and blacks to separate house listings) to preserve the dualistic housing market. The more extremist racial attitude of some Northeast whites is captured in the few blunt words of one resident as quoted by *Philadelphia Magazine:* "Just give them time. If we don't get together real fast and protect ourselves, they'll be up here ruining the Northeast like they've ruined every other part of the city." Though otherwise politically weak in the corridors of a city hall controlled by an inner city Democratic machine, the Northeast has received strong support from Philadelphia officials in the shelving of plans for the extension of the city's subway network into the area, as well as the killing of two of many proposals for locating a possible 1976 Bicentennial Exposition, first near the Byberry State Hospital and then at Port Richmond in Bridesburg. Though both projects might have benefited the Northeast, many commentators have insisted that they were solidly opposed because residents viewed them as leading to the influx of minorities and the construction of low income housing.

Life in most of the Northeast is not without its special frustrations. Little political weight downtown means getting the short end of the stick much of the time. The subway issue and its attendant racial fears aside, surface transportation is probably the single greatest harassment that Northeast residents must put up with on a day-to-day basis. The trip downtown for most is a grueling experience on the still incomplete and jammed Delaware Expressway or on the unlimited access, light at every corner, traffic-choked Roosevelt Boulevard and its distributary routes into the inner city. Automobiles are indispensable, as movement by bus within the Northeast is very inconvenient, and not surprisingly, car ownership rates are the highest in the city (see Figure 39).

SUBURBAN POLARIZATION AND ITS CONSEQUENCES

The lifestyles described above have little relationship to one another. This incompatibility is expressed geographically when the regional mosaic of Philadelphia's suburbs is assembled, and the consequences are seen as a series of sharply defined cleavages among highly fragmented areas in which people of different income groups reside, work, shop, and socially interact. Before examining this internal socioeconomic polarization of suburbia, however, it is worthwhile to look at an even broader metropolitan cleavage—that of suburb and city.

Suburb-City Polarization

Throughout the suburbs these days, one hears residents proclaim that they care little about Philadelphia. In a study of suburban imagery of Philadelphia, Kent Scribner has pointed out that suburbia often found its "rights and privileges" played down in favor of the central city. Therefore, in order to con-

vince society of the importance of its role, suburbia lashed out at the city in three ways—Philadelphia's inferiorities were accentuated; the city's intentions concerning suburbia were exaggerated; and conflicts with the central city were emphasized. By blowing up these things out of proportion in suburban newspapers, a stereotype of Philadelphia was created which Scribner believes functioned largely as a defense mechanism for the psychological self-preservation of the suburbs in the fifties and sixties. To that end, the "straw man" of Philadelphia was used by suburbia to strengthen and unify its weaker and more vaguely defined communities, induce its residents to avoid shortcomings similar to those in downtown, and warn complacent suburbanites to maintain their independence from the city. These sentiments, however, may have abated (Scribner's study was done in 1961); current press reports now indicate the prevailing suburban view of Philadelphia as one closer to total apathy as the central city becomes increasingly irrelevant in the daily lives of suburbanites.

Creating unity and consensus at the local level has not been easy in suburbia. The suburbanite's nonparticipation in local affairs—other than to occasionally complain about some tax, school, sewer, or highway problem which intrudes upon his daily existence—frustrates honest politicians. Indeed, dependence on the supralocal county form of government, which filters down to the people through a fragmented and narrowly defined system of boroughs and townships, has resulted in widespread political excesses. For example, the Delaware County "War Board," the heritage of John McClure's iron-willed Republican machine, still runs the county and remains one of the most powerful political machines in the nation (though current setbacks at the polls are forcing changes). Recently, a local reporter spending a few days observing the "functioning" of Delaware County's government at its courthouse in Media was appalled to discover that whole offices were empty, and those attended were manned by a skeleton crew reading newspapers, eating fruit, and catnapping.

Intrasuburban Polarization

City-suburb divisions continue to grow to the extent that large numbers of suburbanites avoid Philadelphia altogether. However, the dominant cleavages in the Delaware Valley's suburbs are among its own resident income groups. High income regions seek out superior residential amenities; middle income regions cluster as closely as possible to the high status, high amenity locations; and low income regions emerge in the least desirable areas containing the oldest housing, usually near industry and situated along old water and rail routes emanating from the central city. Finally, poverty regions contain dilapidated housing in the most undesirable, out of the way locations. Each group is almost completely walled off from the others, sometimes quite literally in cases where certain high income residential developments are physically segregated from their less affluent surroundings by tall wooden stake palisade fences.

Since desirable and nondesirable residential conditions are scattered instead of being homogeneously distributed in geographic space, existing patterns reveal an intricate balkanization of income groups in suburban Delaware Valley (Figure 25). Let us examine economic segregation in one portion of the suburbs—Montgomery County, northwest of Philadelphia—in order to discern in some detail the nature of the geographical variations involved. High income areas (greater than 50 percent above the SMSA median family income figure of $10,783) abound, due in large part to the concentration and drawing power of great wealth in the Main Line area in the southern corner of Montgomery County. Middle and

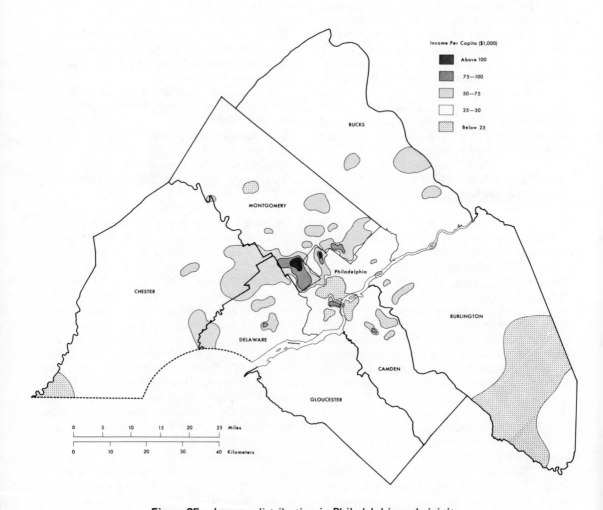

Figure 25.   Income distribution in Philadelphia and vicinity.

upper middle income areas (0–50 percent above the SMSA figure) are seen to cluster around, and fill in the gaps, between those income "peaks." Lower income areas (less than the SMSA median) are largely confined to old railroad and industrial towns such as those in the Schuylkill Valley, and to the rural areas beyond the built-up suburban frontier in the northwestern part of the country.

The evolution of the income distribution observed in Figure 25 is largely a product of the post–World War II automobile era, which witnessed a rapid shift away from axial railroad town development to highway-oriented suburbanization in the interstitial zones lying between the rail corridors (Figure 26). The near total mobility afforded by the automobile enabled the intricate economic partitioning of suburbia in the 1950s and 1960s, with each income group free to locate in a suitable niche. With the growth of large highway-oriented shopping malls in the 1960s, the last remaining function—retailing—has steadily drifted away

from most of the older railroad suburbs, thus abandoning them to the lower income groups. Deterioration would seem to be inevitable, although the revival of some of these towns is conceivable, given their rail access to Philadelphia in a time of uncertainty with respect to future gasoline supplies and prices.

Areas of true poverty in Montgomery County are not captured in the map of median family income distribution. The lowest income census tracts are located in the ghettoes of the two largest towns—Norristown and Pottstown—but do not quite reach the poverty line of two-thirds of the SMSA average ($7,189) used by some urban economists (Figure 27). There are, of course, poverty pockets, particularly in the urbanized inner half of the county. By no coincidence, the poverty map almost without exception describes concentrations of black population, poor quality housing, and low income. These pockets are nearly always walled off in out of the way geographical cubbyholes. Besides the centers of the stagnating railroad

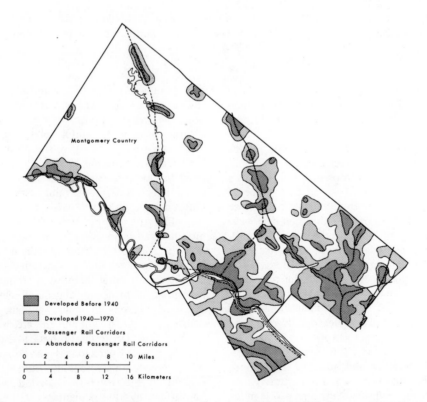

Figure 26. Area development in Montgomery County, 1940 and 1970. Source: Montgomery County Planning Commission.

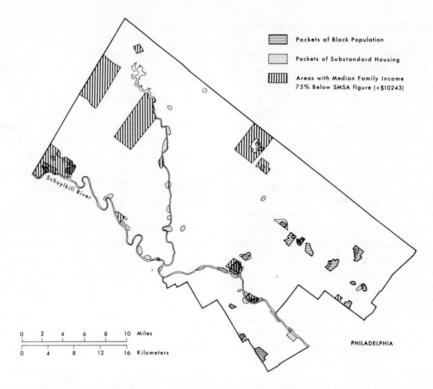

Pockets of Black Population

Pockets of Substandard Housing

Areas with Median Family Income 75% Below SMSA Figure (<$10243)

Figure 27. Social cleavages in Montgomery County in 1970, as shown by pockets of black population, lower income, and substandard housing. Data source: Montgomery County Planning Commission.

towns, small concentrations of blacks are also observed in obscure corners of other municipalities such as Abington, Lower Gwynedd, and Whitpain Townships.

Forces at work to separate income groups also tend to perpetuate racial segregation. Only a small minority of metropolitan Philadelphia's blacks are able to afford the purchase price of *any* part of true suburbia, and most of those who can find the doors closed to them anyway. The percentage of blacks in the suburban counties has remained relatively constant since 1900 (Figure 28). The only significant increase has occurred in the inner cities of the two large satellite urban centers of Chester and Camden. Most other pockets of black population in suburbia have persisted for decades as remnants of nineteenth century trackside shacktown settlements which housed the servants who catered to the wealthy landowners of that period. One notable exception to this pattern is the small town of Lawnside, New Jersey, five miles southeast of Camden in the Lindenwold corri-

dor (Figure 24). One of a handful of all-black towns in the United States, Lawnside has somehow managed to survive for over a century as a fairly prosperous, middle class community. The town grew up as a way station in the pre-Civil War underground railroad, and many migrant blacks were attracted to settle there. The community took root, and established an independence which still persists.

Unlike the nearby New York-New Jersey metropolitan region, which is beginning to witness the spillover of black ghettos into certain inner suburbs, the rule in the Delaware Valley is still almost total stability in terms of the percentage of blacks in suburbia. Excluding the black populations in inner Camden, Chester, Norristown, Pottstown, and the area surrounding the Fort Dix military base in Burlington County, black percentages in Philadelphia's suburban counties rose only from 4.2 to 4.3 percent in the 1960-1970 period. Viewed a bit differently, the percentage of the SMSA's black population living in the true suburbs rose

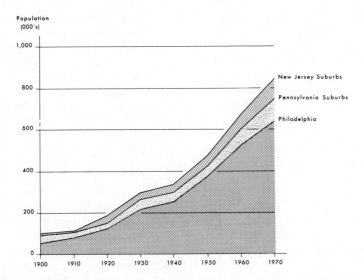

Figure 28. Black population trends in the Philadelphia SMSA, 1900–1970. Data source: Philadelphia City Planning Commission.

from 12.7 to 13.3 percent in the same time period. However, this modest gain pales considerably when it is realized that black rates of entry to the suburbs fell so far behind whites during the 1960s that this minority's rate suffered a slight *decline* when compared to the preceding decade of the 1950s. These observations are supported in a recent study by the Federal Reserve Bank of Boston which showed that Philadelphia's suburbs (and those of many other large cities) became less open to blacks during the 1960s, and that intermunicipal racial segregation of the existing black population actually increased during the last decade.

Dissatisfied with the snail's pace of social change, the office of the governor of Pennsylvania announced in July 1973 a broad new drive for open housing in the suburbs. The commonwealth is now fighting for its right to withhold state government funds from communities that perpetuate economic and racial segregation through exclusionary zoning codes. A crucial test case is underway in the courts over the state's rejection of an application for funds for a park made by an upper income suburban Pittsburgh township. The state has ruled that municipal zoning practices kept out all but upper income whites, and that public funds cannot be used to support such a project. This action has already been upheld by a lower court. The final outcome may be a sig-

nificant legal decision that will affect the provision of certain suburban services for decades to come.

SELECTED GEOGRAPHICAL PROBLEMS OF SUBURBAN LIFE

Despite success in maintaining the social and racial status quo, the Delaware Valley's suburban residents are confronted with a number of other problems. Three relating to spatial organization and behavior in suburbia are dealt with here—geographical disorientation, community structure, and the impact of rising fear.

Geographical Disorientation in the Suburbs

The lack of orderly suburban growth over the last several decades has produced geographical disorganization in every corner of suburbia. The term "suburb" itself, as the reader is by now aware, can apply to a bewildering array of settlements—among them, bedroom communities (Main Line rail station towns); old industrial cities and towns (Chester); sprawling development tracts (most of the land developed in South Jersey since 1950); "instant cities" (Echelon); artificial "towns" centered around a commercial core (Cherry Hill); expanding areas of older housing (much of the Near Northeast); and isolated pockets of blacks and other poor.

Moreover, the three forms of urban sprawl identified by Robert O. Harvey and William A.V. Clark—low density continuous, ribbon, and leapfrog development—are all locally observed in the Delaware Valley. The most gluttonous type of sprawl—leapfrog development—is still evident in the outer suburbs, though the economic downturn of the mid seventies has slowed all new construction. It has most recently occurred in its usual setting along a new expressway corridor, this time the Route 202 Expressway that opened in 1971 connecting the Valley Forge–King of Prussia area with West Chester. At each exit one can see the beginnings of instant development related to land speculation, with intervening land use in the corridor often remaining in a near rural state.

The geographical hodge-podge of suburbia causes problems of disorientation for its residents. Many are even uncertain which township they live in. Vance Packard, in *A Nation of Strangers,* discovered that "finding out where we are" is a ubiquitous problem in an environment where everything looks alike and seems to blend together. The slow process of learning to orient oneself in suburbia involves the formation of a new personal *activity space* —the geographical area one becomes familiar with as one moves about performing such everyday chores as commuting and shopping. Gradually, enough knowledge of the area around one's home is acquired to develop some minimal sense of security and familiarity. This learning process can often be more difficult than it sounds: when Levittown first opened, street signs were scarce and residents often had to ask the help of local police to find their houses (as well as putting up with angry relatives who drove out to visit but were forced to return to the city after they became hopelessly lost in the development). Personal *mental maps* of new areas are usually built up through local searches for food and other necessities. Eventually, as a result of several trial and error attempts, the layout of nearby places is learned. Still, because of almost total reliance on the automobile, the activity spaces of suburbanites tend to become and remain focused upon the most familiar streets and repeatedly traveled routes (Figure 29).

Community Structure

Because of the rapidity of urban development, suburban community organization is often weak. This is particularly true of the post-war auto-oriented suburbs—townships settled hastily and in piecemeal fashion so that they amount to little more than ambiguous accretions of separate residential developments. A South Jersey Unitarian pastor describes the effects of this haphazard community formation: "My congregation comes from 27 different political entities. That's all Cherry Hill is, a group of isolated, fragmented communities. There's just no sense of community anymore."

While the suburban municipality as a form of government should offer many advantages such as proximity to the people, personal contact between citizens and local officials, and manageability of community problems, it has fared poorly as an instrument of local social organization in the Delaware Valley during the last few decades. On the other hand, certain municipal institutions have at least provided partial community cohesion. Outstanding among these are the local schools. If the suburbanite is interested in any local issue it is most likely to be the quality of the school system, more often than not a major factor in the decision to buy into the community in the first place. As the quality of education is partly a function of the local tax structure, suburban schools are directly related to a number of critical economic and social issues, among them the degree of zoning for nonresidential tax ratables (such as shopping centers and industrial parks) and the prices of individual apartments in new multiunit residential developments. Schools are also important as social foci: PTA and other home-school organizations foster contacts among nonneighboring families of school age children; intense sports rivalries with other schools abet local community spirit; and the high school functions as a hangout for youths, though increasing numbers of teenagers take to cars anyway in search of other social experiences.

Social scientists have traditionally defined "community" in terms of either (1) geographical locality or (2) group behavior by people sharing some kind of common outlook, but there is growing evidence that contemporary suburban communities fit neither category. Rather, what seems to be emerging is a complexity of superimposed social networks which function with little reference to distance or territoriality. With the near total mobility afforded by the automobile, suburbanites de-

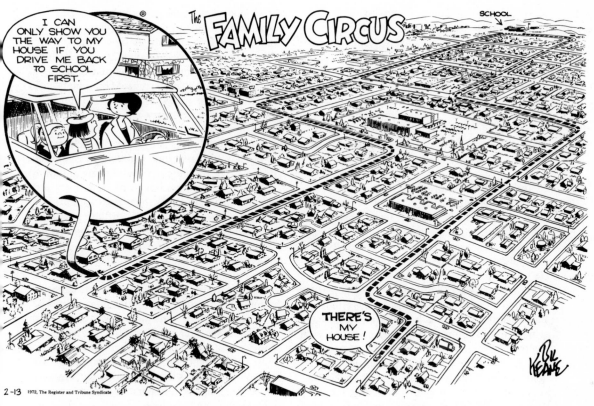

Figure 29. Suburban spatial perception and corresponding behavior. Used with permission of the Register and Tribune Syndicate.

velop ever more widely dispersed activity spaces in which ties with friends, jobs, shopping centers, and entertainment may regularly involve considerable movement in many separate directions—spatial behavior which seems to confirm Melvin Webber's contention that "we are passing through a revolution that is unhitching the social processes of urbanization from the locationally fixed city and region." Increasingly, suburban lives are being lived beyond the local neighborhood. As sociologist Jessie Bernard has put it, we are now living in a post-community society offering "a great locale-independent sea of contact with little vestigial locale-anchored pockets of communities here and there; a great impersonal world where groups, classes, coalitions, and alliances form and re-form, but remain always in flux, unanchored to any settled locale."

While the traditional community appears to be unraveling at the local level, recent developments suggest that suburban social organization is now shifting to a broader scale.

As a growing number of residents seek to put down real roots in suburbia, it is becoming apparent that the necessary "social glue" is largely being provided by the regional shopping mall. Originally built only to turn a quick profit, the newest shopping centers are in fact consciously designed as foci for surrounding residents, supplying social as well as commercial reassurance that they are not stranded in the sticks. In many ways it was inevitable that these large retail centers would emerge as the social as well as economic cores of suburbia. For years the regional shopping mall has served as a most convenient place for friends to meet and for groups to hang out. This is particularly true of teenagers, who often have nowhere else to congregate in a grownup's environment in which no forethought had been given to what would happen when the children of the 1950s and 1960s grew up.

As part of their growing social function, big suburban shopping centers in the Delaware Valley are becoming sites for a rich variety of activities—among them, overnight boy scout encampments, church services, voter registration drives, dances and socials, home base for a county library, outdoor band concerts, political rallies, and psychological counseling. Quite obviously, regional malls are becoming the downtowns and Main Streets of Philadelphia's suburbs by finally revealing a basic order to what had initially been thought a crazy quilt pattern of disorderly urban development.

Insecurity in Suburbia

To the astonishment of many residents of suburban Delaware Valley, fear for personal safety is beginning to impinge upon their relatively stress-free environment. It used to be that the only worries experienced by the suburbanite were related to the posting of a "For Sale" sign on his street ("Who are the new neighbors going to be?" and "How will they affect my investment?"), but the hardening of economic segregation in suburbia and the actions of local realtors in guarding the social status quo have greatly diminished these apprehensions in recent years. Today, however, Philadelphia's suburbanites are increasingly tasting the very real fear they imagined they had left behind in the city forever—the fear of crime. The following excerpt from a letter published in the local press in mid-1973 points up this new stress in the suburban environment: "Many of us [in the suburbs] are those who fled the city, and mainly from black forces. We settled quietly, and suddenly it all erupted. We were back in the big city with juvenile delinquency (perhaps the only creative activity in suburbia), overpopulation (not people, but cars), and good old-fashioned crime."

Recently published crime statistics show that these concerns have a strong factual basis. In 1970, three municipalities outside Philadelphia—Chester City, Bensalem Township, and Cheltenham Township—had higher crime rates (number of crimes per 100,000 population) than the central city. The highest concentrations of crime are located in the inner portions of old suburban towns and in the wealthiest residential areas. Local police officials insist that a correlation exists between crime and accessibility: municipalities closest to expressways and major regional highways show higher crime rates than more isolated communities.

Crime as a problem in suburbia—and it is quietly acknowledged as such these days—is a rather touchy subject. A few years ago, a former mayor of Philadelphia, the late Richardson Dilworth, publicly commented in words to the effect that "what some Main Liners need these days are a few muggings in their own area." This kind of testy remark, which caused a furor in the local press, is indicative of the feelings of city residents who are constantly reminded of their crime problem by suburbanites, a situation which is now turning around to the extent that downtown one now hears such comments as "it serves them right for abandoning the city." This kind of conflicting dialogue recalls Scribner's analysis of city-suburb polarization, apparently borne out by the rebuttal of many suburban officials that recently released crime data are "central city progaganda" which cover up the fact that "most suburban crime is of the minor, shoplifting-type variety."

Regional crime data do tend to show, with such notable exceptions as the 1972 psychopathic mass murder of nine people in a Cherry Hill office building, the prevalence of less serious crime in suburbia, especially burglary. Since burglary is less personal than the more widespread and violent rapes, assaults, and homicides of Philadelphia, many complacent suburbanites delay confronting their newest problem. Affluent homeowners spend vast sums of money to protect their houses with sophisticated electronic alarm systems and surveillance by private security agencies. At the same time, they think so little of the effectiveness of local law enforcement that many municipalities have actually voted down additional police protection.

A recent addition to the suburban crime problem is the proliferation of teenage gangs in certain communities. In some respects suburban gang behavior is similar to Philadelphia's, particularly in terms of malicious mischief such as vandalism and arson, and gang rumbles in which clubs, chains, and knives (but so far not hand guns) are used. However, the nature of the auto-oriented suburban environment has produced an interesting geographical twist in gang territorial delimitation; instead of having well-defined areal boundaries, suburban gang turfs are localized to the defense of hangout points such as shopping centers, highway strip drive-ins, and railroad stations. Moreover, rather than naming themselves after street intersections as is common in the inner city, suburban gangs choose names such as The Undertakers, The Rejected Souls, and Ardsley's Mighty Fighters.

SUBURBAN CORES: THE DECENTRALIZATION OF ECONOMIC ACTIVITY

Thus far, we have been examining suburbia largely as a stable, predictable residential haven for whites from the stresses of life in a complex metropolitan society. The haven function has been characteristic of suburban America for decades, and has taken on added regionwide significance in the Delaware Valley with the postwar tidal wave of migration to the suburbs. Concomitant with the latest influx of population, however, large new concentrations of nonresidential activity began to appear in suburbia in the second half of the 1960s. By the early 1970s, novel geographical arrangements of commerce and industry had emerged throughout Philadelphia's suburbs, with enormous implications for the immediate future of urbanization in the Delaware Valley. The spatial organization of this new activity development is consistent with, and has greatly reinforced, the growing orientation of suburbanites to large regional shopping malls. These centers are now attracting a vast array of other commercial and industrial activities to locate around them. Together, and at great cost to the declining economic base of Philadelphia, they have formed the nuclei of several urban cores or *minicities* which have tremendous drawing power in their surrounding suburban areas. This section will review the growth of regional malls and contiguous employment cores as cornerstones in the spatial reorganization of Greater Philadelphia which is evolving in the mid-1970s.

The Development and Impact of Regional Shopping Malls

In many ways, the growth of shopping malls is the story of suburban development in the Delaware Valley over the last twenty-five years. Retailing is an activity which is highly sensitive to, and an excellent indicator of, the changing distribution of population and income within metropolitan regions. As people and wealth have deconcentrated from Philadelphia to its suburbs, retail trade followed close behind. The sequence of planned regional mall development through 1970 conforms to the two stages of suburban commercial sprawl—consequent and catalytic—identified by Bart Epstein. The first stage refers to the casual outward drift of stores in the wake of pioneer settlers in the early years of postwar suburbanization; the latter relates to the more recent role of major malls as growth poles which actively shape new suburban development by attracting people and other activities to locate in their vicinities.

The stage of consequent suburban Philadelphia commercial development covers the period from the late 1940s to the early 1960s. Initially, there was considerable reluctance to move large stores to the suburbs, perhaps due to the infancy of postwar mass merchandising concepts. As a result, through the late 1950s, the only suburban retail centers were small clusters consisting of convenience or everyday goods establishments like supermarkets, and a limited number of independent shoppers goods stores supplying more expensive purchases such as furniture and appliances for which some comparative shopping is done. The typical commercial development of the 1950s was situated at a highway intersection and contained a food market, drug store, laundromat, and one or two other essential services. No strategies for market development had yet emerged, and many places found themselves without nearby stores. Pioneer Levittowners were forced to drive miles to Trenton for food until the first local supermarket opened in the middle 1950s. The Northeast became the first outlying area in the Philadelphia region to attract large chain department stores in the late 1950s. Lit Brothers and then Gimbels led the way and located, with several small stores, along Cottman Avenue west from Roosevelt Boulevard to Castor. The project was successful and other large stores, particularly such discount chains as Kleins and later Korvettes, soon followed. This period of consequent commercial growth, which was repeated at a lesser scale in other Philadelphia suburbs through the early 1960s, saw shopping centers following residential development. Stores opened only after an area was settled and threshold demands for goods and services were generated by local residents.

Since the middle 1960s, however, catalytic commercial development has prevailed in the Philadelphia suburbs. No longer satisfied to merely follow people to suburbia, large new shopping centers have sprung up in the outer suburbs at highly accessible locations in areas just about to be settled. The big chains and their developers thus gambled, highly successfully as it turned out, that suburban population would be attracted to locate around these new growth points. Catalytic developments were also planned at a very large scale. Department store developers would invite one or two competitors and a complete array of smaller stores to join them, and huge open spaces for parking were set aside.

Cherry Hill—the granddaddy of them all—was the prototype of the large catalytic regional mall in the Delaware Valley. Opened in 1961, it became an instant success and drew in sightseers from all over the Middle Atlantic states. The glamour of the project brought many side benefits to the mall's locality and, later, to most of South Jersey. More than twice the expected number of shoppers and new residents were attracted to Cherry Hill, sparking what was to become one of the most spectacular growth booms in the history of the Philadelphia area. The remarkable success of Cherry Hill led to the rapid diffusion of the regional mall concept throughout the Delaware Valley, a process accelerated by the enormous suburban infusion of affluent migrants with all but insatiable demands for durable shoppers goods. The latter, no doubt, reflected the prosperity of the region's economy in the mid-1960s, as federal funds poured into Greater Philadelphia for the aerospace and Vietnam War–related industries, anchored by such local manufacturers as RCA, General Electric, and the Vertol helicopter division of the Boeing Corporation. What began at Cherry Hill in the early 1960s reached its peak in 1965 with the opening of King of Prussia Plaza near Valley Forge at the intersection of the circumferential Pennsylvania Turnpike and the Schuylkill Expressway to downtown. King of Prussia, which claimed itself "the world's largest shopping center," was the biggest scale application of the multi-department-store mall concept in the United States at that time: no less than five giant retail outlets signed on—Gimbels, John Wanamaker, Korvettes, J.C. Penney, and F.W. Woolworth.

By the end of the 1960s, large regional shopping centers blanketed the Delaware Valley. Large malls continue to be built, but there now appears to be developing a countertrend toward more compact centers. The Rouse Corporation (builder of Cherry Hill as well as Echelon) has spearheaded this movement, and its newest center, Exton Square Mall in central Chester County, is viewed by some as a harbinger of a new generation of smaller scale mass retailing in suburbia. Exton Square marks a return to a single core department store surrounded by numerous smaller quality shops. The latter are particularly important in Exton's plan: lavishly designed storefronts and other accouterments are cleverly integrated to form a classy, sophisticated shopping environment. The desire for smaller scale retailing appears to be growing, because the last few years have witnessed the revival of shopping districts in some all but forgotten older suburban towns. High prestige and wealthy communities—such as Chestnut Hill in northwest Philadelphia, and Wayne and Bryn Mawr on the Main Line—have especially benefited from these developments.

When the regional mosaic of mall trade areas is assembled, the new multinodal spatial organization of suburban Delaware Valley becomes apparent (Figure 30). Data on the drawing area for each center are fairly crude—they were collected by the *Philadelphia Inquirer* in a telephone survey of about 6,000 households—but their mapping reasonably suggests the regionalization of the main trade areas associated with each mall. Retail centers are located at highly accessible sites, particularly at expressway interchanges. Large regional malls dominate the pattern, especially those with the best access and centrality to affluent residential areas. Although Philadelphia's central business district is weaker than it was, it remains the metropolitan region's largest single retail center but with an influence generally limited to the heavily populated and economically weak trade areas of the inner city. The wealthy Main Line area shows little affiliation with nearby malls.

The dominance of regional malls has had a major impact on the spatial arrangement of other retail activities in suburbia. As already noted, malls have siphoned off a great deal of business from older retail centers. Many of these towns have been badly damaged as shopping districts, but, as we have noted, a few are

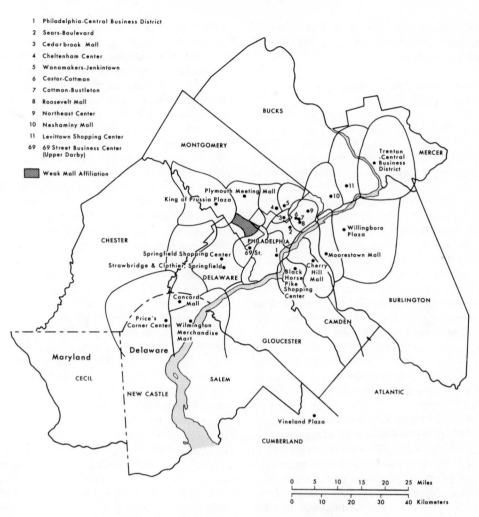

1   Philadelphia-Central Business District
2   Sears-Boulevard
3   Cedarbrook Mall
4   Cheltenham Center
5   Wanamakers-Jenkintown
6   Castor-Cottman
7   Cottman-Bustleton
8   Roosevelt Mall
9   Northeast Center
10 Neshaminy Mall
11 Levittown Shopping Center
69 69 Street Business Center
    (Upper Darby)

Weak Mall Affiliation

Figure 30. Approximate 1969–1970 trade areas of Delaware Valley's twenty-five largest shopping malls. Based on data collected for Retail Trade Area Survey of *Philadelphia Inquirer*, 1971.

beginning to recover. A major factor in such small scale commercial redevelopment appears to be parking: the town of Woodbury in South Jersey discovered that by removing its parking meters it was able to recapture some of its old customers who were driving to a mall twenty minutes away where free parking was assured. In other areas, however, nothing could be done to save the older small store clusters of the consequent commercial development days. The outspoken bitterness of these small businessmen is expressed by an ex-delicatessen owner from the Northeast who was interviewed in *Philadelphia Magazine:* "The centers have ru-

ined everybody. They've put the little guy out of business—not just squeezed him out, but picked him up by the back of the neck and kicked his ass out of the door. First the bastards come in and take all the land, and then they take all the business. The small businessman is dead—cold stone dead."

While some small storeowners were forced out, others discovered ways to survive. Unable to afford the expensive setbacks and parking requirements of big shopping centers, many small businessmen have been able to squeeze onto cheaper land fronting on highways leading to malls. The result has been the proliferation of ugly commercial strips, replete with rows of large signs competing for the attention of speeding motorists.

Employment Cores in Suburban Delaware Valley

With regional malls emerging as the geographical focal points of suburbia, a large number of business and noncommercial activities have been attracted to locate around them since the mid-1960s. Entertainment relocated toward the suburban market in much the same way. Among the many effects of mall core development, however, none has had a wider impact on the lives of people in the Philadelphia region than the rapidly growing number of office and manufacturing firms which have relocated to these suburban minicities.

The locational advantages of minicities for commerce and industry are identical to those for shopping centers—good highway accessibility to the entire region. Modern trucking technology has greatly reduced the cost of road transport in the last few years, and locations anywhere on the metropolitan expressway networks are now at least as accessible to the rest of the Delaware Valley as sites in or near Philadelphia's CBD. As the cost differential for many firms between city and suburb thus becomes neutralized, noneconomic factors such as the high status image of addresses near style-setting suburban malls are now dominant in locational decisionmaking. The growing desire to work in a suburban setting was recently underscored in the local press, which reported that developers of new industrial and office parks are deluged with job applications from surrounding suburban areas; interestingly, it was also observed that a growing number of applicants were apparently willing to take pay cuts in order to work closer to home in the prestigious suburban minicity milieu.

Most suburban employment cores develop near regional malls and usually are built around one or more industrial parks. Until the mid-1960s, industry was often unwelcome in the suburbs. Today that attitude has been reversed, as municipalities have discovered that manufacturing firms considerably ease the local tax burdens of homeowners. In fact, the industrial park concept is ideal for all concerned. For the community, tax revenues and employment climb, and the parks strive to fit in properly

with the local environment while occupying a relatively small proportion of local land. For the manufacturer, most of the locational advantages of the central city are preserved.

Industrial parks in the Philadelphia region show a definite locational affinity for major metropolitan highway corridors and suburban minicities (Figure 31). Locally, economic impacts are favorable as in the case of Montgomery County's recent manufacturing growth: a 1964-1969 expansion of the county's employed labor force which was double the SMSA rate; a near doubling since 1960 of the inflow of commuters from neighboring counties; and a 25 percent increase in the number of housing units—particularly apartments, which are growing so rapidly that the predicted 1968-1980 increase in the percentage of apartments vis-à-vis total county housing units will jump from 27 to 65 percent (Figure 32).

Suburban industrial growth during the 1960s has been dramatic, as has Philadelphia's decline in the same period (Figure 33). The state Department of Commerce reported that between 1962 and 1971, 252 factories employing 17,385 workers left Philadelphia for adjacent Pennsylvania counties. Several thousand others have also been affected by the dispersal of industry to South Jersey as well as to outlying sites such as the Far Northeast within the central city limits. Philadelphia has attempted to stem the outflow by opening its own industrial parks. Through the efforts of the Philadelphia Industrial Development Corporation, which has close ties with the city's financial community, the Northeast Industrial Park and several smaller projects have been successful in recruiting manufacturers, but they have made only a ripple in the overall tidal stream of emigrating companies. The motivations cited by relocating firms fall into two categories—worsening conditions in the city and the attractiveness of suburbia. Among the former, in addition to the grim daily life in a blighted and crime-ridden inner city, are high renovation costs for old plants, lack of space for expansion, high cost of peripheral land for loading and parking, few alternative sites not frozen by zoning or renewal schemes, the lack of even minimally skilled clerical workers, and high taxes, especially Philadelphia's 3.31 percent personal wage tax (scheduled to increase by more than 30 percent in mid-1976). Among the suburban

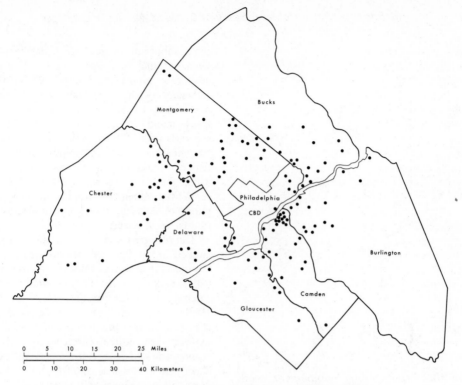

Figure 31. Industrial parks in Delaware Valley, 1972.

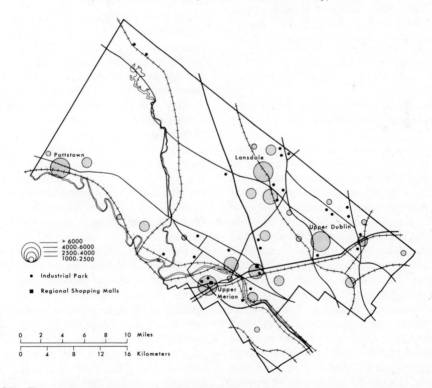

Figure 32. The economic impact of industrial parks in Montgomery County. Data source: *Montgomery County: Economic and Demographic Profile* (Philadelphia: Philadelphia Electric Company, 1972), pp. 85–86, 88.

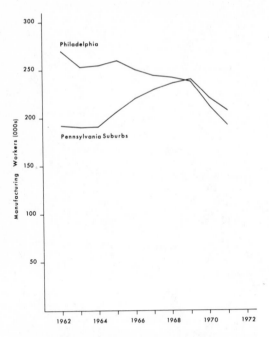

Figure 33. Manufacturing employment trends in Philadelphia and its Pennsylvania suburban counties, 1962–1971. Adapted from the Pennsylvania Industrial Census Series, M-5-71, Bureau of Statistics, Pennsylvania Department of Commerce, 1972.

advantages, in addition to those already discussed, executive convenience and corporate imagery are important.

Vance Packard is but one of many social commentators to recently draw attention to the growing practice of corporate executives moving plants to the suburbs to reduce their own commuting times. Industrial developers often joke that suburban relocation sites are "halfway between the president's home and his country club," but employees and their families who are frequently uprooted in the process find little humor in such situations. These kinds of location decisions, however, are more frequently related to executive efforts to improve the corporate image by moving the establishment to a prestigious outlying area where it can be seen. During its current suburbanization period industry has become more status and image conscious. Sites near glamorous malls or along heavily traveled freeways are prized, and companies will not hesitate to spend lavishly to design and landscape

their suburban properties. These trends have been national in scope, and, as a result, the corporate image of Philadelphia outside the Delaware Valley increasingly has come to rest upon its suburban imagery. Elizabeth Deutermann, in a report for the Federal Reserve Bank of Philadelphia on locating corporate headquarters and branch offices in the region, found that questions relating to suburban business environments, lifestyles, and residential amenities were uppermost in the minds of decisionmakers in corporation board rooms across America.

The office park concept has also been widely applied in the Philadelphia suburbs lately. The Cherry Hill area was one of the first to push office parks, but the Pennsylvania suburbs are catching up with South Jersey. In the late 1960s, large companies such as General Electric, Burroughs, and Prudential Insurance put up vast campuslike complexes. One of the more ambitious recent projects is Valley Forge Plaza just north of King of Prussia, which in a recent ad in the local edition of *Time* advertised itself as combining "the convenience of [downtown] Penn Center with the tax advantages and breathing room of a suburban setting." Another type of pseudooffice park, Decker Square, has been operating for over a decade with a cluster of large buildings in the city-suburb transition zone along the "Golden Mile" of City Line Avenue near the Schuylkill Expressway. Although traffic is heavy, the scheme works, and Philadelphians, despite the bankruptcy of the builder, respect the development. As an example, the Philadelphia-Baltimore-Washington Stock Exchange in 1969 successfully pressured the city into killing a proposal for a 0.5 percent stock transfer tax by threatening to move to Decker Square, literally across the street from the city.

The changing distribution of employment in the Delaware Valley has greatly altered the region's commuting patterns since the mid-1960s. Twenty-four of twenty-five workers residing in the suburbs are now employed outside downtown Philadelphia, with twenty of twenty-five working outside the city altogether. Analysis of journey to work patterns in the early 1970s reflects these changes: in 1972, only 16 percent of the Delaware Valley's work force, including city residents, commuted into central Philadelphia; apart from a sharp rise in reverse commuting from city to suburb, most work trips were intersuburban in nature. Given the region's inferior highway network, hopelessly clogged expressways, and lack of intersuburban rapid transit, average commuting times are surely higher now than five years ago; aside from the normal grumbles about traffic, people seem content behind the wheel for longer and longer work trips, making some observers believe that many commuters would not object to spending more than three hours a day on the road. In light of gasoline shortages and price increases, however, it now appears unlikely that work travel times will be able to increase much more in the future.

The Montgomery County Planning Commission has undertaken a preliminary study of recent changes in county commuting patterns. As jobs have multiplied, so have commuters. From 1960 to 1970 employment increased 63 percent, but the resident labor force, due in no small part to economic segregation practices, rose only by 24 percent. The result has been a massive influx of commuters—140,000 daily, or a net inflow of 32,000. On the other hand, the county's daily exodus of workers to Philadelphia fell from 25 to 19 percent of county out-commuters in the same period; since the resident labor force working within Montgomery County has remained at 59 percent, the 6 percent decline in Philadelphia commuters has been diverted to other suburban counties. At the same time, reverse commuters from Philadelphia to Montgomery County nearly doubled from 19,000 to 36,000 during the decade.

ECONOMIC AND SOCIAL IMPACTS OF RAPID EMPLOYMENT DECONCENTRATION

The rapid deconcentration of jobs from Philadelphia to the suburbs is taking its toll on the city's economy (Figure 34). The city's share of SMSA jobs fell from 61 percent in 1960 to less than 48 percent at the end of 1972 (and to 45% by late 1975). The 50 percent crossover point was reached in mid-1971. Allowing for the ups and downs of the national economy and their impact on local business cycles, Philadelphia has suffered a 2 percent annual job loss rate since the early 1960s. Meanwhile, suburban employment, which accounted for over 86 percent of the SMSA's new jobs since 1960, continues to expand.

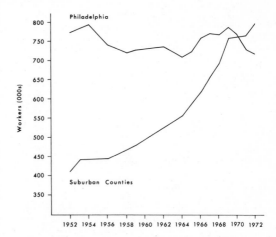

Figure 34. Employment trends in the Philadelphia SMSA, total nonagricultural minus government workers, 1952-1972. Data source: *County Business Patterns*, Bureau of the Census; and *Employment and Earnings, States and Areas*, Bureau of Labor Statistics. We wish to thank Thomas Gizecki of the Mideast Regional Office of the Bureau of Labor Statistics of the U.S. Department of Labor for assistance in preparing this graph.

The economic impact of job decentralization has affected Philadelphia's two major employment sectors—manufacturing and services production—in different ways. Manufacturing has been dropping steadily, and in early 1970 was surpassed for the first time by rising tertiary and quaternary employment (Figure 35).

Since Philadelphia was perhaps the most overindustrialized of the nation's large old cities, it is suffering more than others as its manufacturing plants continue to die or emigrate. In addition to suburban decentralization, industries at the national level, particularly the important steel markets, are shifting away from the resource-poor Atlantic seaboard, with its heavy dependence on imported raw materials in an increasingly uncertain international trading environment, to the resource-rich interior. This change is likely to accelerate as the current environmental and energy crises deepen: with the supply of low polluting fuels available to Megalopolis steadily declining, this densely populated conurbation can ill afford to increase its already dangerous concentrations of atmospheric impurities. Moreover, barely sufficient and increasingly expensive supplies of

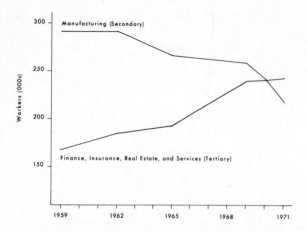

Figure 35. Employment changes in Philadelphia's secondary and tertiary sectors, 1959–1971. Data source: *County Business Patterns.*

electrical power in the Middle Atlantic states will further induce industry to relocate to better energy sources in regions to the south and west. (The possibility of exploiting offshore oil beyond the New Jersey and Delaware coastlines is still many years away). Finally, much of the recent dispersion of manufacturing from Philadelphia would have occurred regardless of changes in national and metropolitan economic geography. Many of the city's aging industrial facilities approached obsolescence by the middle 1960s, and the enormous costs of renovation simply made it unfeasible for most companies to remain when advan-

tageous alternatives existed in suburbia and beyond.

Philadelphia's new employment pattern shows a weakened manufacturing sector but apparent strength in other areas (Figure 36). The recent growth of Philadelphia's finance, insurance, real estate, and service industries sparked a CBD office-building boom in the early 1970s. However, overbuilding has quickly resulted in a glut of downtown office space in the mid seventies, prompting some to point out that the white collar job spurt may only be temporary. Some support for this cautious view is seen in the continuing strong expansion of the suburban white collar sector, and the fact that office firms continue to leave Philadelphia.

The recent expansion of Philadelphia's white collar sector has been a mixed blessing for the city, because the lion's share of new jobs has been filled by suburbanites who possess the education and skills which the city's largely blue collar and lower income populations do not. As a result, the city's resident labor force is caught in the middle as Philadelphia's manufacturing base shrinks without a concomitant growth of replacement jobs. By late 1972, manufacturing dispersal had proceeded to the extent that remaining industrial employment—largely in old plants engaged in apparel, metal fabricating, and electrical machinery production—leveled off. City public relations people were quick to claim a reversal in blue collar loss trends, but more knowledgeable observers realize that the decline was chiefly due to the

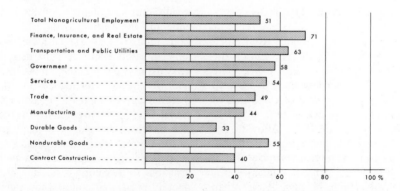

Figure 36. Philadelphia's proportion of SMSA workers in various job sectors, 1970. Source: U.S. Department of Labor, Bureau of Labor Statistics, *Employment Structure and Trends, Philadelphia,* Mideast Region, Report Number 2, September 1971, p. 2.

attrition of relocation-prone factories, and that the remaining facilities, because of long term plant investments and the need for cheap unskilled labor not available in the suburbs, would simply find it too costly to move.

Philadelphia's blue collar lower income wage earners, many of them residents of the old and rapidly deteriorating inner city industrial areas northeast of Center City, have been most adversely affected by shifts in the location of manufacturing. Such industrial migration has heavily affected inner city North Philadelphia, an observation which would undoubtedly be strongly reinforced were complete data on industrial moves available (Figure 37). Be-

cause few replacement jobs can be found in the city, growing numbers of central city workers must now reverse commute to the suburbs. The inner city worker is excluded from living in the suburbs by economic and social barriers, and is thus forced to undertake unreasonably long commuting (Figure 38).

Of the inner city workers, blacks are hardest hit by the uprooting of Philadelphia's industries. Their neighborhoods tend to have the highest rates of outmigration by manufacturers. Moreover, the best chances blacks have at obtaining decently paying jobs are in the blue collar sector, as most lack the education and skills for office jobs downtown. Few migrating

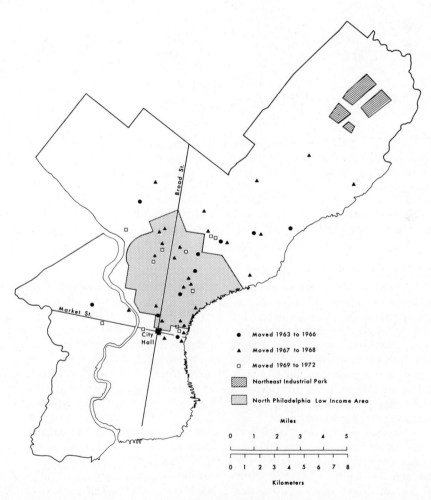

Figure 37. Former addresses of industrial firms which relocated to the Northeast Industrial Park, 1963-1972. Based on survey conducted by Robert Esmond.

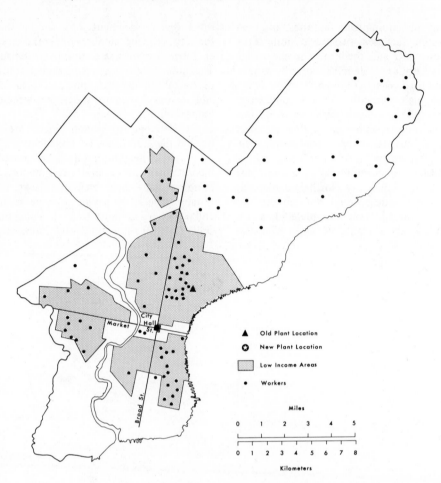

Figure 38. 1973 residential distribution of workers at Hodges Kitchenware Company which relocated in Northeast Industrial Park in early 1971. Data courtesy of William Schur, personnel director at Hodges.

employers have taken specific steps to provide blacks with access to the suburbs. Most blacks have thus been left to fend for themselves in gaining access to jobs in the suburbs, but the low automobile ownership rate for this group as a whole (29 percent versus the citywide rate of 42 percent of auto-owning households) means that few are able to do so. Not owning an automobile means that the black cannot compete effectively in the suburban job market; he is cut off from job information flows, which tend to be confined to suburbia, and low mobility greatly constrains both his search for employment and his daily commuting after being hired. The inevitable result is rising unemployment, as few except middle class blacks can keep up with intrametropolitan job decen-

tralization. Blacks also have to contend with racial discrimination in suburbia, not only in connection with residential segregation, but also on the part of employers. Indeed, several firms have expressed a desire not to "offend" local suburban communities by hiring blacks (even black sales clerks are often discouraged, as store managers claim that their customers want only to deal with members of their own race).

Comparison of existing variations between inner city whites and blacks confirms that the latter are worse off. Among poorer whites median family income in 1969 was $8,160, while for blacks (70 percent of Philadelphia's blacks live in the low income region) it was $6,740, a difference of 21 percent. Employing the urban economists' poverty line of two-thirds the SMSA median family income, or $7,188, blacks average below it while whites are well above. Unemployment for blacks in 1970 was 11.0 percent (34 percent for black teenagers), as opposed to 8.7 percent for all people residing in the low income region. The citywide average at the time was 4.5 percent. Journey to work data showed that black reverse commuters to the suburbs could expect less of a reward than whites: the increase for whites was from $116 per week in the city to $154 per week in the suburbs, but for blacks the increase was only $106 to $121. Work trips for blacks were longer than for whites: 3 percent more whites worked in the

low income region itself, 2 percent more in Philadelphia, but 5 percent more blacks worked in the suburbs. Travel times reflect the same biases: for work trips averaging less than thirty minutes, whites led blacks by 22 percent for the city and 9 percent for the suburbs; for commutes of longer than sixty minutes, blacks led whites by 4 percent for both Philadelphia and the suburbs. Commuting time differences are largely the result of disparities in auto ownership (Figure 39). There is a striking concentric zonation of increasing auto ownership with distance from Center City. Within the North Philadelphia low income region, the boundary between the high and moderately high areas of nonauto households coincides

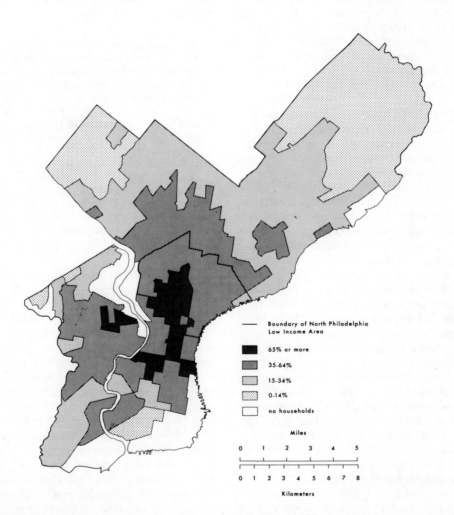

Boundary of North Philadelphia
Low Income Area

65% or more

35-64%

15-34%

0-14%

no households

Miles

0   1   2   3   4   5

0 1 2 3 4 5 6 7 8

Kilometers

Figure 39. Households without automobiles in Philadelphia, 1970. Adapted from map prepared by Kent Johnson.

with the sharply defined north-south boundary between black and white population.

A growing segment of the city's black population is nevertheless resigning itself to the arduous strain of reverse commuting, and most are forced to rely upon public transportation. Suburban mass transit access problems for Philadelphia's blacks begin with the city's transit system, now run by the Southeastern Pennsylvania Transportation Authority (SEPTA). An inadequate subway network means that access to most black residential areas is largely by bus and trolley. Service is often unreliable and it is no secret that SEPTA's poorest equipment is assigned to inner city routes. White collar suburban rail commuters, on the other hand, find good subway connections from downtown terminals; if their jobs are not within walking distance from Penn Central Suburban or Reading Terminals, they can usually get there directly by subway or bus within a few minutes.

The extensive regional rail network in the suburban Pennsylvania counties (also controlled by SEPTA) is heavily biased in favor of same-sector morning in–evening out commuter flows. Reverse commuting is both expensive and inconvenient: rush hour fares are charged outbound in the morning and inbound in the evening, and service is scheduled so that the leisurely non-rush-hour timetable is maintained for opposite direction trains during peak hours.

Final access from suburban rail station to job site is usually the most difficult part of the work journey from the inner city, as suburban plants and industrial parks are highway-oriented. Little thought has been given to planning direct transit access to plants: even when a factory is located near a station or bus stop, obstacles such as fences, roadways, and loading docks remain in the path of commuters on foot. Suburban bus service is insufficient and is not timed to meet commuter trains. In rare instances when direct downtown-to-industrial park bus service is available, trips are unreasonably slow and expensive. A 1971 survey of suburban industrial park access from the inner city showed that only 11 percent of the mass transit work trips (versus 80 percent by car) can be made in less than fifty minutes. A time and cost analysis of these travel patterns showed that most of the inconveniences were caused by transfer waits and frequent stops; express bus service is virtually unknown in the Delaware Valley, even on suburban highway routes.

It would appear that many of the city-to-suburb accessibility problems are the result of SEPTA's slow response to changing travel demands. The transportation agency's policies, however, are determined by the five Pennsylvania county governments in the region. The four-to-one weighting against Philadelphia, combined with the usual hostility and suspicion of the suburban board members with respect to the city, thus ensures continued discrimination against reverse transit commuters. Lenora Berson, writing in *City Magazine,* illuminates the inner workings of SEPTA's decisionmaking machinery by quoting Jerome Shestack, one of Philadelphia's SEPTA representatives:

> We had hoped to develop a program to use SEPTA buses to transport people from North Philadelphia to some of the outlying industrial parks where help is desperately needed. Our plan was to have a series of buses circulate through North Philadelphia picking up passengers in the early morning, take them out to the suburbs, and bring them home after work. We hoped to charge a minimal fare. The plan fell through because we could not get the board members from other counties to go along. They opposed the plan despite the interest of would-be employers. The political pressure against bringing in the poor black workers was too strong.

The rapid decline of Philadelphia's manufacturing base and commensurate increase of inner city unemployment is a crisis of enormous magnitude, as poor blacks are increasingly becoming locked in to Philadelphia's dying blue collar labor market. Solutions to this problem have been proposed, and fall into two categories—industrial redevelopment of the inner city and improved accessibility to suburban plants. The city government is attempting to begin restoration of the balance of employment in the inner city by redeveloping abandoned industrial land, and a demonstration project in the heart of the old manufacturing district will shortly begin operating. This "mini" industrial park will capitalize upon the main locational advantage of the inner city—cheap low-skilled labor for producers who cannot afford higher suburban wage rates. Solutions proposed for improving the accessibility of the inner city labor force to suburban jobs range from government support for increasing auto ownership through free driver training programs; liberal financing and subsidies for the restoration of wrecked and abandoned cars by ghetto cooperatives; organized car pools; and cut-rate public transit for the poor. Furthermore, plans for new mass transit facilities can be speeded up; every county and regional planning agency enthusiastically endorses improved rapid transit as a high priority item, but progress has been virtually nonexistent. The one exception is the Lindenwold Speedline, but industry in that corridor has made no attempt to recruit Philadelphia blacks, most of whom remain unaware of the existence of the facility as a possible commuting link to the suburbs.

THE NEW INDEPENDENCE OF SUBURBIA: MYTH OR REALITY?

Throughout suburban Delaware Valley today one sees signs of a lessening degree of dependency on Philadelphia, and increasingly its residents are asking whether or not the suburbs are still "sub-" to the "-urb." For many residents the break is complete: goods, services, jobs, and entertainment are all available in the suburban outer city and there is no longer any reason to go into Philadelphia.

A major factor in the growing avoidance of Philadelphia by suburban residents is the poor quality of transportation in the Delaware Valley. Some shortcomings of the railroads have already been touched on, and we can add here, from the suburbanite's point of view, inadequate station parking, less than reliable service, often decrepit equipment, and uncertainty due to the fact that both the Reading and Penn Central are in receivership; in fact, it frequently appears as if both railroads, as well as other components of the suburban transit system, were trying to do their best to keep their ridership down to a minimum.

Even if the Delaware Valley had adequate public transportation (the rail network is adequate but service is inferior), a majority of suburbanites would undoubtedly still prefer their automobiles. However, the highway and expressway situation, especially on the Pennsylvania side of the Delaware, is in far worse shape than rapid transit. And the problem grows more serious each year as road construction fails to keep pace with the region's growing and shifting population; the Delaware Valley Regional Planning Commission recently reported that the number of people per car in the SMSA dropped from 3.7 in 1960 to 3.2 in 1970, with the suburban counties averaging between 2.0 and 2.5. Among the grossly inadequate main arteries in the Pennsylvania suburbs, one above all stands out as the object of greatest scorn—the infamous Schuylkill Expressway, which parallels the west bank of that river for most of its route from South Philadelphia to King of Prussia. Obsolete the day they cut its ribbon in 1957, the history of the expressway is a series of legendary traffic tie-ups more often than not the result of truck jack-knifing accidents which released hundreds of gallons of corn syrup (which well-meaning road crews later covered with tons of sand!) or even several dozen squealing pigs onto the potholed roadway. To many suburbanites the Schuylkill Expressway—alias the "Sure-Kill Crawlway"—has become the symbol of the agony of getting into Philadelphia, an altogether accurate perception as a glance at the regional highway map shows no other realistic alternate route to Center City from the northern and western suburbs.

The rest of the regional highway situation is reflected in the driving time map (Figure 40). This already discouraging time-distance map describes the offhours pattern, with driving at peak hours considerably longer in every direction. Unfortunately, the demands of suburban drivers for better expressway access to Center City directly conflict with the interests of downtown residents; as we have already observed in the cases of Society Hill and the Chinese resistance to the Vine Street Expressway, many Philadelphians view such highway construction as a death blow for their neighborhood communities.

A trip to Philadelphia is thus becoming a rarity for a growing segment of suburban society. The *Philadelphia Inquirer* recently quoted the comments of a resident of Bala Cynwyd, whose house is exactly two blocks from the city line: "I'll be doggone, I just can't remember the last time I went into Philadelphia. I remember! We took the kids to the Thanksgiving Day Parade." The same behavior is found among young adults, supposedly the most mobile metropolitan group. Asked how many had not been to Philadelphia in at least six months,

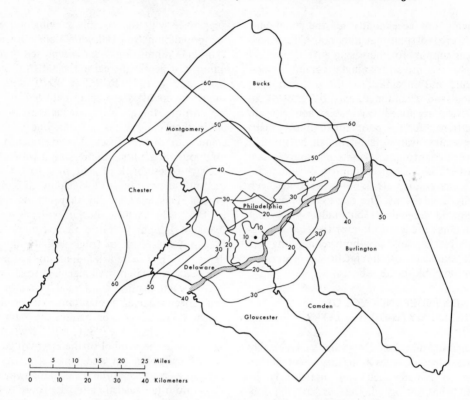

Figure 40. Offhours driving time from central Philadelphia, 1972. Adapted from map prepared by the Delaware Valley Regional Planning Commission, 1973.

a large majority of a class of thirty suburban college students at Temple University's Ambler Campus raised their hands; when pressed more closely, almost all of those who had been to the city had gone only once or twice to engage in some special activity such as Christmas shopping, attending the Army-Navy game, watching the Mummer's Parade on New Years Day, or using International Airport. To counteract the avoidance of downtown, radio ads for a major Center City men's clothing outlet play up its large selection of odd-size garments, maintaining that suburban department stores will not stock as great a variety of items. More recently that establishment has evoked nostalgia for old Philadelphia neighborhoods, and its latest pitch runs something like "I made three trips to the city last year: one to my in-laws, one to make up with my in-laws, and one to Boyd's."

The growing break between Philadelphia and its suburbs is also reflected by factual evidence. The continuing decline of central Phila-

delphia's shopping district, once the Delaware Valley's dominant retail trade core, is a good indicator of recent shifts in population distribution, buying power, and use of shopping centers. As expected, the CBD has suffered as suburban malls opened and thrived, with downtown sales losing more than 12 percent during 1970 alone. The decaying physical facilities of Center City shopping streets attest to the stagnation and low morale of retailers: Philadelphia's main shopping corner at Eighth and Market streets, site of the flagship department stores of the Gimbels, Lits, and Strawbridge and Clothier chains, is falling apart though new construction is finally underway after years of delay. Even the fashionable shops along Chestnut Street have become interspersed with a few seedy discount drug and variety junk stores. Part of this blight is certainly a response to anticipation of commercial renewal associated with the Market Street East plan, an ambitious redevelopment project which is to include a new rail terminal, office buildings, and a multilevel shopping arcade, but much of the structural decline is also due to the changed metropolitan reality.

The problems of the downtown shopping district are mirrored in the *Philadelphia Inquirer's* 1970 retail trade area survey. The CBD is still the largest single regional shopping center in the Delaware Valley, but downtown largely attracts those with only modest buying power. In fact, more than 80 percent of the CBD's clientele is drawn from Philadelphia's lower middle and low income neighborhoods, and the largest single customer source area (16 percent) is the North Philadelphia ghetto, the city's largest poverty zone. The largest suburban drawing area is not on the Pennsylvania side of the Delaware: the Camden suburbs, despite a $1.10 round trip bridge toll, is the highest-ranking outlying area to be attracted. Moreover, many of the suburban CBD shoppers are "captive" in that they work downtown and use the stores only during their lunch hours or to and from their jobs in the mornings and evenings. Indeed, only 9 percent of the CBD's shoppers come from the Pennsylvania suburbs— mostly from southern Delaware County, which has a notoriously poor road network, a large working class population, and few good shopping malls (though two opened in 1973).

Although many in suburbia can live comfortably by avoiding Philadelphia altogether, the question must be asked as to whether or not the Delaware Valley's suburbs are really self-sufficient. Many in the region do not think so, and the gut feeling is expressed emotionally by Mike Mallowe in his *Philadelphia Magazine* piece, "Hell No, I Won't Go":

Just because people who live beyond the city limits can shop in malls instead of on Chestnut Street, or dine out at country inns rather than center city restaurants, an erroneous notion has sprung up that the city, per se, is obsolete. But, ironically, those suburbanites are the very ones who do need the city. The poor black in North Philly or the struggling white in Fishtown certainly doesn't need the city—in his eat-or-be-eaten world very little beyond bed and board is really needed. But that guy out there fortifying his quarter-acre is more dependent on the city and its complex marketplace that buys and sells everything from sin to sodium than he could ever realize and admit. He has

a lifestyle—and a standard of living—that is so precariously balanced that every time a liquor store is knocked over in West Philly, the socioeconomic vibrations shoot tremors through his job, his industry and even his block. Like it or not, he has a stake in the life or death of the city. Very much against his will he's trapped on an economic roulette wheel of interdependency where his number is perpetually in danger of coming up.

These intuitive feelings are supported in a study on interdependencies in the Philadelphia region which was prepared in 1967 by Robert Coughlin and his associates at the Regional Science Research Institute. This survey on the region's economic structure in the mid sixties came to the conclusion that the basic city-suburb interdependency is the key to the Delaware Valley's prosperity. Most important are the services produced by downtown Philadelphia's business community, which were seen to anchor the entire employment base of the metropolitan region. Although there continues to be some outward movement of these activities to the suburbs, it seems unlikely that the central business district will lose this dominance over the region in the immediate future. The spatial "glue" of the CBD that should hold these specialized services in place is a location variable not widely evident in suburbia— the centralization of a complete business community which allows for face-to-face contact on a few minutes' notice. The fact is that important business transactions take place at lunches and other spontaneously called meetings, a form of rapid interpersonal communication difficult to maintain among the widely dispersed concentrations of business activity in the suburbs.

While it is possible for suburbanites to ignore and avoid Philadelphia, many are aware of the regional importance of the central city. The same Bala Cynwyd resident who was hard put to recall his last foray downtown, was quick to add that people in the city "need us, and we need them." Suburban developers readily emphasize accessibility to those Philadelphia activities which appeal to suburbanites; for example, the lavish Echelon brochures underscore with maps and pictures the fact that the development is less than a thirty minute drive from both International Airport and the city's outstanding new Veterans Stadium and indoor

Spectrum arena. Lack of community identification in suburbia can also foster a need to feel a belonging to "Greater" Philadelphia. A former Montgomery County commissioner is quoted by Lenora Berson as follows:

> People who live in the suburbs are conscious of their own neighborhood, but they do not think of themselves as Montgomery, Chester, Delaware, or Bucks County-ites, but rather as Philadelphians. They might not like the city; they may have deliberately moved from it to avoid the problems and unpleasantness; they may increasingly spend their lives outside of its boundaries—but it is still their geographic reference point.

It is clear that a new geographical relationship between Philadelphia and its suburbs is evolving in the mid-1970s. The conditions which created the physical fabric of a tightly centralized core city no longer exist, and we are now witnessing the emergence of new functional interdependencies as the socioeconomic and morphological elements of metropolitan space realign themselves. A full assessment of these trends and their implications must await future analysis; however, educated guesses can be made in light of recent developments. Many of these changes have been discussed in this survey of suburban Delaware Valley. Their consequences were summarized by Arthur Loeben, director of the Montgomery County Planning Commission in an interview with the *Philadelphia Inquirer:*

> Philadelphia will never go back to being the predominant center for jobs, and will never recover its prominence as a center for entertainment, shopping and sports. The traditional concept of the city as hub and the suburbs as appendages is dead wrong. Society is now multi-nodal. Previously each area would center around one node, but now with shopping malls we are in a multi-nodal era.

Looking into the crystal ball, it is his opinion that Philadelphia is not about to die, as its lifestyles will always be desired by enough people to guarantee that large numbers will want to live in and commute to the city. The major change will be that Philadelphia's role as the leading urban center of the Delaware Valley will be increasingly shared with outlying suburban minicities, as the spatial transformation from a single focus to a multinodal metropolitan society is completed.

Final Remarks

This study of the Philadelphia region has been organized around the themes of its diversity and internal divisions, and has highlighted a number of social and economic problems. Today's mass education and mass media have served to increase our awareness of these problems. Richard Schermerhorn reminds us that a situation defined as real becomes real in its consequences—that is, ". . . even social fictions believed to be real will be made the basis for social action on the part of those who believe them. . . ." Our problem, then, is to sort out the real problems from the "social fictions."

The social cleavages that have developed among racial, ethnic, and economic class groups are reflected in patterns of spatial segregation throughout the entire Philadelphia region. These patterns also reveal the tendency for people, as social animals, to associate with others of similar background and common interests. Voluntary segregation need not be a source of intergroup tension and violence if we can learn to believe in the tenets of cultural pluralism. As sociologist Milton Gordon states in *Assimilation in American Life,* the interaction of diversified groups in a social structure consisting of racial and ethnic subcommunities cross-stratified by social class can, and should, result in mutually beneficial relationships. To the extent that segregation is involuntary, however, whether by de jure or de facto mechanisms, it cannot, and should not, be tolerated.

Some of the problems of the Delaware Valley are common to all large urban areas in the United States and can perhaps be attributed to our "age of affluence." While personal expectations continue to rise, their realization has frequently lagged far behind, creating problems that cry for massive social action to eliminate inequities. While there is a level of poverty below which no human being should be allowed to fall, most Americans today enjoy a degree of affluence unparalleled in the history of mankind.

The magnitude of the fear that permeates the city and its suburbs is, in the opinion of many, caused by overreaction to events which, in reality, call for less impassioned responses. Reports of increasing central city crime, however, have led to public outcries for more police, stronger laws, and tougher courts, while private concern is manifested in efforts to increasingly defend space with burglar alarms, guard dogs, locks, and window grates. Given the nature of crime statistics, it is almost impossible to assess the validity of this reaction, and thus to justify vast expenditures of public and private monies to restore effective "law and order."

As people, employment, and retail activities deconcentrate to the suburbs, the central cities of the region increasingly become the home of the poor and other disadvantaged minorities; their demand for housing and services continues while fiscal resources decline. The dual trends of central city office concentration and suburban industrial and retail dispersion have increased the spatial separation between home and work for most people. Thus both the white collar worker, living in the suburbs and working in the city, and the blue collar worker, living in the city and increasingly working in the suburbs, spend ever greater amounts of time and effort commuting to their jobs. Separation from the source of employment has more serious consequences for the growing pool of unskilled labor which resides in the inner city. Lacking adequate mass transit, the resources and opportunity to move to the suburbs, the problem of unemployment and underemployment in the inner city becomes chronic and debilitating.

Some of the problems outlined above are critical, and serious efforts have been made to cope with them. Programs have been proposed in an effort to increase the tax base of Philadelphia, provide more low cost housing, and reorganize fragmented governmental units. Such problems have met with varying success to date.

As economists have pointed out, the disparities between the tax bases of the central city and its suburbs are increasing. Caught in the fiscal squeeze created by the suburban exodus, Philadelphia is actively attempting to attract people and industry back to the city. In terms of population, there have been some notable successes: the Society Hill neighborhood is an example of a high income residential development which has become popular in Center City, and Franklin Town is expected to be similarly successful. We must caution, however, that the true impact of such projects has yet to be realistically appraised.

In terms of industry, which is a much greater potential source of tax revenues, the city's record has not been encouraging. There is no doubt that an increased tax base would help alleviate some of the economic problems of Philadelphia, but we suggest that there is a concomitant need to reassess the city's current fiscal priorities. A critical element in the tax base issue is not only the strength of that base, but also the manner in which city services are allocated among its residents. As geographer Robert Colenutt notes: "If services are inequitably distributed and tend to favor the needs of the rich over the needs of the poor, [then] an increase in the tax base will not change the pattern of relative deprivation in the city."

As long as the poor continue to concentrate in the central cities of the region, there will be a continuing need for low income housing. Since a low profit margin has traditionally discouraged the private construction of such housing, and since demolition for urban renewal and highway construction has removed more low income structures than have been replaced, the need is becoming more critical. Government programs to provide low cost housing have failed on several counts: not enough is being built, much of what has been built is unsatisfactory and not really "low cost," and the location of projects has tended to perpetuate racial segregation in the city (Figure 41).

The Philadelphia City Council recently passed legislation that offers a unique solution, since adopted by other cities to help alleviate the problem of low income housing shortages. Entitled the Homestead Act, this legislation enables the city to sell abandoned, structurally sound houses for $1 apiece to low income families who agree to restore and live in them for at least five years. Given the relatively small number of sound abandoned houses that are available—only 562 have been acquired by the city to date—"homesteading" is admittedly only a partial solution to the housing problem, but it is an indication that positive steps are being taken in Philadelphia to deal with this critical issue.

Metropolitanwide government is seen by many as a means for ending competition among local governmental units so that the region's resources can be pooled and distributed on a more equitable basis. The 1964 Penn-Jersey Transportation Study report highlighted this problem: "... there are not less than 500 major public assistance agencies in the Philadelphia region which have direct control of land utilization through zoning, or indirect influence through taxing powers." Efforts to overcome the problem of governmental fragmentation have been most successful in a planning context. The Delaware Valley Regional Planning Commission has jurisdiction over the Philadelphia Daily Urban System. This agency has drawn up a number of major areawide plans aimed at the regional integration of transportation, land use, recreation and open space, water supply, sewage and solid waste disposal, and utilities. Like most other regional planning agencies, DVRPC has no legal authority to implement its plans. Unlike other planning commissions, however, all major units of local government participate as active members of DVRPC. The direct feed-

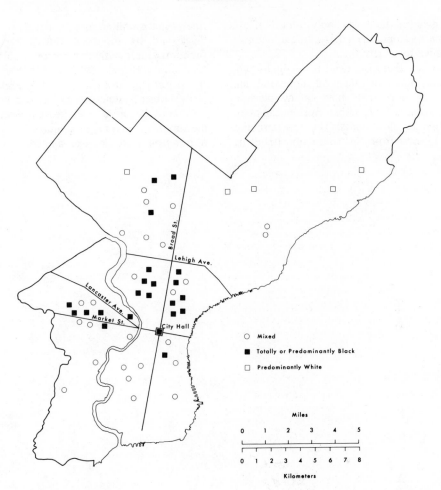

Figure 41. Racial segregation in Philadelphia Public Housing Authority Projects. Source: *Philadelphia Inquirer*, July 15, 1973.

back to decisionmakers that is thus maintained has obvious pragmatic advantages. Increased centralization of government functions, however, carries with it the danger of reinforcing existing inequities at the local community level in all parts of the region. Thus, truly effective government reorganization must be able to balance the economic efficiencies of metropolitanwide control against the social "efficiencies" of community control.

Part of the problem faced by the people of the Philadelphia Daily Urban System is one of large scale and rapid change—the metropolitan resident suffers from an acute case of "information overload." As a result, it is not surprising that simplistic cognitive filters are used to deal with such an overload. Thus many people continue to view the metropolis as composed of distinct parts—the neighborhood, the city, the suburb. More to the point, however, many people consider the "urban crisis" only in these separatist terms. Faced with an increasing sense of alienation and fear, residents of the city continue to flee to the "privatism" of the suburbs, or to withdraw into the "defended space" of the row house or compact neighborhood community of limited liability. To the extent that voluntary segregation represents flight or withdrawal from the problems of the city, it runs counterproductive to real solutions and cannot be tolerated any more than can involuntary segregation. Provincialism in a competitive context can only retard efforts to define metropolitan goals and the cooperation needed to achieve them.

Above all, there is a need to recognize, and to believe, that the residential, industrial, and commercial movements now taking place in the Philadelphia Daily Urban System are essentially *internal* movements. The new structure that will evolve from this space adjustment defines a metropolitan area that is more than the "city and its suburbs," but rather a truly functional unit with one set of problems that can only be dealt with from a holistic perspective. The diversity of the Philadelphia Daily Urban System can and should be tapped so that it becomes an increasing asset of this metropolitan region, and much less a source of nonproductive cleavages and conflicts.

✳

Bibliography

Alexander, John K. "The City of Brotherly Fear: The Poor in Late Eighteenth Century Philadelphia," in Kenneth T. Jackson & Stanley K. Schultz, eds., *Cities in American History*. New York: Alfred A. Knopf, 1972, pp. 79–97.

Anderson, John W. "Little Community in the Big City: Spatial Organization and Community Culture in an Urban Neighborhood." M.A. thesis, University of Pennsylvania, 1969.

Baltzell, E. Digby. *Philadelphia Gentlemen: The Making of a National Upper Class.* Glencoe, Ill: Free Press, 1958.

Bernard, Jessie. *The Sociology of Community.* Glenview, Ill.: Scott, Foresman and Company, 1973.

Berry, Brian J.L. "Contemporary Urbanization Processes." In Frank E. Horton, ed., *Geographical Perspectives and Urban Problems.* Washington, D.C.: National Academy of Sciences, 1973, pp. 94–107.

Berry, Brian J.L., and Cohen, Yehoshua S. "Decentralization of Commerce and Industry: The Restructuring of Metropolitan America." In Louis H. Masotti and Jeffrey K. Hadden, eds., *The Urbanization of the Suburbs.* Beverly Hills and London: Sage Publications, 1973, pp. 431–455.

Berson, Lenora. "Philadelphia." *City,* 5 (January-February 1971): 40–42.

Binzen, Peter. *Whitetown, U.S.A.* New York: Random House, Inc., 1970.

Bittan, David. "Levitt or Leave It." *Philadelphia Magazine,* September 1972, 78–85, 190–195.

Brush, John E., and Gauthier, Howard L., Jr. *Service Centers and Consumer Trips: Studies on the Philadelphia Metropolitan Fringe.* Research Paper No. 113. Chicago: Department of Geography, University of Chicago, 1968.

Bunge, William. Cited in Robert J. Colenutt, "Poverty and Inequality in American Cities." *Antipode* 2 (December 1970): 55–60.

Burgess, Ernest W. "The Growth of the City." In Robert E. Park, Ernest W. Burgess, and Roderick D. McKenzie, eds., *The City.* Chicago: University of Chicago Press, 1925.

Burt, Nathaniel. *The Perennial Philadelphians.* Boston: Little, Brown, and Company, 1963.

City of Philadelphia. City Planning Commission. *Population and Housing Trends: 1970 Census. Philadelphia and Its Metropolitan Area.* Philadelphia: City Planning Commission, 1971.

———. *Population Characteristics: 1960 and 1970 Philadelphia Census Tracts.* Philadelphia: City Planning Commission, 1972.

———. Department of Commerce and Business. *MiniIndustrial Parks Program.* Philadelphia: Department of Commerce and Business, 1973 (courtesy of Jan L. Vagassky, deputy director).

Colenutt, Robert J. "Do Alternatives Exist for Central Cities?" In Harold M. Rose, ed., *Perspectives in Geography.* No. 2. *Geography of the Ghetto: Perceptions, Problems, and Alternatives.* DeKalb, Ill.: Northern Illinois University Press, 1972.

Collura, John, and Schuster, James J. *Accessibility of Low Income Residential Areas* in *Philadelphia to Regional Industrial Parks.* Report Prepared for the Institute for Transportation Studies. Villanova: Villanova University, 1971.

Commonwealth of Pennsylvania. Department of Commerce. *Philadelphia County: 1971.* Pennsylvania Industrial Census Series, M-5-71. Harrisburg: Department of Commerce, 1972.

Conway, W.S. Letter to the Editor, *Philadelphia Magazine,* July 1973.

Cottingham, Phoebe H. "Black Income and Metropolitan Residential Dispersion," *Urban Affairs Quarterly,* 10 (March, 1975), 273-296.

Coughlin, Robert E. et al. *Interdependence in the Penjerdel Region.* Report to Penjerdel, Greater Philadelphia Movement, and the Federal Reserve Bank of Philadelphia. Philadelphia: Regional Science Research Institute, 1967.

Danielson, Michael N. "Differentiation, Segregation, and Political Fragmentation in the American Metropolis." In A.E. Keir Nash, ed. *Governance and Population: The Governmental Implications of Population Change.* Research Reports, Volume IV. Washington, D.C.: Commission on Population Growth and the American Future, 1972.

Davies, C. Shane. "The Reverse Commuter Transit Problem in Indianapolis." In Harold M. Rose, ed., *Perspectives in Geography.* No. 2. *Geography of the Ghetto: Perceptions, Problems and Alternatives.* DeKalb, Ill.: Northern Illinois University Press, 1972.

Davis, Allen F., and Haller, Mark H., eds. *The Peoples of Philadelphia: A History of Ethnic Groups and Lower Class Life.* Philadelphia: Temple University Press, 1973.

Dear, Michael. "Abandoned Housing." In John S. Adams, ed., *Urban Policymaking and Metropolitan Dynamics: A Comparative Geographical Analysis,* ch. 3. Cambridge: Ballinger Publishing Company, 1976.

Delaware Valley Regional Planning Commission. *Highway Travel Time Between Major Activity Centers in the Delaware Valley Region.* A Summary Report. Philadelphia, 1973.

———. *The Delaware Valley Plan.* Philadelphia, 1970.

"Delaware Valley, U.S.A.: An Economic Primer." *Philadelphia Inquirer,* Special Supplement, October 30, 1973.

Deutermann, Elizabeth P. "Headquarters

Have Human Problems." *Business Review* (Federal Reserve Bank of Philadelphia), February 1970, pp. 3-22.

DuBois, W.E.B. *The Philadelphia Negro: A Social Study.* New York: Schocken Books, 1967.

Epps, Richard W. "Suburban Jobs and Black Workers." *Business Review* (Federal Reserve Bank of Philadelphia), October 1969, pp. 3-13.

Epstein, Bart J. "The Trading Function." In Jean Gottmann and Robert A. Harper, eds., *Metropolis on the Move: Geographers Look at Urban Sprawl.* New York: John Wiley and Sons, Inc., 1967, pp. 93-101.

Gans, Herbert J. *The Levittowners: Ways of Life and Politics in a New Suburban Community* (Willingboro, New Jersey). New York: Vintage Books, 1967.

Glantz, Frederic B., and Delaney, Nancy J. "Changes in Nonwhite Residential Patterns in Large Metropolitan Areas, 1960 and 1970." *New England Economic Review* (Federal Reserve Bank of Boston), March-April 1973, pp. 2-13.

Golab, Carol Ann. "The Polish Communities of Philadelphia, 1870-1920: Immigrant Distribution and Adaptation in Urban America." Ph.D. dissertation, University of Pennsylvania, 1971.

Gordon, Milton M. *Assimilation in American Life: The Role of Race, Religion, and National Origin.* New York: Oxford University Press, 1964.

Government Consulting Service et al. *Development of an Antipoverty Program, Montgomery County, Pennsylvania.* A Report to the Montgomery County Opportunity Board, November 9, 1966. Cited in Montgomery County Planning Commission, *A Summary Survey of Housing Conditions and Demand.* Norristown, Pa.: Montgomery County Planning Commission, 1972.

Guinther, John. "The Persistence of Devils in Delaware County." *Philadelphia Magazine,* June 1973, 90-98, 196-205.

Harvey, Robert O., and Clark, William A.V. "The Nature and Economics of Urban Sprawl." *Land Economics* 41 (February 1965): 1-9.

Kron, Joan. "An Infiltrator's Guide to the Main Line." *Philadelphia Magazine,* June 1973, 114-117, 168-171.

Levy, Maury. "And on the Seventh Day,

When the Lord Rested, Man Made the Northeast." *Philadelphia Magazine,* November 1970, 84–91, 139–148.

———. "South Jersey: Too Much, Too Soon?" *Philadelphia Magazine,* April 1972, 78–87, 168–177.

Ley, David. *The Black Inner City as Frontier Outpost: Images and Behavior of a Philadelphia Neighborhood.* Washington: The Association of American Geographers, Monograph Series No. 7, 1974.

Ley, D., and Cybriwsky, R.A. "Urban Graffiti as Territorial Markers," *Annals,* The Association of American Geographers, 64 (December 1974): 491–505.

Lichstein, Isadore, ed. *1973 Bulletin Almanac: A Source of Information About Greater Philadelphia and the United States.* Philadelphia: Bulletin Co., 1973.

Lieberson, Stanley. *Ethnic Patterns in American Cities.* New York: Free Press of Glencoe, 1963.

Mallowe, Mike. "God Isn't Dead. He's Moved to the Suburbs." *Philadelphia Magazine,* June 1973, 124–131.

———. "Hell, No, I Won't Go." *Philadelphia Magazine,* June 1973, 228, 160.

———. "The $400 Million Steamroller." *Philadelphia Magazine* July 1972, 76–85, 110–120.

Masotti, Louis H., and Hadden, Jeffrey K., eds. *The Urbanization of the Suburbs.* Beverly Hills and London: Sage Publications, 1973.

McHarg, Ian L. *Design with Nature.* Garden City, N.Y.: Doubleday & Co., Inc., 1969.

Mitchell, Robert B., ed. "Planning and Development in Philadelphia." *Journal of the American Institute of Planners* (special issue) 26 (August 1960).

Montgomery County Planning Commission. *Labor Force.* Norristown, Pa., 1972.

Morley, Christopher D. *Travels in Philadelphia.* Philadelphia: David McKay Co., 1920.

Muller, Peter O. "Urbanization in Suburban Delaware Valley: The Recent Growth of the Philadelphia Urbanized Area," in Clyde E. Browning, ed., *Population and Urbanized Area Growth in Megalopolis, 1950–1970.* Chapel Hill, N.C.: University of North Carolina, Department of Geography, Studies in Geography No. 7, 1974, pp. 71–83.

The Neighborhoods of Philadelphia. Philadelphia: Bulletin Co., 1969.

Nettis, Joseph, and Burt, Nathaniel. *Philadelphia Discovered.* Philadelphia: Greater Philadelphia Magazine, 1964.

"The New Suburbia." *Philadelphia Magazine,* June 1973.

Newman, Oscar. *Defensible Space.* New York: Macmillan Co., 1972.

Packard, Vance. *A Nation of Strangers.* New York: David McKay Co., Inc., 1972.

Penn-Jersey Transportation Study. *The State of the Region.* Philadelphia, 1964.

Philadelphia: A Guide to the Nation's Birthplace. St. Clair Shores, Mich.: Somerset Publishers, 1974. (Reprint of 1939 volume in Federal Writers' Project American Guide Series.)

Philadelphia Electric Company. *Montgomery County: Economic and Demographic Profile.* Philadelphia: Philadelphia Electric Company, Area Development Department, 1972.

Philadelphia Inquirer, October 26, 1971; February 9, 1973; April 29, 1973; July 15, 1973; July 29, 1973; October 30, 1970; June 30, 1973.

Rabin, Yale. "Highways as a Barrier to Equal Access," *Annals of the American Academy of Political and Social Science,* 407 (May 1973), 63–77.

Randall, Willard. "The Daily Crabgrass." *Philadelphia Magazine,* September 1971, 97–112.

Rapkin, Chester, and Grigsby, William G. *The Demand for Housing in Racially Mixed Areas.* Berkeley: University of California Press, 1960.

Retail Shopping, Purchase, and Service Patterns in the Philadelphia Retail Trading Area. A Report Prepared by the Philadelphia Inquirer Research Department. Philadelphia, 1971.

Report of the National Advisory Commission on Civil Disorders. Otto Kerner, chairman. New York: Bantam Books, Inc., 1968.

Schermerhorn, Richard A. "Minorities: European and American." In Milton L. Barron, ed., *Minorities in a Changing World.* New York: Alfred A. Knopf, 1967.

Schribner, A. Kent. "Suburban Image of Central City as Found in Selected Suburban Newspapers, with Emphasis on the Philadelphia Metropolitan Area." M.G.A. thesis, University of Pennsylvania, 1961.

Sunday Bulletin, June 13, 1971; June 24, 1973.

Taeuber, Karl E., and Taeuber, Alma F. *Negroes in Cities: Residential Segregation and Neighborhood Change.* Chicago: Aldine Publishing Co., 1965.

"This is Delaware Valley, U.S.A." *Philadelphia Inquirer,* October 19–November 2, 1966.

U.S. Department of Labor. Bureau of Labor Statistics. *Philadelphia's Inner City: An Analysis of the 1970 Census Employment Survey.* Mideast Region, Report no. 6. Prepared by Herman P. Miller and Stuart Garfinkle. March 1973.

———. *Employment Structure and Trends, Philadelphia.* Mideast Region, Report no. 2, September 1971; Report No. 14, May, 1975.

Warner, Sam Bass, Jr. *The Private City: Philadelphia in Three Periods of Its Growth.* Philadelphia: University of Pennsylvania Press, 1968.

Webber, Melvin M. "The Post-City Age." *Daedalus* 97 (Fall 1968): 1091–1110.

The Whole City Catalogue. Philadelphia: Synapse Communications Collective, 1972.

Wirth, Louis. "Urbanism as a Way of Life." *American Journal of Sociology* 44 (July 1938): 1–24.

Wolpert, Julian; Mumphrey, Anthony; and Seley, John. *Metropolitan Neighborhoods: Participation and Conflict Over Change.* Resource Paper no. 16. Washington, D.C.: Commission on College Geography, Assoication of American Geographers, 1972.

Wurman, Richard Saul, and Gallery, John Andrew. *Man-Made Philadelphia; A Guide to Its Physical and Cultural Environment.* Cambridge, Mass.: MIT Press, 1972.

Zikmund, Joseph II. "Do Suburbanites Use the Central City?," *Journal of the American Institute of Planners,* 37 (May, 1971), 192–195.

Chapter 5

**From Farm to
Factory to Urban
Pastoralism:
Urban Change in
Central Connecticut**

Introduction

Connecticut is being absorbed into Megalopolis, the vast coalescing urban region stretching along the Atlantic Coast from Washington, D.C., to Boston, Massachusetts. Growth is evident everywhere, the rate of change is accelerating, and there are indications Connecticut's population will double by the end of the twentieth century. Connecticut must plan for and mold the future in order to provide a quality living environment. These issues stand in bold relief in central Connecticut, the four county area of Hartford, Tolland, New Haven, and Middlesex (Figure 1). This urban region contains ten cities and towns with over 50,000 people and population projections by Connecticut's Office of State Planning envision extensive growth; the total 1970 population of 1.8 million is expected to rise to 3.0 million by the year 2000.

The additional 1.2 million people in central Connecticut will contribute to intense pressure for conversion of land from open space use to urban uses such as residential, commercial, and manufacturing. Compounding the pressure for urban development are demands by households for ever larger lot sizes. In a survey of Connecticut households in the early 1960s, only 8 percent lived on lots of one acre or more but 38 percent expressed a preference for such lot sizes. Connecticut's population increased by 20 percent between 1960 and 1970, while land used for residential purposes increased by 53 percent. If existing trends continue, the year 2000 should see a substantial reduction of open space in central Connecticut. Within the northern half of the region it is estimated that the amount of land in urban uses will quadruple between 1960 and 2000.

Central Connecticut must cope not only with greatly increased numbers of people by 2000 but also with a changing population composition. Black and Puerto Rican populations are rapidly growing in the major cities. As their numbers expand, these minorities will increasingly be challenging the rest of the residents of central Connecticut to make good on promises of fair treatment in housing, jobs, and public services.

Can a quality living environment be provided for the residents of central Connecticut under the pressures of growth and change? This urban region is famous for its Yankee inventors and entrepreneurs who played an important role in the industrial revolution in the United States and transformed central Connecticut from a rural landscape to an urban-industrial region. From being in the forefront of social and economic change in the nineteenth century it has become in the twentieth century one of the wealthiest urban regions in the United States. Understanding the process of urban growth in central Connecticut that led to the existing urban mosaic is a prerequisite to answering questions about the future. After identifying present trends in urban development, the existing and possible future urban mosaic will be assessed in terms of its potentialities for providing a quality living environment for the residents of central Connecticut.

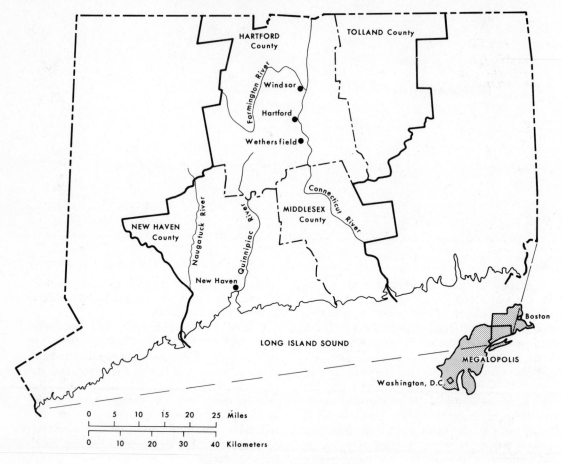

Figure 1. Central Connecticut.

Evolution of an Urban Landscape

URBAN OUTPOSTS

Between 1633 and 1638 Puritan Englishmen firmly penetrated the Connecticut wilderness and settled at Windsor, Hartford, and Wethersfield on the Connecticut River and at New Haven on Long Island Sound (Figure 1). These early settlers had a variety of motives for going to Connecticut, but two stand out—acquiring control over their daily lives in social, economic, and religious affairs and acquiring the resources to achieve the good life. The latter motive was translated into the exploitation of the fertile farm lands especially along the Connecticut River and the development of trade with the Indians. These settlements or towns as they would be called were not run on a democratic basis as we understand it today. The original proprietors, those owning the first shares in land, controlled development of the town by passing on division of land and admitting people to governing power in the town.

The Connecticut towns were areal units which might or might not have an "urban" agglomeration. In the early years the customary method of settlement was the clustering of population in a village, with houses of the proprietors strung along several intersecting roads, farm land extending away from the road, and additional plots scattered outside the village. As new settlers arrived they would be allotted land on the periphery of the settlement; a new cluster of households might develop, call its own minister, and eventually separate from the original town to form a new town.

Thus the settlement of central Connecticut during the seventeenth century was the spread of the town form of territorial organization. Two major cores from which settlement diffused were Hartford-Wethersfield-Windsor and New Haven. Prime targets for the settlers were the fertile valleys of the Farmington, Naugatuck, and Quinnipiac rivers (Figure 1). After 1700, dispersed farms became important because most large tracts of fertile land suitable for occupancy by a group of people living in villages had been settled. The only true urban outposts in this rural landscape were Hartford and New Haven, which contained merchants involved in trade. They accumulated the small agricultural surpluses of subsistence farmers which included grain, pork, and butter and usually shipped these products to Boston in return for clothing, wine, and manufactured articles. But up to the early 1700s even the towns of Hartford and New Haven were chiefly occupied by farmers.

By 1800 expanding markets in the West Indies and increased local agricultural production provided the base for the emergence of three important urban centers—Hartford, Middletown, and New Haven. Each town had a significant proportion of its population living in a village and engaged in nonagricultural pursuits. A visitor to these urban centers would quickly identify their economic function; ships at anchor, sailors, wholesale houses, ropewalks, and shipyards testified to the importance of mercantile activities. Key figures in these urban centers were the merchants who collected surplus agricultural products of the region directly from farmers or through the intermediaries of country store owners in the villages. Merchants exported agricultural staples —including cattle, horses, lumber, grain, butter, and cheese—to the West Indies and imported food and manufactured goods by way of Boston or New York—including molasses, rum, sugar, fruit, dry goods, hardware, tea, and spices.

The populations in the urban portions of the towns in 1800 were about 2,100 in Middletown and 4,000 each in New Haven and Hartford. Compared with populations of 24,937 in Boston and 60,515 in New York, the Connecticut urban places were relatively insignificant, but compared to the villages surrounding the three urban places they were in a different world. In the villages almost all inhabitants were farmers except perhaps the minister. Even blacksmiths, saw and grist mill owners, and carpenters were usually part time farmers; the demand for services was too small to permit more specialized occupations. Of course very small scale manufacturing of buttons, tinware, clocks, and combs existed in some towns but the number employed was seldom a dozen people and therefore did not provide a base for urban growth. The interdependent cities we see today and that were to develop in the nineteenth century were not conceivable in 1800.

THE URBAN TRANSITION

At the beginning of the nineteenth century Connecticut's future was not bright. Most suitable agricultural lands had been settled by the time of the Revolutionary War and many farmers found they could not make a decent living off the hilly, rocky soils of Connecticut. With continued growth of population and inadequate employment opportunities, post-Revolutionary Connecticut residents chose to migrate in large numbers to northern Vermont, Pennsylvania, New York, and Ohio. The result of this extensive migration was slow population growth for the state between 1790 and 1840, averaging 5 percent per decade while the nation as a whole was growing by 34 percent per decade. Within central Connecticut population growth was uneven. Middlesex and Tolland counties, which contained poor agricultural land and isolated semisubsistence farms, grew about 6 percent per decade while

Hartford and New Haven counties, which contained better agricultural land and farms with good access to markets, grew 50 percent faster but still substantially slower than the United States growth rate. Not until after 1840 was there a sharp upturn in population in central Connecticut and this was concentrated in Hartford and New Haven counties.

Although agriculture, the base of the Connecticut economy, was stagnant from 1790–1840 except in the vicinity of the main commercial centers, important social and economic changes were occurring that would transform central Connecticut into an urban-industrial region. Adoption of the Connecticut state constitution in 1818 symbolized the breaking of control of Connecticut life by the Federalist-Congregationalist elite. The church-state alliance was a conservative force that had dominated Connecticut since its settlement in the 1630s. Economic bases of the alliance included people in agriculture and commerce, but with the ascendancy of Republicans in 1818 manufactures were given encouragement by political leaders.

Restrictions on the entry of European manufactures from about 1807 to 1833— including the Embargo Act of 1807, the War of 1812, and passage of tariff laws—were encouragement for the development of local manufactures. Connecticut entrepreneurs were faced with the possibility of competing with foreign manufacturers outside the local Connecticut market and in the New England and national markets.

The response of Connecticut's population to the possibilities of industrialization is legendary. Throughout the nineteenth century Connecticut led all states in the number of patents granted per capita and its entrepreneurs became famous for their shrewdness and ingenuity. Furthermore, the people of Connecticut entered into industrialization with four distinct assets. First, given the technology of the time, early nineteenth century Connecticut contained many skilled craftsmen who provided the essential products for running a relatively self-sufficient economy and therefore had skills that were partly transferable to manufacturing. Second, these craftsmen as well as the general population were highly educated for their time; most native-born residents could read and write, libraries served as reading centers in many towns, and newspapers were widely read and passed around. Therefore new ideas about inventions and methods of industrial organization coming from Europe, other parts of the United States, and originating locally could diffuse throughout central Connecticut. Third, whatever innate aptitude for cleverness, shrewdness, or ingenuity Connecticut residents may have possessed, by 1800 it was also true that Connecticut society viewed these aptitudes as socially acceptable and gave an honorable place to the pursuit of self-interest. These favorable social attitudes provided a climate in which inventors and entrepreneurs could flourish. Finally, those people with capital to invest were willing to support industrial innovation; merchants began to divert capital from trade to the manufacturing of cotton and wool textiles, machinery, and tools.

Infant manufacturing villages and their offsprings, the cities, did not develop in all towns but instead became highly localized. A plausible explanation for the selective nature of urban growth is that inventors and entrepreneurs would not be ubiquitous but would be concentrated in those areas where the economy was productive and released money for experimentation and where the division of labor allowed some people to devote most of their time to skilled crafts. Invention was not facilitated on isolated, self-sufficient farms where all efforts were devoted to surviving. The interesting fact about the industrial regions of central Connecticut as of 1845 was their high degree of localization in the earliest settled areas located within or adjacent to the densely populated agricultural districts along the Connecticut, Farmington, or Naugatuck rivers or near the early important commercial centers of Hartford, Middletown, and New Haven. Isolated, hilly, poor agricultural areas of Tolland and Middlesex counties and northwest Hartford County did not develop an urban base. Of course not all towns with "favorable" conditions developed manufacturing; successful inventors and entrepreneuers were not ubiquitous and therefore manufacturing growth was selective.

For the period 1815 to 1818 it is possible to crudely reconstruct the extent of manufacturing in towns (Figure 2). In only three towns—Hartford, Middletown, and Seymour—were there more than 100 people employed in manufacturing for a nonlocal market in es-

tablishments that were larger than a shop of six to twelve employees and none of these towns had more than 250 factory workers. Hartford's and Middletown's commercial functions were more important than their manufacturing. Only the town of Seymour had a large manufacturing village. The Humphreysville Manufacturing Company operated woolen and cotton mills and sometimes employed almost 200 workers. However, the company and the manufacturing village of Humphreysville which it constructed were unusual for this time, not representative.

Minor manufacturing villages existed in Glastonbury and Vernon (cotton and woolen mills), East Windsor and Enfield (gin distilleries), Waterbury (button and clock factories), and Wallingford (woolen mill, button, tinware and metal spoon factories). New Haven, though an important commercial town, was only a minor manufacturing village with a powder mill, cotton mill, two paper mills, and, just outside the town border in Hamden, the Whitney firearms factory. None of these factories was large and most probably had fewer than twenty employees. Thus in 1818 the manufacturing village was still an unusual feature of the central Connecticut landscape; farming occupied most people.

But a small group of inventors and entrepreneurs were actively laying an important manufacturing base in clock, brass product, tool and hardware, britanniaware, and arms production during the period 1800 to 1850. These were to form the nuclei for the growth of many manufacturing villages into industrial cities. The significant innovations in clockmaking were initiated by Eli Terry who experimented with the large scale production of wooden clocks and introduced the technique of interchangeable parts into clockmaking. Between 1806 and 1809, in a community north of Waterbury, Terry produced 4,000 wooden clock movements on contract with Edward and Levi Porter, merchants in Waterbury, who distributed the clocks through local peddlers. This was an astounding accomplishment since the average clockmaker made fewer than ten clock movements per year. By 1816 Terry had made a revolutionary rearrangement of the clock works that needed a case only twenty inches high in contrast to the usual six foot clock. In his typical fashion he also designed new production equipment and techniques. The next significant development in clock-

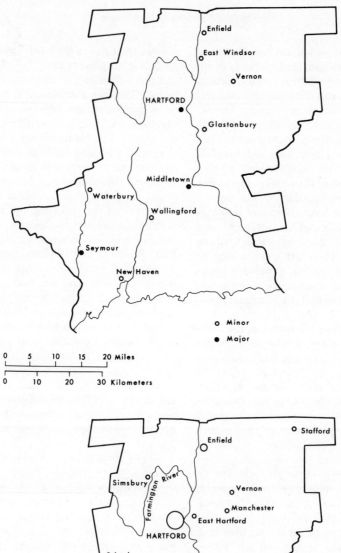

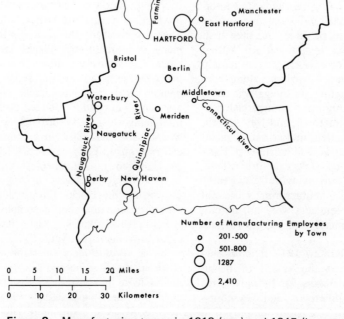

Figure 2. Manufacturing towns in 1818 (top) and 1845 (bottom).

making was Chauncey Jerome's invention of the one day brass clock in 1837 which was substantially cheaper than similar wooden clocks. Jerome had been an employee of Terry but had left to found his own company which by 1821 was located in Bristol but moved to New Haven in 1845. With large profits to be made in clockmaking, numerous competitors were attracted into the business in central Connecticut.

In contrast to important inventions in clocks and innovations in their production by Connecticut residents, growth of the brass industry between 1800 and 1850 was distinguished by shrewd Connecticut entrepreneurs importing machinery, production processes, and skilled labor from England. The brass industry began in Waterbury in 1802 with the founding of a company to manufacture buttons from sheet brass. However, difficulties competing with English buttons initially meant slow growth of production.

During the 1820s the brass industry became securely established and by 1850 additional firms had entered the brass industry in Waterbury, Ansonia, and Derby and diversification grew as new products such as rolled brass, wire, pins, and tubing were manufactured. Stimulated by large profits, the expansion of the brass industry exhibited a circular and cumulative process; growth in demand for brass led to increased production of brass which in turn stimulated production of new brass products which in turn led to growth in demand for brass and so on (Figure 3). The effect of this industrial growth was to make the Naugatuck valley the brass center of the United States.

The tool and hardware industry did not develop on an equivalently large scale as the brass industry during the period 1800 to 1850, but important beginnings were made. Diverse metal products including chisels, nails, hooks, locks, hinges, and buckles had been produced in modest quantities in small shops by 1820 in

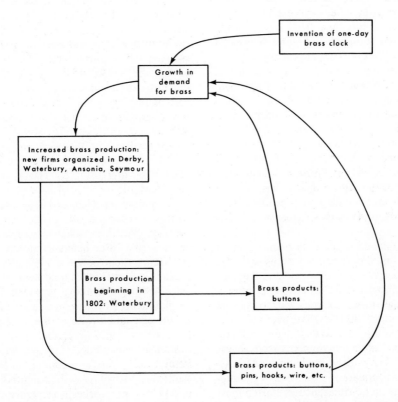

Figure 3. Circular and cumulative process of growth of brass industry in the Naugatuck River Valley, 1800-1850.

the part of Berlin town that is now the separate city of New Britain. Between 1830 and 1850 several firms were organized for the production of locks and house trimmings, but they were small, generally having fewer than twenty employees. The important factor for New Britain's rapid growth after 1850 was that some of these early firms were the predecessors of the future large tool and hardware companies.

Britanniaware production was begun by the Yale brothers in 1815 in Wallingford. They brought to America English workmen who knew the formula for making britanniaware. Other factories soon started in Wallingford and the nearby town of Meriden so that brittaniaware and associated silver manufacturing became highly localized in these two towns by 1850. Other innovations derived from Englishmen such as electroplating and nickel silver were adopted by the britannia companies. Thus, similar to the brass industry, local invention was not an important factor in the growth of industry but shrewd entrepreneurship was.

Although the arms industry in central Connecticut was never large during the period 1800 to 1850, along with other arms makers it made significant contributions to manufacturing technology—the principle of interchangeable parts, development of metalworking machine tools, and the use of precision measurement. Eli Whitney of New Haven, an important leader in advancing the technology of arms production, and Simeon North of Middletown were the major figures in the local arms industry. During this period neither employed more than eighty workers so their immediate impact on the growth of cities was limited. A significant development in the arms industry was to come in 1854 with the founding of the Colt Patent Fire Arms Manufacturing Company in Hartford.

The individual effect of each manufacturing development on the growth of cities was limited, but taken together they laid the base for numerous industrial cities in central Connecticut. Individual inventors and entrepreneuers during the period 1800 to 1850 had no incentive to locate in the same town; scale of production was small, labor requirements were slight, water power was widely available, and transportation was adequate for the limited production. Inventors and entrepreneuers started their manufacturing plants near their home village or in a nearby village. Manufacturing establish-ments gradually expanded at these dispersed locations or new ones were established by local imitators or former employees and the urban settlements grew. By the time the scale of production was so large that new industries needed to locate in large cities, the industrial towns of central Connecticut had grown. Hence the region became characterized by many discrete cities rather than one very large metropolis, and the basic outline of the urban-industrial landscape was evident by 1845 (Figure 2).

Manufacturing was not the only base for urban growth in central Connecticut. Hartford and New Haven were co-capitals of the colony of Connecticut and then of the state until 1873 when Hartford became the sole capital. Prior to 1850 both cities, as capitals, continued to benefit from prestige and access to power as well as government jobs. Commerce, shipping, insurance, and banking were also factors in urban growth, especially in Hartford, Middletown, and New Haven. In the latter half of the eighteenth century these three urban centers had dominated the commerce and shipping of central Connecticut. However, the prosperity of the post–Revolutionary War trade ended with Embargo Act of 1807 which restricted trade with France and England and effectively stopped the important West Indies trade. Following the War of 1812 trade resumed but it did not expand beyond the level of the 1790s and increasing size of ships meant fewer vessels could navigate the Connecticut River to Middletown and Hartford. Middletown, which had specialized in the West Indies trade, declined as a commercial and shipping center while Hartford and New Haven continued to be important.

Increasing specialization of merchant activity was characteristic of the late eighteenth century. Wealthier merchants organized banks and the first three banks to incorporate in central Connecticut between 1792 and 1795 were located in Hartford, Middletown, and New Haven. Although banking provided local urban employment, it was limited in growth potential by the size and wealth of the local population. In contrast, the development of specialized insurance companies that operated almost immediately on a national scale provided significant urban growth potential. Beginning in 1795 the earliest insurance companies specialized in marine insurance, and each of the major commercial shipping towns, Hartford,

Middletown, and New Haven, had companies. However, with the declining importance of foreign trade in central Connecticut these companies had bleak prospects; the future of insurance lay in different directions, especially in fire insurance. In the second decade of the nineteenth century two of the later giants in insurance were incorporated in Hartford, the Hartford Fire Insurance Company in 1810 and the Aetna Insurance Company in 1819. Shortly after incorporation both companies set up an agency system throughout the United States.

In 1846 the insurance business expanded into life insurance with the incorporation of the Connecticut Mutual Life Insurance Company of Hartford. Numerous insurance companies were incorporated in Connecticut, but the most successful ones were in Hartford so that by 1900 the insurance business had become highly localized there. However, prior to 1850 the insurance business was not large and main office operations consisted of little more than a management official and several clerks. Therefore, insurance companies had little direct impact on the population growth of Hartford at this time.

In contrast to Middletown, which declined as a commercial center, Hartford and New Haven were able to solidify their commercial supremacy in central Connecticut from 1800 to 1850 by vigorous efforts at achieving key positions in the evolving transportation system and controlling a productive hinterland. Hartford's and New Haven's function as capitals of the Connecticut Colony had insured their location on the post roads that linked Boston and New York. Besides the post roads, which were usually in poor condition, other roads connected towns, but these were in even worse condition. Connecticut participated in the turnpike rage which swept the nation in the early nineteenth century and chartered 121 companies between 1792 and 1853, not all of which completed turnpikes. At one time during the turnpike rage eight turnpikes entered New Haven. Since most turnpikes were not significant improvements over the old country roads, they did not extend Hartford's and New Haven's control over productive farming hinterlands. These hinterlands usually did not extend beyond twenty miles by land, with extensions where connections could be made to river transportation. In this respect, the location of Hartford at the head of navigation of ocean-sailing vessels put its merchants in a strategic position to control a large productive hinterland bordering on the Connecticut River from Hartford north to Massachusetts, Vermont, and New Hampshire. Although turnpikes did not contribute to extending the range of movement of agricultural goods, they did make it feasible for many small factories to locate at water power sites away from navigable rivers.

During the first three decades of the nineteenth century aggressive actions of Hartford merchants in improving Connecticut River nagivation by constructing canals around falls on the river and financing steamboat companies to operate in the river and coastal trade were instrumental in the maintenance of Hartford's control of Connecticut valley trade in competition with Boston, Springfield, and New Haven. The latter city made an attempt to capture the valley trade by constructing a canal from New Haven, through the Farmington valley, and connecting with Northampton, Massachusetts, on the Connecticut River. This canal was constructed between 1825 and 1835 but it suffered numerous financial problems and was not successful in attracting trade. Although the canal effort was a failure, New Haven gained considerable urban growth possibilities with the steady expansion of its coastal trade. At first agricultural products from its local hinterland dominated the exports, but by 1850 shipments of manufactured products were becoming significant.

The opening of the Hartford and New Haven Railroad in 1838 signaled the end of inland water transportation in central Connecticut (Figure 4). Yet before 1850 the impact of railroads on the growth of cities was slight because the volume of industrial production was small and railroads did not offer significant advantages over other forms of transportation. It was not until after 1840 that the raw material needs of the brass industry around Waterbury were large enough to be a transportation problem. This was solved by completion of the Naugatuck Railroad in 1849 from Long Island Sound near Bridgeport through Waterbury and north to Winsted, Connecticut. Because the railroad improved transportation for the Naugatuck valley brass industry it facilitated the growth of the local manufacturing cities after 1850.

Hartford had railroad connections to Boston, New Haven, and New York by 1850, but it was not a major rail junction. New Haven

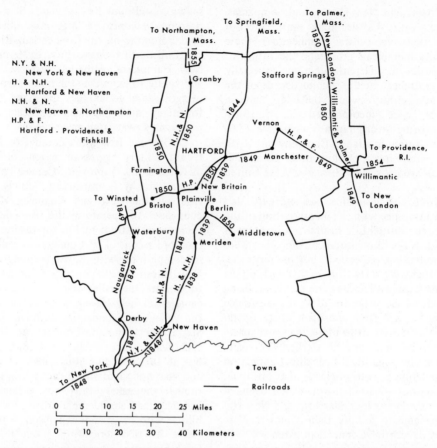

Figure 4. Central Connecticut railroads completed by 1850 (adapted from map by Sidney Withington, *The First Twenty Years of Railroads in Connecticut*).

benefited somewhat more from the railroad because it was the terminus of the Hartford and New Haven Railroad which was extended to Springfield in 1844. Two other railroads built prior to 1850 added to New Haven's importance as a rail center. In 1848 the New Haven and Northampton Railroad was completed from New Haven to Plainville along the route of the defunct canal, but it was not completed to Northampton until 1855. Also in 1848 the New York and New Haven was completed and it served as a collector of the railroads connecting the interior of western Connecticut with Long Island Sound.

Although New Haven developed into a railroad center and thereby benefited from employment in transportation and commerce it could never serve more than the markets of central Connecticut. Railroads required heavy

capital investment and therefore few cities could serve as major railroad centers for larger regions such as New England. By 1860 Boston's aggressive merchant capitalists had insured that it was the most important New England rail hub and to the west New York was dominant, also functioning as the national distributing point for domestic and foreign goods. Hence central Connecticut cities were relegated to being way stations on a larger transportation system dominated by Boston and New York.

THE URBAN EXPLOSION: 1850–1900

For people living in central Connecticut during the last half of the nineteenth century the explosive growth of cities must have been awesome. Lured by opportunities to make large profits in the dynamic American economy, industrialists started new factories and expanded old ones. Economic, political, and religious groups proclaimed their confidence in the future of the cities by constructing three to five story business blocks, impressive court houses and city halls, and elegant churches on the main streets. Street after street of identical wooden tenements were built barely fast enough to keep up with the hordes of immigrant workers arriving to work in the factories. Between 1850 and 1900 Hartford and New Haven grew by over 400 percent and New Britain and Waterbury grew by over 800 percent. Coinciding with this rapid population growth was an increasing concentration of population in a few towns in two counties; 66 percent of the Hartford County population lived in only four of the twenty-nine towns and 85 percent of the New Haven County population lived in just seven of the twenty-seven towns by 1900.

From 1840 to 1900 agricultural towns stabilized or declined in population as the number of farm workers remained relatively constant. Middlesex and Tolland counties were mostly occupied by farmers and their average decadal growth was 29 percent. The turnabout from agriculture to manufacturing in Connecticut was dramatic: in 1840 farm workers outnumbered those in manufacturing by two to one but by 1870 this situation had been reversed; there were twice as many factory workers as farmers, and by 1900 this ratio was four to one.

The type of manufacturing forming the base for urban growth varied from city to city. Of the cities larger than 20,000 population in 1900, Hartford and New Haven had the most diversified industrial base (Table 1). If Hartford had a specialty it was in the broad category of machine tools, machinery, and metal products such as firearms and screws. Production of bicycles and tricycles was also important in Hartford and accounted for about 9 percent of the manufacturing employment. In New Haven hardware and corset industries were large employers according to the published census sources but each accounted for less than 11 percent of total

Table 1. Manufacturing Employment in Selected Industries for Cities with 20,000 or More Population in 1900

City	Industry	Number of Employees	Percent of Total Manufacturing Employment
Hartford	Bicycles and tricycles	1,213	9
	Carriages and wagons	904	7
	Electrical apparatus and supplies	341	2
	Foundry and machine shop products	2,603	19
Meriden	Cutlery and edge tools	376	5
	Hardware	1,102	15
	Plated and britannia ware	2,048	27
New Britain	Foundry and machine shop products	540	6
	Hardware	4,111	49
New Haven	Boxes, fancy and paper	603	3
	Carriages and wagons	724	4
	Cars and general shop construction and repairs by steam railroad companies	1,102	5
	Corsets	1,493	7
	Foundry and machine shop products	911	4
	Hardware	2,110	10
	Sewing machines and attachments	529	3
Waterbury	Brass castings and brass finishing	2,238	15
	Brassware	2,616	18
	Buttons	479	3
	Foundry and machine shop products	720	5
	Stamped ware	820	5

manufacturing employment. Two very large factories in the city, not listed in the census because they were the only ones of their kind, were the New Haven Clock Company employing about 1,000 and the Winchester Repeating Arms Company employing about 1,500 workers. New Haven's function as a railroad center for central Connecticut is exhibited in the 1,102 employed by steam railroad companies.

In contrast to Hartford's and New Haven's varied industrial base which complemented their diverse functions in commerce and finance, the other three large cities were so specialized in manufacturing that nicknames were applied to them. Meriden was known as the "Silver City" for her production of plated silverware, New Britain was known as the "Hardware City" for her production of assorted hardware, and Waterbury was known as the "Brass City" for her production of rolled brass and diverse brass products.

The smaller industrial cities (7,500 to 20,000 population) also specialized in a few production lines. Bristol produced clocks and other brass products and Manchester concentrated on paper and textiles such as knitting, cotton yarn, and silk. City specialties in the Naugatuck River valley included rubber and brass products in Naugatuck; copper, brass, and wire in Ansonia; and iron and brass products and silver novelties in Derby. Wallingford was part of the silverware industry centered in Meriden and produced silver hollowware and eating utensils in addition to hardware. In Middlesex County, Middletown was the only significant manufacturing center and produced suspender webbing, belting, and rubber products and Tolland County's largest town, Vernon, specialized in woolen and silk manufacturing.

Perhaps more dramatic than the expansion in gross numbers of manufacturing employees and their concentration in selected cities was the growth in employment in individual companies to sizes fifty to one hundred times the characteristic employment size before 1850. One of the most dramatic portents of this enlarged scale of individual manufacturing enterprises occurred in 1862 at the funeral of Samuel Colt when 1,500 workmen from the Colt Patent Fire Arms Manufacturing Company in Hartford lined the pathway to his grave. Prior to 1850 companies were seldom larger than twenty employees except in the textile industry. In 1900 the 1,000 employees

of the New Haven Clock Company were not unusual, for the Winchester Repeating Fire Arms Company in New Haven had 1,500 employees and in Waterbury the Scovill Manufacturing Company employed 1,200 and the Waterbury Clock Company employed 700. Ansonia had three large factories—Ansonia Brass and Copper Company with 1,200 employees; Farrell Foundry and Machine Company with 600 employees; and Coe Brass Company with 1,500 employees.

The enlarged scale of manufacturing meant that even one or two companies which located in a small town or which grew from small to large size could significantly affect the town population size. The large size of factories now might inhibit their choice of location. If a factory needed 1,000 employees, the small, rural town was not a feasible location because it would be difficult to find laborers. Instead the large factory became restricted to choosing locations in large cities which had sufficient population from which workers could be drawn. These factors of industrial location tended to concentrate urban growth in the larger towns.

The rapid growth of Connecticut's population from 1850 to 1900 was based on foreign immigrants coming to work in the factories. There were only 38,518 foreign-born people in 1850, comprising 10 percent of Connecticut's population, but by 1900 the foreign-born population had increased sixfold to 238,210 and comprised 26 percent of the state's population. Connecticut's proportion of foreign born in 1900 was almost twice the United States proportion. Yet the impact of foreign immigration on Connecticut's population composition was even greater than these figures suggest. If in addition to foreign born we also count native-born people who have one or both parents born in a foreign country as having foreign immigrant background and term this group people of foreign parentage, then a majority—57 percent—of Connecticut's population in 1900 had a recent foreign immigrant background. At that date the principal places of birth of the foreign-born population in Connecticut were French Canada, England, Germany, Ireland, Italy, Poland, Russia, and Sweden; the Irish comprised twice as many as the next largest ethnic group, the Germans.

Within central Connecticut foreign-born immigrants were concentrated in the rapidly urbanizing counties of Hartford and New

Haven, although by 1900 all of the central Connecticut counties had between 20 and 30 percent foreign born. The cities were the immigrants' destinations; Manchester, New Britain, and the cities of the Naugatuck River valley (Ansonia, Derby, Naugatuck, and Waterbury) averaged one-third foreign born. Although Hartford and New Haven contained the largest number of foreign born their proportions were smaller than most other cities. They were the most diversified in employment and had numerous jobs outside the manufacturing sector in commerce, finance, and the professions. Immigrants were often excluded from non-manufacturing jobs because these presumed different types of skills than many immigrants had and discriminatory employment practices restricted immigrant entry.

The most important countries of birth of immigrants living in central Connecticut reflected the state distribution; Irish were the dominant group followed by Germans. However, immigrant groups differed in their choice of the large cities of Hartford, New Britain, New Haven, and Waterbury. The Irish were the dominant ethnic group in every city and comprised more than one-third of the foreign-born population except in New Britain where they were only one-fifth of the foreign born. In comparison with other cities, New Britain's immigrants were much more dominated by people of Swedish and Polish extraction whereas Italians were few. The latter were most heavily represented among the foreign born in New Haven. Except for the disparity in Italian representation, Hartford and New Haven had similar ethnic distributions. The main difference between Waterbury and other cities was its relatively high proportion of French Canadians and its somewhat low proportion of Germans. The most evenly distributed ethnic groups in relative terms were the English and Russians.

While white foreign immigrants were pouring into Connecticut between 1850 and 1900, the small black population merely doubled in size and declined slightly in proportion to the state population. Blacks comprised only 2 percent of Connecticut's population in 1900 whereas they were 10 percent of the United States population. Within central Connecticut blacks were concentrated in the industrial cities, especially Hartford and New Haven. In 1900 blacks were excluded from most manufacturing jobs, so Hartford and New Haven with

their more diversified employment base were more attractive to blacks than the specialized manufacturing cities.

The composition of the urban population of central Connecticut had been totally transformed between 1850 and 1900. By the latter date persons of foreign parentage were in the majority in Hartford, New Britain, New Haven, and Waterbury. Yet a prominent history written during this period of rapid growth of foreign immigrants, Trumbulls' *History of Hartford County,* was oblivious to this change in population except to note the organization of immigrant churches. Similarly, Clark's *History of Connecticut,* subtitled *Its People and Institutions,* published in 1914 did not even include a discussion of people of foreign parentage who were in the majority in 1900. It was almost as if the Connecticut Yankees were closing their eyes and hoping the immigrants would disappear.

Although immigrants were ignored by local Yankees except when the subject of criticisms motivated by fear of these strangers, immigrants were active in organizing their own churches, especially Roman Catholic, and a wide variety of charitable and self-help organizations. As each Catholic immigrant group became large enough to support its own church, a separate one was formed. Thus, in 1872 a priest was brought in to serve German Catholics in Hartford, in 1886 St. Anne's Church for French Catholics in Waterbury was organized, and in 1895 a Polish pastor was sent to New Britain by the Catholic diocese. Other denominations also served immigrant groups: German Lutheran churches appeared in New Haven and a Swedish Lutheran church and a German Baptist church were organized in New Britain. The purposes of the immigrant churches and self-help improvement organizations were not to challenge the social-political institutions that existed in the cities. For example, the Polish-Catholic pastor in New Britain, Reverend Lucyan Bojnowski, condemned labor agitators and was noted approvingly by an historian of Hartford County. In addition to charitable functions one of the purposes of the Catholic lay organization, the Knights of Columbus, first organized in New Haven in 1882, was to be an uplifting influence in its members' lives.

The most critical transportation problem posed by the rapidly expanding immigrant populations was movement within the cities, not between them. The innovation that was to meet the need for easy movement within cities was the horse-drawn street railway which was first introduced in New York in 1824. The Hartford and Wethersfield Horse Railroad Company, the first street railway to be incorporated in Connecticut, was organized in 1859. In 1860 the second street railway was incorporated in Connecticut to operate in New Haven and was called the Fair Haven and Westville Horse Railroad Company. Hartford added a second street railway in 1863 to run to West Hartford and in 1865 New Haven added two additional ones, but Middletown did not have a street railway until 1871 and Waterbury until 1886. Concentration of the earliest street railways in Hartford and New Haven was probably because they were the largest towns and each had a substantial middle class to demand the service. Sheer size was important in the adoption of this innovation because its success depended on attracting sufficient riders to make it profitable to run. But mere size was not sufficient unless a substantial middle class was present and this prerequisite Hartford and New Haven fulfilled with their large employment in commerce, finance, and professions. Usually the early street railways connected the central business districts with outlying areas and extension and development of lines was closely linked to the opening of new areas of middle class housing. Since central business districts were major middle class employment sites this class had easy access to their jobs from their home in the new "suburbs" and had the resources to pay the fares.

In contrast, manufacturing workers could not as easily move to the suburbs. Factories were not always near the center of town and often existed in several different districts; therefore access by street railway was difficult. Unstable employment with consequent shift in jobs meant that even if a worker found a home in the suburbs along a street railway that connected with the factory, this easy access could be nullified by a job change. Hence the manufacturing workers stayed in the central parts of the town near the factories in what has been called the pedestrian city. In the late nineteenth century this was an area with a radius of at most two miles from the center of town and is evidenced today by the large tenements and three-decker houses in the cities of central Connecticut. The street railway not only linked the new suburbs with central working and shopping areas but also the lines were extended to summer resort locations. By 1870 a horse railway connected downtown New Haven with Savin Rock and the shore at West Haven.

The first introduction of electric street railways in central Connecticut was at Derby in 1888, only two years following their United States debut in South Bend, Indiana. The significant improvement in comfort was probably a factor in the rapid changeover from horse to electric street railways; by 1895 all New Haven street railways used electricity. Electric street railways not only improved intraurban but also interurban transport. Shortly after 1900 many of the towns of central Connecticut were linked by electric railways.

Elaboration of the Urban-Industrial Region

A dominant motif of life in central Connecticut in the late nineteenth and twentieth century has been urban-industrial growth. Since the 1890s the urban counties of Hartford and New Haven have kept pace with the United States population growth rate and since 1940 Middlesex and Tolland counties have begun rapid growth. The basis for their growth has not been due to new economic activities. Instead they have been converted from minor agricultural and forested areas to residential sites for workers in the rest of central Connecticut and are merely participating in the same general urban growth that has been occurring in Hartford and New Haven counties.

Agriculture, the economic activity which had dominated the economy of central Connecticut for the first 200 years of settlement, employed only 1 percent of the workers in 1970. Its chief legacies are the numerous open fields in the valleys and on the hillsides which provide land suitable for residential developments. The industrial character of central Connecticut in 1970 is reflected in the fact that 34 percent of the workers are employed in manufacturing, whereas for the United States the figure is only 26 percent.

The amazing fact about the major urban centers of central Connecticut in 1970, those greater than 30,000 population, is the persistence of the urban-industrial landscape that was evident in 1845 (Figure 2) and more fully elaborated by 1900 (Figure 5). Most of those early manufacturing settlements have formed the lineaments of large cities and towns

of 1970 which stretch approximately on two axes between Manchester and Waterbury and between Hartford and New Haven. The other important urban axis of 1970 which was evident in 1845 but is not evident in the statistics of population size is the axis extending along the Naugatuck River valley between Waterbury and Derby. Major dropouts from the 1845 pattern were the carpet centers of Simsbury and the wool and cotton textile centers of Vernon and Stafford, all specializing in industries that would not form the base for central Connecticut's industrial growth.

Towns which exhibited extraordinary population growth between 1900 and 1970 were usually those adjacent to the large cities of Hartford—such as East and West Hartford—and of New Haven—such as Hamden and West Haven. Industrial activity in these adjacent towns was generally a spillover of the industrial developments in the largest two cities. But West Hartford could hardly be described as an industrial town even though there were 7,890 manufacturing jobs in 1967. Manufacturing is highly concentrated in the southeast part of town in an area called Elmwood which developed in the 1920s along the New York, New Haven, and Hartford Railroad lines; much of the rest of the town is a relatively high income residential district.

Yet 1970 is not just an enlarged replica of the nineteenth century urban-industrial region. A significant development is the conversion of forested and old agricultural towns to residential sites for people working in the greater

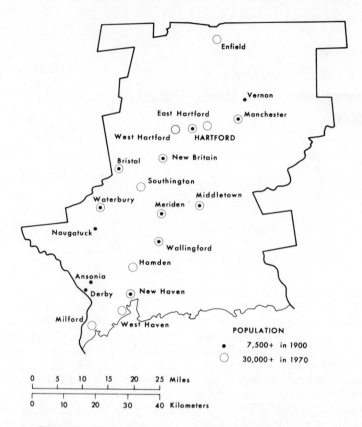

Figure 5.   Town and city population in 1900 and 1970.

urban region of central Connecticut. These towns—such as Haddam, Killingworth, Simsbury, or Tolland—were generally under 20,000 population in 1970 but also included a large town such as Enfield which had 46,189 people in 1970. Some of these towns—such as Enfield and Simsbury—also had small, old manufacturing settlements that are now insignificant. In Enfield's case thèse were Thompsonville and Hazardville and in Simsbury's case it was Tariffville.

Where West Hartford was a rapidly growing town beginning about 1900, towns such as Simsbury and East Windsor near Hartford and Woodbridge and North Branford near New Haven experienced large population increases after 1950 and Tolland, northeast of Hartford, grew extensively after 1960. Over time the towns with large population growth are found at increasing distances from the older industrial cities. In contrast the latter cities have stabilized in population—such as Waterbury after 1930—or declined in population—such as Hart-

ford and New Haven after 1950. The stabilization of population in older industrial cities is mainly a reflection of no space for growth and no pressure for increasing intensity of residential land use because of easy personal mobility provided by the auto. Bristol's continued population growth has been possible because it had large areas of undeveloped land. Declines in population such as Hartford and New Haven have experienced are a combination of the same factors of no space and no pressure for increasing intensity of land use coupled with extensive demolition of housing due to urban renewal and expressway construction.

To say that manufacturing in the various parts of the urban region is the same as in 1900 would be an overstatement. Yet in broad fashion the framework of manufacturing evident in 1900 exhibited an astounding persistence to 1970. The Hartford metropolitan area is still highly specialized in the manufacture of machinery, machine tools, and fabricated metal products such as screw machine products and wire products. The involvement in 1900 in the new industry of electrical products has now increased seventeenfold to 5,700 employees. In the New Britain metropolitan area hardware remains one of its most significant specialties. To this has now been added the production of metalworking machinery, probably a result of the general expansion of machinery industries in the nearby Hartford area. New Haven's metropolitan area continues the production of firearms and of fabricated metal products such as hardware and primary metal industries are a continuation of the pattern of foundries and copper and brass mills in the southern part of New Haven County. Alas, the carriage and wagon industry that New Haven was known for in 1900 was consigned to oblivion by the rise of the auto industry in Detroit. However, the 1,929 workers living in the New Haven area employed in the railroad industry testify to New Haven's modest hold on the regional rail network of central Connecticut. In the Waterbury metropolitan area the brass industry, including the production of brass and diverse brass products, remains important, as does the production of watches and clocks.

United Aircraft Corporation, the largest manufacturing company in central Connecticut, is the cinderella industry of the region and did not exist prior to 1925. Although its activities are obscured in published governmental statistical sources due to disclosure rules, information is available from the company. This corporation provides a case example of the link between present and past industrial developments in the region, the continuing interlocking nature of the metals and machinery industry, and the impact of industrial developments on urban growth.

Its origin dates from 1925 when Pratt and Whitney Aircraft was founded by Frederick Rentschler. His choice of Hartford was dictated by two considerations: (1) the Pratt and Whitney Tool Company had ideal plant facilities and money to invest, and (2) the Hartford area had numerous skilled metal craftsmen and machine fabricating and machine tool companies that could form an important subcontracting base. Aircraft engines were the major product of the company in its early years but expansion into wide applications of turbine power has now occurred. With 72

percent of its $2 billion of sales in 1972 concentrated in turbine power, the early focus of the company remains. Other major components of the company are still linked to aircraft and include flight systems such as helicopters, propellers, and airborne controls and space rocketry systems. The concentration of the corporation on fabricated metal and machinery provides a continuing link to associated industries in central Connecticut. The scope of this link is indicated by the fact that in 1972 it placed orders worth more than $200 million with other companies in Connecticut.

United Aircraft has made a significant contribution to urban growth and the dispersion of employment in central Connecticut and has provided an impetus for the dispersion of residential locations of its workers. Its employment in central Connecticut in 1973 totaled 41,800 and was concentrated in five towns—East Hartford (24,000), Middletown (3,800), North Haven (5,000), Southington (3,000), and Windsor Locks (6,000). Since the company did not exist before 1925 it is not surprising that all of the major employment locations are outside the old, large industrial cities; few large sites for industrial expansion were available in them by 1925.

Although urban-industrial growth has been a dominant characteristic of central Connecticut for more than a century, the growth of the insurance companies in Hartford now provides a significant complement to manufacturing. From the small offices of two insurance companies in 1820 the insurance companies had grown in number and size to such a scale that at the opening of the twentieth century the city of Hartford deserved the name of world's "Insurance City" according to a local author. That insurance was becoming an important source of local employment was testified to by the large insurance buildings in Hartford. The erection of two, four, and six story buildings had begun by the 1870s and the first quarter of the twentieth century saw more extensive expansion of office space. By 1971 Hartford County had 30,975 employees in the insurance industry, making it a significant base for the local economy, while New Haven County followed far behind in insurance employment with 3,659, and Middlesex and Tolland counties had negligible numbers.

Residential Territory in the 1970s

The urban landscape of central Connecticut's past, symbolized by the densely built-up industrial cities that grew rapidly in the latter half of the nineteenth century and early part of the twentieth century, has been transformed into an extensive urban region comprising most towns in central Connecticut. But this transformation has not obliterated the effects of past decisions. The old industrial centers and their dense residential districts have provided a frame for present diverse residential decisions including calculations about available jobs and cheap housing as well as calculations about avoiding all that is considered bad about cities.

LEGACY OF THE URBAN PAST

To enter the industrial cities of central Connecticut is to take a trip backward in time to the latter half of the nineteenth century and early decades of the twentieth century. Although new public housing projects, urban renewal, and expressway construction have obliterated some of the old housing, their past residential character remains vividly imprinted on the urban landscape. In the three largest cities—Hartford, New Haven, and Waterbury—over 60 percent of the housing was built before 1940, while in smaller cities such as New Britain, Naugatuck, Derby, Ansonia, and Meriden, from 45 to 60 percent was built before 1940.

The imperative of accessibility provided a major rationale for the construction of this housing. Multifamily housing built on narrow lots with little or no yard space is a dominant house type because land values were pushed up by the large number of persons competing for central locations near the jobs. Although large brick apartment buildings occur, it is the two and three story houses such as the double-decker and triple-decker houses that provide the consistent visual theme from city to city (Figure 6). Block after block of similarly styled housing testifies to the fact that homogeneous housing tracts were not inventions of twentieth century suburbia.

Most of the old factories in the industrial cities are located in the river valleys and near the cores of the cities factories and housing intermingle on the streets (Figure 7). Much of the other multifamily housing clings to the hillsides overlooking the factories. The close proximity between residence and job in the past often meant a walking distance of a block to at most one mile. Even today near the cores of these cities between 10 and 25 percent of the people walk to work.

Complementing the workers' housing in the industrial cities are the remnants of the middle and upper middle class residential districts; large, well-built homes on tree-lined streets typify this housing. In some cases the old high prestige districts retain their character—such as near Asylum Avenue in Hartford or southwest of New Britain's central business district (Figure 8)—and in other cases the housing has been converted to multifamily occupancy or nonresidential uses.

Figure 6.   Triple-decker housing in New Britain (top) and Waterbury (bottom).

If the large concentrations of old housing in the industrial cities are a legacy of the urban past, it seems a contradiction in terms to find that they also contain the largest concentration of new housing. To be sure, in relative terms the old industrial cities have low percentages of housing built during the sixties, usually under 25 percent, but it is the large cities of Hartford, New Haven, Waterbury, and New Britain that had the greatest amount

Figure 7. Housing and the factory (Waterbury).

of new housing construction during the sixties, not the rapidly growing residential towns. This new housing was single family dwellings built on vacant land left on the periphery of the city and new apartments near the center of the city built on land cleared by urban renewal programs. Except for some instances of upper class apartment buildings replacing slum housing, most of the recent housing construction in the industrial cities reinforces their past character. Public housing replaces deteriorated housing in the cores and new low cost workers' dwellings are built on the peripheral vacant land (Figure 9).

Although the physical legacy of the urban past remains strongly imprinted on the landscape of central Connecticut, past inhabitants have died, moved away, or remain as the aged. Since most housing was originally constructed for manufacturing workers, it was low cost housing. The housing built for the middle class is no longer demanded by them because it is old and not in the style demanded today— a detached house on a large lot. Therefore,

the old industrial cities contain extensive low cost rental housing while the new, high cost rental housing is found in the immediately surrounding towns. As in the past the housing in the older industrial cities is attractive to factory workers for these cities still contain many industrial jobs. The Naugatuck River valley cities, New Britain, Bristol, and Meriden average about 27 percent of their workers employed in manufacturing occupations, while Hartford and New Haven with their more diversified economic structure have a somewhat lower percentage (21 percent).

What most distinguishes the older industrial cities from surrounding towns is that the former are the homes of the poor, the black, the Puerto Rican, and the foreign-born immigrant. The large amount of low cost housing combined with sizable employment opportunities in close proximity form the positive attractions of the older cities for the poor, while discriminating zoning laws and refusal to construct federally subsidized housing outside the older cities ensure that the poor cannot find

Figure 8.   An old prestige district (New Britain).

suitable housing elsewhere (Figure 10). Even within a city such as Hartford there is a differential location of income groups with the very lowest income families concentrated in the oldest housing near the downtown or in public housing near an industrial district in the southwest portion of the city and a small isolated cluster of high income families on the west side of the city (Figure 10).

If you are black or Puerto Rican your most likely residence is an industrial city, whether you are poor or not (Figure 11). Blacks are overwhelmingly concentrated in the cities of Hartford and New Haven and this relative concentration is greater in 1970 than it was at the turn of the century. In Hartford County the percentage of the county's blacks in the city of Hartford increased from 59 to 82 and in New Haven County the percentage of the county's blacks in the city of New Haven increased from 57 to 64. Modest numbers of blacks in towns adjacent to the two large cities are not indicative of racial integration but

merely represent extensions of black residential areas across city boundaries. Although Puerto Ricans are concentrated in the industrial cities their distribution among them is more even than the black distribution (Figure 11).

With the largest number of blacks and Puerto Ricans of any town or city in central Connecticut, the problems facing Hartford's two minorities are microcosms of regionwide issues. Although it is true that the majority of blacks who recently (1965–1970) migrated to Hartford came from the South, the common view that blacks are a displaced rural folk is not accurate. Only 11 percent of the blacks in Hartford in 1970 were recent migrants from other parts of the United States, no different than the percentage for the city as a whole. In contrast, Puerto Ricans in Hartford have arrived in large numbers very recently; during this same five years period (1965–1970) almost 30 percent of them migrated from Puerto Rico.

Both groups are disadvantaged in education and income compared to the rest of the popula-

Figure 9. Modern factory workers' housing in New Britain (top) and Waterbury (bottom).

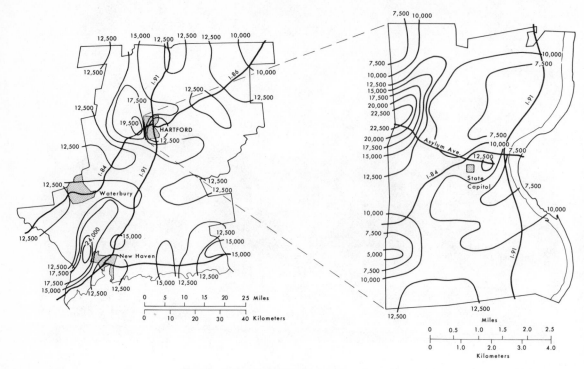

Figure 10. Mean family income in 1969.

tion. Although the median education completed by blacks in Hartford is close to the figure for the city as a whole it is two years behind the figure of 12.3 years for the metropolitan area. Their income deficit is substantial; they make about $5,000 less per family than the typical Hartford area family. Compared to blacks, Puerto Ricans are in even worse shape. They are less educated and have lower incomes than blacks; the gap in education is about two years per person and the gap in income is about $2,000 per family. The serious portent for the future is that the disadvantaged black and Puerto Rican populations are dominated by young people who will have few educational and financial resources to launch them on their careers. About one-half of the black and Puerto Rican population are under eighteen years whereas in the rest of the city's population only about one-fourth are under eighteen.

Within Hartford blacks (Figure 12) and Puerto Ricans (Figure 13) are highly segregated from the rest of the population and their main clusters are segregated from each other. In the case of the black population the highly segre-

gated housing pattern is a reflection of pervasive discrimination in housing. Hartford's housing pattern is typical of numerous cities and towns across the United States for the last one hundred years. In the all-black areas of a city poorer blacks usually occupy the older housing near the central business district and the middle and upper income blacks occupy better housing more distant from the central business district. The latter groups usually form the leading edge of the expanding black housing area. Whether or not the Puerto Rican housing situation develops like the black population's remains to be seen.

Just as they have for the last one hundred years, the industrial cities of central Connecticut continue to serve as the ports of entry of foreign-born immigrants to the region. Hartford was the main entry point between 1960 and 1970 followed by the next three largest cities, New Haven, Waterbury, and New Britain. Contrary to what blacks may anticipate, the second and third generations of these immigrants who attain financial security can expect to find housing in the growing towns outside of the old industrial cities. The two largest

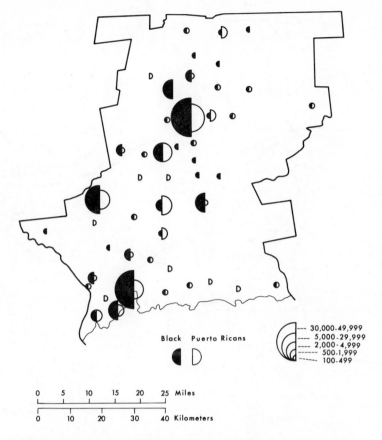

Figure 11. Black and Puerto Rican population by town in 1970.

European-born ethnic groups in central Connecticut are the Italians and the Polish and their concentrations in 1970 are remarkably similar to 1900. The Italians are especially found in New Haven and the nearby towns of West Haven and Hamden and in Hartford and Waterbury, with the chief change since 1900 being the development of a cluster in New Britain. Polish immigrants in 1970 are heavily concentrated in New Britain with a secondary concentration about half as large in Hartford, virtually identical to the situation in 1900.

ACHIEVING URBAN PASTORALISM

If the old industrial towns that dot central Connecticut are the pride of the nineteenth century they now are at worst despised and at best tolerated by the nonpoor. Backs are turned toward the industrial cities and the nonpoor look toward the country as the place to achieve

the good life. Real estate ads in the *Hartford Courant* for new housing in the 1960s and 1970s provide a barometer for estimating what people hope to achieve by living outside the industrial cities.

The country environment that is being sold to purchasers of single family homes in the Hartford area is pictured as being wooded and hilly. Descriptions of the housing and its environment wax enthusiastic about "a breathtaking panoramic view," "an almost unbelievably wooded area, rising and sloping in the midst of open fields," living "in the wooded hills, . . . off Goose Lane," being "nestled in the grandeur of the gently contoured landscape of Wethersfield," "a lush beautifully wooded area," a community "located in quiet elegance in the rolling Connecticut countryside," and "strolls in the woods." To remind prospective homeowners about woods and hills surrounding the homes names may be attached to develop-

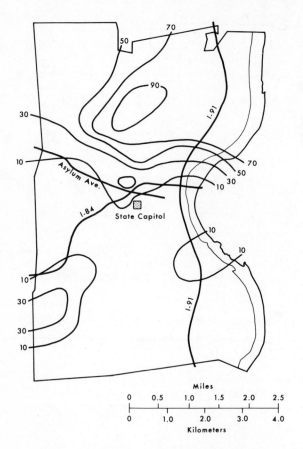

Figure 12. Percent population black in Hartford.

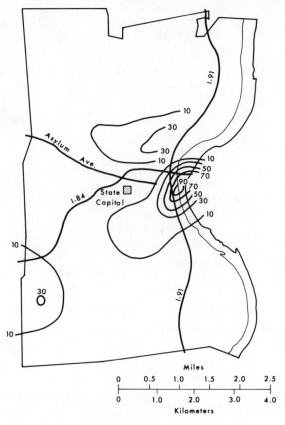

Figure 13. Percent population Puerto Rican in Hartford.

ments such as Maplewood, Hickory Hills, Foot Hills Grove, Red Mountain Estates, Mountain Farms, and Pinewood Acres.

Outside the crowded industrial cities a peaceful, secluded environment can be purchased. Just as on the farm, your home is situated on land that is measured in acres not square feet as in the city. Never mind that you may be buying one-quarter or one-half acre lots, the thought of living on your own "acre" stimulates images of country living. Although no one takes it literally, it is also nice to imagine that one lives like a country gentleman in Birch Hill Estates, Berkeley Estates, Rocky Hill Estates, Red Mountain Estates, or Windsor Estates, even though the "estate" is one acre or less. Imagery of country living even includes symbols of the West; houses are described as ranches or raised ranches. However, this country living is without the real rustics, for if "city water" or "city sewers" are available these are

proudly proclaimed in the real estate ads. The historical heritage, if appealed to in the ads, reaches past the dominant feature of central Connecticut's economic life of the last 150 years—its industrial development—to colonial times when people lived in small villages. Today you can live in a small community of homes in Colonial Village, Windsor Village, Village Gate, or Winthrop Village.

People do not have to live in single family detached homes to enjoy the perceived benefits of country living in the Hartford area; it is also available in apartment developments. In these environments you can "just imagine sitting in your living room looking out at the reflections on the lakes" or "wander down a nature trail and breathe in the solitude of woods and wildlife." Names of apartment complexes evoke a variety of images that are not quite country but definitely not city. Apartments are available in Griswold Gardens, Lakeview, Clearview Gardens, Meadowview, and Park Ridge. It is even possible to live on an estate such as Ramblestone Estates or in a Manor House while living in an apartment. If apartment living carries connotations of the city with its high density living, you can be reassured that in fact you live in a small village setting such as Fountain Village, Gaslight Village, or Nutmeg Village where people are not part of an anonymous crowd.

Although environments of apartments do not precisely duplicate detached single family homes, the recently popular condominiums are being sold as having everything single family homes offer. You can live in "a true country setting," "in the glen," or on an "untouched hill rolling gently toward the Connecticut River." Images of woods and hills abound in condominium developments such as Timber Ridge, Currier Woods, Farmington Woods, and Knob Hill. Condominiums may even call to mind "estate" living with development names such as Royal Villas and Country Squire. An open space atmosphere is heavily stressed and visions of large scale development may be muted by using names evoking images of the intimate, small town village life of colonial times—Milestone Commons, Northfield Green, Talcott Village, and Spring Lake Village.

Although seekers of housing may not literally believe all that real estate ads proclaim, the consistency of the ads over time suggests that they are touching popular, deeply felt demands of residents in the Hartford area and the rest of central Connecticut. From the viewpoint of residents in the region, the pre-eminent role of towns outside the old industrial cities is to serve as living environments that are not the city. They do not have old grimy factories, tenements, poor people, blacks and Puerto Ricans, and slums. Residential environments of the nonpoor are peaceful, elegant, wooded, hilly, estatelike, and replicate the intimate village life of colonial times.

If this is the idealistic image of the urban pastoral environment outside the old industrial cities, it also can be characterized in other mundane but significant ways. An obvious characteristic is that most housing was built since 1940. Near Hartford even the long settled towns of Windsor, East Windsor, and Wethersfield, and near New Haven the towns of Woodbridge, North Haven, and Branford, have less than 40 percent of their housing

built before 1940. Housing construction has frequently obliterated or obscured whatever remained of the old town centers with their stylized greens, churches, meeting houses, and colonial homes. In fact, in many towns surrounding the older industrial cities over one-third of the housing was built since 1960. Even towns which had small, old industrial centers—such as Vernon with its Rockville section—can have their whole character dramatically transformed by new construction so that in 1970 almost half of its housing was built since 1960. The new housing and commercial developments along Route 83 in Vernon are so dominant to the eye that the old Rockville section on the sides of the hills along the Hockanum River seems quaint.

The dominant type of housing in these residential towns outside the industrial cities is the single family detached house sitting on an expanse of grass. In most towns over 70 percent and in some as high as 90 percent are this type. The only breaks in the single family dwelling landscape are isolated pockets of aged, multifamily housing near old factory sites such as Tariffville in Simsbury, Rockville in Vernon, or Thompsonville in Enfield (Figure 14) and new apartment complexes and condominiums. If there is any large age difference in the residential towns it is between the few longtime elderly residents and the many families with children. The latter move to these towns for the single family residential environments they provide. Yet those residential towns that grew rapidly between 1940 and 1960—such as Bloomfield, Newington, and Wethersfield near Hartford, and Branford and East Haven near New Haven—already exhibit a population moving into middle age.

Although the poorest people in central Connecticut tend to live in the old industrial cities, the other towns do not comprise a landscape with a uniform class structure. They vary substantially in luxuriousness of housing and their residents differ in terms of type of work and income. Two large sectors of high paid workers living in expensive housing are found in the region—one west of Hartford including the towns of West Hartford, Avon, and Simsbury; and the other west of New Haven including the towns of Orange, Woodbridge, and Bethany. Workers in these towns are heavily represented in the decisionmaking and nonroutine information processing jobs (quinary occupations)

Figure 14. Housing near an old factory site, Thompsonville in Enfield Town.

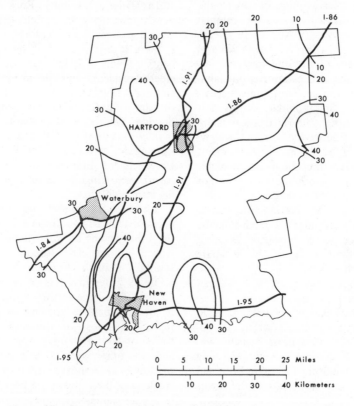

Figure 15. Percent population employed in quinary occupations.

in the financial, insurance, manufacturing, and state government sectors of the economy (Figure 15). Average incomes in the towns were over $17,000 per year in 1969 (Figure 10) and the typical house was built on a large lot set among the rolling tree-covered hills and had a value of over $35,000.

Blue collar and clerical workers tend to live in the towns north and east of Hartford and New Haven. Average family income was below $15,000 in 1969 in towns such as Enfield, Suffield, and East Windsor near Hartford or North Haven, Wallingford, and Durham near New Haven (Figure 10) and consequently housing was generally valued below $30,000. Although the urban pastoral environments of large areas include tract type single family dwellings, such as in the valleys of the Quinnipiac and Connecticut rivers, many blue collar and clerical workers have achieved a housing environment among the tree-covered hills above the valleys.

A Noncentric Urban Region

If central Connecticut in the late nineteenth and early twentieth centuries could be described as a multicentered urban-industrial region, this late twentieth century urban region is amorphous. It is an illusion that the large industrial cities of Hartford, New Haven, New Britain, Waterbury, Bristol, and Meriden are nuclei to which all activity such as work, shopping, and entertainment are oriented. This illusion is fostered by the appearance of their high density housing and specialized land uses of commerce and industry in their cores which are remnants of nineteenth century developments. In fact central Connecticut is characterized by extensive population movements between small towns, between small town and large city, and between large cities. There are no cores in central Connecticut. Rather there are specialized land use activities which the population makes use of; the region is *noncentric.*

The development of public transportation systems with the horse street railway, then the electric street railway, and finally the bus served as a reminder to people that they were interdependent. However, the attraction of the freedom of individual mobility possible with the auto has proved irresistible. The only cities with more than 10 percent of their workers traveling to jobs by public transportation are Hartford with 26 percent, New Haven with 15 percent, and Waterbury with 11 percent.

The commuting patterns of workers are most revealing. The large central city has usually been considered the source of employment for its residents and for those who live outside it, but these commonly accepted generalizations do not apply to central Connecticut. In the six metropolitan areas of Bristol, Hartford, Meriden, New Britain, New Haven, and Waterbury between 30 and 46 percent of the workers living in the central city commute to jobs outside it, and except for the New Haven area, fewer than 30 percent of the workers living outside the central cities work in them.

The movement of people in central Connecticut in 1970 provides another indication of the wide-ranging mobility patterns of the journey to work and movement in general; the area is laced with flows of people with no dominant core (Figure 16). Hartford appears to be a modest core but its position is exaggerated by its location at the intersection of two interstate highway systems carrying traffic past Hartford—Interstate 91 running north-south through part of the Connecticut River valley and Interstates 84 and 86 running south-west-northeast connecting New York State and western Connecticut with eastern Massachusetts.

Yet the commuting patterns are quite understandable because of the widespread use of the auto by workers, freedom of location for industry provided by the truck, and the demand by industry for one story factories on large sites. Manufacturing jobs are especially dispersed throughout Hartford and New Haven counties. The old, large industrial cities of Hartford, New Britain, Waterbury, and New

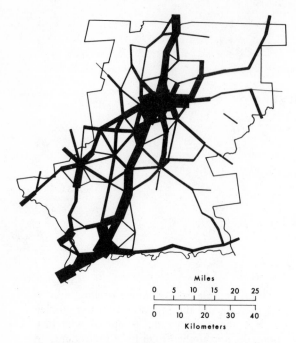

Miles

0   5   10   15   20   25

0   10   20   30   40
Kilometers

Figure 16. Daily person movements in 1970 (adapted from map prepared by Connecticut Department of Transportation).

Haven each have over 10,000 manufacturing jobs but twelve other towns have between 5,000 and 10,000 manufacturing jobs and fourteen towns have between 1,500 and 5,000 manufacturing jobs.

The diminished relative importance of the large industrial cities as sources of manufacturing employment is being reinforced by the establishment of industrial parks, particularly in Hartford and New Haven counties. In 1972, according to a survey by the Connecticut Development Commission, Hartford, Meriden, New Britain, and Waterbury had a total of only five industrial parks with sixty-four industries and Bristol and New Haven had no industrial parks with companies on site. In contrast the towns outside of these large industrial cities had a total of fifty-two industrial parks with 269 industries. The extensive acreage available in industrial parks outside the larger cities can accommodate much future industrial expansion.

Commercial developments in central Connecticut also contribute to the noncentric nature of this urban region. The innovation in retailing of the planned shopping center first arrived in modest numbers in central Connecticut after 1950. This innovation consists of a group of commercial establishments which are planned, developed, and managed as a unit and are situated on a plot of land that includes off-street parking. The development of planned shopping centers is directly related to the increased reliance of people on the auto as a means of travel and to the growth of population outside the industrial cities. For a planned shopping center of modest size containing perhaps twenty stores or more, the population outside the industrial cores had to reach a size large enough to support the shopping center in competition with the central business district stores. It is significant that one of the first planned shopping centers to be developed in central Connecticut was the Bishop's Corner Shopping Center in West Hartford in 1953. West Hartford had over 44,000 people by 1953 and offered the further advantage of containing a large population with a high per capita disposable income.

Because of the dispersed urban population in central Connecticut few regional shopping centers (forty or more stores) had been developed by 1970. One of the three largest shopping centers was in Milford, a city that grew from 12,660 in 1930 to 50,858 in 1970. The other two were in Waterbury which, in contrast to Hartford and New Haven still had vacant land outside the old industrial core available for shopping centers. The remaining planned shopping centers in central Connecticut are either subregional (twenty to thirty-nine stores) or very local (ten to nineteen stores) in market area. They are concentrated in Hartford and New Haven counties and are generally located in towns outside the larger industrial cities or on the periphery of the industrial city but within its corporate boundary. The immediate Hartford area is a good example of the development of planned shopping centers; none with ten or more stores was located in the city of Hartford in 1970, but West Hartford had four and Wethersfield, Windsor, and East Hartford each had one.

With the development of planned shopping centers outside industrial cores it is to be expected that old central business districts, though still the largest commercial centers, contain a relatively small proportion of total retail activity. In the metropolitan areas of Hartford, Meriden, New Britain, New Haven, and Waterbury the central business district retail sales comprise less than 20 percent of metropolitan sales.

Major characteristics of central Connecticut—journey to work, travel, manufacturing location, and commercial activity—indicate that the urban region is no longer organized around the old industrial cities that came to prominence during the nineteenth century. It is not that more large nodes of activity have emerged. Rather, what happened is that many nodes of specialized activities have emerged such as shopping centers and industrial parks. Furthermore, numerous activities have no nodal character or are not concentrated; much retail activity occurs on highway commercial strips and industries are scattered throughout the region outside industrial parks. The result in central Connecticut is an amorphous urban region characterized by extensive movement among a wide range of towns; a noncentric urban region has emerged.

From the Present to the Future

Central Connecticut has not emerged in the twentieth century as a new form of urban settlement that merely replaces the nineteenth century version. Just as in the past, central Connecticut is in a state of continuous flux. The question facing its residents is whether a quality living environment can be achieved in this ever-changing region.

POPULATION GROWTH

One of the most significant forces of change in central Connecticut is the sheer growth in population that is expected by the year 2000. Between 1970 and 2000 the population will grow by 1.2 million people, an increase of 69 percent, with the bulk (38 percent) of the total increase occurring in the Capitol Planning Region around Hartford. Yet the percentage increase for every planning region will be greater than 56 percent and therefore population growth will continue to be extensive in those areas which have been the traditional growth centers since the nineteenth century, approximately equal to Hartford and New Haven counties. An intimation of what may be the future urban growth centers is provided by the large percentage increases expected in the Midstate (130 percent) and Connecticut River Estuary (121 percent) Planning Regions in Middlesex County.

Further intimation of the character of this population growth is gained by examining recent and projected growth of selected towns and cities (Figure 17). Three types of cities

and towns can be distinguished. The first type includes the old, large industrial cities of Hartford, New Haven, Waterbury, and New Britain. These cities have had only minor fluctuations in population since 1940 and will capture insignificant amounts of future population growth. The second type of town is adjacent to one of the large industrial cities such as West Hartford and Wethersfield near Hartford and North Haven and Hamden near New Haven. They were the first to see dramatic gains in population when residents of central Connecticut moved to low density residential environments. Most of them were still showing large gains in population between 1940 and 1970 but their growth will be slowing now because most suitable vacant land has been occupied and much of their contribution to population growth will be completed by 1980. The growth in population between 1980 and 2000 will occur in "rural residential towns" such as Simsbury, Tolland, Woodbridge, and Killingworth where population will grow by 60 percent or more during the last two decades of the twentieth century.

Pressure on open space will be intense in the rural towns and critical for the people of central Connecticut. These towns contain large areas of open space suitable for recreation and water resources. If the population grows as projected then open space resources will be pushed farther away from masses of people necessitating ever longer trips for open space recreation. The irony of the rural towns is that many of the newcomers are moving in because

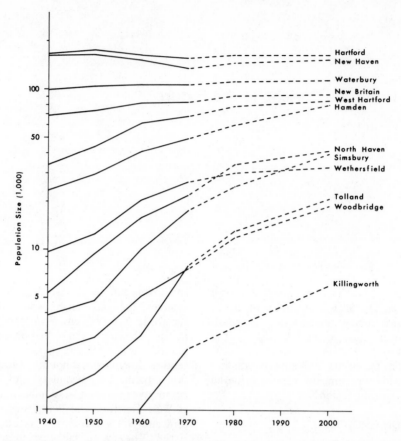

Figure 17. Population of selected towns and cities, 1940–1970, and projections for 1980 and 2000.

of the vast expanses of open space, most of which will be eliminated by the year 2000.

Continued stability of population size in the large industrial cities and the stabilizing of population in adjacent towns by 1980 will probably ease pressure on remaining open spaces. As some of the older two and three family housing is replaced by somewhat higher density housing, the potential exists for adding parks and playgrounds. The latter open space facilities are more usable by the poor in the industrial cities who do not have cars than are more distant parks outside the cities.

Expanding populations in the rural residential towns will increase demands for improved highways but satisfying this demand will involve hard decisions among limited options. Since the wide dispersal of jobs precludes any simple core-oriented highway system, the alternative is a grid of limited access highways covering central Connecticut which by their

nature will destroy the small town atmosphere of the rural residential towns. Furthermore, the construction of highways may only intensify developmental pressures on the rural towns by other residents attracted to highly accessible towns, commerce attracted by markets, and industry attracted by cheap land and good transportation.

REGIONAL ECONOMY

Can the expanding population of central Connecticut look forward to a rosy economic future? As a state Connecticut does an extraordinary job of providing its residents with high incomes. Between 1964 and 1970 Connecticut ranked first in the United States in per capita personal income and third in per household effective buying income. The four counties in central Connecticut had median family incomes in 1969 which were between $1,700 and

$2,500 higher than the United States median family income. Even the very poor are underrepresented in central Connecticut; each county has about half the United States proportion (20 percent) of families with incomes under $5,000. Every county had more than 60 percent of its families with incomes above $10,000 compared to 47 percent of United States' families.

The general wealth that prevails for so many of central Connecticut's residents is moderated somewhat by high living costs. For most families the cost of living is probably about 9 percent higher than the United States urban average, if figures for the Hartford area are representative. Nevertheless, even adjusting for higher living costs the median family income in 1969 was still larger than the United States figure by $780 in New Haven County and $1,471 in Hartford County with the other counties falling in between. Interestingly, the cost of living for higher income families is relatively lower than for other families in central Connecticut.

High incomes for the residents of central Connecticut should continue for the immediate future. During the seventies average annual percentage growth in personal income is expected to be 2.5 times the annual population growth rate in the combined Hartford-New Britain metropolitan areas and 3.3 times the annual population growth rate in the combined New Haven-Waterbury-Meriden metropolitan areas (Table 2). Barring unanticipated economic dislocations, the goal of maintaining a relatively high degree of affluence seems assured.

Table 2. Average Annual Percentage Growth Rates Reported by Connecticut Bank and Trust Company

	Metropolitan Areas			
	Hartford-New Britain		New Haven-Waterbury-Meriden	
	1960-1970	1970-1980	1960-1970	1970-1980
Population	1.8	2.7	1.2	1.7
Personal Income (constant dollars)	6.2	6.7	5.2	5.6

All major sectors of the economy in the major metropolitan areas should contribute to the projected growth in personal income according to figures reported by the Connecticut Bank and Trust Company. It is expected that the growth rate of earnings from manufacturing in the seventies will be substantially higher than in the sixties, placing it among the leading growth sectors of the economy. The extraordinary expansion of services and government during the sixties will moderate somewhat during the seventies but each will remain leading growth sectors. If the projections of the share of total increased earnings contributed by each sector are correct, manufacturing will remain a dominant force in the economy of central Connecticut. In fact the concentration of manufacturing in the top industries of central Connecticut in 1970 will probably increase by 1980. The Hartford and New Britain metropolitan areas will continue, if not actually increase, their specialization in transportation equipment, primarily aircraft engines and related flight and power systems.

Continued importance of manufacturing in central Connecticut, especially the concentration on industries subject to wide fluctuations in demand such as industrial machinery and defense-related industries, means that sharp swings in the unemployment rate will keep on plaguing the area. The experience of the 1960s is illustrative. In 1960-1961 the United States had a recession and unemployment in selected central Connecticut labor markets was high, ranging from 4 percent in the Hartford area to 12 percent in the Bristol area. Following this recession, unemployment dropped and reached a low point during the big Vietnam War build-up of 1965-1968. Unemployment again rose during the recession of 1970-1971 and reached a low of 7 percent in the Hartford area and an astounding high of 22 percent in the Bristol area. Labor market areas with the lowest unemployment and mildest fluctuations in unemployment were the Hartford and New Haven areas, where manufacturing in 1970 comprised only 29 and 24 percent of total employment, respectively. In contrast the Bristol and New Britain labor market areas had 50 and 49 percent respectively employed in manufacturing in 1970 and experienced the wildest fluctuations in unemployment.

Counterbalancing the instability of manufacturing in central Connecticut is the solid growth of the insurance industry. In 1971 about 2 percent of all United States employment was in the insurance industry, but in the Hartford labor market area the figure was 10 percent. Insurance employment has increased steadily; between 1960 and 1971 employment grew from 25,000 to 34,500, an increase of 38 percent. Because they operate nationwide, the insurance companies provide a secure export base for the Hartford area economy. Their impact is suggested by data for 1970 reported by Hellman and Sullivan showing that Connecticut-based insurance companies invested $327 million in the state above what was collected as insurance premiums from state residents.

INEQUALITY OF PROSPERITY

The relatively high degree of affluence in central Connecticut is not equally distributed among cities and towns. There are even signs the gap between various cities and towns is growing rather than lessening. Recent trends in the location of employment opportunities provide one indication of the changes which are occurring in the region.

Probably the most dramatic alteration in the location of jobs in central Connecticut is the rapid decline of manufacturing in the old large industrial cities. Between 1947 and 1967 the six cities of Bristol, Hartford, Meriden, New Britain, New Haven, and Waterbury lost from 24 to 34 percent of their manufacturing jobs. In absolute terms this represented a total decline of 45,192 manufacturing jobs in the six cities during the twenty year period, an average of 2,260 per year. Hartford and New Haven, which had the largest manufacturing employment in 1947, also suffered the largest losses.

Compounding the loss of manufacturing jobs in Hartford and New Haven was their respective decline in retail employment of 21 percent and 15 percent during the period 1948-1967. Part of this can, of course, be attributed to their loss of population. In addition, growth of planned shopping centers outside densely built up portions of the largest industrial cities not only meant newly developing residential areas were being served by different forms of retail activity, but that some shoppers who formerly patronized retail activities in the old industrial city could now patronize planned shopping centers. Industrial cities still growing in population and with vacant land available for shopping centers could exhibit growth in retail employment. Bristol was such a city and showed the largest gain in retail employment in absolute and relative terms. Wholesale employment, which traditionally has been concentrated in the largest cities, revealed a somewhat different pattern of change during the period 1948-1967. Hartford experienced a modest growth of 736 in wholesale employment but New Haven had a dramatic decline of 1,790 employees.

The changing importance of large industrial city employment relative to respective county employment adds a further dimension to understanding trends in inequality of prosperity. In addition to experiencing absolute declines in manufacturing jobs between 1947 and 1967, all of the large industrial cities dropped substantially in the proportion of the county manufacturing jobs contained in them. In the case of the Hartford County cities of Bristol, Hartford, and New Britain the magnitude of the decline was enhanced because total manufacturing jobs in the county increased significantly from 113,840 in 1947 to 150,800 in 1967. New Haven County cities of Meriden, New Haven, and Waterbury did not decline relatively as much because manufacturing employment in the county increased only slightly from 110,611 in 1947 to 114,800 in 1967.

Equal in significance to the relative decline of manufacturing in the industrial cities is the relative decline of Hartford and New Haven as major retail and wholesale centers. As retail centers we can anticipate that within the next twenty years or so Hartford and New Haven will be merely equals with large planned regional shopping centers that will be constructed.

Wholesale activity is operating under different considerations. The decisionmaking and control of wholesale trade may remain in Hartford and New Haven because they are the financial and office centers of the region. However, the warehousing and physical distribution of products is leaving these cities for highly accessible sites along the major expressways of central Connecticut such as Interstates 84 and 91. In the past a location within the two largest cities was the most accessible place for distribution to the region because so much of the population and economic activity was centered around them. With the spread of population, commerce, and industry throughout central Connecticut it is equally easy, if not easier, to reach customers from locations outside of Hartford and New Haven. Large amounts of cheap land needed for one story warehouses and distribution facilities make a location in Hartford or New Haven infeasible.

In spite of declines in manufacturing, retail, and wholesale activity in Hartford and New Haven, their future is not bleak. They are undergoing an alteration of their character which is consistent with their roles for the last three centuries as centers of ideas, decisionmaking, and control for central Connecticut as well as within the national context. Recent data reported by the Connecticut Labor Department show that total employment in both cities is increasing; between 1965 and 1972 Hartford's employment grew by 14 percent and New Haven's employment grew by 3 percent. These increases came at the same time manufacturing declined by 32 percent in Hartford and 23 percent in New Haven.

Growth in nonmanufacturing employment is significant in the city of Hartford; in the period 1965 to 1972 the number of jobs added in the nonmanufacturing sector totaled 23,390. Jobs being added are white collar office employment in finance, insurance, and government and service employment. Government employment in Hartford, the capitol, increased by 9,910 and the combined increase in finance and insurance was 7,730. Employment in services associated with the white collar industries jumped by 6,530.

The continued presence of the insurance industry in Hartford is critical for the future economic health of the city because it is a significant source of property taxes and jobs for city residents. The Hartford area insurance industry is primarily concentrated in the city of Hartford; it had 87 percent of the area's total industry employment of 33,905 in 1972. An indication of the commitment of the insurance industry to remain in Hartford is provided by a Connecticut Department of Commerce study showing that during the year 1972 insurance companies had planned, under construction, or completed office space totaling 1.8 million square feet and valued at $61.3

million. Connecticut General Life Insurance Company, which moved to the adjacent town of Bloomfield in 1957, is the only major company that has left the city.

The decline of manufacturing, retail, and wholesale activity in the old industrial cities with an expansion of manufacturing outside these cities and the growth of white collar employment in Hartford and New Haven pose serious problems for central Connecticut because these changes are occurring in concert with important population dynamics. The nonpoor are moving to urban pastoral environments outside the cities and the poor population within them, especially Hartford and New Haven, is growing. Between 1950 and 1970 family income in both cities declined significantly relative to family income in their respective counties; Hartford's median family income declined from 93 percent of the county's median family income to 76 percent of it and in New Haven the decline was from 94 percent to 80 percent. In 1970 the poor population of the Hartford and New Haven metropolitan areas was overwhelmingly concentrated in the cities of Hartford and New Haven.

These trends in population and jobs means there is an increasing distance between the residences of the poor and potential jobs; the Hartford case is illustrative. The employment sector which is growing is heavily concentrated in white collar occupations—those occupations the poor are least able to enter. With an increasing poor population, the sector that must provide jobs is the unskilled service sector. Although this sector will continue to grow these jobs are low paying and offer no opportunity for advancement. The possibility of a poor person in Hartford finding a job in manufacturing, which may hold some opportunity for advancement, is declining because total manufacturing jobs continue to drop while the number of poor competing for unskilled manufacturing work grows. The likelihood of acquiring unskilled employment in warehouses and distribution centers of wholesale firms is also declining as these activities move outside Hartford along the expressways.

Growing numbers of jobs outside Hartford are beyond the reach of the poor in Hartford. Cars are essential to reach most of these jobs because public transportation does not provide access to them. Since many poor do not have cars, they are restricted to jobs that can

Table 3. Fiscal Disparities Among Selected Urban Places Reported by Connecticut Public Expenditure Council

Selected Revenues and Expenditures	East Windsor		Simsbury		Hartford	
	1970 Per Capita ($)	Percent Change 1960–1970	1970 Per Capita ($)	Percent Change 1960–1970	1970 Per Capita ($)	Percent Change 1960–1970
Revenue:						
Property taxes, interest, lien fees	223	145	256	127	347	102
Expenditures:						
Total	283	119	359	144	486	131
Public safety	7	250	18	260	74	118
Public works	21	91	17	–6	48	85
Public welfare and social services	1	–50	1	0	49	88
Recreation and parks	2	*	2	100	16	100

*1960 base figure too low for meaningful result.

be reached by walking or which are located along a public transit line.

The irony in central Connecticut is that affluence for the majority seems assured but the poor can look forward to an increasingly bleak future where they will be locked into their poverty. Potential for upward economic mobility that manufacturing seems to have provided so well in the past for foreign immigrants to the region is rapidly being eroded. New immigrants—poor blacks and Puerto Ricans—will be forced to rely on public assistance income in order to achieve a subsistence existence with little hope for finding jobs which pay an adequate wage. Of those black and Puerto Rican families in Hartford in 1970 who were below the poverty level defined by the United States government, 45 percent relied on public assistance money to even achieve a poverty income.

The alteration in the economies of Hartford and New Haven holds promise for maintaining vibrant core areas with impressive office buildings but surrounding these cores will be a large ring of poor population whose existence is based on menial jobs available in the business district and who have little opportunity to escape their poverty.

FISCAL DISPARITY PROBLEM

Growing poor populations and aging physical plants of industrial cities are placing increas-

ing demands on their resources while the capability to meet these demands becomes weaker. At the same time the middle and upper classes are increasing the distance between themselves and the poor. Because most non-poor are in different political jurisdictions than the poor the former can avoid the high property taxes needed to provide services for the poor and rebuild the industrial cities. Data reported by the Connecticut Public Expenditure Council (and presented in Table 3) for three selected urban places with different trends in population growth and different incomes provide an example of the increasing fiscal disparity problem: (1) East Windsor, a moderately growing middle income town; (2) Simsbury, a rapidly growing upper middle income town; and (3) Hartford, a stabilized low to lower middle income city.

The property tax burden is much greater in Hartford than in the other towns. As would be expected in towns such as East Windsor and Simsbury with small but growing populations, the per capita property tax increased between 1960 and 1970. Yet Hartford, which had a declining population, had a percentage increase in property taxes that was not far behind the smaller towns. The variation in per capita expenditures on selected items is very revealing. Hartford spends substantially more per capita on public safety (chiefly police and fire), public works, public welfare and social services, and recreation and parks than the suburban towns.

Although expenditure figures for public education on a per pupil basis are not comparable in time to the other figures, they reveal an interesting fact. In the 1972 to 1973 school year the net current operating expenses per pupil for East Windsor, Simsbury, and Hartford were respectively $1,000, $904, and $1,497, representing increases over the 1968 to 1969 school year of 55, 47, and 63 percent respectively. Since the differences among the places in public and private school attendance are not substantial, it seems clear that Hartford has chosen to meet the special needs of its pupils with relatively high expenditures compared to the other towns.

Public revenue and expenditure figures demonstrate that the lower income residents of Hartford have a greater per capita tax burden than the higher income suburban residents in critical areas of public activity. Although the rate of increase in expenditure for some activities was greater in suburban towns than in Hartford, the base from which the increase occurred in the suburban towns was so low that the absolute dollar gap in expenditures between the suburbs and Hartford actually increased between 1960 and 1970. Current trends in population redistribution suggest that the fiscal disparity problem will become worse in future decades.

RACIAL POLARIZATION OF RESIDENCE

The increasing concentration of the poor in industrial cities is being accompanied by a rigid separation between blacks and Puerto Ricans in the industrial cities and the rest of the population outside (Figure 11). Although data on the growth of the Puerto Rican population are not readily available, evidence on the black population provides insight into this major social issue.

The past two decades, 1950–1970, have witnessed an extraordinary growth of the black population in the large industrial cities. During the fifties growth rates of the black population ranged from 95 to 150 percent but during the sixties the growth rates slowed substantially, yet they still were above 48 percent in all of the industrial cities. In contrast to the rapidly growing black population was a much slower growth of the nonblack population in Bristol, Meriden, and New Britain and declines of the nonblack population in the three largest cities

of Hartford, New Haven, and Waterbury. The drop in Hartford's and New Haven's nonblack population of 16 to 22 percent in each of the last two decades could only be described as precipitous.

Relative segregation of the black population in the large industrial cities has actually increased above the extreme levels of 1950. In that year 85 percent of the blacks in Hartford County lived in the cities of Bristol, Hartford, and New Britain and by 1970 this had increased to 88 percent. In New Haven County the percent of blacks in the cities of Meriden, New Haven, and Waterbury increased from 82 in 1950 to 86 in 1970.

To argue that blacks are segregated in the large industrial cities because they have low incomes is incorrect. All blacks, whether poor or not, are severely restricted in purchasing housing. For example, in the Hartford metropolitan area in 1970 only 14 percent of all families with incomes above $10,000 per year lived in the city of Hartford but 78 percent of all black families with incomes above $10,000 lived there. Few blacks are able to overcome the barriers of housing discrimination including outright hostility of whites and difficulties in finding whites willing to sell or rent to blacks.

The main supply of housing available to blacks is on the immediate periphery of the all-black residential enclave. Here is where black demand is focused because of proximity to the safety of the black community and because white resistance is weakest. White demand for housing on the periphery of the black residential enclave is very low or even nonexistent because whites fear residential association with blacks. Since blacks are the only people demanding the housing, it turns over in occupancy from white to black. Thus the black residential enclave usually expands peripherally, block by block, with occasional new outliers developing. This peripheral expansion is clearly illustrated in the city of Hartford between 1950 and 1970 (Figure 18). The main black enclave was on the north edge of the central business district and expansion has occurred north and west.

Blacks have not been able to participate in the move to new, single family houses in the urban pastoral environments of central Connecticut. Instead blacks are restricted to living in older housing, often multifamily dwellings, and at relatively high population densities in the industrial cities. The growth of the black

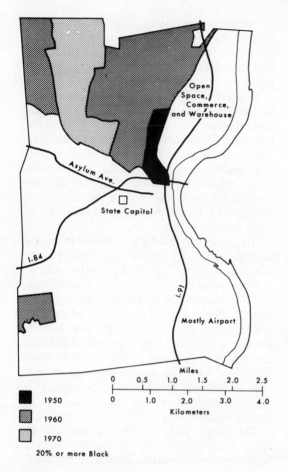

1950
1960
1970

20% or more Black

Miles

| 0 | 0.5 | 1.0 | 1.5 | 2.0 | 2.5 |

| 0 | 1.0 | 2.0 | 3.0 | 4.0 |
Kilometers

Figure 18. Expansion of black residence in Hartford, 1950–1970.

population in a town adjacent to the industrial city such as Bloomfield next to Hartford is merely an instance of the peripheral expansion of black residential areas crossing a city boundary.

Housing segregation for blacks also affects their access to jobs. Because they are restricted to living in the industrial cities they have difficulty finding a suitable residence in appropriate commuting distance of their jobs. Poor blacks living near the central business district have little opportunity for any job but unskilled service work. Black workers in manufacturing may be fortunate enough to find a job in the shrinking manufacturing sector of the industrial city; otherwise they will probably be forced to commute long distances to dispersed manufacturing sites of central Connecticut outside the industrial cities. They

cannot consider choosing a residence closer to their workplace as whites can. With the increasing dispersal of manufacturing, wholesale, and retail jobs, black workers' commuting problems in these sectors will increase. Only black professionals employed in the white collar jobs of Hartford and New Haven will be in close commuting distance to decent jobs. However, this is not by choice, for these same blacks would probably prefer to have a residence in the rural residential towns in the hills and to spend more time commuting.

RESTRUCTURING THE CITY

Growing minority populations, increasing numbers of poor, decaying housing, and declining employment bases in the industrial cities have been a strong impetus for restructuring them. Old buildings have been demolished, highways built, and new retail, office, and housing facilities constructed. Who do these efforts benefit? What do they imply for the future of the city? Hartford, the largest city in central Connecticut, provides a case example of the attempts to restructure the industrial cities.

Major efforts by the city of Hartford to restructure itself began in the mid-1950s and attention focused on the downtown. By 1963 the tone of future development was set with the completion of Constitution Plaza, a complex of eight office and commercial buildings linked by a raised landscaped pedestrian plaza extending the full length of the project (Figure 19). Ten years later the character of the new downtown Hartford as an office (including financial), commercial, and information processing center was being elaborated further. Enhancing this character is a new civic center and additional office and commercial space presently under construction. In addition several hotels and motor inns have been added which provide support for the effort to make Hartford an entertainment and convention city. As much as one-fourth or more of the downtown has been directly affected by urban renewal.

Downtown urban renewal efforts have made possible an enormous concentration of white collar employment in activities which can benefit from close proximity. The tax base of the city has been improved and the prestige of the downtown raised. Unfortunately the ever-increasing numbers of poor gain little employ-

Figure 19. Constitution Plaza.

ment possibilities in the new downtown except as low paid service workers. Only now is the city beginning to direct its renewal efforts toward providing competitive space for industries with its proposals for redevelopment along the Connecticut River.

Major efforts at helping the poor have been aimed at improving housing conditions, not providing jobs. As of 1973 the total number of new units constructed by the Hartford Housing Authority and private sponsors was about 5,700 which comprises about 10 percent of the housing units in Hartford. The two main concentrations of the nonelderly portion of this housing essentially mirror the residential distribution of the low income population of the city (Figure 20; compare with Figure 10).

Housing for moderate income families constructed by the Hartford Housing Authority is all located on the west side of the city away from the main low income population clusters. Since the middle and upper middle income areas of Hartford have been avoided as sites for housing projects, no inroads have been made into the segregation of the population by income. The location of the elderly housing projects is quite different from that of the nonelderly; most elderly projects are situated immediately west of the central business district (Figure 21).

In terms of total number of units, public housing in Hartford is mostly occupied by black and Puerto Rican households, but there are sharp disparities between elderly and non-

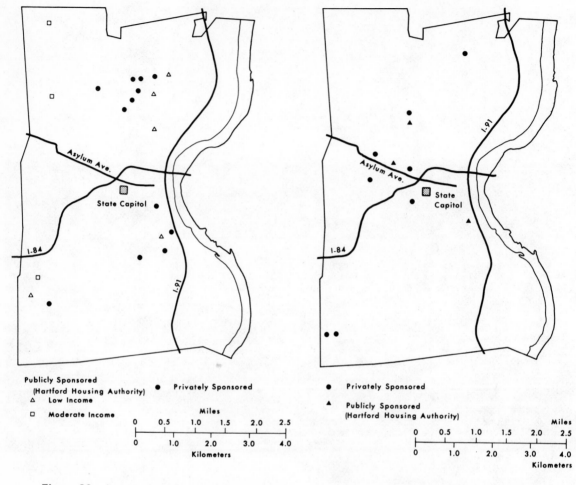

Figure 20. Low and moderate income housing projects for the nonelderly.

Figure 21. Low and moderate income housing projects for the elderly.

elderly housing (Table 4). Black and Puerto Rican households dominate in the occupancy of nonelderly housing, whereas non-Spanish language whites dominate in the occupancy of elderly housing. The dominance of the respective racial groups in various components of public housing seems to be mainly a reflection of the siting of housing projects. Nonelderly housing has been primarily constructed in black and Puerto Rican residential areas and therefore these groups are the principal occupants. In contrast, two of the three elderly public housing projects were constructed in white residential areas and non-Spanish language whites dominate in these. The one elderly public housing project in a black resi-

dential area northwest of the central business district—Mahoney Village—has 78 percent black occupancy. Although figures on racial occupancy of privately sponsored low and moderate income housing were not readily available, it is doubtful if there is any significant difference from the public housing situation.

This strict racial segregation in public housing is not a natural result of differences in income or age among the racial groups. In terms of income, black and Puerto Ricans are substantially overrepresented in public housing based on their respective proportion of low income families in Hartford and whites are substantially underrepresented (Table 5). Even in terms of age, blacks are overrepresented in

Table 4. Racial Composition of Housing Projects of Hartford Housing Authority, November 1973

Project	Number of Occupied Units	Percent Occupied by		
		Black	Puerto Rican	Other
Low Income Nonelderly				
Nelton Court	149	67	17	16
Dutch Point Colony	208	28	28	44
Bellevue Square	451	81	18	1
Charter Oak Terrace	924	35	38	27
Stowe Village	573	75	23	2
Total	2305	55	28	17
Low Income Elderly				
Mahoney Village	49	78	4	18
Kent Apartments	37	16	0	84
Percival C. Smith Towers	199	15	0	85
Total	285	26	1	73
Moderate Income Nonelderly				
Rice Heights	355	50	27	23
Bowles Park	397	78	5	17
Westbrook Village	354	76	6	18
Total	1106	68	12	20
Grand Totals	3696	57	21	22

Table 5. Comparison of Low Income Families in Hartford and Racial Occupany of Public Housing

Race	Number of Families Earning Under $5,000 in 1970	Percent of Total Families Earning Under $5,000 in 1970	Percent of Total Households in Low Income Public Housing in 1973
Black	3149	39	52
Puerto Rican	1237	15	25
Other	3614	45	23
Total	8000	99	100

elderly public housing based on their proportion of elderly in Hartford whereas whites are underrepresented.

Ironically, those groups most discriminated against in the private housing market—blacks and Puerto Ricans—are the ones with the best access to public housing and whites, who theoretically suffer no discrimination in the private housing market, have the least access

to public housing. It would appear that the policy of siting public housing developments has been an important factor in the "discrimination" against whites in public housing. Obviously it is not quite so simple, for the resistance of whites to any public housing in their residential area keeps this housing out, whereas blacks, who have suffered the most discrimination in the private housing market, may be more tolerant of public housing because it provides a source of sound housing that is not otherwise available in the private market.

TRANSPORTATION: SERVING THE NONPOOR

The dispersal of population at low densities, of manufacturing at scattered sites, and of planned shopping centers means that mass transit is rapidly declining as a feasible component of the transportation system of central Connecticut. Mass transit in Connecticut is primarily based on the bus and the general trend in bus patronage between 1950 and 1970 has been down. Although a stabilization of bus patronage occurred in the late sixties, the early seventies exhibited a further decline with the prospect that by 1980 local bus service will be almost nonexistent. Corresponding to declining bus patronage in Connecticut has been a decline in bus service. The Connecticut Department of Transportation reports that miles of bus service have dropped from 21 million in 1963 to 16 million in 1971. The Connecticut Company, the main provider of local bus service in the Hartford and New Haven areas, has had a decline from 36.7 million passengers in 1963 to 29.4 million passengers in 1971, a drop of 20 percent. Bus service of the Connecticut Company has also declined from 12.9 million miles in 1963 to 10.8 million miles in 1971, a drop of 16 percent.

The dominant mode of travel in Connecticut is the car. It accounted for 94 percent of all person trips in 1970 while the regular route bus accounted for less than 2 percent. Because of the dispersal of population and employment, auto driver trips are increasing at a faster rate than population growth as more and more activities can be reached only by car. In the Hartford metropolitan area the population grew 21 percent during the sixties while the proportion of work trips by auto increased from 69 percent in 1960 to 81 percent in 1970. Although the Connecticut Department of Transportation decries the decline in use of mass transit, future planning of the department overwhelming favors highway expansion over mass transit. Of the proposed expenditures for transportation 92 percent are for highways while mass transit (rail and motor carriers) will get only 7 percent.

Connecticut's Master Transportation Plan clearly favors the nonpoor in the low density pastoral environments over the poor in the industrial cities of central Connecticut. The heavy emphasis on highways will not improve transportation for the poor who have no cars. Even the proposed highway program discriminates against the industrial cities in central Connecticut; 82 percent of the funds for highways are to be spent on major capital improvements in expressways which will chiefly benefit nonpoor auto commuters. To make matters worse, 45 percent of the funds for the proposed bus program are to be spent on busways, bus lanes, and railbus improvements that will principally benefit white collar workers commuting from residential towns to central business districts like Hartford and New Haven.

The new express commuter bus service in the Hartford area set up by the Connecticut Department of Transportation provides a good illustration of the proposals which favor the nonpoor. Commuters can park free at a peripheral parking lot and ride to the Hartford central business district for a fare which is no more than the price of gasoline for an auto. The schedules are set up so that it is only possible to go to Hartford in the morning and return in the evening. Within the central business district the buses stop a number of times to make it convenient for the white collar workers.

Rail service improvements will also benefit the nonpoor but not the poor since the proposed railroads are intercity lines which will serve long distance, white collar commuters. The New Haven Railroad serving commuters from the wealthy towns of southwestern Connecticut and traveling to New York City is an existing example of who benefits from rail transportation. Ironically, of the proposed expenditures of $218 million between 1973 and 1990 on mass transit (rail and motor carriers), only 20 percent will be spent on local bus service improvements, the one form of transportation that serves the poor.

Without a drastic resetting of priorities for transportation improvements, the poor in the industrial cities will become increasingly isolated. Local bus service in central Connecticut is primarily limited to the three largest cities of Hartford, New Haven, and Waterbury and portions of adjacent towns (Figure 22). Other bus service consists of radial lines from the industrial cities into the residential towns or bus service between towns with few stops along the way. Compounding the inadequate web of local bus lines is the lack of coordination of bus service; in 1970 no less than thirty bus companies provided some form of local bus service in central Connecticut. If the state of Connecticut carries out its transportation plans there will be little impact on local bus service and, given trends in population redistribution and the use of autos, existing bus service within the large cities will contract. The end result for the poor is to be almost totally immobilized in the industrial cities. In contrast the nonpoor will be served by a fine network of highways and express commuter mass transit service that will make it possible to live in

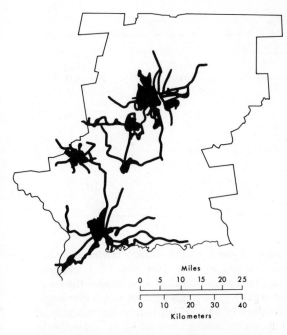

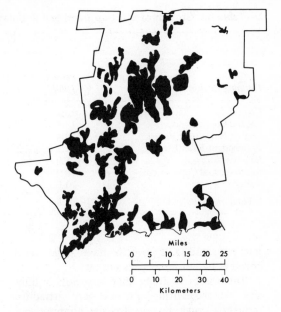

Figure 23. Urban development in 1970 (adapted from map prepared by the Connecticut Department of Transportation).

Figure 22. Local bus transit service areas in 1972 (adapted from map prepared by the Connecticut Department of Transportation).

pastoral environments at ever further distances from white collar employment centers in Hartford and New Haven.

PRESERVING LAND FOR THE GOOD LIFE

Preserving open space land for future outdoor recreation and general aesthetic enjoyment is a major goal in central Connecticut. In attempting to attain this goal, the existing pattern of urban development is a two-edged sword (Figure 23). On the positive side, the scattered nature of the development means open space land is widely available in relatively close proximity to most people. But scattered development also encourages a rapid spread of urban land uses at low densities because sites in between are easily accessible to one or more places containing such activities as employment, commerce, or entertainment.

Providing a sense of urgency to the need for taking action on acquiring open space land before it is too late is the population growth that is expected. But even more critical is the trend for built-up land uses (residential,

industrial, commercial, trades, cultural, and entertainment) to be added at a rate that is two to five times faster than population growth (Table 6). The three major categories of land use—commercial, industrial, and residential—increased in every planning region in central Connecticut by 30 percent or more during the sixties. These increases are consistent with the trend toward planned shopping centers with large parking lots, manufacturing in one story plants, and demands by households for ever larger lot sizes. Because residential land use comprises the largest proportion of built-up land, its rapid growth is the most serious block to preserving open land. During the sixties between two- and four-tenths of an acre of residential land was added for each additional person. Using a rough estimate of three persons per family (a low estimate), this suggests that new housing was being built on sites which averaged between six-tenths acre and one acre. Encouraging the trend toward larger lot sizes for single family dwellings is the practice in most residential towns in pastoral settings of zoning lots at a minimum of one-half acre; some towns—such as Farmington, Granby,

Table 6. Growth of Built-up Land and Population

Planning Region	Built-up Land			Percent Rate of Growth in Population 1960–1970
	Percent 1964	Percent 1970	Percent Rate of Growth 1964–1970	
Capitol	13.1	18.7	42.7	22.6
Central Connecticut	17.8	24.2	36.0	15.3
Central Naugatuck Valley	10.4	20.0	92.3	14.2
Connecticut River Estuary	4.2	9.4	123.8	60.9
Midstate	5.0	8.5	70.0	18.2
South Central Connecticut	18.9	25.4	34.4	13.1
Valley	20.6	27.0	31.1	22.3
Total	12.5	18.7	49.5	18.3

Bethany, and Killingworth—have large areas zoned at two or more acres per lot.

There is little doubt that large lots in hilly and wooded settings provide very attractive residential environments for the nonpoor and that an increasing proportion of the population is achieving these environments. Yet this very success removes increasing amounts of land from open space use and pushes potential open space far from the population of the industrial cities. Given the probably total demise of public transit in central Connecticut, accessible open space for the poor will be limited to their local city parks and playgrounds.

New large open space tracts available to the public will serve the nonpoor who can use their autos. Existing participation in open space programs of the Bureau of Outdoor Recreation, United States Department of the Interior, reveals that the low density residential towns are obtaining large tracts of open space lands but that large industrial cities are not benefiting. This is partly a reflection of the availability of cheap land that is not built up and partly a reflection of the use of open space programs by low density towns to maintain a pastoral environment.

BLUE COLLAR WORKERS AND THE FACTORY IN THE FIELD

The move to urban pastoral environments, wide dispersal of manufacturing, and increasing reliance on the auto pose problems not only for the poor in the industrial cities but also for semiskilled white factory workers. Although the latter are not restricted in their residential choices to the industrial cities be-

cause of race, as the black workers are, they are trapped in twin dilemmas. First, continuing dispersal of manufacturing outside the range of regular mass transit service forces ever larger numbers of semiskilled blue collar workers to rely on expensive commuting by autos. Since their incomes are not high, commuting comprises a significant portion of their resources. Carpooling is difficult because of the wide dispersal of jobs and is chiefly feasible for workers employed at large companies such as at United Aircraft Corporation's main site in East Hartford.

Second, the increasing tendency of towns outside the industrial cities to zone extensive areas for large lots and single family dwellings makes it very difficult for the worker to find low cost housing near the factory. Therefore the semiskilled blue collar worker is forced to live in the industrial cities where cheap apartments are located or to purchase a single family dwelling in the hills long distances from work but where land costs are low and zoning is not yet restrictive.

Although summary data are not available, the most likely situation for the low wage blue collar worker employed outside the industrial city is probably to live in cheap housing in the city and commute by auto to the factory. Information published by the United States Bureau of the Census for a residential area in Waterbury provides a vivid illustration of the plight of these workers. The residential area is located within walking distance of the central business district, adjacent to Interstate 84 which cuts through the middle of the city. Almost all residents are white and they live in old, multifamily housing and pay low rents, about $91 per month including utilities in 1970. The average income of families living here was $9,215 in 1969—about $3,300 below the average for New Haven County. Over half of the workers were blue collar factory employees, almost one-third of those workers employed outside the central business district were employed outside the city, and about half of the workers employed outside the city had jobs that were outside the boundaries of the Waterbury metropolitan area.

THE CHANGE AGENT: GREATER HARTFORD PROCESS

Will relentless forces determine the future of central Connecticut? Business leaders in the Hartford area responded to this question in 1969 by forming the Greater Hartford Corporation, organized, directed, and funded by the area's thirty leading corporations. A major study was funded and two nonprofit public service corporations were set up. The Greater Hartford Process, Inc., was formed to make rational assessments of the capabilities of managing growth and change in the Greater Hartford area, approximately equivalent to the Hartford metropolitan area as defined by the United States Bureau of the Census. It is a regionwide planning and development agency that seeks appropriate approval for specific activities and has representation from business, labor, local government, and planning agencies. The other nonprofit corporation is the Greater Hartford Community Development Corporation, which is the development arm of the Greater Hartford Process. Its function is to obtain financing, acquire land, and engage in site planning, development, and management of the programs suggested by Process, Inc., and approved by residents in the region. The money earned by development activities is to be recycled into other activities in the region.

The key belief behind what has become known as the Process is that a quality living environment can only be achieved if the residents of a region actively influence and manage change and do this on a continuing basis because change is a way of life; the Process becomes a change agent. Process is an attempt to bring people together to assess capabilities, develop a consensus about objectives and

priorities, and act in ways that are part of a coherent approach to needs of the Greater Hartford area. Essential components of the Process approach are views that social, economic, and physical development are inseparable and the scale of action must be large enough to deal with needs and problems on a regionwide scale.

Efforts of the Greater Hartford Process corporations are focused in two directions— creating a New Hartford and building a new community in the suburbs. The creation of a New Hartford is a bold attempt to revitalize Hartford by redeveloping the north half of the city, including the downtown. In relative terms it is probably the largest development effort ever proposed for any American city; it covers half the city's area, 40 percent of its population, and 75 percent of its commercial and office space, and the price tag is estimated at $780 million. The north half of the city was seen as the area most needing action because of deterioration in housing and the concentration of many poor blacks and Puerto Ricans with social and economic problems. A comprehensive approach is being taken including building new housing and rehabilitating old housing; organizing neighborhood life centers which offer a wide range of manpower, health, and social services; redesigning education services, and building new cultural and commercial facilities. The goal is to maintain Hartford as a key center of the region's political, cultural, commercial, and economic life and to make it an economically balanced community in terms of reflecting income levels of the community as a whole.

The other primary effort is focused on building a new community in the town of Coventry, about twenty minutes east of downtown Hartford. Approximately 1,600 acres of land have been purchased by the Greater Hartford community Development Corporation for constructing a new village in the town which will house 20,000 people by the 1990s when it is completed. This new community is to contain housing for families of diverse ages, incomes, and family composition as well as commercial shopping areas, community service facilities, and industrial parks. The goal is to make this new community a prototype for community development in the rapidly growing suburban towns.

Elusive Goals

To say that central Connecticut is in the midst of rapid urban change is to say nothing new to its residents. For more than a century and a half the urban landscape has been rocked by first one change and then another. In the early nineteenth century peaceful agricultural villages began to find themselves next to curious villages that contained small factories and workers' housing. Before having time to adjust to these new villages many of them literally exploded with population, factories, and commercial buildings, beginning around the middle of the nineteenth century, and continued to grow at a dizzy pace for decade after decade. By 1900 the old Connecticut Yankee existed only in people's imaginations; the new immigrants of non-English stock dominated. Yet these densely built-up cities were not to be the forerunner of the future but were instead merely a passing phase which was first hinted at with the horse-drawn street railway and became evident with the auto. In the twentieth century central Connecticut is seeing all who can afford to move to urban pastoral environments. The dynamos of the late nineteenth century—the industrial cities —have become the poor cousins of the twentieth century. Their guts are being removed by urban renewal, housing is deteriorating, and new immigrants are arriving in large numbers. Can a quality living environment be achieved in such a changeable landscape?

ACHIEVEMENTS

The nonpoor are served well in central Connecticut. A high level of prosperity has been achieved for most of the population based on manufacturing, finance, insurance, and government and all trends suggest that this prosperity will continue. An efficient transportation system relying on autos, trucks, and highways has facilitated the dispersion of manufacturing, the spread of population at low densities, and the growth of planned shopping centers to serve this dispersed population. This evolving urban region is infinitely expandable; no one dominant core exists and as new activity centers such as industrial parks or shopping centers are needed they are built on the expanding edge of the urban region.

The easy mobility the auto provides allows households to have a wide freedom of residential choice. The noncentric and replicated nature of the urban region insures that most activities will be accessible to households and frequently they will have a choice among several. Low density development provides a base for what the nonpoor consider to be a pleasant living environment—a house among lakes, woods, and hills.

FAILURES

The spread of population at densities so low that mass transit can not operate efficiently has spelled the death knell for mass transit in the near future. Poor people will be almost totally isolated in the industrial cities. The dispersion of manufacturing to sites accessible only by car is rapidly removing from the poor the possibility of upward economic mobility. Similarly, the semiskilled blue collar worker is forced by restrictive zoning and dispersed manufacturing to live in cheap housing in the industrial cities and commute long distances by auto to the factory in the country.

Agreements over goals for the region may be increasingly difficult to achieve. Spatial polarization is clearly evident at the town and city level between the poor in the industrial cities and the nonpoor in the residential towns, between blacks and Puerto Ricans in the industrial cities and the rest of the population outside, and even between high income people in one residential town and middle income people in another. The only common level of government which can form a basis for resolving fundamental differences between members of the urban region—such as over the siting of expressways, location of power plants, of subsidies for mass transit—is at the state level or higher yet, at the federal level. Hence conflict will increasingly pit organized territorial units (cities and towns) against each other. In this type of conflict costs and benefits may be easier to assign to segments of the population and may become sources of contention because the effects are felt in terms of recognized territorial units.

Segregation of the population by income poses serious problems for the equitable provision of the basic public services such as education, health service, and police protection to all segments of the region's population. Heavy reliance is placed on the property tax and so disparities in wealth from town to town become reflected in the variation in tax burdens. The problem is compounded in the industrial cities where the poor are concentrated because their per capita need for many services is higher than the nonpoor and yet their resources for meeting these demands are lower.

The spread of the population among urban pastoral environments is so rapid that preservation of open space by public policy decisions becomes nullified by private residential, commercial, and industrial decisions. Potential open space is being pushed farther and farther from most of the urban population. Benefits of living in these urban pastoral environments are limited to whites; because of discrimination in housing the black nonpoor cannot equitably share the amenities.

CAN THE URBAN FUTURE BE GUIDED?

An important conclusion about the historical development of this urban region is that urban growth has been incremental; each decision provides a framework for succeeding decisions. For example, the numerous entrepreneurs who set up factories at discrete sites in the early nineteenth century provided a base for the extensive urban growth of the late nineteenth century which in turn provided a frame upon which the wide dispersal of population has been set. An early focus on machinery and diverse metal products that was evident by 1850 provided a basis for the choice of Hartford for the location of an aircraft company in 1925 that now provides high wages and large employment and contributes to the wild fluctuations in unemployment that blue collar workers in the region must suffer through. The founding of two insurance companies between 1810 and 1820 in Hartford is followed by an extraordinary concentration of the insurance industry that then provides a large, secure, and growing employment source for the Hartford area economy.

All of these incremental developments have had a major impact on urban growth and all took over a century or more to become manifest in the region. Such a pattern of urban change forces us to raise serious questions about existing trends because if the past is any guide decisions being made now may benefit or plague central Connecticut into the twenty-first century. The dilemma that past urban growth poses is that prediction of future urban growth is an exercise in gazing into a clouded crystal ball. Who in the nineteenth century could have predicted the future impact of the growth of discrete industrial towns, the machinery industry, and insurance? The difficulty of predicting future urban developments is enhanced by numerous components of the urban region such as households, industries, commerce, and professions, each with its own locational dynamics but all interrelated. It is in recognition of this interrelated complexity that leaders of the Greater Hartford Process have proposed such a comprehensive program of action.

Because of the complexity and incremental nature of urban change, attempts to guide the urban future may need to be comprehensive in a way which has yet to be imagined, even by the leaders of the Greater Hartford Process. One obvious starting point is a set of regionwide land use controls that tries to balance conflicting demands and strives for equity in the allocation of social, economic, and aesthetic costs and benefits. However, the ever present problem in a comprehensive approach is to insure that inhabitants of the region are part of the decisionmaking process rather than having decisions made chiefly by a small elite of professionals.

NARROWING THE GAP BETWEEN GOALS AND REALITY

To be baffled by the complexity of urban change is to do nothing to narrow the gap between the goals (conflicting though they may be) of different segments of the urban region and the reality of urban developments. There are obvious problems that need to be addressed, many of which have been recognized by the Greater Hartford Process.

First, the rapid spread of low density residential developments must be halted. Vast amounts of public resources are used to finance this spread that could better be used to alleviate the problems of the poor in the industrial cities, attack environmental pollution, and provide a higher level of public services. Other means of providing pleasant "pastoral" residential environments can be used, such as the planned unit development of cluster housing, rather than allowing anyone with some money to put his house on one acre of land. Only by halting the rapid spread of low density developments can effective public action to encourage alternative uses such as open space be designed and implemented.

The almost total reliance on the auto for personal mobility must be reduced. Most of the land uses outside the industrial cities—planned shopping centers, industrial parks, and rural residential towns—are based on the assumption that energy will remain plentiful and cheap. If there is anything the energy crisis of the seventies reveals, it is that this assumption may be incorrect. However, to make mass transit a viable option will require strict controls on future residential growth.

The isolation of the poor in the industrial cities must be ended. Improvement in mass transit is one means and another means is to make it possible for the poor to find decent jobs. Instead of focusing all attention on developing glittering central business districts for white collar workers, attention should be focused on setting up competitive industrial sites within the large cities to attract manufacturing. The subsidies for creating these sites would surely be no more than the subsidies given to downtown urban renewal programs that benefit commercial, financial, and other professional interests.

There must be a more equitable match between the demands for essential public services and the resources for meeting those demands. If the separation between the poor in the industrial cities and the nonpoor outside is maintained then there must be major programs aimed at redistributing taxes among the towns and cities from those with the greatest resources and fewest needs to those with the fewest resources and greatest needs.

Housing in the urban pastoral environments must be opened up to the semiskilled workers employed in the dispersed factories. Towns which benefit from the property taxes paid by the factories should be required to remove restrictions against small lot zoning and low cost multifamily housing.

If the black population is ever to find housing that they demand unfettered by racial discrimination, effective public action against discriminatory practices of lending institutions, real estate dealers, residential developers, and homeowners is essential. Existing practices of whites force most blacks to remain in the industrial cities. Although blacks in possible alliance with Puerto Ricans will probably gain political control of Hartford and New Haven by the year 2000, they may be empty prizes except for their downtowns.

To address these problems and provide a quality living environment for central Connecticut's residents will require a recognition of the conflicting nature of goals; only at their most general level of economic prosperity, good housing, efficient transportation, and open space recreation is there little disagreement. Beneath this level there are hard decisions to make concerning where activities should be located, who should pay, who should benefit, and how land is to be used.

Bibliography

Andrews, Charles M. "The River Towns of Connecticut: A Study of Wethersfield, Hartford, and Windsor." *Johns Hopkins University Studies in Historical and Political Science,* Seventh Series (July-September 1889), pp. 1–126.

Bidwell, Percey W. "Rural Economy in New England at the Beginning of the Nineteenth Century." *Transactions of the Connecticut Academy of Arts and Sciences* 20 (1916): 241–399.

Burpee, Charles W. *History of Hartford County Connecticut: 1633-1928.* 3 vols. Hartford: S.J. Clarke Publishing Company, 1928.

Chandler, George B. "Industrial History." In Norris G. Osborn, ed., *History of Connecticut,* vol. 4, New York: States History Company, 1925.

Clark, George L. *A History of Connecticut: Its People and Institutions.* 2nd ed. New York: G.P. Putnam's Sons, 1914.

Connecticut Bank and Trust Company. *Connecticut Business Trends,* 11, 2 (April 1973).

Connecticut Department of Commerce. "Major Industrial and Corporate Office Construction in Connecticut, 1972." Mimeographed. Hartford, n.d.

Connecticut Department of Transportation. *Connecticut Master Transportation Plan, 1973.* Wethersfield, Conn., December 1972.

Connecticut Development Commission. *Connecticut's Industrial Parks, 1972.* Hartford.

Connecticut Labor Department. Employment Security Division, Office of Research and Information. "Total Nonagricultural Employment by Town, June, 1965 and 1972." Mimeographed. Wethersfield, Conn., n.d.

Connecticut Public Expenditure Council. "Municipal Revenues and Expenditures in Hartford County and the Capitol Planning Region." Mimeographed. Hartford, 1966 and 1974.

Countryman, William A. "Transportation." In Norris G. Osborn, ed., *History of Connecticut,* vol. 4. New York: States History Company, 1925.

Davis, William T., ed. *The New England States.* Vol. 2 Boston: D.H. Hurd and Co., 1897.

The Greater Hartford Process. Hartford, April 1972.

Hartford Housing Authority. "Integration as of November 30, 1973." Mimeographed. Hartford, December 3, 1973.

Hellman, Daryl, and Sullivan, John J. *The Impact of the Insurance Industry on the Economy of the State of Connecticut.* Hartford: Insurance Association of Connecticut, n.d.

Lathrop, William G. *The Brass Industry in the United States.* Rev. ed. New Haven: Wilson H. Lee Company, 1926.

Martin, Margaret E. "Merchants and Trade of the Connecticut River Valley." *Smith College Studies in History* 24 (1938-1939): 1–284.

Mitchell, Mary H. *History of New Haven County Connecticut.* 2 Vols. Boston: Pioneer Historical Publishing Co., 1930.

Office of State Planning. "Population and Employment Projections for Regions and

Towns." Mimeographed. Hartford: Department of Finance and Control, State of Connecticut, February 1970.

———. *Proposed: A Plan of Conservation and Development for Connecticut.* Hartford: Department of Finance and Control, State of Connecticut, 1973.

Osterweis, Rollin G. *Three Centuries of New Haven, 1638–1938.* New Haven: Yale University Press, 1953.

The Pratt and Whitney Aircraft Story [East Hartford, Conn.]: Pratt and Whitney Division of United Aircraft Corporation, August 1950.

Roe, Joseph W. *Connecticut Inventors.* Tercentenary Commission of the State of Connecticut, Committee on Historical Publications, no. 33. [New Haven]: Published for the Tercentenary Commission by Yale University Press, 1934.

Trumbull, J. Hammond, ed. *The Memorial*

History of Hartford County Connecticut, 1663–1884. 2 vols. Boston: Edward L. Osgood, 1886.

United Aircraft Annual Report, 1972. East Hartford, Conn.: United Aircraft Corporation, 1973.

United Aircraft Corporation, Public Relations Department. Interview with Frank Giusti. East Hartford, Connecticut, November 1973.

Van Dusen, Albert E. *Connecticut.* New York: Random House, 1961.

Withington, Sidney, *The First Twenty Years of Railroads in Connecticut.* Tercentenary Commission of the State of Connecticut, Committee on Historical Publications, no. 45. New Haven: Published for the Tercentenary Commission by Yale University Press, 1935.

Woodward, P.H. *Insurance in Connecticut.* Boston: D.H. Hurd and Co., 1897.

Index